Unless Recalled Earlier

DATE DUE

JG

Marrow of the Nation

ASIA: LOCAL STUDIES/GLOBAL THEMES

Jeffrey N. Wasserstrom, Kären Wigen, and Hue-Tam Ho Tai, Editors

Marrow of the Nation

*A History of Sport and Physical Culture
in Republican China*

ANDREW D. MORRIS

With a Foreword by Joseph S. Alter

University of California Press

BERKELEY   LOS ANGELES   LONDON

University of California Press
Berkeley and Los Angeles, California

University of California Press, Ltd.
London, England

© 2004 by the Regents of the University of California

Library of Congress Cataloging-in-Publication Data

Morris, Andrew D.
    Marrow of the nation : a history of sport and physical culture
in Republican China / Andrew D. Morris.
        p.   cm.—(Asia : Local studies / global themes ; 10)
    Includes bibliographical references and index.
    ISBN 0-520-24084-7 (cloth : alk. paper)
    1. Sports—China—History—20th century.   2. Physical
education and training—China—History—20th century.
3. Nationalism and sports—China.   I. Title.   II. Series.

    GV651 . M67   2004
    796' . 0951'09   2004001057

Manufactured in the United States of America
13   12   11   10   09   08   07   06   05   04
10   9   8   7   6   5   4   3   2   1

The paper used in this publication meets the minimum requirements
of ANSI/NISO Z39.48–1992 (R 1997) (Permanence of Paper).

For Shaina,
my favorite polar bear

Contents

Figures

Acknowledgments

During this project, I have had the fortune to meet, befriend, and learn from a great number of people. My first and foremost thanks must go to my mentors at the University of California, San Diego (UCSD), Joseph Esherick and Paul Pickowicz, who patiently coached and coaxed a terrified young graduate student who often wondered if he should have stuck with his job at the local power company. Both were truly generous with their time, resources, and ideas, and for this I feel both grateful and fantastically lucky. At UCSD, Dorothy Ko and Takashi Fujitani also inspired and encouraged me and taught me many things. My fellow UCSD Chinese history graduate students, with all apologies to my professors, taught me perhaps just as much. Jim Cook, Julie Broadwin, Josh Goldstein, Michael Chang, Dong Yue, Wang Liping, Mark Eykholt, Charles Musgrove, Sue Fernsebner, Liu Lu, Cecily McCaffrey, and Elena Songster all read long drafts of my work and offered invaluable criticism and suggestions that have made this work much more thorough and critical and hopefully worthwhile. Many thanks are also due to my committee members, Professors David Jordan, Stephanie McCurry, and George Lipsitz, who took the time to press me on the founding questions of this study.

Several other scholars have been of great help in discussing ideas and critiquing my work. Professors Jeffrey Wasserstrom, David Strand, Susan Brownell, Geremie Barmé, Frederic Wakeman, Jr., Mark Elliott, Stephen Averill, Ruth Rogaski, Ann Waltner, Josh Fogel, Robert Edelman, and George Cotkin all provided me with important questions and ideas that are characteristic of their fine achievements.

I would like to thank the University of California Education Abroad Program for a yearlong grant to study and do research at National Taiwan University. The Committee on Scholarly Communication with China's National

Program for Advanced Study and Research in China Graduate Fellowship (administered by the American Council of Learned Societies) allowed me to do a full year's worth of dissertation research at Hangzhou University in the People's Republic of China (PRC). A Summer Stipend from the National Endowment for the Humanities and a Cal Poly State Faculty Support Grant also were invaluable in providing time and resources for the revision of this project.

In Taiwan, Professor Tsai Jen-hsiung of the National Taiwan Normal University (NTNU) welcomed me into his sports history seminars and provided me with the personal networks and knowledge of source materials that made this project much more manageable. His graduate students—especially Liu Chin-ping, Wang Chien-tai, Fan Chuen-yuan, Li Shu-chen, Tan Ching-mei, Liu Hong-yuh, Lee Jane-Shing, and Cheng Kuo-ming—all shared their work and ideas with me and quickly made me feel very much at home. NTNU Professor Wu Wen-hsing was very giving of his time. Professor Hsu I-hsiung of NTNU and his students Hsu Yuan-ming and Chen Jui-fu too were very generous with their work. My (and many others') work has been made much easier by Professor Hsu's bibliography of modern Chinese physical culture sources.

Dr. Yu Chien-ming of the Institute of Modern History, Academia Sinica, was of tremendous assistance, sharing with me her important work on women's physical culture. Professors Chen Yung-fa of Academia Sinica and National Taiwan University (NTU), and Cha Shih-chieh of NTU also gave of their time.

My time in Taiwan was made much more fun by my friendships with Mr. Dong Hanwen and Mr. Li Shiming, both star athletes from the 1930s. (The former is the father-in-law of my undergraduate mentor, Dr. Arthur Rosenbaum, to whom I owe many thanks.) Mr. Dong, eighty-five years old at the time, was mercifully patient with me when I was unable to join the 6:30 A.M. basketball games with his "Old Horses" teammates on the NTU campus. Mornings when I did make it were delightfully concluded with a breakfast and many stories (both always on Mr. Dong) at the McDonald's or Foremost across the street. Mr. Li, eighty-nine years old that year, welcomed me into his apartment and enthusiastically shared his scrapbooks and memories with me. (Mr. Li did not join us for predawn basketball but did adhere faithfully to a six-game bowling regimen every morning. "My arm doesn't get tired," he insisted once, "I used to be a pitcher!") The time spent with these two wonderful men was one of the true highlights of this project.

At Hangzhou University, I am indebted to Professor Zhao Jianhua, who served as my advisor and welcomed me into his home, and Professor Weng

Shixun, who was very generous with his treasured collection of Republican-era sports sources. Professors Zhao Shanxing and Zheng Zhilin, two of the fathers of the PRC sports history movement, were also helpful during my year in Hangzhou. In Beijing, Yan Xuening of the *Journal of Sport History and Culture* was a dear friend who made my stay in Beijing convenient, enjoyable, and productive. Xiong Xiaozheng, chief editor of the *Journal,* also shared his time and ideas.

Mr. Cheng Jinguan of Suzhou is another ex-star athlete that I met through Messrs. Li and Dong in Taiwan. Visits to his home and correspondence through the mail provided some of my favorite moments during my time in China. At a "Jinguan Cup" high school relay race held every year in Suzhou to honor Mr. Cheng's Olympic efforts of 1936, students are told to study Mr. Cheng's "spirit of striving for national glory." I hope these youngsters may also learn from the humility, generosity, and honesty of this delightful man.

Professor Nie Xiaohu of the Chengdu Institute of Physical Education was exceedingly generous in taking my wife Ricky and me into his home and preparing Sichuan-style breakfasts for us every morning. His fellow Professors Tan Hua and Hu Xiaoming took time to meet with me and discuss my research. Professors Zeng Biao of Southern Jiangxi Normal College, Zhou Weiliang of the Jiangsu Provincial Sports Science Research Center, Liang Xiaoming of Shanghai Normal University, Cai Yangwu of the Chinese Sports History Association in Shanghai, and Li Yuming of the Second Historical Archives in Nanjing were all far too generous despite my habit of showing up in offices on embarrassingly short notice. Xia Xiyuan, Su Lifeng, and Shen Yajun of the Zhejiang Provincial Library Classics Section in Hangzhou were always patient and helpful as well.

Dagmar Getz of the YMCA Archives in St. Paul guided me through the China materials housed in that wonderful collection during a short trip to Minnesota during the fall of 1997. Scott Miller was very gracious in allowing me to cite one of his intriguing and appropriate lyrics. I thank Stephen Averill, Melvin L. Adelman, and David K. Wiggins for granting me permission to reprint portions of my articles that previously appeared in, respectively, *Republican China* and the *Journal of Sport History.*

Finally, at the University of California Press, I would like to thank my editor Reed Malcolm, as well as Mary Severance, Colette DeDonato, and Sheila Levine, who was very helpful during my initial contacts with the press.

My parents and brother Jeffrey are always supportive and loving, and to them I owe a world of thanks and appreciation. My sincere love and gratitude is due Ricky, who for thirteen years khas encouraged me, pushed me, consoled me, and made me laugh in different and wonderful ways every day. Finally, Shaina, who was born exactly halfway through this project, has made the second half infinitely more fun and meaningful. Our polar bear adventures in the imaginary tundra of California's Central Coast have made me happier than I ever could have imagined being.

Foreword

Arguably, the late nineteenth and early twentieth centuries defined a period when the "problem" of the body and the "problem" of nationalism came together in complex and interesting ways in many different parts of the world. For example, in numerous ways the so-called Muscular Christianity of nineteenth-century England and the United States is both historically linked with, and structurally comparable to, what might be called "Fascist Fitness" in twentieth-century Europe and Asia. Beyond this, there are striking parallels between fitness regimens in a broad spectrum of state regimes, including those of Japan, Sweden, Israel, and the Soviet Union. Body discipline of various kinds, including physical education and sports, is integral to imperialism and to the way in which various kinds of nationalism developed in the postcolonial world. In this context Andrew Morris's fine-grained and exhaustive study of sport and physical education in Republican China provides an important comparative perspective on both the historicity of physical fitness as a global phenomenon and the local manifestation of this historicity at a time when China was deeply engaged with the problem of nationalism. As Morris makes clear, a very specific problem in the nexus of nationalism, modernity, and the body was making foreign and Western sports relevant to the development of a modern Chinese national identity, even though this identity was defined in opposition to many features of the West and to many kinds of foreign influence. The broader ramifications of this specific problem may be drawn out through comparison.

In 1894, on the occasion of the first anniversary of the Calcutta Mahomedan Sporting Club, Abdus Salam of the Bengal Provincial Civil Service delivered a lecture on physical education in India. Subsequently published as a booklet (*Physical Education in India*, Calcutta: W. Newman, 1895), the lecture is noteworthy for a number of reasons, not least of which is that it draws direct attention to the way in which ethnicity, nationalism, and the body are implicated in questions of modernity. Salam's lecture is wide ranging, rhetorically charged, and deeply invested in the moral priorities of the British Empire while at the same time implicitly working to establish other priorities. In this respect it echoes many statements made by the advocates of physical education reform in Republican China.

One point that seems particularly significant is the way Salam struggles to define the relationships between physical prowess, intellectual strength, and personal character. Set in the context of colonialism, with all but explicit reference to the image of "Indian effeteness" that characterized a certain imperious Victorian conceit, Salam writes:

> Speaking of the Mussulmans in India, and especially in Bengal, their physical deterioration may be briefly, and, at the same time, more or less aptly, described by saying, that they would prefer laying down to sitting, sitting to standing, standing to walking, and walking to running. It may be a painful digression, but I cannot help but remark that this physical attitude more or less represents our present mental attitude! What havoc Time has wrought in our national character! (20)

Referencing his own religious affiliation and lamenting the fact that we have "ceased to pray five times a day, and have thus wantonly deprived ourselves of the physical exercise which the Mussulman liturgy embodies" (18), Salam continues to define what seems to be a key problem in the relationships between sport, athleticism, and national identity:

> We despise, more or less, the indigenous physical exercises of the East, such as wrestling, practice with 'mudghur,' clubs, 'dun' archery, etc., taunting those who practice them as *pahalwans* or wrestlers, and at the same time we have failed to take, like other elastic and less conservative races in India, to the manly Western games, such as tennis, foot-ball, cricket, etc. (18–19)

Leaving aside the knotty question of what counts or does not count as a "manly" game—which would lead into the gendered anxiety of empire itself—the problem is that modernity in general, and nationalism as a specific configuration of modernity, invokes the force of tradition but then seems ambivalent, if not altogether hostile, toward the forms of tradition that are invoked. At the other end of the spectrum there is, to use Salam's apt term, the problem of "elasticity," whereby manly Western games define the form of modernity as an exercise in ever more precise, but never absolute or perfect, mimicry. In many respects, physical educationalists in Republican China took the art of elasticity to new lengths, and—if performance in the

Olympics is the gold standard—established a legacy in which mimesis has produced a better copy than the original.

In all of this, however, it is important to keep in mind the question of class, social status, and perspective—elite, middle-class, peasant—particularly since modernity produces powerful discourses of totalizing synthesis that are, in fact, partial rather than impartial. Who, in other words, is this "we" for whom Salam speaks? Is it, as he seems to indicate at points throughout the booklet, "Indian Youth?" Or is it all Mussulmans in modern India? Or does it extend beyond India—in terms of both time and space—to "Arabia," "Andalusia," "Persia," "Byzantium," and "Central Asia?" These are all places invoked by Salam so as to constructively "turn back Time," as it were, and thereby reflect an image of Mussulman men who might prefer running to lying down, and who might, also, not despise "the indigenous physical exercises of the East."

The point here is significant in general but also important in terms of defining a comparative frame of reference for understanding the relationship between the body, discourses about the body, and nationalism. With an excellent sense of how and why the precise details matter, Morris clearly points out that those who were concerned with the development of sport in early-twentieth-century China struggled with the meaning of sport, and the relationship between Western and "traditional" sports, as well as the distinction between sport, physical education, and physical culture. But they did so, for the most part, from a perspective from which it was both absolutely necessary—and strikingly unproblematic—to speak for all Chinese. The dominant trend in this totalizing discourse was to define *tiyu*—translated as body cultivation involving sports, gymnastics, drill regimens, and calisthenics—as relevant to Chinese modernity and as a key mechanism for transforming effete self-serving subjects into manly citizens with a single, common purpose. In a curious way, the more problematic it became to define and institutionalize *tiyu* as such, the less problematic it became to frame the debate as one that was relevant to all Chinese.

One wonders, in this context, about the extent to which the body of the citizen is itself subject not only to a regimen of training but also to a regimen of discursive appropriation. The actual discipline of bodies on the playing field provides those who write about *tiyu*—in great detail, with considerable rhetorical flourish and with both totalizing and teleological logic—with something that is very elusive in nationalistic rhetoric: a singularly signified material referent that is also powerfully evocative. As in the case of the many public statements made by reformers in China, Abdus Salam's lecture was addressed to a group of athletes. But as a lecture it framed their bodies—and appropriated the strength and skill of those bodies—in terms of language and rhetoric. This is an obvious point, but one that tends to get overlooked, since the body itself—unlike history, nostalgia, art, or other products of culture that take on national significance—is thought of as something that can represent itself rather than a thing in need of representation. An important elision of difference and representation is made possible by the relationship between embodied personhood, body discipline as such, and the discursive form of that discipline.

What is interesting about this, at least in part, is the way in which the relationship between the body and discourses about the body—both rhetorically embellished and institutionally pragmatic—establishes a framework for thinking about the way in which nationalism invokes the force of tradition but is highly ambivalent about the form and content of the tradition so invoked. In much the same way as Salam draws attention to the power of the *pahalwan* ("traditional" Indian wrestler) only to point out how he was taunted and despised by modernity, many of the early Republican advocates of *tiyu* refer to *wushu* (the "traditional" martial arts of China) only to point out that they do not fit into the framework of modern physical culture and are irredeemably anachronistic.

This starkly structured discourse of opposition notwithstanding, it seems that things are much more interesting in practice, and Morris hints at this. He writes that during the early period of the Republican era the martial arts seemed to be "destined for the garbage bin of history" on account of being feudal and infused with superstition. Then they reemerged through "hybridization" and formalization during the Pure Martial Era and under the rubric of the State Guoshu Project of the Nanjing Decade. This raises a series of questions: Who speaks, from either within or on the precipitous edge of the garbage bin, for the broad range of people who embody *wushu* in terms that are meaningful to themselves rather than meaningful to the state? What is the relationship between the *wushu* body and the *tiyu* body? Most significantly, is there a history of *wushu* that stands in a different relationship to modernity than one defined by nationalism? Andrew Morris has grappled with these issues and is keenly aware of the complex mimetic relationship between *wushu* and *tiyu*. However, it would be interesting to pursue the question further, and more explicitly, not simply to pick through the trash, as it were, but to point out the contingency of clear distinctions. Stepping away from the figure of the *pahalwan* as a "traditional athlete"— provoked to trenchant surliness and formidable excess on account of being "taunted and despised," as Salam put it—it is useful to consider the case of yoga in India. This is not because it is the "Hindu" equivalent of Salam's "healthy" Mussulman liturgy but because it compares more directly to *wushu* as a form of what might be called "metaphysical fitness." In other words, what forms of practice like *wushu* and yoga do is render the whole category of sport and physical fitness somewhat problematic.

Yoga, like *wushu*, can be understood to be a form of physical education and physical self-cultivation or to be nothing of the sort. It all depends on how the body is represented and experienced. And that is the point. Yoga and *wushu* are domains of experience and practice that are highly problematic for nationalism to engage with in terms of modernity. This is not on account of their being "anachronistic," although that is a factor. It is because of the way in which they problematize the body, as this problematization of the body makes body discipline relevant to other cultural configurations. One could extend this vector of comparison to other areas of the world and periods of time as well. For example "running" as a form of whole person eco-spatial exercise among Native Americans in the Southwest is directly relevant to questions of identity. It is both like and very unlike sport and physical exercise. And if "running" seems at least logically in the domain of physical fitness, there are so-called "medical" systems that are concerned more with immortality and the perfection of the body than with curing diseases. How are these forms of medical practice—if that is really what they are—to be understood in relation to comparable forms of practice that are defined as physical culture? To pose the question in terms of uncertain classification is exactly the point.

Given the way in which yoga defines the body in terms of metaphysical fitness, the history of yoga is directly and unambiguously linked to transnationalism and the global flow of cultural information about health and well-being but is very ambiguously connected to Indian nationalism as such. This is not because it has been represented as mystical and transcendental but precisely because it was defined, as early as 1920, as a holistic form of physical education capable of training both body and mind. Thus yoga was used to resolve the key problem articulated by Salam in 1894 concerning the relationship between physical, intellectual, and moral character development in the domain of physical education, but once it had done so it immediately crossed the borders of India to become, over the past seventy-five years, a truly global phenomenon. My sense is that *wushu*, regardless of the extent to which it was or was not uninvented, invented, and reinvented as a tradition in the 1920s and 1930s, co-opted the domain of physical fitness in the way yoga did by being incompletely co-opted by sport and physical education as such. Most certainly both yoga and *wushu* are more emblematic of transnationalism and globalization than nationalism. At least in part this is because they do not so much build the body as put a twist on it, on the nature of its power, and therefore on the dynamic relationship between embodied power and the power of states to control bodies, both in fact and through discursive representation.

The history of sport and athleticism in India follows a trajectory that seems to be parallel to the history of *tiyu* in China, almost to a point that would seem to demand cross-cultural historical comparison, particularly with regard to the important role of the YMCA, the emergence of national bodies bent on institutionalizing formal sports policy, ambivalence about the place of "indigenous games," and the militarization of drill regimens by hard-line nationalists. Many of these themes—if not the way they play out—are characteristic of modernity at large and are not at all unique to China or India. On this level scholars working on the history of sport and nationalism beyond Asia will find rich and stimulating material in this book.

What is specifically significant in the local arena of Asia, however, is that a history of *wushu*—embedded as it is here in the history of *tiyu*—can deconstruct sport as a stable category. This points toward a range of possible comparative perspectives on parallel phenomena in other regions. Yoga, like *wushu*, has become a form of physical fitness training that is linked to issues of regimentation, health, and discipline. In a few relatively rare circumstances it is even practiced as a competitive sport. But yoga is equally linked to embodied ideas about supernatural perfection, immortality, and transcendence. Whether yoga can effect immortality is immaterial, as is the same question with regard to *wushu* in the context of Taoist self-perfection. What is concretely material is that those who engage in these forms of practice embody the tension between ideals of health and fitness on the one hand and transcendental, metaphysical self-awareness on the other. As such this provides for new and interesting ways to think about the relationship between nationalism and transnationalism as this relationship is negotiated in embodied terms.

Joseph S. Alter
Professor of Anthropology
University of Pittsburgh

1 Introduction

In 1914, Wu Tingfang, a former ambassador and minister of justice under the Qing dynasty (1644–1911) and the young Republic of China, turned his thoughts to sport and culture in his book *America through the Spectacles of an Oriental Diplomat*:

> Perhaps in nothing do the Chinese differ from their Western friends in the matter of amusements more than in regard to sports. The Chinese would never think of assembling in thousands just to see a game played. We are not modernized enough to care to spend half a day watching others play. . . . I much doubt if [sports] will ever be really popular among my people. They are too violent, and from the oriental standpoint, lacking in dignity.[1]

Clearly, a visitor to 1914 America—Wu was horrified by the tobacco smoke that clogged churches, lecture halls, homes, and offices[2]—could be excused for making comparative overestimates of "oriental" dignity. In any case, Wu's judgment of his fellow Chinese and the modern nature of their interests was spectacularly wrong. As the world now knows, the people of China now are as "lacking in dignity" as any other when it comes to emphasizing, cheering on, and excelling in modern sports.

It wasn't just Wu's prognostications that were wrong. The brilliant scholar-statesman also failed to notice the trends sweeping through the cities of early-twentieth-century China. By 1907, staff at the Tianjin Young Men's Christian Association had formulated a provocative challenge meant to stimulate the modern and nationalist sentiments of their Chinese charges:

1. When will China be able to send a winning athlete to the Olympic contests?
2. When will China be able to send a winning team to the Olympic contests?

1

3. When will China be able to invite all the world to come to Peking for an International Olympic contest, alternating with those at Athens?[3]

As famed missionary C. H. Robertson observed, these three simple but weighty questions had the power to "grip in a remarkable way the heart and imagination of Chinese officials, educators, and students."[4]

Missionaries were not the only ones who could challenge Chinese people in this way; the last years of the Qing saw the development of Chinese sporting media that could ask similarly painful questions. *Physical Education World (Tiyujie)*, the first Chinese physical culture periodical, was established in 1909 by Xu Yibing, a member of the Tongmenghui Revolutionary Alliance (a radical anti-Qing organization based in Japan) who returned from Japan to China to found the Chinese Calisthenics School (Zhongguo Ticao Xuexiao) in Shanghai. Indeed, Xu's opening essay left no doubt as to the real importance of physical culture in those times:

> The people of our nation are weary and spiritless, our bodies emaciated by disease. We trudge on towards death, and if we bother to find out why, we see that it is nothing else but the harm from our abandonment of *tiyu* [physical culture]. . . . Alas! These deficient, weak, exhausted bodies—what in the world would happen if they were pushed into the unforgiving competition of men in this evolutionary world of strong countries and strong physiques?[5]

More than Robertson and his YMCA students could ever know, such questions, or at least different versions of them, would continue to obsess Chinese elites for the remainder of the twentieth century. It is a measure of the turmoil of twentieth-century Chinese history that no one associated with the Tianjin YMCA in 1907 could have dreamed that China would have to wait until 1984 to collect its first Olympic medals and that it would be a full century before Beijing would host the games in 2008. Nevertheless, despite its Olympic shortcomings, China eagerly participated in the sporting revolution that spread throughout the world during the twentieth century.

One of the amazing cultural developments of the twentieth century was the popular acceptance and integration of modern sporting and physical culture forms, developed in particular western European contexts during the mid–nineteenth century, in virtually every nation on earth. Spurred on by the Olympic movement—that new tradition of fair competition between friendly nations—modern disciplines of sport, physical education, exercise, and physical fitness now are understood as universally relevant pursuits advanced by any worthwhile modern nation-state. Many indigenous physical forms—dances, races, bouts, and games with specific ritual functions—live on today, but they are almost always understood or studied as traditional artifacts that, in contrast to the modern sports that thrive on the athletic grounds and schoolyards of any nation, have a place only in the museum.

In China, these once-Western physical culture forms have now been welcomed, accepted, and understood for nearly a century simply as *tiyu*, a very broad category whose name translates as something like "body cultivation," "physical education," or "physical culture." China boasts a long history of physical endeavor, from the Confucian arts of archery and chariot riding, to the kickball games used in military training, to aristocratic polo and golf games, to the wrestling and "ice frolic" processions so popular with the royal spectators in the Qing dynasty court, to the storied and diverse history of Chinese popular martial arts.

However, the modern physical culture introduced to China in the late nineteenth century was a decisive break from these previous modes of physical endeavor. During the early years of the Chinese Republic (1912–49), Chinese scholars began to classify premodern physical activities as "ancient" or "traditional" *tiyu*. These elites intentionally posed contrasts between traditional Chinese exercises and competitions and the Western forms of ball games and Olympic-style competitions being promoted in China as endeavors required of a modern and healthy populace. This early Republican discourse was clearly part of the project to reinsert "China" into an international narrative of history and progress. Yet this book also suggests that the modern physical culture so quickly accepted as *tiyu* was novel for its systematic teleology of the relationship between individual strength, discipline, and health and the military, industrial, or diplomatic "strength" of a national body. Even the functions of the human body—from the physiological systems imagined in terms of specialized machinery, to the brain and central nervous system's "command" over the entire body, to the immune system's ability to defeat hostile invaders—were described and codified in terms of the nation and its citizens' political responsibilities. This book aims to show how the all-embracing "body cultivation" that *tiyu* offered the Chinese was a key concept in plans to transform the hoary Chinese imperium into a modern and fit nation-state.

Modern physical culture has always fit perfectly with the nation-state project and its notions of discipline, progress, and modernity. Its accepted rules and regulations, the limits that it sets for bodily motion and behavior, uniforms emblazoned with national symbols, quantitative measures of success, and images of battle and war so closely associated with competition have for over a century made these connections intuitively commonsensical all over the world. The values of the fit body and the strong nation took hold easily during the Republican period, as patriotic Chinese searched for anything that could finally make China the equal of the hated and envied imperialist powers.

The Janus-faced rhetoric of modern sporting ideology, with its constant tension between familiar Little League terms of sportsmanship and generosity and "playing fields of Eton" discussions of sport as metaphor for conquest and domination, also was mastered long ago in China. A current example of the view of competition as a benign stimulus to achievement that produces respect and cooperation among contenders is the official Beijing 2008 Olympic "vision," which states, "With our motto 'New Beijing, Great Olympics' and our goal to host a 'Green Olympics,' a 'Hi-tech Olympics,' and the 'People's Olympics,' Beijing is ready to become a truly international city. . . . We see the Olympic Games as a catalyst for exchange and harmony between various cultures and peoples."[6] But such ideological rhetoric goes back a hundred years, as shown by the effusive praise of the new athletic culture in a 1906 article by a Chinese contributor to the magazine *Tientsin Young Men:*

> "Competetion [*sic*] is the life of trade." . . . "The spirit of contest is the joy of exercise." . . . These and many others are fragmantary statments [*sic*] of a great and universal truth. . . . [T]hey are all related because they have to do with a great principle the meaning and extent of which the world has not yet been able to state nor even to conceive in its entirety. . . . A manifestation of one phrase of this great principle among men is included in the word "athletics."[7]

Similarly, the framing of modern sports competition in terms of confrontation and conquest has a long history. When Zhou Ming, the People's Republic of China (PRC) National Swim Team Head Coach, commented in 1997, "Just as our women [swimmers] dominate you now, so will our men dominate you in four, five, six years, and so too will we dominate you in world economics,"[8] he was merely stating in a more bellicose way what Y. Y. Hsuh, a student at the Shanghai Patriotic Girls' School, meant when she wrote in 1925, in English, "[O]ur country men, make up your mind, and try your best to improve athletics. In this way, China will some days be the strongest nation in the Far East, and in the world too."[9]

Although modern sporting ideology has long been part of Chinese popular discourse, Western historians and cultural critics have been slow to address this fact. English-language scholarship has never produced a substantive history of the Republican-era *tiyu* project or a sophisticated critique of the rise of Chinese physical culture.[10] The fullest work to date on Republican-era *tiyu* is Fan Hong's 1997 *Footbinding, Feminism and Freedom*, a dramatic recounting of sport's role in "the liberation of women's bodies in modern China." Fan's aims are to tell "the astounding history of [Chinese women's] struggle to reclaim their bodies, to reject mutilation on a gargantuan scale, to achieve physical normality, and finally, to seek through the exercise of their released bodies, health, pleasure, confidence, independence and achievement."[11] In many ways Fan is right about the significance of women's physical culture in China; I have discussed elsewhere how the liminal realm of physical culture and its relation to body, race, and nation became an important site for the late-Qing discussion of Chinese women, their bodies, and their role in a Chinese national future.[12] However, as Joan Judge has demonstrated, early-twentieth-century Chinese women's "new role as 'female citizens' was open to limitless manipulations,"[13] many of which were designed more to achieve national ends than to address the identities that these women might be shaping for themselves. Indeed, the optimistic narratives of progress and liberation that guide Fan make her work a tribute to the "liberating" aspect of modern sport that I mean to challenge here.

Anthropologist Susan Brownell's *Training the Body for China*, an account of sport, "body culture," and morality in the PRC of the 1980s, is the most thorough English-language investigation into Chinese physical culture to date. Brownell's notion of a "body culture" that "reflects the internalization and incorporation of culture" and her assertion that modern sports are an important site for the observation of Chinese "public culture" are useful ideas that have aided my inquiry into the *tiyu* of the early twentieth century.[14]

Brownell's description of the mania that greeted the PRC women's volleyball team's victory in the 1981 World Cup vividly illustrates her thesis. The university student who wrote to the team, solemnly asserting that their victory had allowed him for the first time to feel "the honor of being human,"[15] was expressing a sentiment that, while surely sincere, was hardly original. Since the end of the Qing dynasty, it had been widely accepted in China that modern physical culture was the truest indicator of national strength and health. Specifically, this quality was envied in the western European, American, and Japanese powers, which seemed able to expand their empires at will. Modern-minded Chinese wanted what these powerful nations had and thus were very amenable to the new sporting and exercise forms that seemed, from their first use, to inculcate the values and attitudes needed to create a nation that could work and struggle as a team for the cause of victory. Just as the modern global nation-state system into which Republican Chinese entered was based on particular rational models for organizing the state, its industry, and the lives of its citizenry, so was modern physical culture based on dominant models of rational organization.

Two nations had early-twentieth-century physical culture programs and ideologies that were strikingly similar to China's modern *tiyu*. One was the Soviet Union, where two instances—Lenin's faith in sport as a form of character training to mold the "all-around individual of communist society" and the Communist Party's 1925 description of *fizicheskoi kul'ture* (physical culture) as promoting health, fitness, the development of individuals' harmonious personalities, military training, and group identification[16]—strikingly mirror the development in China, during the 1920s and 1930s, of a "revolutionary" physical culture still influenced by earlier bourgeois YMCA-type notions of the complete modern individual. These similar patterns of development are best understood as a result of similarities between Soviet and Chinese concerns about military strength in the face of increasingly ambitious imperialist neighbors and as a reaction to the absolute power and pressure of the global nation-state system.

Chinese *tiyu*, however, owes its greatest debt to modern Japanese physical culture. Recent work by Douglas Reynolds and Lydia Liu has allowed us to see how crucial the Japanese presence and experience was in "translating" modernity into forms and language acceptable and comprehensible to Chinese modernizers.[17] As is true in so many other cultural, intellectual, and political realms, it is almost impossible to imagine a Chinese physical culture shorn of its early Japanese influence. The very terms of Chinese physical culture *(tiyu; ticao,* "calisthenics and gymnastics"; *yundong,* "exercise/sports")* were direct translations of Japanese terms *(taiiku, taisō, undō)* developed in the Meiji era.[18] Japan is also the site where many progressive Chinese got their first taste of the addictive modern discipline delivered by German- and Swedish-style calisthenics and gymnastics.

The Meiji Restoration provided the context, as in almost every other realm of Japanese culture and society, for the reconfiguring of "traditional" forms to meet the urgent needs of the modern era. Although *sumō* wrestling is now identified as the Japanese "national sport," the feudal connotations of traditional *sumō* organizational structures, the "embarrassing" nakedness of the wrestlers, and their "barbarous" topknot and swords all presented challenges to the Meiji "enlightenment" project.[19] Kanō Jigorō was celebrated in the twentieth century for his work in transforming the ancient martial art of *jūdō* into an international competitive form that still managed to retain "Japanese" notions of honor and composure.[20] The Chinese

TABLE 1. Physical Education in the 1904 Educational System

Level	Age	Year	Activities	Hours / Total per week
Kindergarten (Mengxuetang)	5–7	1–2	Games	1
Lower primary (Chudeng xiaoxuetang)	7–12	1	Exercises, Games	3/30
		2–5	Exercises, Games, Calisthenics	3/30
Upper primary (Gaodeng xiaoxuetang)	12–16	1	Calisthenics, Exercises	3/36
		2–4	Calisthenics, Exercises, Military Drill	3/36
Middle School (Zhongxuetang)	16–21	1–5	Calisthenics, Military Drill	2/36
Higher-level school (Gaodeng zhongxuetang)	21–24	1–3	Calisthenics, Military Drill	3/36

counterpart to these changes, as described in Chapter 7, was the widespread effort beginning in the 1910s to modernize, unify, and "scientize" the diverse body of Chinese martial arts in one educational, sporting, and healthy discipline known as *wushu*, or later, *guoshu*. Like the Japanese, who had also faced national and racial "extinction" at the hands of rapacious free traders, Chinese saw the cultivation of a healthy and manly national body as a priority of the age.

The first genre of modern physical culture to develop in China was *ticao* (from Japanese *taisō*), a program of calisthenics and gymnastics inspired by Swedish and German models, stamped with the impressive Meiji pedigree, and adapted by Chinese reformers and educators concerned about the health of their nation-race.[21] In the first years of the twentieth century, *taisō* students returning from Japan provided a crucial impetus for the expansion of this vigorous culture—translating Japanese treatises on physical education, sponsoring calisthenics meets, and founding physical education institutes throughout the empire.[22] Qing officialdom was quick to respond to this popular demand; the 1902 and 1904 Educational Systems included a significant emphasis on "soft calisthenics," gymnastics, and military drill at each level of education up through the higher-level academy (Table 1).[23] The calisthenics and gymnastics of the *ticao* regimen were so popular with young Chinese people that when students at the Shantung Christian University began a boycott of classes in November 1906, one of their demands was the appointment of a teacher in athletics and military drill.[24]

Thus modern *tiyu*—taught by progressive coaches, trained in specialized schools, sponsored by farseeing governments, and supported by enthusiastic fans—became an important element of Chinese culture in the early twentieth century. Since the early nineteenth century, the Qing dynasty had been beset by a series of domestic crises and often-related foreign threats that long before would have destroyed any lesser regime. The new physical culture seemed just the remedy for these national agonies. The drills and sports learned from German, Swedish, Japanese, British, and American models were understood in terms of discourses of self-strengthening in Confucianism and later in terms of important Social Darwinist and Spencerian ideas. They provided new and spectacular forms of individual participation in the new national program and were highly significant for how a modernized Qing China would relate to the established nations of the world.

Modern *tiyu* by no means represented the beginning of Chinese physical culture. Rituals and performances involving what some would now call sportlike contests were an important part of imperial culture for thousands of years. Studies of China's diverse and fascinating "ancient physical culture" (*gudai tiyu*), as described in Chapter 2, were undertaken for nationalistic reasons in the first decade of the twentieth century and still constitute a thriving nationalistic industry today. (One dramatic example was G. G. Tan's midcentury rhetorical question: "Who can deny that these changes and modifications [to "the art of ball games"] might not have been derived from the Orient, and more specifically, from China thousands of years before Christ?")[25]

Yet the forms of *gudai tiyu* were so numerous and so varied—originating in different parts of China or coming to China from different parts of Asia, used in different rituals to express different beliefs and hierarchies, and allowing their participants to relate to and present their bodies in different ways—that we cannot accurately characterize them as a single "ancient physical culture."[26] The premodern period offers no analogue to the totalizing modern physical culture introduced to China in the late nineteenth century as part of the modern world system of nation-states. Whereas ancient Chinese physical genres emphasized in different proportions martial manhood, aristocratic privilege, local flavor, and cosmological and calendrical patterns, the modern physical culture known as *tiyu* was one systematic ideology invested with specific ideals of the relationship between the individual and the national body. The modern *tiyu* was to these old physical cultures what the idea of nation-state was to the old imperial notion of *Tianxia*—

that the Emperor ruled "all under heaven"—a drastic break in the old order, instigated in the name of international standards, commerce, and engagement. Modern notions of physical fitness and strength rendered virtually all of the diverse forms of Chinese physical culture obsolete and relegated them to history. Although the genres known as "martial arts" were kept alive by proud nationalist activists, and a few games that were dubbed "traditional" sports were allowed to survive as quaint Oriental living relics, modern forms of physical culture predominated in the national realm.

National narratives from the PRC era typically portray the 1840s as the dawn of modern Chinese history, and PRC histories of tiyu tend to conform to official periodization by placing the beginnings of modern Chinese physical culture in that decade as well. Secondary sources predictably cite as watershed moments the heroic resistance, during the Opium War, of the "British-Quelling Squads" (Pingyingtuan) recruited from martial arts bands in Sanyuanli, Guangzhou, in 1841[27] and Wei Yuan's writings, in the 1840s, on Western methods of military training troops.[28] This exaggerated commitment to modern and national political correctness in PRC sources— in part structural, since Chinese *tiyu* historians work not in history departments but in physical education departments, where there is a very clear sense of the role of *tiyu* in the national enterprise—makes much of PRC *tiyu* scholarship analytically problematic, if still providing useful guidance on chronology and bibliography.

The great majority of the source materials drawn upon for this volume are books, scholarly journals, popular magazines, and newspapers dating to the Republican period, mostly during the 1920s and 1930s. One of the thrills of this project was to be able to pore over the many hundreds of sporting books and magazines published during the Republican era that have never been examined by Western historians. The mountains of *tiyu*-related materials that I was able to locate in libraries and archives throughout China quickly erased any doubts I had as to the feasibility of this research project, or, more importantly, to its significance for understanding the culture and thought of the Republican period.

Perhaps my most important finding is the degree to which physical culture was not only an instrument useful in creating the modern state and citizen but a vital element of this transformation itself. It was taken for granted that *tiyu* did more than make Chinese citizens muscular and fit; only this new bodily science could teach the values—competition, sportsmanship, confidence, awareness, discipline—that would create a new China. The two-character phrase *tiyu*—used first in its modern sense in Yan Fu's "On Strength" (1895)[29]—is a direct reimportation of the characters used in the

Japanese *taiiku,* itself an early-Meiji translation of Herbert Spencer's concept of "a physical education."[30] To Spencer, and to his Japanese and Chinese disciples, this education via physical gestures, movements, and control (which joined with a moral and an intellectual education to complete the whole self) was much more broad and totalizing than simple exercises in gym class.[31]

The specialized *ticao* academies[32] that began springing up all over China during the last years of the Qing demonstrate this trend (Table 2). Little is known about the exact curricula of most of these schools, but a 1907 entry in *Shibao* shows that the Chinese Calisthenics School's one-and-a-half-year program included training in military drill, gymnastics, calisthenics, games, judo, fencing, education theory, ethics, physical education theory, physiology, medical theory, military theory, surveying, drawing, and music.[33] This was hardly mindless body-drilling, but rather a truly physical education that would prepare China's young generation for the modern era by linking their fit individual bodies to a society governed by rigorously scientific standards.

In line with this new social consciousness, modern physical culture now became a public spectacle, a demonstration of a new China where the "public" and its opinions now mattered. The viability of the new Chinese nation was related to what Bennett has termed the "exhibitionary complex"—"the opening up of objects to more public contexts of inspection and visibility . . . which simultaneously helped to form a new public and inscribe it in new relations of sight and vision."[34] Thus the large-scale public athletic meet (*yundonghui,* from Japanese *undōkai*) became a common part of the Chinese educational and social landscape beginning in 1905. The first Chinese-run athletic meet was a massive affair put on by the Chengdu Military Academy in November 1905. There, 3,281 student-athletes from forty-one academies participated in various footraces, calisthenics, and military drills, helping China finally to join "the world trend that only competition can ensure survival."[35] That this brand of athletic meet spread to Guilin in 1907 and even to Chishui County, Guizhou, in 1909[36] testifies to the popularity and power of the message delivered by the new public-spirited *yundonghui* meet.

The very nature of this modern physical culture and the large public venues it created also opened up new spaces for explicit political discussion and action. The crowds that these athletic meets drew, and the spontaneous collective energy they inspired, combined to create atmospheres buzzing with public and political concern. For example, at a Suzhou meet in 1909, after the completion of the four-hundred-yard dash, "mountains and oceans of people" seized by enthusiasm for progressive political reform left their seats

TABLE 2. Sampling of Qing-Era
Physical Education Training Schools

Name of School	Location	Founded
Hangzhou Educational Association *Tiyu* Institute	Hangzhou	1904
Military Academy *Ticao* Research Institute	Changsha	1904
Fengtian *Ticao* Training School	Shenyang	1905
Shanghai *Ticao* & Games Institute	Shanghai	1905
Sichuan Chengdu Zaiwu Academy *Ticao* Academy	Chengdu	1905
Songjiang Prefecture Louxian County Study-Promotion Society *Ticao* Institute	Songjiang	1905
Sichuan Higher Academy *Tiyu* Academy	Chengdu	1906
Sichuan *Tiyu* Training Academy	Chengdu	1906
Ticao Training School	Kunming	1906
Chinese Calisthenics School	Shanghai	1907
Fujian Normal Academy *Tiyu* Training School	Fuzhou	1907
Henan *Tiyu* Training Academy	Zhengzhou	1907
Summer Women's *Ticao* & Games Lecture Series	Suzhou	1907
Wang Family Shuren Academy *Ticao* Program	Zigong, Sichuan	1907
Chinese Women's *Ticao* School	Shanghai	1908
Chongqing *Tiyu* Academy	Chongqing	1908
Study-Promotion Society *Ticao* Research Institute	Tianjin	1908
Fengtian Official *Ticao* Training School	Shenyang	1909
Shouzhou *Ticao* Training School	Shouzhou, Anhui	1910
Fujian Provincial *Tiyu* School	Fuzhou	1911
Short-Session *Tiyu* Instructors Training School	Changsha	1911

SOURCES: *Shenyang shi tiyu zhi* (Shenyang: Shenyang chubanshe, 1989), 189; "Xuebu caijing," File 241, First Historical Archives, Beijing, China; Qiao Keqin and Guan Wenming, *Zhongguo tiyu sixiangshi* (Lanzhou: Gansu minzu chubanshe, 1993), 180; Zhang Weidai, "Yunnan minzhu geming de xianxingzhe, jindai tiyu de kaituozhe—Yang Zhenhong," *Kunming tiyu wenshi* 2 (1987), 79; *Tiyu wenshi* 49 (May 1991), inside front cover; Zheng Zhilin and Zhao Shanxing, "Zhongguo ticao xuexiao jianjie," *Tiyu yundong jiaoxue cankao ziliao* 15 (May 1982), 12; Sun Bailu, "Zhongguo zui zao de tiyu xuexiao," *Shanghai tiyu shihua* 12 (December 1985), 22; Tan Hua, "Jindai tiyu yundong zai Sichuan de chuqi chuanbo," in *Tiyushi wenji* (Chengdu: Chengdu tiyu xueyuan tiyushi yanjiushi, 1983), 203; Hunan sheng difangzhi bianzuan weiyuanhui, ed., *Hunan shengzhi, di ershier juan: Tiyu zhi* (Changsha: Hunan chubanshe, 1994), 114–115; Lin Mingyi, "Qingmo xuexiao tiyu," 23; Tianjin shi difangzhi bianxiu weiyuanhui, ed., *Tianjin tongzhi: Tiyu zhi* (Tianjin: Tianjin shehui kexueyuan chubanshe, 1994), 124; Fujian sheng difangzhi bianzuan weiyuanhui, ed., *Fujian shengzhi: Tiyu zhi* (Fuzhou: Fujian renmin chubanshe, 1993), 361; Zhang Tianbai, "Zhongguo zui zao de tiyu xuexiao bushi 'Songjiang Fulou xian Quanxuehui ticao chuanxisuo,'" *Tiyu wenshi* 52 (November 1991), 59–60.

to sign a petition circulated by students from the Higher Academy and Public Middle Academy in support of a National Assembly.[37] Similarly, a meet held in mid-1911 at the Middle/Elementary Girls' School in Shanghai included, amidst the calisthenics and dance routines, events listed as "Recover Sovereignty" (effective sovereignty over the areas of coastal China that the Qing had lost) and "Seeking Donations for the Jiangbei Flood"; after the second of these, "the spectators untied their purse strings to help."[38] Such athletic meets, which invited crowd participation in the form of cheering and rooting for particular athletes or sides, encouraged the intimate involvement of a "public" in the political affairs of the nation.[39] The spectacle of the new physical culture, much more than any military drill imposed by the commands of a single leader, made it possible to imagine a China where the people (even if only the middle-class crowds who could pay for entry) finally could take an active role in steering the movements and business of the nation.

Studying modern Chinese *tiyu* also brings out China's ambivalent relationships with the Western nations, who worked just as hard to spread these modern ideologies as the Chinese did to integrate and adapt them. The last two decades of the Qing dynasty saw the introduction of the "Anglo-American" model of "sport" (track and field, team sports) into Chinese schools and urban settings, a trend that had greatly influenced development of a modern Chinese physical culture in the early years of the twentieth century. While many argue over who was first to import sports into China—which missionaries or which Chinese returning from Southeast Asia—there is little question that the YMCA made great and lasting contributions to Chinese sport. Christian manhood was the prescription delivered by these medics of national health; as described above, they felt that Japanese and Western critics would never again ridicule China as the "sick man of East Asia" after they were finished training, building, and perfecting the new Chinese man. The YMCA's timely emphasis on physical fitness in the Darwinist world of the nineteenth century was surely one of the reasons for its great success, first in the West and then elsewhere. In China, it also probably did not hurt that the Y's "three-self" formulation of the complete individual, healthy in body, mind, and spirit, introduced in 1895, matched perfectly the Spencerian ideal so influential in Yan Fu's China.

For all their well-known hubris, the YMCA missionaries' commitment to the status and identity of a Chinese nation was remarkable. This agency was the driving force behind the organization of the first Chinese national athletic meet, the First National Athletic Alliance of Regional Student Teams (hereafter referred to as the First National Games), held on the grounds of the Nanyang Industrial Exposition in Nanjing in October 1910.[40] This great celebration of the construction of a capitalist economy, a capitalist labor discipline, and a modern ethos of production and consumption in China seemed the perfect moment for such a public and spectacular breakthrough in Chinese national strength and unification.[41] Indeed, the YMCA magazine *Association Men* reported "monster gatherings" at the meet's basketball and soccer games and a first-day crowd of "16,000, mostly college boys."[42] Fong F. Sec, a Chinese convert to Christianity who would later be chairman of the YMCA National Committee, expressed his appreciation of the event in self-Orientalizing terms: "Those sturdy athletes, wearing spikes and running gear, as they strained every nerve and grit their teeth in order to win honors for their college or section, formed a strong contrast to the gentlemen with long finger-nails, large goggles, and round shoulders—the typical Chinese scholar of the old school."[43] To many of Sec's fellow modernizing Chinese, the most powerful symbol of the obstacles blocking the development of a strong and masculine China was the queue, the humiliating "pigtail" that Manchu rule required all male subjects to wear. Remarkably, eight athletes on the North China team felt so liberated by their upcoming participation in this national meet that they cut off their queues completely on their way to the ancient southern capital.[44]

The most impressive example of the transformative tension of this moment was Sun Baoxin of Tianjin, a standout Putong Academy student and, as the holder of six North China athletic records, one of the finest athletes in all China.[45] But "on account of opposition from his family," Sun could not convince himself to join his dangerously open-minded teammates in liberating himself from this symbol of Manchu rule. His hesitation would cost him days later. On the first day of the meet, Sun faced tough challengers from Shanghai and Nanjing in the high jump competition. When it came his turn, sporting tragedy struck. Sun's strenuous jump was enough to clear the bar, but his long swinging queue knocked the bar to the ground. Encouraged by a meet official who barked at the disappointed Sun, "Cut it off at once!" Sun took the drastic step that he had once feared. Now with victory and national fame on the line, Sun "hacked his queue off that night, with the declaration that the next day he would jump higher than any one ever jumped before in China. He made good on his boast, setting the excellent mark for future competitors of 5 ft. 5¾ in."[46] Buoyed by newfound manhood and ambition, Sun went on to win seven National Games medals and make his name as a true pioneer of Chinese masculinity and modernity.

There could be few finer symbols of the drive, the initiative, and the personal and national tensions of the new sports physical culture than Sun's performance in Nanjing. He and his teammates achieved a real measure of individual self-definition and confidence via this new system of bodily discipline and expression passed on by their YMCA coaches. The fact that the new culture originated in England and not in China does not make this transformation, or the transformative experiences of millions of others involved in the *tiyu* movement, any less worthy or genuine. Lazarus's recent commentary on Adorno's thoughts about "hating tradition properly"—what better example than privileged athletes who cut off their queues on board a train to a national track meet?—is useful here in explaining just how "profoundly ruptural"[47] this moment of entry into the modern can be. For a long time, access to the institutions, facilities, ideologies, and commercial paraphernalia of modern physical culture had much to do with class and privilege; the Chinese athlete, every bit as much as Adorno's "African students of political economy [and] Siamese at Oxford,"[48] was a member of the bourgeois class who had much to gain by manipulating and channeling the "native" adoption of modernity. Yet dismissing participation in this vital new culture as some corrupt elitist monopoly on the spoils of cultural imperialism would be shortsighted. Lazarus's rethinking of how to "hate tradition . . . [in order] to keep faith with true universality"[49] allows us to see the attraction of the new tiyu.

At the same time, explaining modern Chinese *tiyu* also requires more than a defense of the nation, like Jusdanis's recent claim that nationalism is "an attempt to interpret and participate in modernity." His contention that "nationalism actually mediates in the interaction between the self and the other, between the individual and the universal, the old and the new" is helpful in understanding the role of the nation in shaping modern Chinese physical culture.[50] But it still does not capture the fundamentally and radically inclusive ideology of the (sometimes exclusive) *tiyu*, which came to represent a crucial site for the dissemination of modern knowledge, values, and skills. Modern physical culture was uniquely suited to this task, as its self-consciously modern, and simultaneously disciplining and "liberating," movements and gestures provided an opportunity to participate in and receive the important "body cultivation" that *tiyu* promised by its very name. At a time of claims that the modern newspaper could create a "new citizen" and ensure national survival,[51] that the art of public speaking could "raise morale high and low and target the soul of the nation,"[52] and that a Commercial Press textbook series could spread crucial "knowledge of human life" to a new Chinese reading public,[53] it surely seemed believable that the new physical culture could transform the youth of the Republic, programming into their bodies nationalist reflexes as immediate and unconscious as their muscles' responses to training. Little idle "imagining" would be necessary to convince a generation of physically active modern citizens that a new Chinese community was being built.

The chapters that follow trace the many national, racial, sexual, social, and political threads of discourse that came to interrogate and define the realm of physical culture in Republican China. Chapters 2 through 4 explain the evolution, from the 1910s to the 1920s, of a liberal democratic *tiyu* dominated by Anglo-American "sports" and this culture's totalizing notions of teamwork, sportsmanship, the competitive instinct so necessary for success in the "fair competition" under which capitalism justified its global expansion, and more strident post-May 30th nationalism. The fifth and sixth chapters explain the dual and contradictory 1930s foci of building a *"tiyu* for the masses" and fostering elite competitive sport, and they explore the implications of elite Chinese athletes representing the nation in the Far Eastern Championship Games and the Olympics. Chapter 7 turns to Chinese martial arts *(wushu, guoshu)* as a case study of the nationalizing trends I have described here in a realm that was thought to be hopelessly backward, too dependent on oral transmission and too fragmented into diverse and incompatible traditions to be of any use in the modern age. Finally, Chapter 8 describes briefly Chinese physical culture during the war years, 1937–49, suggesting that many of the Guomindang's measures in promoting a mass *tiyu* made possible the organizational and philosophical directions of the Chinese Communist Party's later "red" physical culture.

The history of Republican-era Chinese physical culture was shaped by many trends that were diverse in origins, goals, and sites of performance. Whatever the outward forms of these different *tiyu* models, however, they always shared two tenets: that the Chinese nation would be based on a citizenry who would learn the art of self-discipline and attention to the larger consequences of all their actions and movements and that this could be taught only through a program of physical education or "body cultivation." For decades, historians of modern China have paid attention to the importance of the New Culture and New Education movements and new philosophies of the Republican era and how these all influenced the Chinese nation by influencing the ways Chinese talked and thought. Rarely, however, have we bothered to see how new ideas of physical fitness, physical education, physical exercise, and physical competition shaped the Chinese nation by influencing the ways in which Chinese understood and presented their bodies to fellow citizens and to the outside world. This is the impetus for this book—a history that examines the relationship between physical culture and the modern nation-state's concern with the individual citizen's every move and the way in which individuals' movements acquire new meanings in the context of twentieth-century nationalism.

Finally, a note on *tiyu* and my working terminology. Despite the insistence of many scholars, the term *tiyu* covers far too vast a terrain to render simply as "sport," "athletics," "physical education," "physical fitness," or any combination of the above. The English term that comes closest, regrettably, is "physical culture"—a somewhat ham-fisted and literal translation of *Körperkultur* that does cover a wider range of activity than the more convenient but too-specific English "sport." When not addressing more specific subdisciplines of *tiyu* that can be translated more faithfully as "sport" or "physical education," for example, I use the term *physical culture* to encompass the larger mission that modern *tiyu* represented in Republican China. Translation difficulties aside, the Chinese term *tiyu* also carries specifically modern and totalizing meanings that are central to my investigation into this topic. This project focuses on the connections between Chinese ideas and practices of physical culture and notions of the nation, modernity, and a modern citizenry. *Tiyu* was about more than just sports, physical education, fitness, or any combination of these; its *yu* (educational/cultivating aspect) was an important element that would transform modern physical culture, with its scientific legitimacy, its clear rules regarding physical movement, and its emphasis on rational record keeping, into a set of lived and played moral teachings designed to shape a new self-conscious, self-disciplining citizen.

2 "Now the Fun of Exercise Can Be Realized"

From Calisthenics and Gymnastics
Ticao *to Sports* Tiyu *in the 1910s*

Urban China in the 1910s was a world of exciting philosophical, educational, political, cultural, literary, and scientific explorations. One aspect of the new freedom experienced during China's first republican decade was a fascination, among many Chinese citizens, with physical education and body cultivation. Among the many modern concepts that quickly became widely accepted in the Republican era was that the national body would be strengthened and unified by a fit, competitive, disciplined citizenry that could work and play together as a team.

If the connection between physical exercise and a strong Chinese nation seemed obvious during the 1910s, there was still much debate over the merits and ideological implications of the different forms of modern *tiyu*. Discussions usually centered on two main types—the *ticao* of German and Swedish gymnastics and calisthenics and the Anglo-American team sports of ball games and track and field—although a third type created especially for schools, "calisthenics and games," had evolved from these two dominant forms. By the beginning of the nationalist and antitraditionalist "Chinese Enlightenment" known as the May Fourth Movement of 1919, competitive team sports had emerged as the strengthening and unifying *tiyu* of choice, with *ticao* calisthenics lingering on as a disciplinary supplement. Absent from virtually all of the mainstream debates were the traditional Chinese martial arts *(wushu)*, which many of these modern-minded Republican patriots simply ignored. Their nationalism tended to be less essentializing than that of many of their contemporaries, and their aversion to Chinese feudal and unscientific forms led them to construct *tiyu* forms based on modern (European-American-Japanese) definitions of bodies and nations.

At the end of the 1910s, the forms of physical exercise and recreation in

China marked by the term *tiyu* greatly resembled Western "sports" or "athletics." Remarkably, since the early debates, this definition of *tiyu* as "sports" has persisted, altered only minimally up to the present. Given the significance of physical culture and physical fitness in twentieth-century China, this poses two important questions: What was the power and attraction of this new Western *tiyu,* and how did it become so wrapped up in the Chinese nation?

I do not share the assumptions, so common to sport sociology, that Anglo-American "sports" are natural forms of societal organization or that there is a basic human evolutionary need to participate in public rituals of competition and teamwork. However, interrogating the supposed universality of these games forces one to question why so many peoples all over the world *have* taken to the Western athletic forms as universal. The Anglo-American sports are a particular form of physical activity, developed at a specific time in a specific place as part of a specific worldview. How have these values managed to endure as the Chinese *tiyu?*

The prevalence of a fairly uniform standard of physical activities and competitions around the world is closely tied to the fairly uniform standard of the modern nation-state that transcends any official ruling ideology of the twentieth century. Indeed, it seems almost impossible to imagine modern athletics without its national foundation and functions. China was no exception to this model. Chinese *tiyu* was built along with, and in, the new Republic of China founded in 1912, and it refracted external influences in similar ways. It was in the name of the Chinese nation that physical culture developed in the ways it did. Likewise, the competitions, struggles, and lessons of China's athletic grounds in the 1910s influenced how many Chinese people saw their future as a nation. The world systems of athletics and of the nation-state worked in parallel, positing the athletic arena as a representation of the nation. By May Fourth, urban elites from all over China, presented with the foreign details of both systems, had already worked to build the Chinese nation around them.

COMPETITIVE SPORTS IN THE EARLY REPUBLIC

The Anglo-American model of competitive athletics, though introduced to China some decades after the military drill, flourished in many Chinese cities by the end of the Qing. Christianity, a can-do spirit, and physical wellness were all part of this missionary *tiyu* package that established itself as the Euro-Japanese *ticao*'s competitor for the loyalties of physically active Chinese.

The YMCA, as described in Chapter 1, taught sports as a way to transform China, starting with its individual citizens, into a nation recognizable to Western eyes. Men would be conditioned morally, mentally, and physically by competitive sports, as women, trained by caring missionaries in the domestic womanly arts, watched in appreciation their understanding of team strategy, individual discipline, and fair play.

Sports also held opportunities for salvation on the national level. The Chinese non-nation, consigned to limbo by the rational and strong nations of the West and Japan over the previous decades, could finally enter the light in the domain of sports. The 1910 national athletic meet held in Nanjing gave the first glimpses of what sports held in store for the nation. Athletes from different corners of China, skilled in similar universal arts, came together of their own accord to be judged, timed, measured, and rated and to be cheered on by appreciative crowds with the foresight to understand the importance of these events. Only a few venues could provide these truly national experiences for modern-minded young Chinese. Three of these important meets, described below, were the Second National Games of 1914 and the Far Eastern Championship Games of 1913 and 1915.

The early career of sports in China was perhaps aided by their exclusivity. For privileged university youth of the 1900s–1910s, adoption of the new Western/modern ideology of sport and its knowledge of the body and its movements was one more conspicuous way to display their elite status. Alumni later remembered fondly that "[f]or a time people were able to 'spot' a St. John's student by the way he walked and by the way in which he carried himself when walking."[1] Access to modern *tiyu* soon became much less exclusive, but by then its associations with the nation allowed it to maintain its relevance in the Republican era.

The Second National Games, 1914

The magic and fun that graced China's ancient Southern Capital, Nanjing, in 1910, when the First National Games were held there, came to Beijing four years later with China's second national athletic meet. As befitted the new Republic based in the Northern Capital, changes were made from the format of the first national meet sponsored by the now-defunct Qing. First was the name of the meet itself—it was now the First National United Athletic Meet (Di yi ci quanguo lianhe yundong dahui, but conventionally referred to as the Second National Games), signaling the beginning of a new Republican sporting era.[2]

Organized by the Peking Athletic Association, which had close ties to the Beijing YMCA, the games had a new host site as well: they were unexpectedly moved from the Nanyang Industrial Expo, where they had been held in 1910, to Beijing's Tiantan Park. The museumified "Chineseness" associated with what one observer called "the historical grounds of the world-famous Temple of Heaven"[3] hardly evoked the atmosphere of progress and industry that had enveloped athletes and spectators alike in Nanjing four years before. Perhaps with this in mind, the games' sponsors provided the trappings that could bring a modern national spirit to the capital. The games' second day featured not only music by an official Presidential Palace marching band but also a thrilling air show put on by the Nanyuan Aviation School, whose planes showered games leaflets and colored confetti over the crowd of fifteen thousand people gathered at the Tiantan grounds.[4]

The choice of Tiantan as host to the games is fascinating. Were participants in a national athletic meet held in the Temple of Heaven supposed to sense a connection with the storied Chinese past as they competed in events not long removed from their Western origin? Or was the meet a deliberately formed "striking" contrast between progress and tradition, like later tokenizing pictures of rickshaw men standing next to shiny new automobiles? Brownell suggests another possibility: that the YMCA's blatantly untraditional use of this area as a sports field—reminding observers of the new primacy of Western culture all around the world—was similar to the symbolic revenge enjoyed by American and British troops who vandalized and desecrated these sacred Qing temples after the end of the Boxer siege in 1901.[5] Yet all of these explanations share the radical notion that, in different ways, the new *tiyu* was qualified to stand on its own in the long shadow of the Temple of Heaven.

Other adjustments were made to the original national meet format to republicanize the 1914 games. In line with an evolving sense of the importance of teamwork and team spirit, the second games added baseball and volleyball to the track, tennis, soccer, and basketball of 1910. The first meet had hosted competitions on three different levels: sectional (open to all), intercollegiate, and middle school (ages fifteen to twenty). In the new Republican age, these divisions, which reflected on the athletes' level of schooling (and ultimately their socioeconomic status) in a way that worked against impressions of national unity, seemed inappropriate. Furthermore, three distinct divisions of competition could not provide *one* winning team. Nations competing against each other for economic or military domination could not share victory; only one nation could win, and the "practice struggles" of athletics had to reflect that larger reality.

Finally, the regional divisions for athletes were also completely redrawn here and generically named East, West, South, and North. The groupings of 1910 had divided the nation into three specific, central metropolitan regions (Shanghai, Nanjing/Suzhou, Wuhan) and two amorphous stretches of South China and North China. The new lines of 1914 represented a tremendous change: defining regions only by compass directions "leveled" the nation, replacing regional favoritism with an objective, scientific classification in a new nation of equal citizens.[6]

Many celebrated the second national meet as another step in Chinese society's march "in the direction of progress and rejuvenation." One YMCA observer commented on the significance of the athletes' scantily clad public performances:

> Nothing [in the past] would have degraded a student more in the eyes of his fellow students and friends than the participation in a game of football or a contest on the athletic field. To doff the long flowing gown and don in its place the short shirt without sleeves and the short pants without leggings and run about in the full view of spectators would have given as much a sense of pain and mortification to the actor and as great a shock to the spectators as would be the case if a guest were to appear in his nightgown in the drawing room for a dinner party. Such would have been the attitude of the students a generation ago, and for hundreds of generations back. Today we see just the reverse of the case. The students now come from all over the country and go into athletics with zeal and enthusiasm. The victorious athlete becomes the adored hero of his college and the happy recipient of admiration and praise from all his friends.[7]

The new Chinese student, as strong mentally as physically, and freed from the "effeminate influence"[8] of imperial society, was thus the crowning achievement of the YMCA in China. Concerned less with the elitist nature of the national meet, which drew only from the small and privileged population of college students, than with the fact that these respectable men were actually running around in their underwear like Western amateur gentlemen, nation-minded observers like the YMCA could take much pride in the universally defined progress China was making in its early Republican years.

The First Far Eastern Championship Games, 1913

Modern competitive sport gave the Chinese the opportunity not only to hold national events but also to engage in international competitions where they could display the abilities of their new nation. In 1913 Manila, Philippine Governor-General W. Cameron Forbes welcomed them onto this new stage. Dressed for the colony's spring weather in a white suit and white shoes,

Forbes stood on a small platform decorated with red, white, and blue bunting and seating several Western men and women in wicker chairs. Forbes proclaimed, white hat in hand, to the athletes gathered before him:[9]

> In the name of the Government of the United States and the Government and people of the Philippine Islands, I stand before you, the athletes of the new Republic of China and of our sister nation, the Empire of Japan, and of the Philippine Islands, and extend to you all a hearty welcome. I hope that all your contests will be carried on in the spirit of fair play, which in after years may govern your conduct in business and other vocations of grown-ups.[10]

With this condescending allusion to the universalizing ideologies of free trade and fair play began the First Far Eastern Championship Games and the international athletic debut of the Republic of China.

The Far Eastern Games, originally called the Far Eastern Olympic Games, were the brainchild of Elwood S. Brown, the YMCA physical director in Manila. An annual Manila Carnival every February had featured informal athletic events (including athletes from Japan, Hong Kong, and Singapore) for several years. In 1909, when YMCA officials became concerned about the adverse moral effects of paying athletes to participate in these events, the carnival games were promptly put under the jurisdiction of the Philippine Amateur Athletic Federation.[11] Brown took the next step, traveling to China and Japan in 1911–12 to secure the participation of YMCAs and government agencies there[12] and forming a Far Eastern Olympic Association.[13] In 1912, he reported back to YMCA headquarters on his efforts: "It seems well worth while to arouse the Oriental millions to a realization of their athletic possibilities, both from the standpoint of individual competition and of general athletic development."[14]

In short, these games were put on by white men[15] for the edification, masculinization, and Westernization of their weak Oriental pupils. They hoped that the games could be a place for the athletes to learn and live Governor-General Forbes's fair play and capitalist spirit. One observer in Manila gushed,

> The Far Eastern Olympiad is quite the most significant event that has touched Oriental peoples in united action. They have never met before for united action on any other basis than athletics. The Olympiad is democracy in itself. . . . The Far Eastern Olympiad is the outward manifestation of the spirit of the younger generation. The "effete, effulgent East" of the poets is passing away and the rise of the common man and the solidarity of nations is coming apace.[16]

The games were meant to spread the benefits of Western morality, masculinity, and the nation-state system to places still mired in more backward folkways. Agents of the West had to bring safe and recognizable notions of modern man and the nation (embodied here in the international Olympic movement) *to* Asians, avoiding the risk that they might come up with their own and unknown forms. Governor-General Forbes's banal speech at the games award ceremony at Malacañang Palace underscored even further this theme of an Asia inscribed by Western visions of amateur purity, universal progress, and modern commerce:

> Victory on the athletic field reveals the germ of success in the victor and points to greater triumphs later on in life. But do not let the pursuit of the dollar enter into and corrupt your sports. I hope that this meet just closed will be the forerunner of others in which the peoples of these neighboring countries may mingle . . . and develop closer business relations, so that the vast watery desert of the Pacific may in time become alive with the ships of these countries plying in the international commerce.[17]

The imperialist framework of these early *tiyu* efforts provides little inspiration for a strong Chinese nationalistic spirit—which is one reason that they have attracted little attention in PRC historiography. However, the historian with less of a stake in reproducing contemporary Chinese chauvinistic nationalism would not want to conclude that athletes participating in the Far Eastern Games were somehow deluded into selling out their national identity. Indeed, it would be hard to discount the great pride these athletes must have felt representing their nation (actually personifying it, not just training to defend it, as in the calisthenics of *ticao*) under the national flag, before tens of thousands of people in cosmopolitan Manila.[18] The preliminary competitions held to determine who would represent China in the games and the traveling done to reach the competition site must have impressed the athletes with the immensity of their task—that of inserting China, via their own bodily exertions, into the struggle that modernity posed for all the world's nation-states.

Thirty-six Chinese athletes[19] made the trip to Manila to compete in track and field, swimming, soccer, basketball, and volleyball competitions against 103 Filipino and thirteen Japanese athletes.[20] The Chinese team managed to capture second place overall, their performance winning much praise among Westerners fascinated by the phenomenon of real live Chinese athletic bodies. One reporter wrote, "Altogether, [the Chinese athletes] are lads who present a pleasing spectacle on the athletic field. The majority are well above medium height, possess clear, healthy complexions, and have 'athlete' stamped all over them."[21]

Chinese understandings of their first international competition did not always fit perfectly into the categories originally built into this recent form of organization. On one hand, Chinese observers could rejoice, using Western-inspired terms of progress and international friendship, in the great step that these games represented for their nation. Shanghai's *True Record* commented, "These Far Eastern Championship Games give rise to the hope that someday [China] will join the International [Olympic] Games *(huanqiu da yundonghui)*. . . . These Far Eastern Games should be sufficient to arouse the athletic spirit in the people of our nation, and to join in friendship and polite relations with the youth of other nations."[22] Other times, very literal Chinese interpretations of the games and their significance caught Western organizers off guard. The best example of this was a "ticklish question,"

> arising out of the protest of the Chinese soccer football team, which played a match yesterday with the eleven representing the Philippines. The visitors point out that, whereas they are pure-blooded Chinese, the eleven sent against them are not pure-blooded Filipinos, but are mestizos, and add, with a great deal of justice, that it would have been possible for them to have brought down a team of Eurasians, if they had not been convinced that pure Chinese, Japanese, or Filipinos only would be allowed to compete.[23]

With this soccer protest, the Chinese let the embarrassing genie out of the bottle: that the national struggles that international competitive sport represented were also racial ones. Once the Chinese had brought up this complicated race/nation question, there was little that Western observers could do but praise their reasoning. The lead *Manila Times* editorial of the next day read, "There is much justice in [the Chinese] contention. . . . [T]hey fully understood that they were to meet none but pure-blooded orientals. The authorities are confronted with the necessity, therefore, of making a ruling which shall settle the status of the man of mixed blood, the Eurasian, or, in local terminology mestizo."[24]

The Chinese delegation's frankness on this matter was clearly related to the close overlap between ideas of race and nation in the early Republic. Frank Dikötter has explained thoroughly the many ways in which race was nation and nation was race, national pride racial pride, and national danger racial danger.[25] These connections surely were not foreign to the Western observers so startled by the controversy, although their relief at its resolution speaks to just how awkward the question of "race eligibility" was. There is no record of how the Far Eastern Athletic Association ruled on this issue, but the Chinese did not even wait for such a decision, electing to make arrangements on their own terms. Team management reported to games authorities that the Chinese "would be willing to let the championship game stand if the mestizo players questioned would declare themselves Filipinos."[26] In the end, then, all the Chinese asked for was symmetry, Chinese versus Filipinos, fair and square. A simple exercise in rectifying names was all it took to resolve this contradiction between race and nation, as the Chinese players were perfectly willing to admit defeat to a truly national (read racially) Filipino team.

The foreignness of the Far Eastern Games did not prevent them from quickly becoming significant for a modern Chinese worldview. Obviously the games were a "foreign-run" affair, from the YMCA organizers to the "Yankee Doodle" and "Aloha Oe" calisthenics routines performed by Manila children during the opening ceremonies.[27] But in a world dominated by political and economic systems designed by these same foreigners, few could find fault with productive training rituals like the games, which provided a site for Chinese actors to articulate their ideas about these modern forms. Indeed, Francis Wilber of the Guangzhou YMCA wrote some months after the Manila meet of the lasting "keen" interest and "athletic prestige" associated with the games.[28] No matter who put on or refereed the Far Eastern Games, the act of leaving China for a foreign land, or of competing with representatives of other nations in one's own homeland, could confirm that China now belonged in the world. And no matter who had taught the athletes the connections between nation and physical exertion, their sweat and strain in these international settings could never have seemed more valuable to their beloved China.

The Second Far Eastern Championship Games, 1915

The coming of the Second Far Eastern Games to Shanghai in 1915 was widely seen as another glorious stride on the road to real nationhood. In his opening address, Foreign Ministry representative Yang Cheng, representing President Yuan Shikai, proclaimed:

> This is an age of young men—young men, to take the responsibility which will soon be yours as leaders of the nation, must have strong bodies. To get strong bodies you must be active and energetic, and there is nothing that will help, both in the development of the body and in the development of character, like competitive athletics . . . [The games] offer the opportunity for you to measure your strength against foemen worthy of you. The champion athletes of three nations are here assembled. May your time and energies be spent in healthful competition, striving for mastery without feelings of enmity against your brother man. You are representing the best men of your nations, and it is reasonable to suppose that in time you will become the representatives of your nations and will take your places in the world's conferences

to solve the great problems of mankind. . . . I wish you success in the development of the highest type of manhood.[29]

This manhood would be the currency in which China proved its ultimate worth as a nation. Among these young Chinese men, crewcuts and muscle-revealing tank top jerseys and shorts replaced the queues and robes that had kept alive the image of an effeminate China in a world of men and their nations. It took real men to rehearse, on the playing fields, the international struggles that all good Social Darwinists knew to be imminent, and it took the new sports *tiyu* to put the focus on this type of struggle.

Preparation for the games was grounds for much excitement in Shanghai. Daily updates in *Shenbao* and the *North-China Daily News* began several days before the actual competitions began, and the Shanghai Tramway and Nanjing-Shanghai Railroad adopted special schedules to accommodate fans attending the meet. Shanghai's Commercial Press donated a thirty-inch-high silver cup to serve as a perpetual trophy for the Far Eastern soccer championships,[30] and President Yuan Shikai presented a large trophy in the shape of the ancient edifices of Beijing's Temple of Heaven to be awarded to the decathlon champion. Western organizers, eager to rebuild China in their own image, were also thrilled by what they saw as the "deep interest which the approaching Games have awakened," and the new "picture" it evoked for them "of a Young China nurtured in a love of sports for sports' sake."[31]

There were even more immediate reasons why stakes were so high by the opening of these Second Far Eastern Games—only six days had passed since Yuan's decision to accede to Japan's predatory Twenty-One Demands, that nation's wartime attempt to vault to the forefront of imperialist exploitation of China's markets and environment. Predictably, the meet quickly took on a more nationalist tone. Probably hoping to save some measure of prestige, Yuan personally put up five hundred *yuan* (U.S.$285) to bring the standout Honolulu Chinese Base Ball Team to represent the motherland in the games.[32] At first, Yuan's strategy looked worthwhile. The Honolulu Chinese, preparing for the Far Eastern Games, won eight games in a row against the Shanghai-based U.S. Navy team and the practiced Shanghai Americans.[33] Unfortunately, this desperate move was a clear violation of the Association Constitution ruling on territorial representation, and the Honolulu Chinese were disqualified anyway after it was found that many of the players were professionals.[34] Yet the presence of the team clearly provided an inspiring taste of pan-Chinese nationalism for athletes and fans alike. As one patriot wrote of the Honolulu Chinese, "[W]e feel certain that they worked with hearty goodwill for the honour of China. . . .

If some of them are professionals, it cannot alter the fact that they are all Chinese."[35]

The weeklong meet proved to be an important opportunity for the people of Shanghai and nearby environs to show their feelings of national unity. The great crowds massing at the newly built stadium adjacent to the Hongkou Target Shooting Grounds totaled an estimated one hundred thousand over seven days.[36] These enthusiastic fans were grateful for any chance to exult in a national victory, rare in the humiliating years of Yuan's rule. They had much to cheer about during this special week in Shanghai, when regional and political differences could be put aside for the sake of the nation and all Chinese could be proud of being simply Chinese. J. H. Crocker, the YMCA's national physical director, wrote, "For the first time men from the north, south, east and west stood together and cheered for China, and it mattered not whether an athlete was from north, south, east or west, so long as he had the [national flag] five-barred ribbon on they cheered him."[37] Dr. Elwood S. Brown of the Philippine delegation, founder of the Far Eastern Games, compared the enthusiasm in Shanghai to that of the biggest American college football games:

> I have never seen such enthusiastic rooting and cheering in my life at any athletic event. . . . [When the Chinese soccer team scored a goal to tie the Philippine team,] instantly that whole Chinese crowd rushed from all four sides out into the field, thousands of hats sailed into the air, the Chinese players were lifted up. . . . It was fully ten minutes before the officials could clear the grounds and allow the contest to go on.[38]

And when the soccer contest ended with a win for the Chinese eleven (an all-Hong Kong team), many in the Shanghai crowd poured onto the field to carry their victorious "countrymen" off the field on their shoulders.[39]

It was a liberating experience for these Chinese spectators finally to see their young men—and clearly "their" young men included any Chinese, whether from Hong Kong or Honolulu, the category being racial as well as national—win their battles with foreign forces. The Chinese volleyball team, a Cinderella squad made up of Guangzhou and Hong Kong players and coached by Francis Wilber of the Guangzhou YMCA, faced the powerful Filipino team in the finals. Wilber, in a letter to his parents, described these games as "about the most exciting + busy week I've had in Chiny." He continued in embarrassing detail about the volleyball match, when his players "ran up 10 straight points before the inimy could stop them. That just took the liver out of those brown-skinned proteges of Uncle Sambo, + after that there was nothing to it. . . . And say, it would have done your heart good to have heard those Chinese rooting in the bleachers. They did as noisy + effective work as any gang of American school boys I ever saw."[40] The eight-mile "marathon" race also provided an inspiring moment for Chinese spectators in Hongkou Park. J. Wong-Quincey provided this thrilling narrative:

> Taku of Japan came in an easy first. . . . Takatsu, another Japanese, was about half a lap behind the first when he entered the track on the return from Kiangwan. Nearly a lap behind Takatsu came the Chinese representative Pai [Bai Baokun, of St. John's University]. It was evident to all that Takatsu was nearly exhausted. There were two more laps to run, and Pai made the desperate resolve to overtake Takatsu and secure the second place. It *was* a desperate resolve seeing that he had to gain nearly one lap with only two laps to run. As soon as his intention was known to the spectators he became the cynosure of ten thousand pairs of eyes. He somehow managed to forget that he had already run nearly eight miles, and indulging in a spirited dash which fascinated the beholders he gained upon the Japanese and at the last quarter lap passed him. Never was a second place more strenuously earned; and the frenzied applause which greeted the finish threatened to unroof the substantial grandstand.[41]

This exuberance at Chinese triumphs was not the only brand of audience participation at the games. If international struggles in sport were meant to be merely preparation for the real thing, the distinction escaped the attention of many Chinese fans carried away in a fever of nationalist sentiment. Fights between Chinese and Filipino players marred their second soccer contest, and when Chinese spectators joined in the violence against the visitors, the game had to be postponed.[42]

These amazing crowds, the first of their kind in China, were as much a focal point of the spectacular games as the sports themselves. Wong-Quincey wrote proudly, and with keen analysis, of the significance of the crowds:

> This huge gathering of Chinese of all classes had nothing of the stolid and unemotional passiveness which is so often characteristic of old China. It was essentially an enthusiastic, gesticulating and vocal crowd who could shout and roar, clap and stamp and generally work itself up to bursting point. All these things it did and kept on doing at every manifestation of Chinese success or prowess. This wild enthusiasm meant that the Chinese spectators were keenly interested in the Games, but it meant infinitely more. Its true significance lay in the fact that the Games furnished a convenient occasion for a wild expression of pent-up patriotism, of a bruised and wounded nationalism which had not time to recover from the shock and humiliation arising from the Sino-Japanese crisis.[43]

The sight, sound, and feeling of the gathering of thousands and thousands of Chinese, as a unified people rather than what Sun Yat-sen had famously described as "a sheet of loose sand," seemed as much worth celebrating as the triumphs of Chinese student-athletes.[44] Hosting such a meet, and having the world come to China, provided a whole new realm of national possibilities.

Other events at the games accentuated notions of mass solidarity. The opening ceremonies, beginning with a slow march around the playing field by athletes grouped by nation, set the tone for serious competition between these men as real representatives (no longer mere citizens) of modern nations. The opening ceremonies also included a mass "soft calisthenics" program performed by seven hundred boys from the Nanyang Public School and the YMCA, providing a "mass" element on the field that team sports could not.[45] A highlight of the games' fourth day was a Boy Scout competition featuring some five hundred Scouts from Shanghai and Guangdong. The program included events like building bridges, marching, archery, pitching tents, flying model airplanes, and even a flag routine promoting use of the *baihua* vernacular.[46] Demonstrations like these highlighted the youthful strength and modern creativity of the young men of China and provided useful reminders of what could be accomplished by properly unified Chinese.

A final example of this new spirit of mass expression came at the end of the games. After Chinese volleyball and swimming triumphs on the meet's fourth day clinched the overall games championship for the host nation, the call was made for mass lantern processions *(tidenghui)* to be held in Shanghai and all over China to celebrate the momentous victory. An appeal was made for Chinese of all occupations to gather at the Chinese Park on North Suzhou Road and other starting points at 6:30 P.M. on 26 May, four days after the games' conclusion. The main Shanghai procession, to be organized by bureaucrats, merchants, and students, would be led by Wang Zhengting, games chairman and vice speaker of the National Assembly. Winding around the French Concession, the procession would conclude at the Zhang Gardens, a popular site during the Qing for the voicing of anti-Russian and anti-Manchu protest, as well as for public gatherings of all sorts.[47] This dramatic "traditional" event would assume new modern meanings as members of different strata of society took to the streets to celebrate a truly national victory. Authorities sensed danger, however, even in this celebration of a rare international victory for China. The powerful Songhu Police Prefecture flexed its muscles, reminding citizens of the statutes in place against "gathering under false pretenses and causing disturbances," and procession organizers had no choice but to cancel the powerful celebration.[48]

The Second Far Eastern Championship Games, held in Shanghai in 1915, demonstrated to hundreds of thousands of spectators and newspaper readers the power and the promise of international athletic competition. Only these games could bring healthy men of rival Asian nations to Chinese shores for fair competition under international rules. And only these games could present the spectacle of thousands of Chinese coming together, finally (ostensibly) stripped of all regional and class consciousness, to cheer on their own young men. As important as previous "national"-level competitions in Nanjing and Beijing had been, it was the international games in Shanghai that taught Chinese the future that competitive sport could build for their nation. Despite the games' foreign sponsorship, few could walk away from them without an appreciation of what these youth of China, aided by recognized and standardized international forms, were doing powerfully and fearlessly to create a strong and masculine nation-state.

CALISTHENICS AND GAMES
IN THE CHINESE SCHOOL SYSTEM, 1912–19

The competitive sports introduced in the last years of the Qing today form an important element of contemporary Chinese nationalism and engagement with the outside world. The late Qing and early Republic fostered another form of *tiyu*, however, that enjoyed a less prominent career than military drill or sports. This "calisthenics and games" mode, a modern form invented for use in schools, drew more on indigenous sources than the foreign models described above. "Soft" calisthenics routines and games were designed to fit younger students' psychology and explicitly teach children about their future roles in society. Although its influence waned by the 1920s, the calisthenics and games movement provided its own connections to science, modernity, and national strength for educators and students searching for efficient and healthy roads to individual fitness, hygiene, and a promising national future.

Whereas the military drill implemented visions of anonymous masses moving as one, educators who advocated this more enlightened mode of physical education took the individual child as the main subject of the exercises. In a 1913 article entitled "On Physical Education for Children," one author claimed, "[C]hildren are the most precious thing in the world. . . . [W]ithout children there is no humankind." Rejecting the normal military themed calisthenics that "exhaust the brain and deform the body," this author called for more "useful" forms of physical education that would concentrate on individual bodies and hygiene at the age when children were "blossoming gloriously like spring flowers, progressing day and night."[49] Drawing on the work of foreign educators, another author stressed the need for games to have strong physiological and psychological uses, so that "the body and the mind *(shenxin)* can develop evenly."[50] And in 1918, another New Culture educator reminded physical education instructors that *ticao* instruction should not be too team centered, lest "students think that the group is the only important thing and forget about the individual." He pointed out that "respect for the individual" was the key to aiding students' physical development and added that a good teacher would have to pay attention to each student's level of "self-awareness" *(zijue)* in learning the exercises.[51] These scientific-minded physical educators of the 1910s, working with the new unit of analysis known as the "individual," thus had strayed far from the group mechanics of the old military drill.

Republican-era educators advocating the softer games and calisthenics also saw their work as potentially having great influence on the family life of their young students and sought ways to rearrange and reform their students' households. One author wrote on the need for "family games," played inside or outside the family courtyard, that would bring into children's home life the lessons of morality and physical exertion that teachers could only demonstrate for two or three hours a week.[52] Another educator, citing Western family norms, pointed out aspects of Chinese family life that were unhealthy and destructive to individual physical fitness. The Chinese "customs" of bundling up babies, constant snacking, parental threats and intimidation, and bad habits of filth and disorder all harmed children's physiques. This educator demanded that Chinese families learn from their Western counterparts about raising children to be self-reliant, self-confident, self-disciplined, and hygiene-conscious.[53] All the efforts of diligent physical education instructors like these would be wasted if the healthy habits they cultivated at school were canceled out by chaotic and unhygienic home life; the family had to do its part to ensure that children would be ready to face and build the new Chinese society.

Physical educators of the 1910s designed their calisthenics and games to teach at an early age lessons about republican society and its basis, work. Just as proponents of sports *tiyu* often described it in terms associated with commerce, fair trade, and free capitalism, proponents of "calisthenics and games" often applied their notions of *tiyu* to the organization of modern society and its workforce. One educator, writing on "The Value of Physical Education," discussed the uses of *tiyu* in promoting cell reproduction and the replacing of old cells with new. He then applied this physiological model to the societal body, describing how healthy physiques allowed individuals in society to work together, pooling their energies, "no differently than the countless numbers of cells that are working together in our bodies."[54] Thus only a scientific understanding of the workings of the individual body could provide the foundation for a healthy and rational social organism.

Within modern republican society, of course, there would have to be divisions of labor, and many physical educators used their discipline to prepare their young students for these realities. One student in Nanjing Higher Normal's Physical Education Department saw as a "most suitable type of exercise for mankind . . . games that instill professional confidence. Putting professions into games allows for the enjoyment of work, while introducing play into a profession . . . allows the work not to become drudgery."[55] Games, depending on the specific subject matter, and if taught correctly, could give children the tools they needed to become biologists, merchants, farmers, artisans, military officers, mining engineers, and botanists, all professions important to the functioning of society as a whole.[56] A student from Fengtian, in an English-language essay submitted to the *Students' Magazine*, wrote of a routine performed at his school's annual track meet that was rooted in these notions of playing out the roles of different segments of society: "[W]e had an after-piece which was made by ourselves with various figures, such as monks, statues, farmers, merchants and a ragged beggar. Besides these, old ladies, girl students and children."[57] Thus even by this early date games and bouncy calisthenics routines had become an important way of teaching China's youth about the hierarchies and organizing structures of republican society.

Physical education was also a realm in which women could make a statement about their contributions to China's society and economy. At the Second Jiangsu Provincial Women's Normal School Meet, held in Suzhou in May 1915, a Women's Professional Group put on a spectacular calisthenics routine made up of the motions of thirty-four types of women's work grouped into five categories: household, agricultural, industrial, commercial, and educational/public work. After watching this thrilling reenactment of women's work from washing rice to spinning cotton to selling poultry to rope making to selling government bonds, one observer wrote, "With this kind of authentic presentation and imitation down to the last detail, there was not a single moment when the audience was not applauding loud as thunder."[58]

Philip Deloria has described similar games utilized by the American Camp Fire Girls to "inculcat[e] a belief in the nonmonetary rewards of domesticity and the essentially domestic destiny of women."⁵⁹ Indeed, the larger society took for granted the everyday real execution of these tasks—working to sell government bonds being a notable exception to the otherwise domestic nature of the chores—by millions of women all over China. Yet the gripping mimetic performances inspired and validated by the name of modern *tiyu* garnered much gratitude and appreciation in a China where physical education was understood to have such a great influence on society and its methods of organization.

Th calisthenics and games mode, besides teaching valuable lessons about the individual, the family, and greater society, was a powerful way of expressing sentiments about the Chinese nation. Its theorists characterized the workings of the new nation in physiological terms that brought notions of *tiyu* and the modern nation-state closer together than ever. The first issue of Changsha's *Tiyu Weekly* featured a piece on a recent "Human Body Peace Conference." The "Central Government (the brain)" first sent telegrams (*dianbao,* "electric messages," a pun understandable only to those with a modern understanding of the human nervous system) to all parts of the body. Soon after, "representatives" from the body's different organs and systems met in the chest cavity to "discuss healthy ways of working to protect the survival of all."⁶⁰ This creative piece, serialized over the first four issues of *Tiyu Weekly,* shows that physiological theories preoccupied many imaginations of the modern nation and that national visions influenced how many intellectuals understood their very bodies.

Games for children could also be designed to bring out, through the pleasurable motions and sensations of play and physical exertion, awareness of the Chinese nation's past, present, and future. A series of "competitive games" introduced in 1914 by the Shanghai *Journal of Physical Education* included games called "Well-Field" and "Telegraph." Designed by students at the Chinese Women's Ticao School in Shanghai, these games would use the thrill of competition to teach students about China's superior ancient forms of social organization and an "unbelievable" product of scientific development (the telegraph) of great use to the unification of the new China.⁶¹ Other games were invented to teach students about aspects of the new nation in whose governance they would someday participate. One game designed for use in the fifth and sixth years of elementary education was called "The Republic of the Five Races" *(wuzu gonghe).* Here, students holding red, yellow, blue, white, or black flags (to represent the Han, Manchu, Mongolian, Muslim, and Tibetan "races" that combined to form a single Chinese people) competed in a five-team relay race. The game, engineered to teach participants that "those who quit halfway will always lose due to their cowardice,"[62] would also allow students to live out the central paradox of a united nation made up of five competing races.

Wang Huaiqi, a physical educator from Jiangsu who went on to write fifty-nine books on physical education, published in 1916–17 descriptions of two physical education activities he had thought up to heighten students' awareness of China's national and international struggles. One was "May Ninth Calisthenics," which commemorated 9 May 1915, that "disgraceful, shameful day . . . etched deep in the minds" of all Chinese, when the Yuan Shikai government agreed to Japan's Twenty-One Demands.[63] In this flag calisthenics routine, thirty-eight students, all holding a Chinese national flag in their right hand and an army flag in their left, moved through fifty-nine motions to their teacher's timed flute calls. The grand finale left the students, armed raised, in a formation that spelled out the Chinese characters *wu jiu*, or May Ninth, capping in spectacular style their long effort to create a somatic memorial to the shame suffered by their nation.[64]

Wang's second nationally themed activity brought into his school's P.E. curriculum the epic struggles undertaken against Yuan Shikai and his aborted attempt to take the throne as Emperor of a Hongxian (Great Constitution) dynasty in 1916. In the game "Songpo-ball" (named for the revolutionary hero Cai E, also called Songpo), students could use the motions of their bodies to strike blows against the feudal archenemy Yuan. In a game much like German handball, players moved a ball from the Uprising Circle at midfield, attempting to throw the ball at and knock down the stakes in their opponents' Hongxian Dynasty Circle,[65] thus allowing each team to relive, through this strenuous ballgame, Cai's struggle to save the Republic from Yuan's mercenary forces.

Such games, whether addressing elements of China's glorious past, its troubled yet thriving present, or its future greatness, provided wonderful opportunities for China's physical educators and their students to play out the myths and experiences that made up their beloved Chinese nation. Thus the games and *ticao* routines could provide even more immediate connections to the nation than military drill or sports *tiyu*. Military drill presented an abstract model of unity and a keen shared awareness. In sports, athletes and spectators could participate in disciplined modes of competition that invoked the rigors of the modern systems of the nation-state and of modern commerce. But calisthenics and games went sports one better by actually teaching students through direct experience the story of their nation. Whereas sports were limited to a few standardized and internationally recognized forms, the domain of calisthenics and games was unlimited, allowing for great creativity in designing explicitly national activities that posed students as participating subjects in processes of imagining, building, preserving, and defending the Chinese nation-state.

Other qualities of the educational calisthenics and games movement besides its nation-centered performances carried powerful national meanings. This realm of *tiyu* was unique in that it was understood to be just as, if not more, open to girls as to boys. Republican-era military drill was explicitly a male domain, training China's men of the future to defend the nation. Sports, as described above and in Chapter 1, were also strictly defined as male activity, for experts of the time understood the rough-and-tumble intense movement of sports to be just as unsuitable for women as the commercial and capitalist competition that sports invoked. Games and "soft calisthenics," however, were the standard mode of physical education for girls and young women, as well as younger boys, in the early Republic and beyond. By allowing a healthy mixing of boys and girls and a realm of expression for progressive-minded women and girls, the calisthenics and games movement could make claims to national advancement and modernity that even the successful sports *tiyu* could never reach.

Many meet spectators came away more impressed by young women's calisthenics and games than by men's sports. One educator in attendance at the Second Jiangsu Provincial Meet agreed with "those who say that girls' school physical education is more successful than boys' school *tiyu*. When girls' feet are not bound, their bodies grow full and strong, and their faces are a healthy dark shade. But schoolboys' complexions are always pale and white. This is true, if only because girls mature sooner."[66] The presence of soothing, optimistic, cooperative women's games like "Mencius's Mother Moves Three Times," "The Republic of the Five Races," and "Fields of Human Compassion" allowed those in attendance at the Changshou (Jiangsu) Athletic Meet of 1915 to take pride in the productive and positive nature of their gathering. One educator wrote,

> There was none of what is called *tiyu* [sports] here. . . . But the content of these meets [the Changshou Meet and the Second Jiangsu Provincial Women's Normal School Meet] was what should be called *yundong*, more than those simple skills-for-sale athletic meets, where School A competes with School B, or Student B competes with Student C, that just lead to turmoil and disturbances, and that can never be an educational form of exercise.[67]

Thus many saw the games and calisthenics movement, which seemed to encourage participants' "feminine" qualities, as saving physical culture from the competitive excesses of sports.[68]

Other meets were held specifically for women's schools. One of the largest was the Second Jiangsu Provincial Women's Normal School Meet, held in Suzhou in May 1915. An elementary school teacher who attended the meet recorded the scene, which drew over one thousand spectators from nineteen schools from Wuxian and nearby counties: "In front of the gate, sedan chairs were crowded thick as fog, and everywhere were skirts and shoes as people made their way into the stadium." Banners hung on the athletic grounds' main gate proclaimed, "The nation is peaceful as these rains wash away our humiliation in East Asia" and "Women teachers stride forward, witness the spirit of a military march, enough to wipe away the smoke in our eyes."[69] Forty-two separate calisthenics and games demonstrations thrilled the audience, and "Every single [spectator] marveled that women's physical education is not inferior to men's *tiyu* after all."[70]

However, this otherwise positive atmosphere could be disrupted by spectators who were unsure exactly what to make of these tremendous displays of the female "wonderful, active, disciplined, and courageous spirit." The crowd at the Jiangsu Women's Meet was originally quite orderly as it took in these demonstrations.

> But after twenty events, the men's seating area had become a chaotic, disorderly mess. And after thirty events, there were disturbances in the VIP seats and government officials' sections. All kinds of debates and opinions were heard. Some said [the meet] was proof that women could serve in the military. Others said that this was just converting the Chinese *(Xia)* to barbarian ways and was a type of education that would surely lead the nation to ruin. And these are things that the upper classes of society said.[71]

The calisthenics and games movement created a vibrant space for women's and girls' participation and expression in the physical culture world. Yet as the account above implies, many people, even many urban liberal elites, who would have supported women's *tiyu* in theory, were taken aback, even disturbed, by the sight of these visibly active women, a fact that hints at the complexity of the phenomenon. Still, these calisthenics routines, thanks in part to their inclusion of and "suitability" to women and girls, occupied a unique and important position in 1910s China's public culture.

Restricted to the educational system, calisthenics and games never enjoyed the spectacular career of competitive sports, which became an important avenue of Chinese engagement with the world, but they formed an important part of Republican-era school physical education. For decades, teachers committed to healthy and wholesome physical education devoted great effort to designing and publishing pleasurable and productive games and calisthenics routines. The ability of these games and calisthenics to summon and create notions of the individual, his or her place in Chinese society, structures of work and labor discipline, the Chinese national past, present, and future, and male-female equality and complementarity was the key to the success of this branch of physical culture in the 1910s and 1920s.

THE BARBARISM OF MILITARY DRILL
IN THE REPUBLICAN AGE

While new scientific notions of education spurred many Chinese educators to design "natural" or "healthy" *ticao* routines for their young citizen-students, the martial spirit that surged after the 1912 overthrow of the Manchus did allow an official revival of notions of "military citizenship education" and military calisthenics *(bingcao)* during the 1910s.[72] Before long, however, the Qing militarist origins of the *bingcao* caught up with it, and Republican educators began seriously to question this mode of instruction. Xu Yibing, the late-Qing founder of the Chinese Calisthenics School and of China's first *tiyu* journal, *Physical Education World*, found the spotlight again in 1914 with a new publication, *Journal of Physical Education*. The lead article in that publication's first issue was entitled "The Differences between Physical Education and Military Force." In it, Xu wrote:

> Since the founding of the Republic, the government has trumpeted military citizenship education as the guiding philosophy of the nation's educational system. It is the same approach as in the [Qing] dynasty. All would agree that physical education is the backbone of the nation. But year after year, if we ask how to implement a proper *(zhengdang)* *tiyu,* . . . the so called military *tiyu*-ists stick with the exercise they are paid so well to teach, practicing their beating and pillaging skills—it's really just another kind of barbarism.[73]

A self-consciously scientific-minded educator, Xu imagined and worked tirelessly to teach norms of order and hygiene using games and soft calisthenics regimens, well researched by physical education specialists and designed with the specific physiological and psychological needs of the students in mind, that would thus allow "the fun of exercise to be realized."[74] Trained at Tokyo's Ōmori Physical Education School in the mid-1900s, Xu was a firm believer in the use of scientifically sound calisthenic exercises in building a strong body and healthy, disciplined mind and outlook. For Xu, *bingcao*'s militarist and imperial connotations disqualified it from the role of educating the bodies of China's future citizens. The military *ticao* seemed a barbaric relic of past abuses and ignorance, unfit for use in a Republican era.

Military drill continued as part of the Chinese *tiyu* enterprise for several years into the Republican period. Supporters of the military models of physical education, however, were forced to redefine their arts in more fashionable *tiyu* terms. The National Education Conference held in Tianjin in 1915 called for instituting military citizenship education in China's schools but conceded that the martial spirit could be developed not only by fencing, judo, and boxing but also by baseball and swimming, activities associated with Anglo-American models of fair and natural play.[75]

Another sign that the military drill was losing its popularity was a 1915 article by Jia Fengzhen in the *Chinese Educational Review*. The author, though a staunch supporter of military drill, confessed that the philosophy of "military citizenship," which asserted that all citizens had a duty to acquire a military education, threatened to make Chinese people as cruel and suspicious as the foreign imperialists. Instead, he suggested what he called a practical "training-ist" *(duanlian zhuyi)* education. Here, activities like hiking, fencing, swimming, cold showers, and tennis would provide for a "total development of the mind and the individual nature" while still training the body with movements useful in resisting the foreign imperialists.[76] Finally, *bingcao* enthusiasts had to be disappointed with the events of the Third Jiangsu Provincial Games of 1916, where the execution and discipline of the drill performances just were not what they used to be. A panel of displeased judges agreed that there were six major weaknesses in almost all of the drill exhibitions and that some, like crooked line of forward march, dirty gun barrels, and the tendency to turn one's back on the "enemy" when returning to position, even augured "great danger."[77]

Military drill—taught by characters whom Xu Yibing described as "your average unintelligent, immoral soldier right out of the barracks . . . ineffective and worthless . . . heavy drinkers and mad gamblers, who love to fight like wolves and whom nothing would be below"[78]—no longer seemed important to young Chinese looking to physical culture as a means of building a strong China. *Bingcao* aimed for physical readiness in the case of battle with a national enemy and a constant mental awareness of the nation and its interests. But its discipline, barked orders, and strict cadence could not have made much sense in a world where all was now fluid, progressing, evolving. More than a strong military, China needed a new type of community, where the skills necessary to survive in the world could be fostered by friendly competitions at home.[79] Drilling involved a collective focus on the leader, but it could not arrange the friendly micro-struggles between schools, cities, provinces, and soon nations that sports *tiyu* could. Only sports could focus the gaze of its participants on the transcendent concept of victory. Teamwork and sports teams' travel across distances to compete with each other provided a sense of a larger community striving for this singular goal. The timing, measuring, and official rules allowed for structured ways to evaluate improvement and progress, so crucial to survival in the modern world. And the crowds that attended the games gave the athletes a sense of performance, drama, and tension that would have seemed appropriate as the very future of their nation was being decided in the great international struggles of the world.

Offering nothing like the *yu* (nourishment, education, uplift) that came with this new ideology of physical culture, the one-dimensional *bingcao* could only *cao* (drill or control) the body. The June 1917 issue of *Association Progress,* the normally bland YMCA newsletter, included a critical piece by Yun Daiying, a student at Zhonghua University in Wuchang. Yun, who later became a Communist educator-agitator-organizer, attacked the military drill currently taught at his university. He admitted that "every student of our nation is a weak sissy *(wenruo)*" but saw great problems in how drill classes demanded "overexertion that can injure [students'] internal organs or limbs and torso, bringing no benefit and only harm." Yun claimed that in the current system of martial education, students "didn't learn any more than if we were just listening to some army commander's barked orders." He demanded of Chinese educators: "Transform the jerky, inconsistent *tiyu* into a progressive *tiyu*. Transform the listless and dry *tiyu* into an interesting *tiyu*."[80]

If China's New Culture endangered military drill, the outcome of the First World War delivered its deathblow, given how closely its traditions were identified with a German origin. In 1919, a Changsha author exposed the horrible consequences of the sadistic military *tiyu* training curriculum: "[M]ilitary citizenship physical culture *(jun guomin tiyu)* betrays perfectly and absolutely the goals of 'satisfaction in life.' Where one should be seeking life, he is taught to work toward death; where one should be enjoying life, he is taught to savor death."[81] A contributor to the "Enlightenment" *(juewu)* section of the *Republican Daily News* in 1920 also critiqued military drill instruction, writing that military titles, weapons, and uniforms had no place in schools. "The European War is over; shouldn't we be acting together to oppose militarist nationalism?" He concluded, "Our ideal *tiyu* must be based on [concepts of] universality and freedom."[82]

Changsha's *Tiyu Weekly* published an issue devoted almost solely to the question of military drill training and its future in the schools of China.

Readers were invited to express their opinions on the subject, thus creating a public forum where physical educators could imagine themselves contributing to the future of the nation. Zhang Baochen, a drill instructor at the Zhejiang Seventh Normal School who probably feared for his livelihood, submitted an article in which he wrote mockingly,

> Recently your typical oversensitive youth will take the German-Austrian defeat and the Allied victory [as an opportunity] to . . . say smugly and complacently that justice has triumphed over authoritarianism and that militarism *(junguo zhuyi)* has been extinguished, that world wars will be no more, that a utopian world is on the way, and thus that the military drill instructors in our nation's schools can be eliminated. This kind of superficial observation, these deceptive and untrue explanations, never even take into account the status and condition of the nation.[83]

Still, the majority opinion tilted heavily against those, like Zhang, who still sought to define the nation through militarist discipline. A Nanjing Higher Normal School *tiyu* coach opposed military drilling, as its great emphasis on obedience killed students' initiative *(ziqixin)*, a value vitally important to the national project.[84] *Tiyu Weekly* editor Huang Xing urged a reasonable debate but came down clearly on the side of the *tiyu* progressives, concluding that military drill instruction was good only for teaching students about war.[85] Even more than the contents of these pieces, the very act of holding such a forum in print spoke to a new progressive era in which militarist practices would not be relevant.

This new May Fourth–inspired concern with the orientations and priorities of Chinese *tiyu* targeted not only military drill but many of the ideas and attitudes of the Anglo-American sports *tiyu* as well. Many credited democratic *(pingmin zhuyi)* ideology with having brought down military drill. They recognized, however, that it had also contributed to the selfish and materialistic approaches of "trophyism" *(jinbiao zhuyi)* and the "athlete system" *(xuanshou zhi,* where schools paid nonstudents to compete on school teams).[86] Some went so far as to condemn the whole sporting enterprise as "the birth of vanity" in modern Chinese schools, where athletes spoiled by their special privileges often became "plain hoodlums."[87] Many students felt that there was still a shortage of qualified P.E. teachers and that those who were properly qualified put too much emphasis on winning, harshly criticizing or even beating students who fell short of their high demands.[88]

These faults, however, could not budge sports *tiyu* from its place of dominance by the end of the 1910s. Educators and students enlightened by the whirlwind developments in China and abroad could no longer imagine a place for military drill in their physical culture and moved almost unanimously to banish it from the new progressive realm. Their work was efficient and thorough. By the very early 1920s, military drill was already nearly obsolete. What some called the "odious double-track system" that concentrated equally on military drill and more modern *tiyu* forms ended around 1922, when the "stale and hackneyed" military drills were removed from the required curriculum and *ticao* "coaches" *(jiaolian)* were officially replaced by *tiyu* "teachers" *(jiaoyuan)*.[89] And a sure sign of the passing of *bingcao* was the 1922 call by the Education Department's Physical Fitness and People's Recreation Conference for the use of new "modern" sports *tiyu* even in military and police training, sites that were bastions of the old martial drill.[90] These forms would be brought back, though in altered forms, circumstances, and contexts, as one element of a "militarized *tiyu*" advocated by Nationalist activists of the 1930s. The career of an independent *bingcao* discipline was over, however, as the Chinese physical culture community broke with the forms that had characterized Qing-era worldviews and programs in favor of the progressive impulses that would be delivered via sports, games, and soft calisthenics.

WRITING *TIYU* INTO HISTORY

The awakenings of the late 1910s left one final task for this early Republican *tiyu* community: rewriting the history of physical culture. The powerful and transfixing forms of the nation-state, including the dramatic and cathartic competitive sports *tiyu*, led many educators, students, and urban observers to ask about these institutions' predecessors in imperial times. New histories had to be written to make sense of China's dynastic past in Republican terms. The New Culture and May Fourth Movements asked that national sense be made of *tiyu*, that its location and role in Chinese history be explained.

The task of assigning *tiyu* to its rightful niche in the world of things Chinese was delicate. Crucial to the effort of placing physical culture in the account of China's historical progress was the fact of the modern *tiyu*'s ultimately foreign (and Western) connections. Frantz Fanon has written of a mode of anticolonialist "nationalist culture" in which, to fight off the colonizing power, native intellectuals "relentlessly determine to renew contact once more with the oldest and most pre-colonial springs of life of their people."[91] However, Chinese nationalism did not require denying any points of commonality with the foreign. The very idea of making China a nation and the modern nationalism it had to achieve were based on a specific western European Enlightenment example of power and a will to progress.

Prasenjit Duara observes that while "nation-states glorify the ancient or eternal character of the nation, they also seek to emphasize the unprecedented nature of the nation-*state,* because it is only in this form that the people-nation has been able to *realize* itself as the self-conscious subject of History."[92] This model works well in explaining early Republican ideas of *tiyu* and history. Competitive and rational *tiyu* belonged to, and was understandable only in the context of, the nation-state. By May Fourth, modern physical culture had provided gratifying, energizing, and liberating experiences for many Chinese people for more than two decades. Yet its heyday could begin only when the momentous national and international meets of the 1910s brought this national context to the forefront. As the nation needed the masculine, muscular boost that was *tiyu,* so did *tiyu* need the nation and its (imported) structure. That modern physical culture was not totally a "Chinese" invention was, by definition, an integral part of this narrative, and a truth that emphasizes more forcefully Duara's point about the great break that the nation could appear to represent in Republican China.

All agreed that *tiyu* could take China to the promised land of progress and international community, but an inspiring tradition and history, which China certainly had at its disposal, also would be necessary to draw upon. As Ernest Renan famously stated, knowledge of "common glories in the past" is as crucial in forming a nation as "a common will in the present."[93] Those looking for *tiyu* in China's past sought a new understanding of the achievements and the wonders of ancient China that could blend with modern appeals to progress and international kinship.

Xu Yibing's 1909 essay "The History of Physical Culture," the first *tiyu* history piece written in China, presented sport as yet another innovation to be credited to the great Chinese race.[94] The 1910s saw further attempts at a history of China's "ancient *tiyu.*" Xu, back with his new monthly *Journal of Physical Education,* in 1914 began a much more thorough investigation of China's *tiyu* past. The first two issues of this new journal contain a ten-page "Chapter 1: Ancient *Tiyu*" of Xu's new "History of Physical Culture." These are the only two *Journal* issues still extant in China, so we may never know the full scope of Xu's effort. However, the first chapter is instructive. Xu conceded that in terms of developing disciplined, regulated competitive sports like the West's, which represented only a "narrow" view of *tiyu,* China had little to brag about: "Our nation does not have this [Western] type of *tiyu,* as our education and scholarship through history have obviously never been as transparent or systematic as that of the

West."[95] However, as he demonstrated with his detailed discussions of ancient hunting, archery, music and dance, mastery of swords and other weapons, and Zhou dynasty education—all manifestations of Xu's "broad definition" of *tiyu*—China was indeed heir to a rich tradition of physical culture.[96]

Another discussion of "ancient Chinese physical culture" was published in the Nanjing Higher Normal School Physical Education Research Society's massive 266-page collection of essays, published in 1918. An author scolded his peers for their ignorance of their own nation's *tiyu* past: "Ignorant students, their minds drunk with the spirit of Europe, still say that China has no *tiyu* history of which to speak. Ah, how could they be so wrong?" Not only did China's ancient archery competitions "possess the same significance, only in microcosm, of the West's Olympic Games," but the *cuju* kickball games seen in the *Historical Records* and the *History of the Later Han* were the equal of modern soccer. Ancient Chinese sword and martial arts were likewise "qualified to be part of *tiyu*," as they taught discipline and skills of self-defense, just like the intense competitive sports of the modern West.[97]

These investigations thus incorporated premodern imperial forms of physical culture into a linear progressive history leading to the modern physical culture of the republican 1910s. In their formulations, the *tiyu* of the twentieth century was the completely logical successor to the games, rituals, and military training of imperial China.

Also important to the narrative of *tiyu* progress was the question of why this superior modern form was late to evolve in China. "Why Chinese *tiyu* has not developed" was one of the first points Guo Xifen addressed in his 1919 *History of Chinese Physical Culture*. Guo placed the peak of "ancient *tiyu*" in the military training competitions and exercises developed during the Spring and Autumn period (eighth to fifth century B.C.E.). After reaching these great heights, however, China unfortunately went into an extended physical slump of some 2,500 years. Generations of weak Confucian scholars who "emphasized study and detested the martial," and for whom "drinking wine and being lazy was the highest achievement," could do nothing to end the decline. Thus only in the first decade of the Republic could Chinese people "awaken from their delusion."[98]

Guo, a professor of *tiyu* history at Shanghai's East Asia Physical Education Training Institute, was not only known for his research into physical culture. Under the name of Guo Shaoyu, he worked closely with Gu Jiegang in the study of folksongs, pioneered the study of ancient Chinese proverbs, and later founded (with Zhou Zuoren) the Literary Research Society at Beijing University.[99] This impressive pedigree allowed Guo, an expert on popular culture through the ages, to define an essentialized Chinese culture that "emphasized the literary and neglected the martial." This became the accepted explanation for the Chinese people's "failure" to develop the physical culture that Westerners and Japanese had to bring to them. Springfield College graduate Hao Gengsheng later referred to a decline of three thousand years, placing what he imagined as the peak of Chinese *tiyu* in the late Shang dynasty![100] Another author later provided a shorter but more vivid estimate when he referred to this Qin-Qing interregnum as a "2000-year deposit of misguided sloth."[101]

If this theory of sloth and weakness was true, what had happened in the world of Chinese physical culture during all those millennia? Guo's 160-page book on Chinese *tiyu* surely had to be about *something*. As he explained, somehow in these thousands of dazed and lethargic years, many Chinese games and exercises had developed. And these games were amazingly similar to the sporting forms spreading so rapidly in Guo's Republic; he identified one finite "quality" or "nature" that characterized the development of *tiyu* all over the world. For example, the old *cuju* "kickball" was "similar" to modern soccer, and the old "hit-ball" game of *chuiwan* was "similar" to baseball. Guo not surprisingly concluded that "Chinese and Western [*tiyu*] are kindred, these are not two different principles." The only difference he pointed out between these two traditions was that "Western games emphasize rules and simply do not have this [Chinese] sort of grace and elegance."[102] In 1919, Guo thus established a comprehensive way of looking at Chinese *tiyu*, identifying it as an entity that (in keeping with the new progressive histories) had been suppressed by the backwardness of imperial rule but that at heart was always following and developing along the universal line of *tiyu* to which the West had (re-)exposed China in recent years.

This moment of comparison between ancient and contemporary *tiyu*—the consciousness of what had come before and the interrogation of its implications for the national present and future—was extremely important. The comparisons reflected a need to create for the young nation a transition from old to new. Pierre Bourdieu writes convincingly of the impossibility of making comparisons across the break at which older precapitalist games or rituals become "sports." He suggests understanding sport as correlative with a break "with activities which may appear to be the 'ancestors' of modern sports, a break which is itself linked to the constitution of a field of specific practice, endowed with its own specific rewards and its own rules, where a whole specific competence or culture is generated and invested."[103]

There is no question that, as Bourdieu writes, these old and new activities are seen by participants in fundamentally different ways. From a critical position, it is easy to see that the cosmological meanings of *cuju* kickball games were a world apart from the sporting values of modern soccer and that the ritual meanings of Zhou dynasty dance were far out of step with modern scientifically designed calisthenics routines. However, these connections were exactly the ones in which many Chinese of the early Republic believed as they authored new linear histories that emphasized the relation of the new Chinese *tiyu* to the physical forms that preceded it.

Tiyu and the nation as written by May Fourth participants like Guo Xifen recalled aspects of the old China in a way that, "feudal" as they may have been, shared (and even foreshadowed) aspects of a universal development with the dynamic and advanced West. The *tiyu* community that coalesced in the 1910s never shared the unquestioning faith in the West and universal condemnation of all things Chinese that many May Fourth writers expressed, and thus they saw the nation much more broadly. Modern *tiyu*'s inclusion in the story of the Chinese Republic dictated that the nation would have to be more flexible and syncretic, incorporating modern Chinese improvisations on Western traditions as well as indigenous Chinese forms recently legitimated by Western developments. These were the core assumptions of *tiyu* histories of the 1910s (capped by Guo's in 1919), which hailed Chinese ancient glories while equating them with irreproachable notions of progress, achieved by the peoples of the West and now emulated by China's Republican citizens.

CONCLUSION

As I will show in Chapter 7, the imagining of the modern Chinese *tiyu*/nation described above was possible only with a modern attempt to erase the very ambiguous tradition of the Chinese *wushu* martial arts. *Wushu*, part and parcel of China's imperial past and lacking any conceivable connection to the modern and progressive West, represented a perfectly negative and opposite image of the China that the modern New Culturists and May Fourthers hoped to build. The superstitious, decidedly unscientific martial arts, practiced and taught by dispossessed rural elements, and fragmented into numerous clashing traditions and schools, had little to offer the architects of a China for the twentieth century. Thus these new linear *tiyu* histories sought to write *wushu* out of existence, actively denying and forgetting it, as they remembered new modern styles of *tiyu* into Chinese history.

The China of the late 1910s was one that did not have to be so martial, or even so "Chinese." Things clearly not Chinese could become Chinese, and things clearly Chinese were scorned as "feudal" or even forgotten completely. Such is the arbitrary process of creating a nation. At the same time, however, with hindsight the process actually seems somewhat predictable. Put simply, how many other ways were there for nations-to-be to become so in the early twentieth century? The nation was a means of ending the unequal treaties and fighting imperialism in China, of winning respect from the strong nations of the world, and so was created in their image. The power of modern *tiyu* forms—whether in gathering athletes from all over China to join in friendly but intense competition, offering visions of a new Chinese man willing and able to meet men of other nations in sporting battle, or teaching schoolchildren the history and future of the Chinese nation through imaginative games and calisthenics routines—trumped any essentialized "Chinese" value that indigenous forms like martial arts could offer.

Joseph Levenson's description of the late Qing use of the *ti-yong* model— referring to reformers' hopes that the Chinese structure *(ti)* would be strengthened by strategic use of Western methods *(yong)*—is helpful here. He reveals memorably the "fallacy" in this use of the formerly Confucian formula, namely that "the *yong* of modern techniques could not defend the Chinese *ti*, as advertised, but only change society so that the old *ti* would have a rival instead of a shield."[104] Levenson thus reads this strategy as a mockery of Confucian statecraft tragic in its implications for the modern fate of Confucian China. However, by the late 1910s, nation-minded students, educators, reformers, and modernizers likely would have found the injection of Western *yong* a blessing rather than a curse. The popularity of modern forms of physical culture fit perfectly with the trends of New Culture, as nationalists of all stripes worked desperately to save China from what they saw as certain destruction.[105] It was these impulses and stimuli that allowed the progressives of the 1910s to write the Chinese nation so skillfully as a mixture of consciousness of the old and knowledge of the new, transforming into agents of Chinese modernity inventions and ideologies of very un-Chinese traditions.

3 "Mind, Muscle, and Money"

A Physical Culture for the 1920s

> Physical education, as has been proved by the majority of civilized nations, is a definite means to afford the human race the knowledge of how to live a happy and active life. . . . Can China follow the same path on which America has built her national physical life? . . . Or can China afford to live in this twentieth century without adopting any modern physical educational system?
>
> GUNSUN HOH (HAO GENGSHENG),
> *Physical Education in China*, 1926

Chinese modernizers of the 1920s saw their mission as going beyond the soul-searching and antitraditional critiques of the 1910s to create a society like those of the "civilized nations." Many were certain that a modern physical culture would be an integral facet of this society that could provide "a happy and active life" for all of China's citizens. Men like Hao clearly failed to recognize that the material "happiness" of the Western nations was in many ways a direct result of centuries of imperialism, which was in turn the model for many of the sports taking Chinese urban society by storm. Yet this was perfectly consistent with *tiyu*'s purpose—to make the Chinese the happy, active, wealthy equals of their imperialist rivals.

But how? The year 1919 saw the eruption of "May Fourth," an epoch-making movement that began as an anti-Japanese, antigovernment protest and quickly evolved into a totalizing condemnation of the "old ways" that cursed the young Chinese Republic. Just weeks after its explosive beginning, an explanation using the logic and language of this new era appeared in *Tiyu Weekly*, a Changsha, Hunan-based journal founded and published by the physical educator Huang Xing.[1] In a short piece entitled simply "What Is *Tiyu?*" Huang declared that *tiyu* stood for both "(1) *Physical* education, research into its use vis-à-vis human physiology, and (2) Physical *education*, research into its use with regard to humankind and social life. . . . We can say, 'Physical education is the correct means of developing the individual's body and is a requirement for adjusting to life in the human community.'"[2] Chinese physical culture activists were now ready to develop the connections between their discipline and the needs of a growing modern citizenry.

In the 1920s, *tiyu* would be marked by a more sophisticated approach to the relationship between the bodies of Chinese individuals and the Chinese nation. Many of the older, more blatantly militaristic and Social Darwinist forms of nationalism had been discredited by the late 1910s, but newer national formulas were available. New discourses allowed the imagination of a nation defined by both the human need for community and individual rights and freedoms. *Tiyu*, long conceived as a means of somatically imprinting an awareness of the nation on the minds of citizens, now would become a physically experienced link between citizens' dual responsibilities—to keep healthy and fit in body and mind and to work and unite with their fellow Chinese.

Besides these philosophies of what I call a new liberal democratic *tiyu*, this chapter explores several other aspects of the Chinese physical culture of the 1920s. For a time, Chinese citizens and their Western *tiyu* mentors and coaches were able to mix with and observe each other in an "intercultural zone" outside national narratives until more stridently nationalistic forms of *tiyu* organization made this kind of contact impossible. Physical culture was presented as an innovation that would allow China to share in the modernity of the West. But at the same time it could be integrated into nationalist narratives because its rational, scientific trappings—standards for accurate measurement of young citizens' physical performance, the explication of *tiyu* as a legitimate scientific discipline, and the professionalism of physical education training schools, organizations, and publications—made it seem so objective and universal as to appear to transcend specific cultures. Finally, Chinese physical culture was closely tied to commercialism and became an important element of conceptions of capitalist labor discipline of modern China.

LIBERAL DEMOCRATIC *TIYU*

In September 1919 Shanghai's *Chinese Educational Review* featured an article entitled "Democracy and Training," in which an author using the pen name "Great Profundity" set forth an ambitious vision for 1920s physical culture. He described the abuses of the current physical training system rooted in a Chinese custom of "sacrificing the individual will to accord to that of the group." The author criticized the Spartan model of citizen training once so popular in Chinese intellectual circles, writing that "the goals of this model are to breed obedience to force and to one's commanders, the submersion of soldiers' individual will, and machinelike passive movements."[3]

Extensively quoting Nicholas Murray Butler's work on post–World War

I education in Britain, the author argued instead for a democratic training, born of "high morals and social evolution," that would "utiliz[e] children's play instinct to encourage the training of the will via children's physical and mental activities" and would "develop free will and self-restraint." "I am by no means advocating the dissolution of rules and authority," the author continued. "I am saying, however, that rules and discipline must be rational and clearly understandable to achieve currency in the schools."[4]

This individualistic yet disciplinary approach meshed perfectly with the missionary E. D. Vernik's prescriptions for teaching group athletics in China, published in the journal of the missionary-led Educational Association of China:

> Modern athletics or physical training . . . places it's [*sic*] emphasis upon the development of the man who is subnormal in an effort to make a normal man of him. The aim of Modern Physical Training is not to make a star athlete of any man but to take the body every man has and make it an efficient serviceable machine which is capable of standing the wear and tear of his ordinary life. . . . [I]t must be a program calculated and so arranged that it will foster the spirit of group loyalty, develop the ability to co-operate with other boys toward a common end, instill within the boy a sense of mutual trust and dependability. It must be a system in which every boy can feel that he is an essential unit and is contributing some essential element toward its success. It must be a program in which the boy is taught to assume practically the whole responsibility for its working. . . .
>
> [In a 1919 program established in a Beijing mission school,] [e]very individual in each group is obliged to compete in every competition unless physically disabled. If he is absent or does not compete his team loses. . . . [H]e can always know that it may be just his one point that is needed to win the competition for his team.[5]

This missionary, like "Great Profundity" above, envisioned a physical culture that could create "normal" Chinese citizens, not by imposing order upon them, but by cultivating an individual awareness of one's own role in the larger community. Chinese reformers and Western missionaries alike saw this potential for a democratic system of "soft" discipline, based on rationality, tolerant of the individual citizen's free will, but dependent upon his or her self-restraint and ultimate commitment to order and an orderly nation, to shape a progressive China.

B. A. Garside of Shantung Christian University wrote on a similar experiment conducted at the Point Breeze Academy in Weixian County, Shandong, to "get the entire student bodies of the schools to participate in their sports and games with the most zest and interest. . . . [I]t was planned to provide a track-meet in which every boy in school would participate in every type of event for which his age and size fitted him."[6] The meet was also set up as to foster the sense of personal responsibility so important to the modern nation-state: "Before the race, each boy was asked to note as he finished who was ahead of him, and in general they gave us the correct order of their crossing the finish without trouble, although having several assistants to help with judging the finish always served to prevent disputes."[7]

The Chinese reformer and Western missionary visions of the Chinese nation converged and fit together quite neatly despite the hostility between members of the two camps. If missionaries felt directly threatened by manifestations of Chinese *nationalism*, they still hoped to make contributions to Chinese *nationism*—the drive for a China that could stand as one nation under God (indivisible, with liberty and justice for all, as the Chinese reformer would have added). Both reformer and missionary understood the new physical education system as a "modern" solution to older problematic programs in both cultures; Chinese modernists wanted a democratic alternative to the constraints imposed by the German-style military drill, while American missionaries hoped for a more egalitarian solution to the defects of a (U.S.-style) star sports system that ignored the skill levels of the majority. These visions meshed perfectly, as both configured young Chinese men as contributors to a greater modern and masculine nation-state whose harmonious working would be ensured by notions of individual normality, mutual trust, and a combination of "free will and self-restraint."

This was a new conception of the social body of the modern nation-state. In these postwar times, it was no longer efficient to attempt to build national strength by brute force, by shackling the individual's body and subjecting his will to a national body and will. Instead, a new model would have to be established and followed—what Takashi Fujitani has called "the positive deployment of power into the soul of the individual" or (paraphrasing Michel Foucault) the "individuation of the nation's subject-citizens."[8] Indeed, a graduate of the Beijing Higher Normal School Physical Education Department, Zhi Yongqing, in his 1924 book *Games and Sports*, criticized the monotonous military drill that was never able to "capture the student's interest." Zhi insisted that a modern physical education be created that accorded to physiological principles and "[took] the student as the subject (*zhuti*)."[9]

In his work on Meiji-era military conscription, Fujitani reminds us that "no modern regime has ever articulated its enterprise of constructing the nation-state as a project of limitations and restrictions."[10] Both the Western missionary and Chinese reformer clearly would have agreed—what

China needed was a nation of individual citizens who, rather than being forced, actually *wanted* to work together and play together as a team. But the survival of this team, as the missionary Vernik explained, would utterly depend on each individual's willing dedication to the whole, his determination to fit in as normal, and his knowledge that he was "an essential unit . . . contributing some essential element" to the whole and that he had "practically the whole responsibility" for its success. This was a world that required, again quoting Fujitani, "constant attention to the self."[11] Only by constantly monitoring his own performance, dedication, and normality could a young Chinese ensure that his slip-ups would not cost the nation its final victory. Physical culture was perhaps the finest classroom for the instruction of this system of "free will and self-restraint."

Thus in 1921 Wu Yunrui looked to modern physical culture to teach the "fighting spirit" that Chinese citizens would have to master for the nation to survive.[12] Wu, hailing from Xiaoqi Village in Jiangyin County, Jiangsu, graduated from Jiangsu Normal School's Physical Education program in 1915. He soon entered the new two-year Physical Education Program at Nanjing Higher Normal School and was a standout member of the first graduating class of 1918. In spring 1919, Wu entered the Shanghai YMCA Physical Education Training Program, and by that summer, he was hired to teach human kinetics *(renti yundongxue)* and gymnastics at Nanjing Higher Normal. Months after writing on *tiyu* and the fighting spirit for the YMCA journal *Association Progress,* Wu entered Southeastern University's P.E. Department and became one of China's leading *tiyu* voices during the 1920s and 1930s.[13]

In his 1921 piece, Wu took a page from Germany's defeat in the Great War to justify a new vision of Chinese physical culture. He noted that the Germans' "physiques might well be crowned world champions" but explained that "[those who] have fighting skills but do not possess the fighting spirit can only be called an unorganized mob *(wu he zhi zhong)*." The strong individual body thus had a double potential: not only to unite the nation in envisioning a future China but also to drive the nascent nation downward into chaos and mob rule. Wu classified fourteen elements of a disciplined fighting spirit that would be necessary for saving China—cooperation, courage, initiative, perseverance, obedience, coordination, training, sacrifice, group loyalty, honesty, firm will, self-restraint, determination to win, and fortitude—and described how different types of sport and exercise could breed all of these qualities.[14]

Wu closed his article with the well-known historical anecdote of Wellington attributing his victory at Waterloo to the lessons his men learned in playing *kelikoutuo* (cricket); he concluded that "each type of team sport is a factory for the manufacture of martial citizens." Like Chen Duxiu's attacks on feudal Confucianism for obstructing individual independence, Hu Shi's emphasis on the pragmatism so missing from Chinese thought and philosophy, and Ding Wenjiang's writings on (Western) science, Wu's article clearly indicated that the survival of the Chinese nation depended on a direct transfusion of knowledge developed in the aggressive and enterprising West. For Wu and many others, sporting "factories" were among the most important technologies to be transferred from the progressive West to an "unenlightened" China.[15]

TIYU AS AN INTERCULTURAL ZONE

Interestingly, however, the world of postwar Chinese physical culture was remarkably free of the thought that supposed a great and absolute dichotomy between China and the West. The whole history of *tiyu* in modern China, after all, had been one of finding similarities with the West and envisioning a place for China in a Western framework of history presumed to be universally applicable.

In this section I will borrow from Michael Taussig's ideas on what he calls the human race's "mimetic faculty"—"the faculty to copy, imitate, make models, explore difference, yield into and become Other"—to explain the ways that Chinese and Western cultures interacted in postwar Chinese *tiyu*. Like Taussig's work on the Cuna Indians of Panama's San Blas Islands, a history of modern *tiyu* presents a need to understand "the unsettling confrontation of the West with itself as portrayed in the eyes and handiwork of its Others."[16] Traditional historical models of contact between imperialist and the imperialized, or colonizer and colonized, have been framed in terms of one-dimensional "acceptance" and/or "resistance," and the history of Chinese sport has often been read in this way. However, use of Taussig's "mimesis" model reveals a much more complicated contact between Western spreaders of sport and their Chinese students, a contact that created in athletics "an intercultural nexus, a new cultural zone . . . for discovering strangeness and confirming sameness."[17] The world of *tiyu* created an entirely new cultural space, where both Western teacher and Chinese student were able to use *tiyu* in exciting ways—as Taussig says, "slipping into Otherness, trying it on for size."[18] One of Taussig's most useful contributions is to suggest that this mimetic faculty emerges only in certain historical circumstances. The postwar, post–May Fourth early 1920s seem to have been a time when conditions were ripe for an explosion of mimesis in China's *tiyu* community and young Chinese athletes and their earnest Western teachers embraced this "welcome opportunity to live subjunctively as neither subject nor object of history but as both, at one and the same time."[19]

Language Appropriation and Mimesis

One aspect of mimesis in the tiyu of the early 1920s was the very common use of English sports terminology, not only within Chinese books and articles on *tiyu*, but on the playing field itself. Several elderly interviewees, ex-athletes who began their sporting careers in 1920s China, remembered their experiences largely in English terms. Dong Hanwen began playing soccer in junior high school in Shenyang in the mid-1920s; when asked about it now, he speaks proudly of his skills at "center half."[20] Li Shiming joined his Shenyang junior high school baseball team in the early 1920s and, after moving to Dalian, joined a "Sports Club" organized by Japanese and Chinese merchants there. His reminiscences about his sports career in Liaoning are studded with Japanese-accented English terms like *baseball, pitcher, running,* and *skating.*[21] Cheng Jinguan, a hurdler-sprinter on the 1936 Chinese Olympic team, began playing soccer in middle school in Shanghai. Although he was a standout athlete, later playing on Fudan University championship soccer teams while still in high school, he described his soccer talent to me (in a burst of fluent English) as "natural, I never practiced."[22] The fun of this new world of sport could even include taking an English name; in 1925, the Shanghai College annual praised two standout freshmen athletes on the track and field team, Amoeba Wu and Longfellow Chen![23]

Spectators could get in on the act as well. A. B. Davis, headmaster of the Hankou YMCA Commercial School, wrote an account of China's Third National Games, held in Wuchang in 1924. He marveled at the way in which Chinese sports fans cheered on their teams:

> The manner in which the athletes went at their jobs, and their comments on the games, were much the same as those of Western youths. The Chinese students seem to have largely adopted English phraseology in some of their sports; and in the races it was not uncommon to hear such remarks as, "Come on, boy, you can beat him!" "Hurray! North China comes in one, two, three"; while the spectators at the basket-ball games frantically encouraged their players with, "Shoot, shoot!" "Take it away from him!" "Too bad you missed that one." At the baseball games, even a dyed-in-the-wool fan could shut his eyes and listen to the talk, and imagine himself comfortably seated in the bleachers somewhere back in America.[24]

This use of spoken and written English is a telling element of this era of Chinese physical culture, and far too important to explain away as a simple instance of creating distinctions and class hierarchy through the use of a few foreign words. No one who has played baseball in rural Taiwan and heard children yell out their calls "Stu-rike-uu" and "Out-tow," local variations on Japanized baseball terminology still used more than fifty years after the departure of the colonial power, would deny that language appropriation allows us to see real and complicated historical factors at work, whether in contemporary central Taiwan or 1920s urban China.

In a 1926 school publication on Nankai *tiyu*, Zhang Jiwu, physical education director for Nankai University and High School, quoted—in English without Chinese translation—F. H. Robertson that "man is the sum of his movements" and William James that "intrepidity, contempt of softness, surrender of private interests, obedience to command, must remain the rock upon which states are built."[25] A journal published by the Patriotic Girls' School Physical Education Research Society in June 1925 included three articles written in English by Chinese *tiyu* activists in Shanghai. Yi Liang Chang wrote that the school was "widely reputed for its special attention to the physical education of girls. Either a graduate or an undergraduate, after having been well trained, is very active, sound in body and mind, and able to accomplish every thing as a man."[26]

In fall 1923, Shen Guoquan took a job as professor of physical education at Nanyang University, only months after he graduated from Nanyang and completed a soccer career so outstanding that he was "worshipped by the entire school as a master sportsman."[27] That winter, he told a *Nanyang Weekly* reporter, "The West has a saying: 'If we want to have a truly great citizenry, we will have to train and turn out individuals who have the three Ms,' where these three Ms are *Mind*, *Muscle* and *Money*. The meaning of this saying is not too far removed from our three types of education, the moral, intellectual, and physical *(de-zhi-ti sanyu)*."[28]

Thus English was being used to communicate an astounding range of ideas, from James to Spencer. Some may see this type of quoting as a way to show off one's class status. We also see the acceptance of English as a recognized common language and most precise body of terminology in the field of world physical culture, akin to the use of Latin as a worldwide standard in the natural sciences.

Yet there is another process going on here as well. Walter Benjamin, in describing humanity's "powerful compulsion" to see resemblances and produce similarities, has written on the magic of written language and its ability sometimes to achieve what he calls a mimetic "flash." He describes how "the coherence of words or sentences is the bearer through which, like a flash, similarity appears."[29] This formulation works here with a slight adaptation. What I propose is that in this instance it was the incoherence (an understood, even expected incoherence) of mixing English words and phrases with Chinese that brought Benjamin's flash, conveying the sense that perhaps even a lowly Nankai High School student in 1920s Tianjin could actually live in another transcendent world of "physical health and intelligence"[30] along with all those moderns in the West so fit in mind and body.

Shen's exposition on the "3 Ms," for example, was more than his wish for a fit and wealthy China "translated" into English. If the medium is the message, then the English language here *was* quite literally Mind, Muscle, and Money and the way in which all of these could be achieved. Bodily mimesis—imitating, practicing, mastering the poses, gestures, and movements of the Western athlete/teacher—allowed the Chinese Other to enter this world of physical fitness and commitment to a national community via a learned self-control.[31] The use of language to produce similarities between China and the West allowed Chinese youth to move past these physical horizons to an entirely new frontier of sportsmanship, fair play, and all that was sporting about the fabulous West.

Westerners Become Other

Also drawn to this exciting frontier were the Western physical education experts who came to China in the early Republican period to spread their philosophies of fit bodies, minds, and nations. The most famed of these foreign experts was Charles Harold McCloy, who became known almost exclusively by his Chinese name, Mai Kele. In 1913, at the age of twenty-seven, the Marietta, Ohio, native graduated from Johns Hopkins Medical College and was immediately appointed Secretary of the Department of Physical Education in the National Council of the YMCA of China.[32] Upon his arrival in China, McCloy began proposing reforms to the military drill-dominated physical education he saw as so "monotonous and dull, almost totally lacking in educational value,"[33] "purely passive," authoritarian, antidemocratic, and actually harmful to students' health. By the early 1920s, Mai Kele was an institution in the world of Chinese physical education, publishing several articles a year and an occasional book, all written in Chinese. He taught a cadre of loyal students at National Southeastern University in Nanjing, where he was director of the School of Physical Education from 1921 to 1926. His 1916 book *Gymnastics Nomenclature (Ticao yiming)* was the standard for Chinese authors translating English works.[34] Ex-students like Wu Yunrui and Shao Rugan, whom "Professor Mai" taught during the

1910s at Nanjing Higher Normal School, were major figures in the Jiangsu-Zhejiang physical education community. McCloy's journal *Physical Education Quarterly*, founded in 1922 and printed by Shanghai's Commercial Press, was China's largest and most influential physical education journal in the 1920s. And McCloy was a force behind the three most important *tiyu* organizations of the late 1910s and early 1920s—the Jiangsu Province Educational Association, the Chinese Educational Reform Society's Physical Education and Citizens' Recreation Section, and the China Amateur Athletic Union.

McCloy's range and energy in his promotion of Chinese *tiyu* was astounding. He might invoke the work of Liang Qichao as he exhorted Chinese to lead a "New People" through their efforts in *tiyu*. Or he might summon up the legacy of May Fourth, as in his article "*Tiyu and De-mo-ke-la-xi*."[35] He was invited to speak at the Shanghai Wushu Association's January 1921 winter graduation ceremony, where he fit perfectly into the ranks of Chinese reformers and their historicization of Western claims of Chinese weakness: "Chinese people during the Qin, Han, and Tang dynasties were complete in emphasizing the scholarly and the martial. Thus, the country flourished and grew in power. But then the Song arrived and [Neo-Confucian] *lixue* philosophy prospered, and the people began to take after the ideal of the weak scholar. The [overformalized] eight-part essay convention was instituted [in the official government exam system], bequeathing its harm to future generations, a problem which to this day has not been solved."[36]

McCloy's journal *Physical Education Quarterly* afforded him the perfect chance to leave the strict confines of his persona as a YMCA missionary and fulfill his role as Mai Kele, accomplished Chinese *tiyu* activist; in fact, McCloy seems to have ended his formal contact with the YMCA in 1921 when he took his position at Southeastern University.[37] In 1922, he expounded upon the formation of ideals of "sportsmanship" in Europe and America. He translated this concept into Chinese as *junzi de jingshen*, literally, "the gentlemanly spirit," explaining, "We should know that when Europeans and Americans were still in the barbaric ages, Chinese already had the concept of the natural and perfect gentleman *(junzi haoran)* as explained by Confucius and Mencius, but had not yet discovered the gentleman's spirit as applied to competitive sport."[38] In the same issue, McCloy joined his students in the routine work of translating into Chinese the second of five parts of a long English article entitled "Appropriate Exercise Regimens for Male and Female Higher Primary School Students."[39] A year later in his journal, McCloy ventured into the realm of culture, suggesting thirteen standards by which Chinese and any other culture could be evaluated and the relationship between *tiyu* and achieving these standards.[40] He could also work out the most basic details of the Far Eastern Athletic Association and China Amateur Athletic Union's switch to the metric system. He discussed its near-worldwide use and its use in the Chinese railroad and postal systems and modern military, explained how to design running tracks to accommodate metric distances, and gave eight conversion factors between the metric and English systems of measurement.[41]

Two examples above all show how deeply McCloy had become involved in his role as Mai Kele. In 1922, *Shenbao* published a large volume entitled *The Past Fifty Years*, which featured sixty-seven essays on the changes in China since the newspaper's founding in 1872. Articles were contributed by luminaries in every field in China—Hu Shi on Chinese literature, Sun Yat-sen on the revolution, Liang Qichao on China's progress, Cai Yuanpei on philosophy, and Ding Wenjiang on China's mining industry. Alongside these greats was Mai Kele, who wrote a piece listed in English as "China's Physical Culture & Athletics for the Past 50 Years." The English "Contents" page compiled by *Shenbao* Secretary Francis Zia romanized the author's name ("Me K'e-lo") in the same fashion as it did Sun's and the others; there was no sign that this authoritative author picked to define Chinese *tiyu* over the last fifty years was a "Westerner."

McCloy's article traced Chinese *tiyu* from high antiquity all the way through to the present activities of the Jiangsu Educational Association and emphasized the need to understand the "historical process" involved. Reading the article, one finds it hard to blame Secretary Zia for thinking Mai Kele was another in a long line of Chinese reformers. The *tiyu* history McCloy described included an early "class schism" between *shi* elites and *nong* peasants, between those who labored with their minds *(xin)* and with their bodies *(li)*. He celebrated the "complete" Confucian ideal, which combined the scholarly and the martial, and then mournfully narrated its two-millennia-long decline brought on by the First Qin Emperor's anti-Confucian campaigns and sustained by Buddhist and Daoist teachings on purity and nirvana and nonaction, the elitist abuses of the examination system, the inherent degradation of Manchu Lamaism, and the practice of women's foot-binding.[42] McCloy simply outdid himself here, explaining recent martial arts history, describing his hopes for Chinese *tiyu* in the next fifty years, and explaining why Chinese *tiyu* had to be developed in a form suitable to "the nature of the Chinese people *(Zhongguo minxing)*."[43]

Mai's readers would have found themselves in a fascinating, not gray but swirling black and white, zone between China and the West. This zone was opened up to all by an American writing, under a Chinese name, for a Chinese audience about China's progress (in Western-defined terms as read by Chinese reformers) in both *tiyu* physical culture (Western in origin but capable of expressing the strength and vitality of the Chinese nation) and martial arts (a "sport" Chinese in origin and thus lacking the modern rational and educational values that China desperately needed).

A second example of McCloy as Mai came in a long article called "The Significance of These National Games," written in Chinese by McCloy in 1924 for the official publication of the Third National Games at Wuchang. His opening was typical of his earlier English-language work in its discussion of the disastrous results of an education that neglected the physical:

> Say you have [a student] who is very intelligent, accomplished in scholarship, and clear-minded. But he will still lack something in terms of life. He will fail because, besides the intellectual, even if mentally he is perfect, the other aspects of his character are not developed. Take his judgment and adaptability—he will lack judgment and be unable to adapt. In discouraging situations, he will completely lose spirit. He will never be a self-starter, he will lack initiative or any fighting spirit. His psyche will be on the edge of disaster. He will never be able to relax and will easily sink into anxiety. These qualities all come back to his poor physical condition. And he will probably be unable to relate to others. Without a social conscience, without sincerity, and without any leadership ability, it will be hard for him to have any efficiency in any social conditions.[44]

McCloy's emphasis on statistics and their use in measuring the spread of Chinese *tiyu* was characteristic of his work as well:

> The correlation between Olympic point totals and national population is 84 percent. I have also computed the relationship between scores in American track meets and university enrollments, which correlates at 82 percent. So what does this mean? It just shows that the more athletes there are, the more great athletes there will be. . . . So one great use of these [National] Games will be to give us a measure of how widespread *tiyu* is in China and how efficient physical education has been.[45]

But it is between these points in this article when McCloy truly became Chinese *tiyu* master Mai Kele:

> The Chinese upper classes traditionally emphasized scholarship and neglected the martial, and had no concept of a healthy character. Any nation in this situation would begin to regress—but this regression is not a regression in character; rather, it is just that the natural instinct has not yet been developed. It is like a village full of hundreds of poor

people who have right under their feet a huge gold mine. If they can develop this mine, they will all be rich. *We Chinese (Women Zhong-guoren)* need only recover this hereditary instinct and develop it, and we can achieve this healthy character, these lofty morals and abilities.[46]

If McCloy's emphasis on statistics, healthy initiative, and physical fitness as material wealth had seemed "Western," it was really only an illusion, or only as "Western" as Chinese reformers had tried to sound for decades. For Mai was now fully able to lead, as one of "we Chinese," this search for untapped Han instincts of chivalry and competition.

I am fascinated by McCloy's thirteen-year role in China as Mai Kele[47] and by what it meant for McCloy, as Mai, to pass on this body of knowledge to the Chinese *tiyu* community in the Chinese language. Again, McCloy was doing more than merely "translating" this Western discipline from English into a written language that Chinese people could understand. If Mai Kele's medium was the message, then it was one of great consequence for the future of Chinese *tiyu*—that this "physical education" belonged to China as *tiyu*. No longer did Chinese intellectuals have to search for China's place within universal history, for *tiyu*'s place within universal sport and its history. As McCloy abandoned his position as the Western physical education teacher for a role as Chinese *tiyu* doyen, he helped bring to many Chinese this new world, this space beyond the powerful West and weak China, and beyond histories of Western masculine initiative and Chinese feminine passivity.

Indeed, it was possible for Western missionaries, once in the intercultural zone, to forget even their calling, the reason for them to be in China. Dr. J. H. Gray was a leader of the Chinese YMCA Physical Education Section for several years, coming to China in 1920 after twelve years at a similar post in India. Gray penned an article or two under his Chinese name, Ge-lei, but he never took to this Chinese persona as McCloy had to Mai Kele. Gray more than others insisted that *tiyu* was something only Westerners could teach and that Chinese could only be their pupils; he was roundly execrated in 1923 when he insisted on serving as leader of the Chinese team at the Sixth Far Eastern Games in Osaka. Yet it seems even he was able to forget these distinctions, writing, "The avidity with which [China] has adopted [the athletic movement] and made it her own clearly indicates that it was not built on national or even racial lines, but on instinctive and fundamental human traits, and can, therefore, be claimed by China as inherently hers, as it can be by any other people. It *remains*, therefore, an inherent expression of Chinese life."[48]

An extreme case of mimesis in Chinese physical culture can be seen in the brief history of American football in China.[49] In November 1926, a football playoff was held in Shanghai between the Shanghai American School and two Chinese teams. The Huaimei School from Yancheng, northern Jiangsu, sent their team, founded in 1923 by an American principal who had been a gridiron star in the States.[50] St. John's University was represented by the Shanghai Chinese American-Football Team, established just that fall by William Sung (Shen Siliang, recently returned from study at Springfield College), with American ex-footballers Portfield and Gilliam as coaches. After the Shanghai Chinese team soundly defeated the Shanghai Americans at this tournament, the American school's young cheerleading squad dedicated a transnationalistic cheer to the victors, of which even May Thirtieth activists would have been proud:

> What's the matter with China?
> She's all right!
> Who's all right?
> China who won the game, China![51]

Chinese students as American football players and American cheerleaders as Chinese nationalists—seldom could there have been acted out more convincingly this model of Chinese *tiyu* as what Taussig would call a "welcome opportunity to live subjunctively as neither subject nor object of history but as both, at one and the same time."[52]

This model of mimesis and *tiyu* is hardly meant to ignore more brutal elements of the cultural imperialist project in China or to confuse an "intercultural zone" with some imperialist utopia, where a Chinese nation-state is built to perfectly conform to Western criteria. Early 1920s Chinese *tiyu*, for all its engagement with the West, was more than a domain of acquiescence to hegemonic Western formulas of modernity. I understand it as a zone where all were finally free to engage with, and even become, their Others as a way to escape confining imperialist and nationalist narratives. How else should one explain events like the amazing transvestite baseball game, joined in by some twenty Chinese and foreign "members of the teaching staff of Yenching University, Peking, in which men impersonated women, and vice versa"?[53]

Taussig writes that "modernity provides the cause, context, means, and needs, for the resurgence—not the continuity—of the mimetic faculty."[54] If we take this to mean not just the modern condition in general but the specific historical conditions of modernity (and of modern China in particular), then we can see why this zone of mimesis would look so inviting—both for Chinese tiring of imperialist intrusion and for Westerners starting to question their historical roles and activities atop the imperialist order. In the intercultural zone, all these boundaries could seem to dissolve as Westerners came face to face with themselves, their language and motions, portrayed by the Chinese Others they taught and coached. Chinese youth had been testing the waters of the intercultural zone for years now, but these Westerners' immersion in Chinese *tiyu* only accelerated its transformation into a domain where all were free to cast off the weight of national and modernist narratives and to "[slip] into Otherness, [try] it on for size."

PHYSICAL CULTURE AND MODERNITY

By the early 1920s, physical culture occupied a significant space in Chinese conceptions of modernity and of a modern China. If this modernity was based on the science, health, wealth, and progress that had fueled the industrial and imperialist triumphs of the Western powers and Japan, it was never seen as culturally bound to these foreign societies or histories. Likewise, modern physical culture was seen as a proven formula, so empirically sound and theoretically scientific that it could be imagined to transcend culture. By the mid-1920s the "intercultural zone" had become hard to locate, replaced by a strident *tiyu* nationalism brought on by the May Thirtieth massacre of Chinese demonstrators by British-commanded International Settlement police in Shanghai in 1925, and also by developments in the world of physical culture itself. (I discuss the nationalist mode of *tiyu* in Chapter 4.) Yet the basic physical culture structures and organizations, many of which had been developed by foreigners working and teaching in China, were scientific and modern enough that they were never questioned by even the most nationalistic *tiyu* activists.

Tiyu activists worked to portray physical culture as a fully modern and modernizing enterprise. For example, physical culture had been one of eight main topics of the Ministry of Education's program of mass education lectures, delivered to illiterate audiences by educators, college students, and local leaders, since 1915.[55] Another example was the Changsha journal *Tiyu Weekly*, which fully adopted modern attitudes, carrying advertisements for other self-consciously modern periodicals like *National Salvation Daily*, *Current Events*, and *Hunan Commerce*,[56] and featuring translations of important English- and Japanese-language pieces like Yoshida Akinobu's "Sports Physiology" and Henry S. Curtis's "Games Instruction."[57] Editor Huang Xing even contributed a short article on the scientific basis for the use of firecrackers in New Year's celebrations.[58] And it did not seem out of

place for another *Tiyu Weekly* author using the pseudonym "True Inten-
tions" to propose physical games and activities that could convince the public to abandon the lunar calendar and instead celebrate New Year's according
to the solar calendar.[59]

Many aspects of *tiyu* revealed its emergence as a self-consciously modern discipline. Below I focus on five—the push for universal numerical standards, the positing of *tiyu* as a modern science in its own right, and the emergence of specialized physical education schools, public organizations, and
media—that were crucial in shaping *tiyu* as a field of knowledge thoroughly
qualified and crucial for a modern Chinese age. At the same time, the mod-
ernization of China—in particular, developments in the creation of a new
public culture, bureaucratization, and commercialism—also influenced the
directions in which this physical culture would grow. Indeed, *tiyu*'s exclusive patent on new ways of disciplining the individual "subject-citizen" was
a crucial element of the modern Chinese nation-state.

Establishing Standards

> Perhaps the most important thing that has been done this year
> is the enormous amount of research conducted by Professor
> C. H. McCloy. . . . A study of weight for body types has been
> completed. . . . A study of chest measurements has been made. . . .
> The chest index as a basis of a test for hereditary stigmate of
> degeneration has been made. . . . A study has been made of the
> vital measurements and school grades to see what the relation
> might be. . . . A new weighting for age-height-weight and athletic
> performance has been devised.
>
> W. TCHISHIN TAO AND C. P. CHEN,
> *Education in China*, 1924

The establishment of standards—ranging from physical checkups of students, to evaluations of students' physical skill levels or physical education
teachers' effectiveness, to standards of *tiyu* ethics—was crucial to the 1920s
establishment of *tiyu* as a truly modern discipline. In fact, in an article proposing national running, jumping, and throwing standards for girls and boys
of all ages, Huang Binsheng wrote that it was the lack of proper testing standards that prohibited the spread of physical fitness throughout China.[60] Another book, entitled *Physical Education Standards Testing*, began:

> Examinations are an important science in modern education. Only
> with examinations can we know the extent of an individual's abilities,
> the strength or weakness of his body and mind, who is better and who
> is worse, who is strong and who is weak. . . . [I]n physical education,
> without these exams, it is very difficult to determine or compare the

measure of an individual's physical stamina, the strength or weakness
of his physique, or the level of his physical skill, and much of the
efficacy of education is lost.[61]

Invasive regimes of measurement and normalization were an integral part
of the modern *tiyu* discourse, even if they were discussed in very liberal
terms. The above authors' proposed testing battery—six skills tests in soccer, ten in basketball, two in softball, five in volleyball, five in tennis,
twenty-five in track and field, and six in gymnastics and martial arts; four
body measurements; and evaluation of ten qualities of "sportsmanship"
(yundong pinxing)—would "bring out students' competitive spirit, enable
the development of *tiyu*, and . . . give educators a set standard for praising
and criticizing as well as scoring students."[62]

Tellingly, Charles McCloy, as Mai Kele, led this Chinese search for reliable and accurate *tiyu* standards of all types. One of his contributions was
a long article called "How to Conduct Physical Examinations"; its thirteen-
page third installment included a table of 111 measurements, evaluations,
and entries to make during each student physical, along with descriptions
of how to carry them out and graph the results most precisely.[63]

Students were not the only individuals coming under the new normalizing gaze. The Chinese National Tiyu Research Society, formed in 1923,
published a finely tuned set of standards by which any physical education
teacher could be categorized in one of fifteen rankings from "High-1"
through "Basic-5."[64] This set of rankings, said to be "absolutely fair and
without bias," was designed to "help motivate instructors to work hard to
make progress," with certificates bearing the proper classification distributed to each teacher. The highest ranking, High-1, required graduation from
a specialized physical education school, three years of teaching experience,
participation in summer instruction training sessions, participation in two
physical education conferences, *tiyu*-related writings of five thousand characters or more, and ownership of at least six books on physical education.
At the other extreme, any instructor with only the following qualifications
would be classified as a lowly Basic-5: graduation from high school or its
equivalent, five years' experience participating in physical exercise, twelve
weeks of instruction in physical education, participation in one P.E. conference, *tiyu*-related writings of one thousand characters, and possession of four
books on physical education. (Unfortunately, however, the authors lamented
that "we fear that China at present has not a single person worthy of the
High-1 ranking.")[65] Besides illustrating the standardizing, normalizing impulse of the age, these standards for physical education instructors indicate
the power of ideals of specialization and professionalization—of imagining

a China where even the least qualified physical education instructors would engage in scholarly research and participate in conferences in their field.

This vision of standards and normalization of Chinese bodies and their motions seems to have been most effective when it was applied to the individual citizen. Now, fulfilling the responsibilities of citizenry depended on scientific evaluation of one's own performance in, and even attitude toward, physical exercise. Participants in the modern *tiyu* became "subjects of self-knowledge," or "self-disciplining subjects." As with Fujitani's new recruits into the Meiji-era Japanese military, proper participation in the world of modern *tiyu* "demanded constant attention to the self" and was "characterized by the minutest attention to the customs of the body."[66]

Xie Siyan's 1927 book *Track and Field Theory and Practice* began with the author asking each reader to locate him- or herself on a spectrum ranging from the true athlete to the common itinerant martial artist.[67] Besides challenging his readers to evaluate their knowledge and their "gentleman's" or "sportsman's" spirit, Xie put the most emphasis on a strong body. And this meant not only a body strong on the outside but a body healthy inside and out. Xie cited the shocking example of a Japanese Olympic athlete who disgraced his nation when he was diagnosed with worms during a routine physical checkup in Europe—clear evidence of the need to truly understand one's own body, health, and diet.[68]

Wang Huaiqi and Zou Falu's book *Physical Education Standards Testing* included a "Student Performance Diary" allowing young athletes to record their daily performance and progress on sixty physical tests.[69] Also included was a "Sportsmanship Self-Evaluation Record" *(yundong pinxing ziping jilu)*, on which the *tiyu* consumer could evaluate him- or herself monthly for six years on ten aspects of sportsmanship: honesty, obedience, enthusiasm, loyalty, morality, humility, politeness, courage and preparation, neat dress, and respect for rules.[70] Also included in the book were twelve perforable copies of an overall score sheet on which students would record their physical measurements, gymnastics, ball sports and track and field scores, and sportsmanship evaluations by semester. And for good measure, each sheet had several different *tiyu*-related homilies printed on the back, such as "A healthy body is to be respected, while weak muscles are shameful," or "Knowledge is the goods, the body is the boat; if the boat is wrecked it will not be able to deliver the goods."[71]

Again, it was not only youth participating in *tiyu* who had to pay such close attention to their bodily motions and rhythms. Conscientious physical education instructors also tormented themselves over their own performance. Huang Xing of Changsha wrote a painful article of confession in late 1919, in the hope that other instructors could learn from his "past sins" committed as a calisthenics instructor.[72] Huang calculated that in his seven-plus years as an instructor, he had taught some nine hundred thousand student-hours and had taught some individual students for up to 480 hours over four years. However, Huang saw this long span of instruction as full of harm for his students on account of his three sins—not thinking enough about his teaching, assuming that his students understood him and not asking if they had any questions, and spending more energy on theory than on practice. He then gave nine examples of the grievous harm done by his sins. In 1914, a good athlete got married a month before his school's Autumn Meet; Huang did not put pressure on him to stay out of the meet after his honeymoon, and as a result of competing in a spent state he was now sick with tuberculosis. In 1916, a good athlete under his charge was masturbating regularly, and Huang was never able to tell. In 1919, a student of Huang's came down with gastritis and then more serious stomach ailments and eventually died because of his habit of eating hot peppers. Huang lamented, "These children gave me their precious time, and they all became sacrifices to my experiments—sacrifices to my vanity."[73] This agonizing attention to all one's thoughts and actions was crucial in creating citizens capable of measuring, evaluating, and disciplining themselves.

Through these endless self-evaluations, students and other *tiyu* participants were now expected to induct themselves into the totalizing systems of discipline upon which the modern nation-state was premised. As the world of Chinese physical culture world shifted more and more from militaristic *ticao* drilling to these "liberating" scientific forms of exercise, the *tiyu*-minded individual was forced to commit to more and more intense forms of self-discipline and self-understanding. The result, of course, as in other areas of society, was the increasing disappearance of externally imposed power, now that many urban Chinese were capable of disciplining themselves far more strictly and religiously than any imperial regime ever could. This was part of the modernizing process by which China began to achieve the conditions necessary to function as a nation-state integrated into a new world order.

The Science of Physical Fitness

Many in the physical culture community also made efforts to establish *tiyu*'s modern credentials by showing its direct relationship to the world of science. Luo Yidong's *The Science of Physical Fitness* (1924) described *tiyu* research as being most closely related to physiology, anatomy, and hygienics but also requiring an understanding of biology, evolution, genetics, and anthropometry. For example, Luo's book included chapters on the relationships between exercise and the human muscular, nervous, circulatory, respiratory, digestive, and excretory systems.[74] Other, similar books on physiological aspects of physical fitness were published in the early 1920s as well: *Diagrams of Muscles and Practical Movements during Physical Exercise,* by Mai Kele (Mc-Cloy) and Jiao Xiangzong; Cheng Hanzhang's *Exercise Physiology;* and Zhang Shouren's translation of Gulick and Cromie's *Muscle Development.*[75]

The *tiyu* community staked a claim to evolutionary science as well. In 1923 an article by Huang Binsheng introduced fifteen "competitive games," such as "hand-pull wrestling" (adapted from Western "Indian wrestling"), "knock off his cap," "chicken fight," and "the dog pulls the cave-tiger"—all two-person games suitable for boys or girls, and containing the "natural motions of climbing, hitting, and throwing [that] are all the most critical factors in the 'survival of the fittest.'"[76]

Social science research was also key to establishing *tiyu* as an agent of national modernity. Zhang Liuquan wrote a long article for the *Chinese Educational Review* in 1925 analyzing high school students' recreational habits. He distributed more than two hundred questionnaires at five Nanjing high schools, asking students detailed questions about their own, family members', and neighbors' participation in fifty-two types of activities, from playing soccer, to barbecuing sparrows, to visiting prostitutes, to newspaper reading. These data were then presented in tables, bar graphs, and ratios of correspondence demonstrating family and neighborly influence during both summer and winter vacation. Zhang concluded that "harmful activities" (visiting prostitutes, gambling, smoking) should be replaced with games and sports as a means of suppressing adolescent desire and that concentration on physical exercise in schools could help cultivate "fine and reliable recreational habits."[77] The legitimacy of social science and investigation was thus also invoked to construct the modern ideology of better living and community through team sports and natural outdoor movements.

Specialized Physical Education Schools and the Jiangnan Model

Meeting the increasingly specialized needs of physical education and research also meant establishing specialized programs and schools to train Chinese youth in this field. As mentioned in previous chapters, China's earliest specialized physical education schools were established in the late Qing dynasty, almost exclusively in the Jiangnan area. This Jiangnan concentration continued into the 1920s, but physical education schools and departments were being established in different areas of China as well. Of the twelve founders of new *tiyu* schools who are listed in Table 3, six were graduates of Shanghai's Chinese Calisthenics School. Five others had graduated

TABLE 3. Sampling of Physical Education Schools
Founded 1920–1927

School Name, Location	Date	Length	Founder (if known)
Chengdu Higher Normal School P.E. Department	1920	2 yrs	Lu Peixuan
Hangzhou Women's P.E. School	1920	1 yr	Wu Wenmei
Shanghai Liangjiang Women's P.E. School	1920	2 yrs	Lu Lihua
Zhejiang P.E. Normal School (Hangzhou)	1920	2 yrs	Cai Juezai
Shanghai P.E. Normal School	1921	2 yrs	Wu Zhi
Yueyun High School P.E. Department (Hunan)	1922	2 yrs	
Zhongshan P.E. Vocational School (Suzhou)	1923	2 yrs	Zhu Zhongming
Fengtian Private P.E. Vocational School	1924	2 yrs	
Shanghai Hujiang Women's P.E. Vocational School	1924	2 yrs	Sun Hebin
Soochow University P.E. Department	1925	2 yrs	Xu Minhui
Southwestern P.E. Vocational School (Chengdu)	1925	2 yrs	Liu Shenzhan
Chengdu YWCA Music & P.E. School	1926	2 yrs	Fu Ziyun
Liaoning Provincial Normal School P.E. Dept.	1926	3 yrs	
National Chengdu University P.E. Department	1926	4 yrs	
Republican University P.E. Department (Beijing)	1926	2 yrs	
Sichuan Provincial Fourth Normal School P.E. & Arts Program (Wanxian)	1926	3 yrs	
Xiachu High School P.E. Department (Hunan)	1926	1 yr	
East China P.E. Vocational School (Shanghai)	1927	2 yrs	Zhang Dongping
Shanghai Chinese P.E. School	1927	1 yrs	Gu Jilai

SOURCES: Sasajima Kōsuke, trans. by Wu Enlian, *Jindai Zhongguo tiyu yundong shi* (Zhongguo tiyushi xuehui bianjibu, 1985), 155–157, 179–182; "Zhejiang jindai de tiyu xuexiao," *Tiyu yundong jiaoxue cankao ziliao* 12 (June 1981), 19–21; Hunan sheng difangzhi bianzuan weiyuanhui, ed., *Hunan shengzhi, di ershier juan: Tiyu zhi*, 115; Sun Zhongda, "Xingxue yilai Sichuan tiyu shizi peiyang," *Sichuan tiyu shiliao* 4 (December 1983), 3; Guo Hengda and Liang Shuyuan, "Sichuan zaoqi nü tiyu laoshi Fu Ziyun," *Sichuan tiyu shiliao* 22 (February 1988), 26–27; Yu Jianmin, "Sichuan shengli di si shifan tiyu yishu zu jianjie," *Sichuan tiyu shiliao* 3 (November 1983), 27.

from other Jiangnan physical education institutions founded in the late Qing or early Republic—Jiangsu Higher Normal School P.E. Department, Zhejiang Physical Education Vocational School, and the Shanghai YMCA and YWCA Physical Education Normal Schools.

The nationwide influence of Shanghai's specialized physical education training is also shown by the roll lists of the Shanghai East Asia P.E. School. Its first two graduating classes, admitted in 1914–15, included twenty-one Jiangsu natives, three residents of Zhejiang, and two from Anhui. But by 1920, more than 22 percent of the school's ninety-five students came from outside the Jiangnan belt. They hailed from, and would take the knowledge of modern *tiyu* back to, Henan, Anhui, Guangxi, Fujian, Guizhou, Jiangxi, and Gansu.[78] Meanwhile, Sun Wangqiu of Hangzhou's Zhejiang P.E. School could boast in 1928, "Since our school was established in the early years of the Republic, over one thousand students have graduated from our degree and extension programs. Except for Tibet, Mongolia, and Xinjiang, every province in the nation is home to one of our alumni."[79] The modern Republican educational system—which provided these novel and exciting opportunities for young people to work and learn across regional and provincial lines—thus also helped to define the modern ideology of *tiyu* as a unifying and nationalizing form.

The Trend toward Formal Organizations

Another element of *tiyu*'s drive toward modernity came with the trend of establishing public organizations devoted to the study and propagation of sports and physical fitness programs. In a time of governmental impotence, endless warlord battles, and factional strife, these organizations' neutrally nationalistic stands made them self-conscious beacons of a modern and healthy China where all could come together to work for a strong national body.

YMCA directors in North, East, Central, and South China had established regional athletic organizations in the 1910s, but the first sports organizations to have a national scope and to be directed by Chinese came in the 1920s. The history of the China Amateur Athletic Union (CAAU) (Zhonghua yeyu yundong lianhehui) demonstrates this trend well. The CAAU was first established in 1919 to administer sending a Chinese national team to the Fourth Far Eastern Championship Games in Manila. Twenty-five delegates representing (mostly YMCA) athletic organizations in Jilin, Shenyang, Tianjin, Beijing, Ji'nan, Baoding, Taiyuan, Kaifeng, Chengdu, Wuchang, Nanjing, Suzhou, Shanghai, Hangzhou, Fuzhou, Xiamen, Kunming, Canton, and Hong Kong attended two meetings that year, adopted a twelve-article

CAAU Constitution, and appointed an Organizing Committee consisting of three foreign and two Chinese YMCA *tiyu* personnel.[80] When the CAAU met in Shanghai in 1921 to prepare for the Fifth Far Eastern Games, forty-nine members elected a new nine-man Organizing Committee made up of six Chinese and three foreigners.[81] The CAAU lasted until 1924, when it was merged into the more outwardly nationalistic China National Amateur Athletic Federation (Zhonghua quanguo tiyu xiejinhui); these events are described in the next chapter.

Such organizing was the next logical step as more and more Chinese came to see *tiyu* as a unique field of knowledge to be investigated and disseminated among the nation's citizenry. The 1920s saw the founding of dozens of formal physical culture organizations, both official and otherwise, from the Changsha Tiyu Study Society and the Chinese Bookstore Tiyu-for-Morality Association (Shanghai) to the Beijing Elementary School P.E. Research Society and the Yunnan Tiyu Federation. These organizations, besides confounding traditional notions of the boundaries between state and society, worked to constitute *tiyu* as an important part of urban culture, and to establish *tiyu* as one more modern domain subject to the rules of specialization and formal study.

The Emerging Tiyu *Press*

> Why do we advocate the sports movement? Because sports are a magic potion to cure our weak and decrepit China!
>
> Why do we worship stars from the sports world? Because sports stars can win glory for the nation and wipe away the humiliation of the Sick Man [tag for China]!
>
> . . . People in society who worship athletes and want to know more details about their lives and the glories they have won for the nation don't think that this is impossible. It is true that athletes are a little too distant; if you want to look up and see their dashing appearances for yourself, you may not be able to. Thus Shanghai's Young Companion Printing House is providing just what society demands with our publication of *Sports World*. There is no major star, minor figure, or news item in China or abroad that our pictorial, more than one hundred pages long, will not report on.
>
> Advertisement for *Tiyu shijie,*
> in *Liangyou* 12 (15 January 1927)

The propagation of *tiyu* knowledge also depended on a steady written stream of information on physical culture to convey both this knowledge and the sense that this realm was a deserving and valid part of Chinese modernity.

The 1920s saw a rise in the amount of material published on physical culture, as readers were instructed in print and pictures concerning the most effective ways of exercising their body and improving their fitness (to be citizens). The epigraph above clearly illustrates the selling point of the *tiyu* press as a means for modern (and quickly alienated!) sports fans to finally get to "know" their dashing and distant athletic idols.

The 1920s saw a great increase in the number of books published on topics in physical culture in China. A recent and surely incomplete index compiled by the Beijing National Library on holdings in the Beijing, Shanghai, and Chongqing Libraries lists 109 books published on physical culture between 1920 and 1927,[82] an increase of more than 50 percent over holdings from the 1910s. Some sample titles—*The Athlete's Guide, An Illustrated Guide to Boy Scout Calisthenics, Strong Bodies for Boys and Girls, The Newest Girls' Basketball Games, Illustrated Explanations of Tai Chi Steps*—can suggest the nature of this young *tiyu* press—not just popular but accessibly pedagogical, giving Republican China's young teachers and consumers the knowledge they needed to transform and discipline their bodies in new and fun ways.

Besides book publications, several specialized physical culture periodicals were introduced during the 1920s. These periodicals—for example, *Tiyu Research, Tiyu Weekly,* and *Sports World*—were devoted to specific topics like competitive sports, physical education, sports science, and martial arts and were published in Shanghai, Nanjing, Beijing, and Qingdao. In addition to these specialized journals, Shanghai's *Shenbao* published a weekly "Education and Life" supplement in 1923–24 with a two-to-four-page *tiyu* column edited by Jiang Xiangqing of St. John's University. Mainstream periodicals like the *Ladies' Journal, Young Companion, Life Weekly,* and *Pei-Yang Pictorial News* all gave regular attention to physical culture, while other periodicals like *Association Progress, Students' Magazine, Nanyang Weekly,* and *New Education* all published special *tiyu* issues during the early 1920s.[83]

These *tiyu* publications of the 1920s posited physical culture as a unique realm that could serve as a subject of serious scientific and national-minded study at the same time that it could constitute a new element of China's rising popular culture. Both capacities of *tiyu* were fully in line with physical culture's role in building a Chinese modernity—healthy entertainment for healthy body–maintaining citizens and an explication of what the human body could achieve if coached and directed in scientifically approved motions. Finally, many of these periodicals, even those published by university P.E. departments, were fully enmeshed with the commercial apparatus thriving in the cities of the new Republic.

COMMERCIALISM AND THE CAPITALIST LOGIC OF *TIYU*

As discussed above, 1920s Chinese physical culture could in many ways be imagined to transcend culture and national boundaries. At the same time, many Chinese could take pride in the growing similarity between their nation's physical culture and that of the strong, wealthy, and modern Western and Japanese powers.

Further similarities can be seen in these modern sports' roots in capitalism and in their magnetic attraction to commercial interests. At times, Chinese *tiyu*'s ties to capital could appear to be above national boundaries. Yet the idea of fair competition between free equals came to China only with modern physical culture and the global capitalist system. Such Western concepts were foreign to premodern Chinese physical cultures. Rather, military, aristocratic, imperial, and/or ritual ideals were the basis for the physical games and contests of China before the late Qing. Furthermore, the formal hierarchies of Confucian society meant that one rarely even came into contact with an "equal"—according to ideals of society and family, the individual had to face almost any other individual as a superior or inferior (or a mixture of both). Like modern sport, capitalism's main selling point was that it provided a space to enter into competition as equals, exceeding one's limits and pushing one's opponents to exceed theirs. If this ideology is taken for granted now, and was in 1920s China, it is still historically situated, and it came to Chinese *tiyu* via modern Western physical culture.

China's modern physical culture provided the arena for the Darwinist practice struggles that Chinese reformers had been recommending for decades. These micro-struggles, experienced not only mentally but physically, were expected to cultivate the competitive instinct necessary for survival in the modern world. Bodily involvement in these struggles also worked to condition the players and spectators for the ideologies of "friendly struggle" and "fair competition" under which capitalism justified its global expansion.

The connections between capitalism and modern physical culture were made on many different levels. The *tiyu* scientist Luo Yidong provided the most fundamental link between physical fitness and the economy, explaining how the weakness of an individual can hurt familial and national economies.[84] A *Shenbao* reporter wrote in 1921 on the values that a physically fit citizenry could bring to a commercialized nation in the forms of healthy trade and peace through strength.[85] No less a figure than General Feng Yuxiang, in a 1927 speech at the Xi'an Political Education Academy, used the subject of modern sports to attack the imperialists' penetration of Chinese markets:

The new-style sports *(yundong)* are fine, but they all use foreign goods. When you are kicking around a soccer ball, the ball is foreign-made and the shoes are imported goods. When you play tennis, the net and the racket are all from the United States. Volleyball, baseball, basketball—not a one is different. I don't oppose playing ball in the least, but I do oppose this feverish consumption of foreigners' goods.[86]

And in 1920 the national track star Chen Zhang'e ran a race against a train; his reputation soared after he defeated the train and proved the Chinese/human body's capacity to better even this ultimate symbol of modernity and commerce.[87]

The specialized agents involved in disseminating sporting knowledge throughout China also modeled their physical culture agenda and philosophies after those of modern commerce and industry. A 1920 *Republican Daily News* editorial hailed the work done by the writers at Changsha's *Tiyu Weekly* and their motto "Let work be our exercise."[88] This approach could be seen in *Tiyu Weekly* founder Huang Xing's 1919 article "Road Construction." After describing the great importance of roads to the modern nation's culture, economy, defense, and employment programs, Huang stated, "The main reason I bring up the question of road construction today relates to physical culture. What I have been working to advocate is a physical culture characterized by 'economy of time' and 'economy of effort,' or a 'physical culture of production.' . . . Now does anyone still doubt the relationship between road construction and physical culture?" Huang went on to make a dazzlingly modern comparison of roadwork with calisthenics and sports, explaining how these activities all exercise the four limbs and the internal organs, teach good posture, and develop a true spirit of competition.[89]

Mai Kele, or Charles McCloy, penned an article in his *Physical Education Quarterly* entitled "The Reasons for Failure" on the substandard performance of China's physical education instructors. Citing a recent American newspaper report describing the eleven main causes of commercial, industrial, and professional failure, Mai described how four of these reasons could be applied directly to physical education instruction: lack of qualifications (which caused 38.2 percent of all economic failures), lack of capital (30.2 percent), lack of experience (5.6 percent), and lack of determination (1.7 percent). "The physical education instructor's capital is his specialized knowledge," wrote Mai, as he encouraged his readers to eliminate 75.8 percent of the cause of *tiyu* failure by remedying these four deficiencies—clearly, it was understood that any question of physical culture by its very definition was a question of commerce and industry and was subject to the same capitalist forms of logic and organization.[90]

Wang Huaiqi's book *Starball Regulations*—rules for a soccerlike game more appropriate for women and children—is another example of the interplay between modern sport, commercialism, and capitalism. The cover of the pocket-sized rulebook featured an advertisement for the regulation ball used in his game, "a durable little leather ball" with the official "Domestic Goods" *(guohuo)* stamp, produced by the Tan Kah Kee (Chen Jiageng) Corporation. The text provided several plugs for the Tan Corporation, mentioning that balls for use in this new sport of starball "can be bought in any foreign goods mart—they have a 'K' printed on them, but these are Japanese-made. There are now Chinese-made balls being manufactured by the Tan Kah-kee Corporation." Wang also mentioned that other items needed for the game—goals, flags, whistles, caps of various colors, and shoes—were also being produced by the Tan Corporation.[91] *Starball's* conclusion made fascinating and disturbing connections between sport and the workings of capitalism:

> Our research into physical culture is absolutely no different from the hard work done by laborers. . . .
> Early *tiyu* was in the form of empty-handed calisthenics, but it only reached a certain level. Without the supplement of equipment, it cannot be truly efficient. For sport, if there are no open grounds, one must exercise alone. But if one wishes to have sport with a great group of people gathered together, how can this be managed? By the unbiased investigations and criticisms made by engineers—are the responsibilities of an engineer and a sports referee any different? And athletes' rules-respecting participation in sports is just like the work done by laborers to produce goods. The ultimate victory or loss in sports, and the ultimate quality of a manufactured product; are these not exactly the same thing? Moreover, there is also the matter of athletes' respect for the rules. Whether in defeat or victory, there will always be some violation of the rules. Again, how much does this resemble the factory discipline that all must follow?[92]

Wang was one of the most influential physical education figures of the 1920s, publishing forty-nine books on subjects in *tiyu* by 1927;[93] it is instructive that the most mainstream of *tiyu* figures envisioned modern physical culture in such an unapologetically mercantilist way. *Tiyu* was an industry that consumed products of other industries, like sporting goods or apparel factories, in China, Japan, and the West. Growing numbers of modern Chinese citizens consumed physical culture, whether through state education, the morning newspaper, or active spectatorship at sports events. But the *tiyu* industry was expected to turn out a unique product—disciplined, self-disciplining individuals willing to sweat in labor or in play for the sake of a greater Chinese nation.

Finally, the tradition of spectatorship that came with these sports played into the rising commercialism and consumer culture of early Republican China. Almost any major meet held in an urban setting could attract thousands of paying spectators. The *North-China Daily News*, usually hostile to Chinese athletic activities held without Western supervision, estimated a crowd of twenty thousand Wuchang fans attending the Third National Games' final day.[94] The second day of the Seventh Far Eastern Championship Games National Selection Meet, held in Shanghai in June 1925, attracted five to six thousand paying spectators.[95] At the Eighth Far Eastern Games held in Shanghai in 1927, sixteen thousand fans paid to watch the China-Philippines soccer game, and eight thousand paying fans attended the China-Japan baseball contest.[96] Eight thousand more paid to watch the China-Philippines basketball game, and Boy Scouts and police had to apprehend several more ticketless fans attempting to break down the fence to get into the event.[97]

China's paying spectators bought tickets in several different classes. For example, at the Fujian Provincial Games of 1921, sports fans could choose from five types of tickets. Tickets were sold in advance at fifty-three stores, banks, pharmacies, bookstores, and teahouses in and around Fuzhou city, each of which kept 15 percent of the ticket proceeds.[98] Tickets for the 1921 Far Eastern Games, held in Shanghai, were also sold in advance at convenient locations such as the Ningbo Guild, the Jiangsu Educational Association, the Wing On Company, the Commercial Press, and the Moudeli Foreign Business Agency. Thus even the initial purchase of the tickets involved individual interaction with one of these agents of capitalist modernity. Once at the window, tickets were sold in five classes, from a one-hundred-*yuan* family pass for the whole games to a student 0.20-*yuan* one-day ticket.[99] These different classes of seats enabled paying fans to experience, through their purchases and through their consumption of these physical contests, clear differences in status, and in discipline and supervision, as Boy Scout and police peacekeepers predictably were stationed in the heaviest concentrations in the cheap seats.

Official material on the Eighth National Games of the People's Republic of China, held in October 1997, erroneously describes how "[f]or the first time, the national games will adopt the advertising method, that is, using the names of sponsors or trademarks, to name the trophies and medals of various competition events."[100] With apologies to the architects of socialism with Chinese characteristics, "advertising methods" actually were no stranger to Chinese national meets even in the 1920s. The Hankou YMCA Tiyu Department funded the official publication of the Third National Games of 1924 with the help of twenty-eight advertisements, including fourteen for banks and other ads for Sincere Company Snow Cream, Girl Brand Beverages, the Hankou Commercial Press, Shell Oil, and Socony.[101]

Sporting images were used to sell products, as in the Quaker Rolled White Oats ad featuring a muscular, tousle-haired Chinese soccer player, ball at his feet, clutching a trophy with Quaker's Chinese brand name inscribed on the cup.[102] The Commercial Press had its advertisements all over *tiyu*-related books and magazines. One of its favorites was Nanjing's *Physical Education Quarterly*. In this journal's August 1922 170-page issue, 21 pages were covered with 25 different Commercial Press ads. In its April 1923 issue, 18.5 of 136 pages were filled by 21 Commercial Press ads, which provided a virtual walking tour of Chinese capitalist modernity. Products sold by the Commercial Press included commerce classes by mail, magazines *(Ladies' Journal, Youth Magazine, English Weekly, Science Magazine, Students' Magazine)*, Wright and Ditson-Victor Co. tennis rackets, Zhao Yuanren's set of eight phonograph records of modern Mandarin pronunciation, eight books on *wushu* martial arts, and filmstrips (in six categories: education, *tiyu*, current events, famous scenery, new drama, ancient drama).[103] The Commercial Press did not supply the emerging sports world with this patronage for free, however—at the 1921 Far Eastern Games, Commercial Press photographers were the only Chinese press allowed on the Hongkou Park field.[104]

CONCLUSION

The heavy identification of 1920s *tiyu* with aggressive capitalist players in China is no coincidence. Nor is this a simple case of savvy media agents working to create a new discipline of knowledge and news coverage, "inventing stories," as it were. Modern *tiyu* came to China at roughly the same time, and for the same reasons, as the globalizing system of capitalism and the nation-state. Modern *tiyu*, the reification of the body and its functions as observed in direct competition, was part of capitalism. Its invention of new ways of disciplining the individual subject-citizen was part of the modern nation-state environment that capitalism needed to thrive. The most celebrated sports moments, like these international meets, provided the rare opportunity to purchase a view of international struggle through the fair competition of *tiyu*. And what a deal! For just the price of a 0.20-*yuan* ticket one could witness sports' most valuable contribution to the nation-state—the reduction of normally complicated and overwhelming competition between nations to a duel between a few selected individuals. And to the winners, of course, went the spoils—here, however, not the right to pillage and dehumanize one's vanquished enemy, but a prize trophy, medal, or banner donated by capitalist firms or bourgeois government leaders.

These connections between physical culture and capitalism should hint at Chinese physical culture's fundamental ties to histories of cultural and economic imperialism—histories from which many had looked to the fun and freedom of modern sports to escape. Chinese of all political stripes hoped to be part of a China that could create, as American-educated physical education expert Hao Gengsheng called it, a "civilized nation . . . a happy and active life" for all of its citizens. Most, if not all, of those who hoped to achieve this goal via physical culture began by looking to the achievements, formulas, and philosophies of the Western nations' physical culture programs. Some were carried away by this world of play, fun, and sport and could imagine themselves and their China as part of the modern West. Others resented Western intrusions and missionizing and hoped to create a Chinese *tiyu* impervious to cultural imperialism. But all partook of the same modern, globalizing system of physical culture. Its obvious ties to Western societies and histories were easy to ignore because its trappings of modernity were accepted as scientific, empirical, and transcending national and cultural boundaries. The next chapter covers another aspect of Chinese *tiyu* in the 1920s by foregrounding the power relations that were typically naturalized and made "invisible" and by showing where these manifested themselves in Chinese physical culture.

4 Nationalism and Power in the Physical Culture of the 1920s

The awakening of nationalist and anti-imperialist sentiment among the urban masses of modern China is recognized as beginning with the May Thirtieth massacre of 1925, when British-commanded International Settlement police fired on Chinese antimilitarist and anti-imperialist demonstrators in Shanghai. However, a traumatic and transformative nationalistic "awakening" had occurred in the Chinese physical culture world fully two years earlier, at the Sixth Far Eastern Championship Games held in Osaka in May 1923.

Since the First Far Eastern Championships of 1913, American YMCA officials had customarily served as heads of the Chinese athletic delegations. By 1923, not surprisingly, many Chinese had tired of this humiliating tradition. Dr. J. H. Gray, secretary of the China Amateur Athletic Union, angered many in the months before the Sixth Far Eastern Games by dismissing—as "political" and not sportsmanlike—nationalist demands to boycott the games to be held on the soil of China's imperialist archenemy Japan.[1] Then, when Gray insisted on leading the Chinese team at the 1923 Games at Osaka, the *tiyu* world reacted with fury. The humiliation was doubled by its occurrence before Japanese fans and media, who jeered at the Chinese for this embarrassing lack of sovereignty.[2] For many in the Chinese *tiyu* community already eager to take back control of this vital realm from the foreigners, the YMCA staff's insulting action was the last straw.

In July 1923, an organization called the Chinese Athletic Association (Zhonghua tiyu xiehui) was established in Shanghai to struggle against the YMCA-dominated China Amateur Athletic Union.[3] A diverse group consisting of individuals from the mainstream physical education community (Wang Zhuangfei, Tang Hao) and the Shanghai martial arts community (Lu Weichang, Chen Gongzhe, Ma Zizhen, Wu Zhiqing), and even a former

CAAU Organizing Committee member (Hao Boyang), the new CAA quickly linked up with nationalist elements in other areas of China. By early 1924, the Hong Kong South China Tiyu Association and the Guangdong provincial women's teams had agreed to a boycott of the Third National Games to be organized by the CAAU in Wuchang that May.[4]

Faced with this nationalist challenge, the CAAU establishment had to act quickly. It recruited six national figures to serve as honorary committee members—the political giants Yan Xishan and Wang Jingwei and the famed educators Huang Yanpei, Zhang Boling, Chen Shi, and Yan Xiu.[5] Jiang Xiangqing, St. John's *tiyu* instructor and *Shenbao* sports editor, wrote an open letter requesting that the CAA end their dissent, citing the importance of the National Games with regard to a strong performance in the next Far Eastern Games of 1925. CAA leaders Lu Weichang and Zhou Xisan traveled to Wuchang on the eve of the games for a meeting with Gray; when the missionary asked for their cooperation in working to send a strong team to the next Far Eastern Games and promised that the foreign role would be limited to consultation only, the boycott threat was abandoned. But the CAAU had clearly outlived its usefulness; it was dissolved at the July 1924 meeting of the Chinese Educational Reform Society and merged with the CAA into the new China National Amateur Athletic Federation (Zhonghua quanguo tiyu xiejinhui), which presided over official Chinese *tiyu* affairs until 1948.[6]

The boycott is a perfect example of the important transformations taking place in mid-1920s Chinese physical culture. Liberal models, described in Chapter 3, which promised national salvation (from such problems as warlordism and imperialism) through democracy and international standards of fun and skill, were quickly revised to accommodate the aggressive nationalism that events in greater Chinese society and the *tiyu* sphere provoked. Modern times seemed to call for strong, often explicitly masculine, nationalist forms to stand up to the imperialists and their ravaging of China's society and economy.

NATIONALIST PHYSICAL CULTURE AND THE THIRD NATIONAL GAMES

The Third National Games, held in May 1924 in Wuchang—home of the Revolution of 1911 that overthrew the Qing dynasty—can be seen as the beginning of the nationalist era of Chinese nationalist *tiyu*. Originally scheduled for 1920 Canton by the CAAU,[7] these first National Games held since the 1914 meet at Beijing's Tiantan were the first Chinese-run National Games and the last to be associated with the YMCA. Of the games' four main planners, only two were YMCA men—Hankou YMCA Physical Education Director Hao Gengsheng and Wuchang YMCA Director Song Ruhai.[8] J. H. Gray, humbled and perhaps edified by the CAA boycott threat, now acted only as "technical adviser" during the planning process, and that mostly from his CAAU office in Shanghai.[9] A list of seventy meet officials and judges listed in *Shenbao* included only six foreign names; besides Gray's charge of the two-team baseball competition (Zhejiang vs. Zhili), the other Western YMCA staff members served as finish line judges, a race starter, a doctor, and a leader of a children's games demonstration.[10] The Wuchang meet thus was a great step away from the swirling "intercultural zone" described in Chapter 3 and toward a more linear national mode of physical culture. Most national narratives of modern Chinese *tiyu* also take the 1924 Games as a turning point—one recent official history praised the 1924 switch to the metric system from the English system of measures and described the games as the "outcome of the post–May Fourth trend of taking back *tiyu* from the hands of Westerners."[11]

The meet featured 527 participating athletes from thirteen Chinese provinces and a Manila Chinese YMCA team—which again reveals much about the racialized notions of the nation in early Republican China. The teams were again divided into four regions—North China, South China, East China, and Central China—although now each team represented both home province and region. The Third National Games featured teams like "Zhili, North China" (Huabei Zhi), "Jiangsu, East China" (Huadong Su), and "Wenhua University, Hubei, Central China" (Huazhong E Wenhua).[12]

Original and idealistic plans described a twenty-two-province games with six divisions, but the West and Northeast China divisions were canceled when these provinces were unable to send teams. The one exception was a Guizhou squad, originally in the planners' West division. After the provincial government ignored the invitation sent them by the National Games Committee, nine Guizhou students studying at Wuchang Normal University and Wuchang Higher Commercial School established their own Guizhou Province basketball team. They sought and received an eight-hundred-*yuan* contribution from the Guizhou Affairs Office in Wuchang, a unit loyal to Zhou Xicheng, a powerful warlord in the Guizhou-Sichuan border region. The Guizhou team was assigned to the South China division, but on May 22 they unfortunately lost their only game to the Manila team by the lopsided score of 97–3.[13]

Besides the new Chinese organizational presence and the "national" scope of the meet as described by the divisional alignment, many other elements of the meet provided strikingly modern national moments. The meet got off to a roaring start, literally, with the May 22 opening ceremonies at the Hubei Public Recreation Grounds. As *Shenbao* described them, "[W]ith the red and green flags billowing, the tremendous sounds of the military bands, the scene was transformed into a grand celebration, the likes of which Hubei has not seen for some years."[14] A warship docked in Wuchang's Jiangkou port sounded ten cannon blasts. This was followed by a spectacular airplane flyover of the stadium, as the Central Air Force craft *Weimei* made ten loops over the stadium at an altitude of just some two hundred feet.[15] The plane dropped ten thousand brightly colored copies of Hubei Provincial Military Governor Xiao Yaonan's best wishes to the athletes (reading in part, "[M]arch toward Europe's status and surpass America, love and cherish this progress, one thousand miles in a single day") over the stadium and the city. The Peacock Moving Picture Company of Shanghai filmed the games for national distribution by the YMCA.[16] Thus it was now possible to extend this sporting experience as far as the YMCA reached and to flash it before the hopeful eyes of young YMCA participants all over China.

The Boy Scout presence was also a key element in the efficient, national atmosphere of the games. The Scouts were in charge of accompanying athletes to the stadium, maintaining order while referees held discussions on the field, keeping food peddlers out of the stadium (there were four official concession booths inside), and resolving any disturbance on the grounds, even those involving friends of athletes or meet officials. Indeed, order was of the highest importance at Wuchang; the Boy Scouts were joined by police and soldiers as they guarded the fenced-off perimeter of the competition area.[17]

The Scouts also were charged with announcing by megaphone the results of each competition to facilitate reporters' speedy telegraphing of the games news back to their home newspapers; *Shenbao* cited the necessity of having Scouts who could speak more than just Hubei dialect so that reporters from all over China could understand them.[18] Modern technology was another proud feature of the Third National Games: a field telephone system was installed so that messages could be sent all over the stadium, and a loudspeaker was fitted on top of a wooden tower for broadcasting competition results and other announcements. A wireless station was even constructed on the grounds, with a signal conspicuously received from Wuchang's main wireless station at noon each day of the meet.

These were also the first National Games to include women's sporting events. Hubei, Hunan, Jiangxi, and Jiangsu provinces were all represented by women's basketball, volleyball, and/or softball squads. Women's teams were welcome to show their skills in special "female" adaptations of these sports (smaller playing areas, different rules), exhibiting the fitness of the new modern woman. However, these were only unscheduled exhibitions and did not count toward the overall championship to be decided by the struggles between China's new men.[19]

Martial arts also made their first National Games appearance, in a three-day program of what were called *guocao* (national calisthenics) demonstrations. Organized by Chen Tiesheng of Shanghai's famed Pure Martial Athletic Association (Jingwu tiyuhui), the program consisted of 107 martial arts exhibitions, all scored on the basis of five standards: orderliness, spirit, strength, posture, and dress. Participants came from ten Wuhan-area schools and the men's and women's Pure Martial branches from Hankou, Nanchang, and even Kuala Lumpur. Representatives from other Pure Martial branches throughout South China and Southeast Asia were also in attendance as the Pure Martial Association used this National Games opportunity to exhibit its own brand of scientific national physical culture.[20]

Tiyu's inherent modernity was also made clear in more ugly, violent ways that seemingly only the national era can manifest. Decades later, Chief Games Planner Hao Gengsheng recalled his many difficulties, namely the grueling all-night meetings with the corrupt, emphysemic, opium-smoking Hubei Military Governor Xiao Yaonan. Especially annoying to Hao were the benighted local citizenry, who "were not open to the new winds of thought and not only did not support this great celebration of a healthy citizenship but in fact used many pretexts to oppose and obstruct it." The new Hubei Public Recreation Grounds were to be built on the site of an old horse training area in Wuchang and in the standard design of a running track that enclosed basketball, volleyball, and tennis courts, and a soccer field. Hao, a P.E. specialist educated in the United States, objected because this design "could not meet the games' needs, to say nothing of international standards. At the same time, I hoped to use this unprecedented opportunity to go even further and leave the people of Wuchang a permanent sports stadium. Therefore, I insisted that we expand the area under construction."[21] One problem, however, was that a memorial arch would have to be destroyed for the grounds to be built according to Hao's plans. Once this news got out,

> The people of Wuchang, young and old, male and female, united to express their opposition, saying, "That memorial arch is connected to the *fengshui* of the entire county, and if it is torn down, then plague, war, and floods will be delivered to all the people of the county." This clearly was an unreasonable appeal, and there was certainly no room

for one to dispel this superstition with a clear argument. But interestingly enough, several youth there believed in these things as well. To protect the memorial arch, they began striking against the National Games Planning Committee, trying negotiations, debates, petitions, protests, all sorts of measures, but none of them were of any use. In such an unfriendly atmosphere, my policy was "Push on and fight for the cause of reason; the plan will absolutely not be altered."[22]

Hao's ironclad commitment to rationality was equaled by the locals' commitment to their memorial arch. One day Hao received a letter that read, "Hao, if you keep on with your plans to tear down our arch, to destroy Wuchang's *fengshui,* and to endanger the common people of the entire county, then we apologize, but we will have to take action and ask you to eat bullets!"[23] The bullets never came, the games went on (the cannon blasts and airplane flyovers no doubt posing even more frightful threats to local *fengshui* and underlining exactly where power lay in this dispute), and Hao went on to promote physical fitness and rational public citizenship to a ripe old age.[24] But the point was made to all involved that in the Chinese *tiyu,* modernity and the nation were paramount—no longer could they bow to irrational or un-national concerns.

RECLAIMING *TIYU* FROM THE IMPERIALISTS

During the early 1920s, as discussed in the previous chapter, Chinese *tiyu* represented to many a magical means of escaping the ugly truths of history and the popular discourse on a weak and dying China. At the same time, however, physical culture proved to be just as effective in the opposite capacity and became an important feature of urban nationalist and antiforeign movements.

Chinese physical culture narratives, then as now, are almost universal in emphasizing a theme of the Chinese sporting community rising up to "take back" physical culture from the hands of the imperialists and missionaries. Despite the suspicious tidiness of this account, the fixation on the Western role in Chinese *tiyu* was no nationalist pathology. The Chinese sporting world was a favorite target of ridicule for Westerners, whose assumptions of supremacy were increasingly being challenged. In 1924, two weeks before the Third National Games, Wuchang educational officials organized a Wuhan area meet on their own for the second straight year. One Western journalist, miffed that foreigners had been left out of the process, wrote that under Chinese management "the result was an even more glorious hotch-potch than last year." His article, sarcastically titled "China's Sovereign Rights on the Athletic Ground," reported that the lanes for races and field events were so narrow that one thrown discus had landed on a spectator's umbrella. He sniffed at the soldiers, police, and Boy Scouts on hand to keep the great crowds off the playing fields and found utterly ridiculous the fact that a dog ran one lap around the track, "urged on by the cheering of the crowd," jeering that "the enthusiasm of the spectator knows no bounds."[25]

There were other insults as well. In 1923, the South China (Nanhua) Soccer Club of Hong Kong was invited to visit Australia for a three-month series of friendly matches. Star player Li Huitang, just eighteen years old at the time, remembered a cartoon published in an Australian newspaper caricaturing the South China team as a pack of rail-thin, sickly, queue-wearing opium addicts.[26] After Nanhua won several of these games against Australian teams—their record on the tour was eight wins, nine losses, and seven draws[27]—the locals' view of the Chinese changed. They gave young Li the nickname "Asian Football King," and one Australian newspaper referred to the team as "not merely . . . 17 players but 'ambassadors' from the oldest country in the world to the youngest to bring forth friendship and better understanding."[28] Li also established the new Chinese masculinity in other ways, starting a serious relationship with a young Australian woman who got his attention by cheering for him, "Go, Number 9," and ended up following Li and the Nanhua team around the country.[29] Still, the Chinese *tiyu* community would not forget insults like the cartoon above and were keen on turning this once-"Western" domain of physical culture against the imperialists.

The early socialist movement in China also included instances of a nationalist anti-imperialist physical culture agenda. As early as 1923, the Socialist Youth League of China at their Second National Conference called for the "Sinicization" of physical education and sports, for Chinese schools and individuals to take the leading role in promoting *tiyu*, and for the exclusive use of Mandarin terminology by referees and officials.[30] The same year, the Socialist Youth Brigade's mouthpiece, the *Pioneer*, included a Chinese translation of a Comintern Youth League resolution that condemned capitalist physical education and sport as "masking itself as a neutral organization, encouraging proletarians to join in, and then eating away at their class consciousness and their courage to carry on class struggle. . . . In the end, [these sporting proletarians] become simply an advance force for the capitalist counterrevolutionaries."[31] And Yun Daiying, eight years after his important article in the YMCA's *Association Progress,* in 1925 drew on his experience with Communist ideology to again blast the role of foreign schools in the Chinese *tiyu* world: "Sometimes [mission schools] will select a few athletes for special cultivation, nourishing them with milk and cookies so that they will excel in track meets or in soccer games, thereby serving as a signboard advertisement for the school. From the time when we began to be in contact with outside commerce, foreign capitalists have always needed to find within China a few 'compradors' . . . to serve as their slaves *(yangnu)*."[32]

Yet the impulse to nationalize *tiyu* was hardly limited to the radical left. When the Chinese Educational Reform Society P.E. and Hygiene Division—whose five head members included Mai Kele (Charles McCloy)—was founded in 1925, one of its first acts was to call for the creation of a unified Mandarin *tiyu* terminology to replace the jumbled mixture of English sports terms and Japanese drill commands still in use. The division explained the urgency behind this nationalist decision: "[I]f we do not work fervently to unify terminology, then in the future there will be no hope of progress or improvement. . . . [W]ithout [this unification] each discipline will break away *(yangbiao)* and travel down its own road, influencing the whole *tiyu* project."[33]

Schools, so central to the dissemination of *tiyu* knowledge, also produced much of the nationalist fervor. In 1925, anti-imperialist and anti-Christian sentiment was so strong in Sichuan that the Provincial Games held that year prohibited the participation of any students from Christian schools.[34] That same year, there was great controversy at St. John's University in Shanghai, where school President F. L. Hawks Pott did not allow students to fly the national flag at half-mast following the May 30 massacre. When Pott closed down the entire university days later, many students and faculty left the school and formed the new Guanghua (Radiant China) University. The implications of these changes affected the Shanghai sports world as well. Nanyang, Fudan, and Southeastern Universities immediately pulled out of the Oriental Eight Athletic Conference of which St. John's was a member and joined with the new Guanghua University to form the Lower Yangtze Athletic Conference.[35]

Physical spaces of *tiyu* could be nationalized as well. In 1922, the North Boulevard Sports Grounds was constructed north of the Bell Tower in Xi'an, funded by Military Governor Feng Yuxiang and Provincial Tax Board/ Tobacco Monopoly Director Xue Ziliang. Besides basketball, tennis, soccer, gymnastics, and boxing facilities, the grounds featured

> a map of national humiliations, with big lettering to explain each one. There is a world park, with flowers and trees planted in the shape of

each nation. As China has been carved up at so many times owing to so many different events, in the center there is a Patriots' Pavilion with pictures of events involving famous patriots, copies of several couplets of admonishment *(quanjie duilian)*, and a newspaper reading room. As there is this recorded knowledge . . . there are set rules on the field, with an appointed leader serving as guide. In games too, people must follow the rules and cannot be disorderly.[36]

Considering the arguments made in the last chapter on *tiyu's* ability to serve as a space for mimesis and intercultural play, the emphasis here on a nationalist, anti-imperialist physical culture may seem incongruous. In fact, it is difficult to isolate a single pattern of *tiyu* discourse when the realm seems to produce such different positions—for instance, engagement with the West versus "Yanqui go home." And in the 1920s, when anti-imperialist and antiwarlord activists were working to create a single Chinese nationalism out of what Prasenjit Duara has called "nationism"—the faith that the modern nation-state is always the most desirable form of political organization—the same could be said regarding discourse about the nation.[37] Further, *tiyu* discourse is so varied because of the mixed nature of *tiyu*—physical education and competitive sports—itself. Modern sport (and might this be the reason for its adoption all over the globe?) is full of what seem to be glaring contradictions—among them, the individual versus the team, the importance of victory versus ideals of sportsmanship and "fair play," myths of free or natural movement versus the bodily discipline and specialized movements that sport requires, and claims to be the key to health for the larger population versus the need for this population to sit and consume sport (and be consumed by it). It should not seem strange that while some Chinese might envision a Chinese nation built on "teamwork" with the West, others might envision a strong nation only as a Chinese anti-imperialist "team."

Some may have seen Western physical education experts as benevolent coaches and their discipline as transnational tough love. Others saw the foreigners as imperialists hoping to create a China that could be exploited even further by the West. And although some Chinese athletes might have taken seriously the ideal of being a "good sport"—improving oneself by competing whether one wins or loses—it is likely that just as many others wanted to break through this hypocrisy and just beat the imperialists, soundly at that. Chinese physical culture sprang from all of these notions. By the mid-1920s, the nation, modernity, and *tiyu* had become so intertwined that there could be no separating them, only attempts to push this ideology in different directions.

SOARING, AWE-INSPIRING, FASCINATING: MODERNITY AND THE WOMEN'S PHYSICAL CULTURE MOVEMENT

Chinese *tiyu*'s greatest claim to modernity in the early 1920s was the growing inclusion of women and girls in the world of physical culture. The modern Chinese nation was to be inclusive, requiring contributions from all its able-bodied citizens—as everyone knew, a healthy China could be achieved only when the whole population was healthy and fit. As Chinese men began to assert their control over administering and theorizing physical culture for the nation, they were careful to include within this grasp the important realm of women's *tiyu*. Physical education expert Xie Siyan (a man who posed shirtless for the frontispiece photo of his book, *Track and Field Theory and Practice*) wrote in a 1923 issue of the *Ladies' Journal*,

> The necessity of women's physical education is something with which anyone with just a bit of commonsense will agree. But I will not be superfluous or wordy here, instead offering a few examples:
>
> (1) Our nation's citizens make up a population of four hundred million, and two hundred million of these are women; now why would one want to promote [*tiyu*] for the two hundred million men while resigning the two hundred million women to enfeebling despondence and lethargy? . . .
>
> (2) Speaking from the standpoint of reproduction, the pain a woman experiences while giving birth cannot be imagined by men. But if a woman is always sick, and her body is weak at the time when she is to give birth, then this is even worse—it is a sure thing that the son or daughter born will not be strong and healthy.
>
> (3) From a genetic standpoint, the power of men's and women's genes is equal. But the male has less to do with passing on physiological traits, while the female is much more involved in this.
>
> (4) Looking at it from the perspective of education, no one can match the educating emotional influence of the mother. . . . [T]he emotional power of a mother can work on any kind of person—so a woman's physical fitness *(tiyu)* is extremely important to her children as well.
>
> (5) Looking at it in terms of the woman problem, those who speak of this question always go on and on, exaggerating its importance. But if [women] do not train their bodies and sharpen their spirit, then it does not matter what you say about all those minor issues. If we do not start from the point of women's *tiyu*, I am afraid that even if we talk until our tongues are weary and our ears are deaf, it will not be of any use.[38]

Society, science, and social science—these self-consciously modern fields of knowledge could all be enlisted in an odd discourse of equality, which in Xie's words here worked to exclude and mock any feminism not founded on the tenets of modern physical fitness. It is transparent that the notions of equality and inclusion, like the discourse of physical fitness that was a principal element of these ideas, were elements of a male-gendered project of building a modern Chinese nation. Tani Barlow's model of the "Chinese intellectuals' appropriation of the imperialists' sex binary"[39] explains well the work by anti-Confucian male members of China's physical culture community to bring *tiyu* to their nation's women—a physical culture that would condition women's bodies according to rational assessments of the Chinese nation and its needs.

Wang Zheng has questioned the significance of Barlow's model by pointing out how May Fourth feminists, empowered by humanist discourses of equality between men and women, created their own access to the power and privileges claimed by modern Chinese men.[40] Revealingly, of Wang's five "forgotten heroines" of Chinese feminism, two—Lu Lihua and Chen Yongsheng—were closely involved with the women's physical culture movement. In China during the 1920s many women like Lu and Chen chose to become more and more involved in this culture of health and the body. Wendy Larson has also shown how, following older bodily markers of femininity like chastity and confinement, women's physical fitness became a site for May Fourth women authors to debate ideas of women's moral virtue.[41] The larger *national* narrative of *tiyu* at the time, however, mirroring the nation-building project as a whole, by definition placed little importance on women's own definitions of physical endeavor. In a modern physical culture based on Western notions of masculinity and the nation, the men in charge of planning this course to nationhood saw little direct national significance for women's participation. Despite the important and transformative work of female activists during the 1920s to claim this realm for themselves, the greater liberal promotion of women's *tiyu* was in fact part of another process, the extension of dominant national gazes to the bodies of Chinese women.

Graceful Sights to Behold on China's Tiyu Grounds

At the Third National Games held at Wuchang in 1924, discussed above, male Chinese athletes competed in seven medal events: track and field, swimming, soccer, basketball, volleyball, baseball, and tennis. Other events were called mere "demonstrations," and it is instructive to see which areas of *tiyu* were not recognized as authentic National Games. The dozens of martial arts and calisthenics demonstrations by male athletes were not deemed proper enough *tiyu* to deserve medal attention; nor were the junior high school girls' dance programs described by caption writers at the journal *Tiyu* as "soaring, moving, awe-inspiring, fascinating."[42] More noteworthy exceptions were the women's competitions in basketball, volleyball, and softball, which were not recognized as medal events either.[43] It was accepted that these ball sports were crucial in developing a Chinese populace that could work and play together as a team. (Volleyball was even known then as *duiqiu*, or "team-ball"). But the logic by which women's efforts in these games were not judged worthy of official National Games mention seems fairly transparent: Of what *national* use would a team of disciplined, willed, unified, strong women be?

National Games organizers were not alone in this way of thinking. The Far Eastern Championship Games featured women's tennis and volleyball as nonmedal events beginning with the Sixth Games held in Osaka in 1923.[44] (Only at the 1934 Tenth Games at Manila were women's events recognized as official medal events.) The *Ladies' Journal* celebrated this milestone in their July and August 1923 issues, publishing pictures from the women's tennis and volleyball competitions of the Chinese athletes in their uniforms of loose white blouses and dark bloomer short pants.[45] Yet the odd status of women at these international games points to an ambiguous position for women's *tiyu* in Chinese nationalism—in particular, the relative insignificance, from men's viewpoints, of women's team sports and their potential to enhance the competitiveness of the modern nation.

Volleyball (with nine to sixteen players per side) was often the first sport introduced into women's physical education curricula. Pan Zhiben's piece "A Game for Women—Volleyball," published in the *Ladies' Journal* in 1922, opened:

> Ball games suitable for women are quite rare; in tennis too few people can play, so it cannot be popularized. Basketball is too intense, as sometimes people may fall down. Thus volleyball is the only game really suitable for women. There is no physical contact *(chongtu)* to speak of with the opponent, and since every person covers her own zone there is not too much running involved. [Women's] using both hands to hit the ball is a graceful sight to behold.[46]

This new participation of women in competitive sports is usually cited as a sign of social progress in China—Chinese women "gallantly ascending the stage of history," as one official history puts it, via their participation in team sports. Likewise, Fan Hong's history of Chinese women's liberation through athletic activity is based on "the essential point that the pursuit of physical freedom was an integral part of women's emancipation in China."[47] Progressive or not, it was an important change; women's participation in competitive sports become much more common in the early 1920s.

However, women's participation in athletic meets was still frequently limited to group demonstrations of what was known as "soft calisthenics" *(rouruan ticao)* or dance. The most celebrated of these demonstrations was the debut of Chinese women in the Far Eastern Championship Games in 1921. Led by Vera Barger, Celia Moyer, and Yuan Baozhu of the Shanghai YWCA, some 830 young women from fourteen Shanghai schools thrilled the Hongkou Park crowd with their mass calisthenics demonstration. Dressed in identical white hats, white long-sleeved blouses, and black bloomer skirts, stockings, and shoes, these women performed a mass routine mimicking the motions of "modern form[s] of recreation," beginning with baseball and swimming and then performed individual selections based on the movements of tennis, tug-of-war, basketball, climbing stairs, fishing, and soccer. These exciting routines were recorded on film, "including many 'close-ups' as well as covering the mass formations," for distribution in China's interior.[48] Women's physical fitness was clearly a priority now in China. However, the distance that modernist men supposed to exist between women and real sport can be measured by the importance they placed on these thrilling mimetic performances of the disciplined and masculinized movements of modern sport. In terms of competing as representatives of the nation, Chinese women athletes would still be allowed only to go through the motions of the *tiyu* realm softly and gracefully.

The All-Southern Sichuan Athletic Meet, held in the spring of 1922 and organized by Yun Daiying (then teaching at Southern Sichuan Normal School), also displayed tellingly modern attitudes toward women. Posted all around the sporting grounds were sets of two posters reading, "My husband Commander Yang supports women cutting their hair short!" and "Female compatriots, once your feet were bound; now liberate your feet!" signed by Yang-Tian Hengqiu and Yang-Liu Gufang—two of the many wives of Games Chairman and Second Corps Commander Yang Sen. (Yang's commitment to women's equality and physical exercise was genuine and enigmatic; Kristin Stapleton relates the story of his forcibly unbinding the feet of one hundred female spectators at another athletic meet in Luzhou in the early 1920s.)[49] This meet featured track and field, soccer, gymnastics, and martial arts competitions for men only, but girls from the Women's Study Society Elementary School and Women's Normal School Elementary School were among students from ten schools performing group calisthenics as side demonstration events.[50]

The eventual inclusion of women in competitive sports in the mid-1920s was not unanimous. There was apparently enough popular opposition to women's participation in track and field events that Zhang Ruizhen, writing in the *Chinese Journal of Physical Education* in 1923, felt it necessary to answer six common misconceptions about women, their bodies, their manners, and the dangers of track and field. To those who protested that "women were naturally disposed toward refinement and quiet and do not enjoy intense exercise," Zhang contended that in this century of sexual equality, to restrict women's sporting participation would "hurt women's self-respect and be unconducive to notions of male-female equality."[51] Many argued against female participation on the basis of physiological difference; Zhang did not refute this claim but rephrased the question enough to answer: "The citizen's martial spirit is learned so much more in the home than in school. If a household has a father and mother who are richly endowed with this martial spirit, then it naturally will be cultivated in their children, who will then flower into martial citizens themselves. That said, who wouldn't work to promote women's participation in track and field?"[52]

Records reveal that many men would have named themselves in answer to Zhang's rhetorical question. A series of reports from the Third Central China Games (Huazhong yundonghui), held in Nanchang, Jiangxi, in April 1925, portrayed an atmosphere of mockery and hostility toward female athletes by men scandalized, or maybe simply aroused, by this new public realm of women's activity. During an opening ceremonies mass dance titled "Heavenly Women Scattering Flowers," performed by Baoyun Girls' School, "at once [several men] stampeded down onto and around the field to watch; it was no small number of people, and the scene became quite chaotic." The reporter then editorialized, "Every time there is a women's performance at an athletic meet, the men all get carried away and rampage about, as if they were rushing to get home upon the death of their parents, and the meet loses all sense of order." Later that day when female swimmers from Hunan arrived at the Nanchang pool, the packed crowd grew even more restless; "fortunately the Boy Scouts were on hand to keep order."[53] And during a women's sporting event, when one of the teams began singing the team song, "several spectators began shouting, 'Well done! Well done! Sing another! Sing another!' their attitudes, language, and gestures mocking and undignified."[54]

This critique of Nanchang boorishness may be partly rooted in a Shanghai prejudice toward inland Jiangxi, but the hinterland was not the only site where these new female roles were rejected. At the Eighth Far Eastern Championship Games held in Shanghai in 1927, the Eastern Chinese women's volleyball team ended their demonstration match prematurely after being subject to jeering and insults from rowdy "undesirables" in the crowd.[55]

The new and large presence of women at regional and international games seems to have been revolutionary, and it is certain that these meets allowed women athletes to formulate their own new ideas of participation in the creation of a nation built on strong bodies and the sporting spirit. However, men's loutish response to women's mere presence at the games demonstrates the fragility of the new gender order in Chinese sport and the extent to which the exclusive male right to team sport still seemed an obvious proprietary claim. I read this popular unrest as yet another attempt to maintain physical culture as a male preserve, to remind women athletes at every turn that their participation in this realm was still to be defined and measured by men, whose real job it was to save the nation.

The Contest to Define a Women's Physical Culture

If women's role in competitive athletics was somewhat contentious, attention to women's physical fitness in general, since the last decade of the Qing dynasty, was an indisputable part of the modern agenda. The point of women's *tiyu* was not exactly competition in the name of the nation but rather a "healthy beauty" *(jiankang mei)*[56]—a concept that was as much a commercialized notion of women's proper appearance as a solution to eugenic worries about the condition of the bodies of the present and future mothers of China.

In 1921, a series of *Ladies' Journal* articles on the connections between women's exercise and "healthy beauty" included a "Beauty Exercise Regimen," whose inventor wrote:

> The health of one's body and the beauty of one's deportment are very closely linked. If one hopes to achieve a healthy body, exercise cannot be ignored. Our nation's women have long ignored exercise, so most women's bodies, if not too skinny and feeble, are too full and fat, and neither of these [physiques] can be counted as a mark of health. The three types of [balancing and stretching] exercises described below are all very simple. If women practice them faithfully for long, they can make their bodies not only more healthy but also more attractive and beautiful *(yanmei)*—yes, there are more than superficial rewards to be gained![57]

A thoroughly modern publication, the *Ladies' Journal* published other articles on exercise for professional women. As Xiao Liu noted in 1922, concerns about the alienating new customs of the modern business world were not only a male province: "Exercise can strengthen the body, this everyone knows. Professionals *(you zhiye de ren)*, no matter how busy they are on the job, simply need to take some time out every day to do a little exercise for their body's sake. And isn't this a time of great debate on the issue of women professionals?"[58] Yang Binru made a similar claim to women's crucial role in China's modern society and economy, pointing out in 1924 that "[w]ith modern transportation growing more convenient, our daily affairs become more and more varied, and there are more and more professional women in society every day. Thus women's *tiyu* needs to grow by the day as well."[59]

As such calls demonstrate, modern Chinese women in the 1920s maintained their own positions in the public and national discourse of physical culture—positions defined by their own ideas about beauty, convenience, work, and modernity. These were women who would not have accepted assumptions that modernity or its physical culture was inherently masculine. At the same time, however, the domain of modern Chinese *tiyu*—as defined by the publishing houses, educational institutions, and branches of government responsible for it—was still largely subject to the scientific authority of foreign authors and Chinese men.

In 1924 Chen Yongsheng, one of Wang Zheng's May Fourth protagonists mentioned above, published *A Regimen for Women's Beauty Exercise*. Here she discussed a "beauty ratio" formulated by the American women's health expert/entrepreneur Annette Kellerman, such that a woman's weight should equal the sum of her height and chest measurement divided by 240. Hastings's "Ideal Ratio of Femininity" (translated by Chen as *nüxing zhishu*)[60] was based on the dubious formula

$$\frac{\text{chest} + \text{buttocks} + \text{thigh}}{\text{neck} + \text{hips} + \text{wrist} + \text{ankle}} \times 100$$

This attempt to scientifically define women's *tiyu* often in fact precluded any departure from foreign models; Gao Shilin had to base her 1921 *Ladies' Journal* article "Why We Should Exercise" almost solely on the opinions of Drs. Henry G. Beyar and Thomas D. Wood.[61]

The discourse of women's physical fitness and corresponding fitness as citizens produced a new space for Chinese women to express their own ideas about their bodies and lives, but often in terms not totally their own. Thus narratives of emancipation like Fan Hong's, which depict women's physical culture as significant for having "provided a psychological confidence that spilt over into other areas of life,"[62] seem somewhat incomplete. For the emancipation and opportunities that did come from women's *tiyu* were also accompanied by new limits and constraints. Fan addresses these obstacles but in May Fourth fashion merely blames "outworn social values and sanctions" belonging to "feudal society."[63] Yet feudal, Confucian, and backward bogeymen aside, it quite obviously was rather the dark angels of science and modernity that sustained men's efforts to retain the upper hand in this *tiyu* discourse. The extent of this male concern about female bodies can be seen in a Beijing *Morning Post* discussion of "Women's Physical Culture," where a writer using the pen name "Profound and Deep" set forth seven main problems with Chinese women's bodies, including the following:

(1) Women's lower extremities—their legs and feet—are always crooked. . . .

(3) The chests of our nation's women are extremely narrow and flat. . . .

(4) Of our nation's women there is not one without a crooked back and a bent-over figure.[64]

This profoundly shallow columnist and others who took women's *tiyu* literally as a "bodily education" understood this realm as theirs in which to lecture on the defects of women's bodies, quite possibly without the least consideration of women's liberation, identity, or even personal feelings.

It was difficult to create a space for women's physical culture outside a narrow zone hemmed in by American and German beauty ratios, Japanese ideals of domesticity that informed other articles,[65] and self-Orientalizing notions of Chinese feminine weakness through history. Agnes Fung's elitist (English-language) analysis below also illustrates the tremendous authority of male reformers' discourse about the pitiful condition of traditional Chinese women and the importance of their learning from healthy Western women:

[F]or several thousand years [Chinese women] had been in bondage, and naturally the encumbrance though removed, still leaves its shadow. . . . For the foreign woman there are all sorts of recreation, such as tennis, swimming, riding, bicycling, hiking, and what not. . . . But for the Chinese woman, there are no such sports. She is shut up in her house, and does nothing, there being the servants at her beck and call, except to play mahjjong in order to pass her time. Naturally sitting in a crammed position can do no good to her body, yet she does it because it is custom. Only the more modern ones dare to give their legs some exercise by doing the Charleston, the others must be content with sitting.[66]

The realm of men's physical culture, as discussed in Chapter 3, could for a time serve as a magical zone of play in which could be seen China's future, free of troubling Chinese-Western historical dichotomies. But Fung's words here express how the image of the Western woman, even when invoked by Chinese women themselves, still served only to show up the supposed weakness and inferiority of Chinese women through the centuries.

On the eve of the Third National Games in 1924, Lu Lihua, founder of Shanghai's Liangjiang Women's Tiyu Normal School and another of Wang Zheng's May Fourth "heroines" cited above, called for more formal research, textbooks, periodicals, and classes by mail on women's physical fitness and for parks and exercise equipment for women down to the village level. But to justify her program, which was quite progressive at the time, Lu also had to draw on the familiar stereotypes invoked by male reformers in China. She criticized Chinese women's "worship of pensive serenity and their understanding of softness and weakness as noble virtues." And even Lu could not avoid recourse to the hackneyed formulation popularized by men like Yuan Shikai: "To strengthen the nation we must first strengthen the race, and to strengthen the race we must first strengthen the women who will be breeding *(yuzhong)*—we women are the mothers of citizens."[67]

Despite such ideological constraints, some women did succeed in incorporating into the *tiyu* discourse original critiques of Chinese society in the 1920s. Xiang Fuchun, a member of the Physical Education Research Society at the Shanghai Patriotic Girls' School, wrote a daring piece in 1925 in which she explicitly gendered *tiyu* by referring to it with the feminine pronoun *(ta)*. Xiang explained that physical culture was meant "to strengthen the spirit, so that one would finally be able to handle any matter or situation in society, not being defeated by the attacks of the outside world." This observation, easily read as a critique of the obstacles that women faced in modern Chinese society, was accompanied by a more sarcastic and powerful condemnation of male-defined twentieth-century modernity: "The more civilized *(wen)* the world gets, the more lazy people's thinking gets. The more machines are developed, the more people's bodies degenerate."[68]

Ding Zengfang, another member of this Shanghai group, used her writings on physical education to formulate explicitly political critiques. Countering the arguments of those who would still blame China's semicolonized status on the weakness of its women, Ding explained how "China's weakness" was basically the fault of the rapacious warlords who destroyed China's populace and industry. Women, as "the mothers of the nation," were surely responsible for not hurting China further by raising "morons and lunatics," but they had to shape up their bodies so that their minds would be fit to process the important democratic and scientific ideas so important to their nation.[69]

These subversive ideas could well have represented common popular attitudes; it is certainly easy to imagine girls and women in P.E. classes all over China wondering what was in this realm for them as girls and women. Analyses by women working outside the 1920s physical culture orthodoxy only went a step further to represent a more emancipatory "break."

Many have assumed that Chinese women, merely by going through the motions of Western sports and exercises, could cause great commotion and thereby make great progress for Chinese womanhood by refuting hegemonic Confucian ideals of female modesty and obedience. But such activity did not necessarily constitute any kind of inherent rebellion or rupture. In fact, the dominant discourse on women's *tiyu* in the 1920s still consisted of impatient and paternalistic exhortations that women make themselves stronger for the sake of the Chinese nation, which was embarrassed and weakened by its feeble women. Western-imposed, scientifically "proven" models of masculinity and nation had such hegemony in this realm that they defined even the work of pioneering May Fourth "heroines" like Lu Lihua and Chen Yongsheng.

Kathleen McCrone has discussed the scientific debate on women's physical culture in late-nineteenth- and early-twentieth-century Britain. Scientific "evidence," modern romanticized notions of "womanhood," and Social Darwinist concepts of "motherhood" combined to impose hegemonic limits on women's sport and exercise that were hard for British women to transcend.[70] Similarly, in the discourse of Chinese *tiyu* in the 1920s, there was little room for women's contributions to a strong China besides the eventual duty of breeding a healthy next generation of Chinese boys. On the whole, China's male managers of physical culture during this period regarded women's *tiyu* with at best mildly liberal condescension. Wang Huaiqi's 1928 explanation of his motivation in designing the original game "starball" (a miniaturized and "peaceful" variation on soccer, a sport seen as too intense for women) illustrates perfectly women's mildly "liberated" position in late 1920s physical culture:

> Soccer has a very intense quality to it; young men naturally are quite interested in this type of competition. But children or weak women surely cannot take this kind of excitement. . . . Since soccer has become so popular, schools have strictly forbidden women and children from taking part in this kind of sport. . . . It does not make sense that there should be sports for men that women cannot practice. Men's and women's bodies, however, are naturally different, so their exercises and sports have to correspond to these different levels. This is well-nigh impossible to avoid. So, when appropriate, games should be designed for women to participate in.[71]

INTERNATIONALISM AND NATIONALISM

A final aspect of Chinese *tiyu*'s appeal to nationalist elements was the promise sport offered for an international presence—a theme played up by architects of modern physical culture dating back to the Olympic founder Pierre de Coubertin.[72]. International sport obviously assumes the nation; in fact, the purpose of international athletic competition was to provide an opportunity, via this new realm of modern sport (or its visual consumption), to train citizens for real competition between nations. Without the international context there would be no need to create a modern Chinese nation, and without the nation and its need to impress itself on the minds of all modern citizens, no one ever would have thought to organize, participate in, or pay to view institutions like the Olympics or the Far Eastern Games.

Chinese athletes' and spectators' first introduction to the international world of sport was via the Far Eastern Championship Games—namely the Second, Fifth, and Eighth Games hosted by Shanghai in 1915, 1921, and 1927. By 1921, many Chinese were very clear about the national and international meanings of sport; a *Shenbao* author took a hard line on that year's games, writing that

> [t]he spirit of struggle in athletics is the same as in war. If one is defeated in war, territory is lost. If one is defeated in athletics, reputation is lost. And of territory and reputation, no one yet knows which is more important. . . . We need to be able to perform in athletics before we can talk of war. A nation needs to be able to fight before it can talk of peace. World peace begins with athletics.[73]

The prominent international role of athletics also made it imperative that all Chinese learn the international rules of proper sporting decorum. After finally ascending the international stage, no Chinese wanted to be immediately laughed off it for unbecoming conduct. Another writer worried about "foreigners laughing at our citizens for our lack of common sense . . . immoral and improper applause [when opposing athletes made mistakes]." At the 1921 Fifth Far Eastern Games in Shanghai, workers were even stationed in the bleachers to announce that "clapping in these situations [when opposing athletes err] is a form of ridicule, and . . . we must abide by the morality of the athletic grounds. By doing this we can avoid the censure of foreigners and the loss of national prestige."[74]

Apart from such worries about spectator etiquette, *Shenbao* reports dwelled on internationalist triumphs in the games environment. After the first day of competition, one writer praised the sportsmanlike spirit of fans who cheered for Japanese athletes during the opening ceremonies.[75] (If Chinese fans were disappointed to learn that the Japanese team included four Taiwanese athletes,[76] no mention was made of it.) Another report commended the contingent of Japanese fans attending the games at Hongkou Park; led by a cheerleader, their yells ended with "Philippines *banzai!* China *banzai!* Japan *banzai!*" Unwilling to let this conspicuous show of international sportsmanship go unanswered, a good part of the Chinese crowd cheered, "Japan *wansui!* Philippines *wansui!* China *wansui!*"[77]

Sports' capacity to transcend national boundaries was not lost on one anarchist group in Shanghai working to realize their own internationalist vision. Six Hunanese anarchists were arrested outside Hongkou Park after one of them fired a gun during the Boy Scout demonstration, closing the games on 4 June. Thousands of anarchist pamphlets seized by French and Chinese detectives contained materials on the great East Asian revolution to come and directly referred to the connection between athletics and international politics. According to their rhetoric, it took "the strength of athletes" for Chinese to attack capitalism and overthrow the government. The slogan on one banner confiscated at the site shrilly incited spectators to "punch the capitalists and kick the government!"[78]

Yet despite attempts to promote international cooperation and goodwill, the Far Eastern Championship Games were often marred by the ugly nationalism and racism that these competitions were supposed to extinguish. Before the Seventh Games, held in Manila in 1925, several poems were published wishing the Chinese athletes well. One poem, "On Sending off the Athletes," included the notable lines, "Annihilate those of the eastern islands, / Conquer those from the South."[79]

Such images of conquest were common; Shanghai soccer player Sun Jinshun remembered being inspired at the 1925 Games by the great Magellan, who four hundred years earlier had triumphed in Manila.[80] This was not a good omen for the games, the most noted event of which was the boycott by members of Japan's track and field team after sprinter Noto Tokushige was stripped of his silver medal for elbowing Garcia, a Filipino opponent.[81] The president of the Japanese Amateur Athletic Association immediately telegraphed the team, threatening to ban boycotting athletes from any future competition.[82] Japan's *Asahi Shinbun* blasted their lack of sportsmanship, and the Chinese delegation filed an official protest over their conduct.[83] Thirteen athletes, including team captain Tani, maintained their walkout; photographs exist of them singing the Japanese national anthem in tears after hearing that they were barred from the national team.[84]

The general environment at the Eighth Games, held in Shanghai in 1927, was unfortunately not much better. Chinese organizers got things off to an internationalist start, awarding a baseball autographed by Babe Ruth, walking symbol of 1920s commercialized sport, to the hitter slamming the first home run of the games.[85] The hosts demonstrated their hospitality by sending Chinese athletes to an official welcome for the Philippine delegation.[86] The Chinese-Philippine soccer game, however, as it always seemed to do, quickly demolished the carefully polite facade that had been constructed at the games' beginning. When the two teams came to blows, the Chinese crowd became violent, throwing bottles, hammers, knives, and sticks at the opponents. Some fans even surged down onto the field to join the brawls; Boy Scouts, police, and meet officials eventually broke up the fights. The Philippine team forfeited the match rather than continue under these conditions but then decided to play the second half of the game anyway to avoid provoking more violence from the crowd of sixteen thousand paying fans.[87]

For the most part, the media refused to be good sports and forget these clashes; the next week the *Pei-Yang Pictorial News* printed a Philippine team picture with the caption "the brutish and violent *(chengxiong ouren)* Philippine soccer team."[88] Hostility toward the Filipino athletes (perhaps dark-skinned reminders of the Asian "backwardness" that the Chinese hoped to escape through modern sport) even found its way into a banquet held after the games to honor the five-hundred-plus visiting Japanese and Filipino athletes and officials. During a lively dance number, many of the Filipinos began "crazily shouting, toasting and drinking." At that point the head games organizer Shen Siliang stood up and made an important announcement, casting aside diplomacy in the face of a much more important and frightening racial threat: he warned the Chinese and Japanese women in the crowd not to leave that night with any Filipino men. The *Shenbao* reporter in attendance saw Shen's warning as quite unnecessary, but for reasons other than we might expect—he reminded readers that most Chinese women simply had more taste than to leave with "pitch-black Filipinos."[89]

CONCLUSION

Such blatant racism—an integral part of the Far Eastern Championship Games—seems an appropriate place to end this chapter, for it illustrates how harsh the nationalist vision of the Chinese physical culture community had become by the mid-1920s. The period of Chinese *tiyu* that began in 1920 and ended with the establishment of the Nationalist regime at Nanjing in 1928 was one of transition from the liberal democratic thought of May Fourth to the aggressive nationalism of the Nanjing Decade and was thus a site where trends of both of these eras were at work—sportsmanship and national conquest, pan-Asian friendliness and racial viciousness.

This was also the last era in which Chinese physical culture was not enlisted and constrained by explicit party-political "isms." Chinese *tiyu* activists borrowed from Western models of the relationships between individual and national bodies, and with these models they attempted to construct nationalist physical cultures that would allow China to repel aggression by the imperialists who had invented them. *Tiyu* made it possible to imagine the Chinese nation as an underdog team of determined individuals who could battle back from previous humiliations and adversity to recapture international honor. Whether couched in terms of a scientific modernity that transcended culture or a specifically nationalist and anti-imperialist program for a strong China, the 1920s drive for *tiyu* "body cultivation" became a widely accepted component of future Chinese nationalisms of all stripes.

This physical cultivation would soon take on different characteristics as the Guomindang state of the late 1920s and 1930s introduced new forms of, and new methods of distributing, a "mass physical culture" for all of Chinese society. The ideals of sportsmanship and individual responsibility to the team would fade with the 1930s aspiration to realize a strong unified national-racial body. But the steps taken in the 1920s, including the liberal use of Western physical culture theory and practices and the switch to a more nationalist mode of *tiyu,* were necessary preludes to the militaristic physical culture programs and ideals of a Guomindang state facing very different conditions.

5 "We Can Also Be the Controllers and Oppressors"

Social Bodies and National Physiques

The glittering beauty of the lake,
Burning with the spirit of the early Xia dynasty.
How many young men and women are there,
Who have mustered their energies one by one, never letting us
    down?
Hurry, with your bronze tendons and iron chests,
Come together in sport, but ask if the land of today's China is well.
Yet to exchange our antiques for the golden cup
All depends on the bodies and skills of our youth.
How brave the struggle! How fierce the soldiers!
Willing someday to put on the cap and begin the long march,
To fight with one's sons against the common enemy.

> Official Song of the Zhejiang Provincial Games,
> 1937 (He Yousheng and Wu Mengfei,
> "Zhejiang quansheng yundonghuige")

THE FOURTH NATIONAL GAMES AND THE GUOMINDANG'S FORAY INTO PHYSICAL CULTURE

On April 1, 1930, Chiang Kai-shek, chairman of the National Government, stood before a body of 1627 national-class athletes on the grass field of the Zhejiang Provincial Stadium in Hangzhou. In his role as honorary chairman of the Fourth National Games, Chiang declared,

> Today the masses from all over our nation have come to join in this athletic meet. But what kind of influence will these National Games have on the Chinese nation-race *(minzu)?* I am here expressly to report on this. The Chinese nation's population of four hundred million and vast territory are unrivaled in the entire world. But the Chinese nation's status in the world, its international ranking, is not even third class. This is our Chinese nation's greatest shame. And the reason is that our national physique *(minzu tizhi)* is weak, causing people of other nations not to take us seriously. Today's meet shows the true spirit of the Chinese nation's wish for liberty and equality. It is also the ardent expression of support by outstanding elements nationwide

for the national government. So the significance of today's National Games is to set a new national record for the health and success of our national physique(s) *(minzu tige)*.[1]

With all of modern *tiyu's* contradictions laid out before these athletes—the tension between the nation-race built from strong individual bodies and the fascist dream of a united national-racial body, the assumption that 1,627 athletes' bodies represented the health and strength of some four hundred million, the conflation of quantifiable categories of elite competitive *tiyu* ("new national records"[2]) with abstract notions of a national suprabody—China's Fourth National Games began. These 1,627 athletes (1,163 male, 464 female) came to Hangzhou to represent thirteen provinces, six cities, Hong Kong, and the Chinese population in Kobe, Japan. More than three times as many athletes participated as in the last games of 1924, but fourteen provinces were still unrepresented, reflecting accurately the extent of the new Nanjing regime's control over the Chinese interior.[3]

Zhu Jiahua, commissioner of the Zhejiang Provincial Department of Civil Affairs, was planning director for the games, and one of many who described the meet as a true watershed moment in the official world of Chinese *tiyu*. In an essay written on the Fourth Games, Zhu referred to "the one or two previous National Games, which were merely embellished facades." He continued, "These games are different. From the earliest planning to the closing ceremonies, one sees in every way the government's promotion of *tiyu* and its true concern for the people's spirit." Zhu praised the government's efforts to make the games so inclusive—"no [locale] was too far away to be reached"—and congratulated the women athletes present who would "give hope to the fragile and weak women of China."[4] In another essay, Zhu went further in discussing the Nationalist government's contribution:

> In the past, the average athlete had incorrect ideas like "sport for sport's sake" or "playing sports just to win prizes." But "sport for sport's sake" is just as meaningless as talking about "eating for eating's sake" or "studying for studying's sake." And "playing sports just to win prizes" is like talking about "studying just for an exam or just for a diploma"—even more ridiculous. The goal of sports, narrowly defined, is to develop the individual's physical fitness. But people cannot exist outside society. Thus we can go even further and say that besides aiming to develop the individual's fitness, [sport] aims to develop the fitness *(tiyu)* of the entire body of society *(shehui quanti)*. We hope that the athletes in this meet can dismantle the old incorrect ideas and know that the guiding principles of this meet are to develop citizens' physical fitness and arouse the national-racial *(minzu)* spirit.[5]

The term *minzu,* used constantly in Nanjing-era discussions of a national physical culture, is crucial and, coming from the Japanese *minzoku,* itself a translation of European concepts of racial nations and national races, is as hard to define exactly in Chinese as it is to translate into English. I see the vagueness of the term, its position between the idea of a modern nation-state and the idea of a primeval race descending from the Yellow Emperor, as a key to its popularization in the 1930s. Since it carries too much national significance to translate as "race," far too much racial significance to translate as "nation," and far too much passion and richness to dismiss with a boring "people" or "folk," I usually translate it as "nation-race." Other terms could be used besides Chiang's "national body" *(minzu tizhi)*—like Zhu's "body of society" *(shehui quanti)* here—but these metaphors of a Chinese *Volksgemeinschaft* clearly carried the day in the new era of unified Guomindang rule.

Held in conjunction with the Zhejiang Provincial Exhibition at West Lake, the Fourth National Games marked the new Nationalist government's entry into the sports world. The China National Amateur Athletic Federation (CNAAF) had twice awarded the Fourth National Games to the city of Guangzhou (for 1926 and then for 1929). However, when the Zhejiang Provincial Government proposed holding a National Games as part of their West Lake Exhibition, Nanjing ordered the CNAAF to cease their planning work. The Guangzhou bid was rejected, and the games were given to the Zhejiang government to promote as a Guomindang (and not a CNAAF) sponsored event.[6]

These games did not represent the first physical culture work done by the new Nationalist government after it hijacked the Chinese revolution in 1927. The government's most celebrated involvement in *tiyu* was the Central Martial Arts Academy established in Nanjing in 1928 and discussed in Chapter 7. The new Education Department's National Education Conference, held in 1928, passed eight resolutions on physical education, from the reintroduction of military training into high schools to the call for public athletic grounds to be built at the county level throughout China.[7] In April 1929, Nanjing issued the new Citizens' Physical Fitness Law, which made parents and guardians responsible for giving their children a physical education, strictly prohibited any customs or practices harmful to the health of young people, and ruled that each hamlet, village, town, and city was to build a public athletic ground.[8] A Central Tiyu Research Society was established in Nanjing in 1929, with its own journal, *Physical Culture.* However, it was the Guomindang's heavy investment in the Fourth National Games that brought its involvement in the sports world to the forefront of the revolution. And it was these games that Wu Zhihui of the Central Reconstruction

Commission called in his speech "the starting point for the Chinese nation-race's *(minzu)* recovery of strength and vigor."[9]

But although the Guomindang attempted to make the games a display of nationalist bravado and to redirect their focus toward national-racial goals, it was impossible to keep the bourgeois capitalist values of the nearby West Lake Exhibition from entering the games. The main planner Zhu Jiahua was fascinated by the similarities between the National Games and the West Lake Exhibition's contributions to the development of Chinese industry and commerce.[10] The editor of Shanghai's *Young Companion* could describe the realm of sports only in blatantly corporate terms:

> The special thing about modern competition is that it combines many smaller strengths into a larger strength and combines larger strengths into even larger strengths. Every kind of sport thoroughly proves this principle. We can extend this principle to the modern business world and see similar trends. Look at the film industry, where MGM and Paramount merge, as do Paramount and Warner Brothers. . . . We must emphasize organized sports training.[11]

The Fourth Games were full of these contradictions. Planning Director Zhu ridiculed the idea of participating in sport just to win prizes, but the Prizes Section was established specifically to distribute the 1,192 prizes (including silver cups, portable muscle trainers, copies of *The Three People's Principles and Utopia,* and pen sets) donated by private companies, government bodies, and enthusiastic pro-*tiyu* elites.[12] The Games Publicity Section circulated thirty-two nationalist slogans, many of which, like "Without healthy citizens we will never create a strong nation and race," emphasized the "mass" nature of a healthy physical culture for China.[13] Shao Yuanchong, representing the Central Party Department, similarly emphasized the importance of *tiyu* for the "masses" when he told the opening ceremonies crowd:

> We should know that in the past, when the masses were interested in physical fitness and martial arts, they always paid attention to the individual rather than the entire society's physical fitness *(shehui tili)* or competition with other nations of the world. Now we must make sure that physical fitness and martial arts are taken to the masses and that the masses pay attention to physical fitness and martial arts in order to make the *minzu* healthy and strong. This will be the success of racial nationalism *(minzu zhuyi).*[14]

Yet at the same time, the Fourth Games gave birth to a sports hero-worship never before seen in China. Two of the Republican period's greatest stars first became famous there: the male sprinter Liu Changchun, from Dalian, who won the one-hundred-, two-hundred-, and four-hundred-meter races, ran anchor on the winning Liaoning 1,600-meter relay foursome, and captured the track and field overall men's individual championship, and the women's track and field individual champion, the female sprinter Sun Guiyun, who won two sprint events (fifty and one hundred meters) and ran the anchor leg for her co-champion Harbin two-hundred-meter relay team. Hangzhou's city fathers were so struck by Liu's and Sun's performances that they dedicated a "Changchun Road" and a "Guiyun Bridge" near the Provincial Stadium to the two stars.[15]

These were the contradictions that would characterize Chinese physical culture in the 1930s and that highlighted the historical contingency of the Guomindang's framing of *tiyu*. Organized sports, born long ago in industrializing England and America, would always draw participants and spectators toward the globalizing doctrine of capitalism—free competition between individuals free to sell their labor (or to exchange it for trophies and prizes). Statist forces, however, would never give up on this domain of physical discipline and the promotion of health and strength, seemingly tailor-made for national goals.

An atmosphere of cooperation and shared commitment to modern ideals infused Hangzhou's National Games. Athletes bunked in converted military barracks furnished with newspaper reading rooms and telegraph services and watched modern-themed evening entertainment, like a film on the recent U.S. National Track Meet at Chicago or the Jinling Drama Company production of *After Returning Home*, a play about a modern youth and his old-fashioned family.[16] Participating in or watching the games themselves—whether a soccer game between Liaoning and Zhejiang or a women's volleyball game between Beiping and Jiangxi—presented a chance for the sporting elites of China to mingle and engage in fair competition and to teach and learn from each other in the modernizing atmosphere of Hangzhou. At times the inequalities between coastal and inland areas of China were too clearly highlighted—for example, when the Tianjin men's basketball team defeated the Jiangxi squad 153–4. But despite this fantastic disparity, the official report on the games tried to put a positive national spin on the beating: "This kind of score is unprecedented. But both teams competed with all their might. The one side was not arrogant and proud in victory; the other was not discouraged or despondent in defeat. Both teams struggled to the end; this will and spirit is genuinely admirable."[17]

Yet somehow this vision of a sporting, modern-minded nation was not enough for the Guomindang at the Fourth National Games, and through the 1930s it became increasingly insufficient for their mobilizing goals. As Zhu

Jiahua wrote, the 1930 Games, by bringing together and displaying so many healthy Chinese bodies, would allow the Chinese to begin to prove that the epithet "Sick Man of East Asia" was now just an outdated joke. But to truly prove it false once and for all would require "a healthy and flawless spirit, which requires a healthy and flawless physique. Only by gathering tens and tens of millions of citizens with healthy and flawless physiques can we have a healthy and flawless *minzu* and culture."[18] However, the Guomindang's goal was to create not only strong individuals who could then work together to form a strong nation (the "liberal" model) but also a strong *minzu* nation-race that could far surpass the accomplishments of mere individuals. Lloyd Eastman and Frederic Wakeman have discussed the fear of liberalism and its attendant individualism among fascist elements in the Guomindang.[19] The same distrust can be seen in the Guomindang's handling of Chinese physical culture during the Nanjing Decade. Chinese sport was explicitly politicized for the first time, as weighty *minzu* "nation-race" meanings were imported to obscure the liberal nation-state notions inherent to modern sport.

Sport and physical exercise are clearly prime sites for the production of liminal moments outside conventional social structures of power and authority. As explained in Chapter 3, modern *tiyu* sometimes was an arena where authoritarian systems of rule could be questioned and temporarily cast aside in favor of fun and individual competition. Thus the Guomindang state had to politicize this bodily realm, imbuing it with meanings of a Chinese nation-race whose millions could move as one, maneuvering vigilantly through a world rife with dangers of imperialist aggression and national extinction. The liberal democratic *tiyu* of the 1920s was based on notions of the self-disciplining capacity of a modern citizenry. But now Guomindang agents, understanding the fundamental unreliability of the easily distracted or misled individual, aimed to centralize this realm, making *tiyu* a new arm of the state with disciplining and stabilizing functions. Finally, the quest for "mass" forms became much more urgent after 18 September 1931, when Japan began its fourteen-year military adventure in China with the provocation of a military "incident" in Manchuria, soon followed by the conquest of the three northeasternmost Chinese provinces and a continuing southward march that threatened the Chinese nation itself.

A NEW MASS PHYSICAL CULTURE

Perhaps the most significant development of Chinese physical culture in the 1930s was the invention of a new "mass *tiyu*" to correct the problems inherent in Western bourgeois forms of sport that had largely attracted the elites of Chinese society. Whereas the privileged sons and daughters of urban China defined sports largely as a mode of consumption, agents of the Guomindang state sought to introduce a productive component to physical culture.[20] *Tiyu* discipline in the 1930s was centered on the concept of spreading *(puji)* physical culture to all elements of the Chinese population, creating a *"tiyu* for society" *(shehui tiyu)* or a *"tiyu* for the masses" *(minzhong tiyu)*. This mass *tiyu* was designed to strengthen the national and social body by extending the benefits of scientific physical training and education not only to national-class athletes but also to China's common people, who, as one author explained, "120 percent need *tiyu* to improve and transform their lives."[21]

The foremost leader in mass *tiyu* was Wang Geng, a native of Yunyang County, Jiangsu, and a student of Charles McCloy. After graduating in 1926 from the Southeastern University Tiyu Department, Wang served as *tiyu* director of the Shanghai Provincial Second Normal School, Zhejiang Provincial Fourth and Tenth High Schools, and the Jiangsu Provincial Mass Education College.[22] In a 1931 book, Wang asked, "What is *tiyu* for society?" and answered:

1. *Tiyu* for society increases the health rate of the masses *(minzhong zhi jiankanglü)*. . . .

2. *Tiyu* for society is a benefit *(fuli)* given to the masses. Of all the most terrible suffering in our nation today, none is worse than poverty. But the basic causes of poverty are disease and weakness. . . . If we promote *tiyu* for society and enable the masses to have healthy bodies and minds, this kind of suffering will end.

3. *Tiyu* for society cultivates a strong will among the masses. . . . [T]he bad habits of fatalistic resignation [to arrangements that are] against one's principles *(gou'an)*, fear, and oversentimentality will all be wiped away.

4. *Tiyu* for society gives rise to the special characteristics shared by our nation's people since antiquity. . . . [B]enevolence, righteousness, loyalty, honesty, and perseverance will flourish even more with the power of *tiyu*.

5. *Tiyu* for society leads to a peaceful society. The unpeaceful elements in society consist mostly of the unemployed. The reason they have no work is usually physical defects or weakness. But these defects can all be corrected with the power of a *tiyu* for society.[23]

Wang's specialty was the design and maintenance of public athletic grounds *(gonggong tiyuchang)*—an important element of the project to pacify, discipline, normalize, and strengthen Chinese society, half a century before "midnight basketball" programs were established for similar reasons in American cities. As another specialist wrote, "Each person who comes to the athletic grounds is one less person in the teahouses, taverns, gambling dens, and brothels."[24]

The Education Department's 1934 yearbook contained twenty-five pages of statistics on public athletic grounds in twenty-four Chinese provinces and six municipalities, listing budgets, facilities, and personnel information for 1,110 such grounds nationwide (Table 4).[25] At the high end were facilities like the Jiangsu Provincial Public Athletic Grounds at Zhenjiang, located outside the old city's South Gate. Blessed with annual funding of seventeen thousand *yuan* (U.S.$5,800), the grounds extended thirty-seven thousand square meters and were furnished with track and field, soccer, basketball, tennis, gymnastics, and ping-pong equipment.[26] Even management was top-notch; Grounds Director Wu Bangwei, a graduate of Nanjing Higher Normal School, taught and served as P.E. director at Fujian's Jimei School, Nanjing's Southeastern University, and St. John's, Guanghua, and Ji'nan Universities in Shanghai before taking the new Zhenjiang Grounds post in 1930.[27] The seventeen thousand *yuan* Wu had to work with in Zhenjiang could have funded some of China's lower-end public athletic grounds for centuries— like Guangxi's Tianhe County Public Grounds, built in 1931 with an annual budget of five *yuan* (U.S.$2) or Yunnan's Huaping County Public Grounds, which got by on twenty-two *yuan* (U.S.$8) a year.

Public athletic grounds were built and maintained for the purpose of creating through sport and physical exercise a healthy, disciplined, and occupied citizenry. As Director Shang Shumei of the Shandong Provincial Public Athletic Grounds explained, "The entire district should be treated as a school, and the entire population as students. One should give advice, assist, and teach in the beginning, with voluntary participation and self-administration as the goal."[28] In 1931, the Education Department's Directive #669 contained instructions on what events to include in the yearly "mass amateur sports meets" to be held at city- and county-level grounds. Martial arts, track and field, swimming, basketball, volleyball, soccer, baseball, tug-of-war, and weightlifting were suggested, although events could be added or eliminated according to "local conditions."[29]

The bodies of China's urban residents received the most attention, as the possibilities of unrest in the cities posed the greatest threat to the state. Expert Wang Zhuangfei saw cities like his native Shanghai, with their population density, oppressive jobs, and moral decay, as "great ovens that can destroy the human vitality passed down for millennia," leading to suicide,

TABLE 4. Statistics on Public Athletic Grounds, 1934

Province/City	Number	Budget (yuan)	Avg. budget/site
Sichuan*	327	24131	73.80
Shandong	79	22063	279.28
Henan	66	13027	197.38
Jiangsu	61	108211	1773.95
Hebei	59	26840	454.92
Guangxi	57	18879	331.21
Guangdong*	56	19440	347.14
Guizhou*	55	730	13.27
Hunan	49	11121	226.96
Shaanxi	42	5726	136.33
Shanxi	39	4196	107.59
Anhui	31	7706	248.58
Gansu	31	2946	95.03
Fujian	29	24569	847.21
Xikang*	22		
Yunnan	21	34045	1621.19
Jiangxi	16	3550	221.88
Chahar	16	1950	121.88
Zhejiang	10	22497	2249.70
Ningxia	9	1760	195.56
Rehe	8	127969	15996.13
Qinghai	6	95	15.83
Shanghai	6	9792	1632.00
Liaoning*	5	600	120.00
Beiping*	4	120	30.00
Nanjing	2	54	27.00
Qingdao*	1		
Harbin	1	17000	17000.00
Hubei	1	1840	1840.00
Tianjin	1	20000	20000.00
Total	1110	530857	478.25

* 1929 data (1934 data unavailable)

crime, vagrancy, and poverty.[30] Public *tiyu* facilities thus were of vital importance to the urban order that the state hoped to build; as Wang wrote,

> The laborer and merchant communities need free-time exercise *(yeyu yundong)* just as students need extracurricular sports; we are all human and all deserve the equal right to pursue health and happiness. And the laborer and merchant communities of [Shanghai] need free-time exercise even more urgently than do the laborers and merchants of other areas. This city is China's foremost marketing and commercial center, so if the hundreds of thousands of workers and merchants are not able to find health and happiness, this will pose great danger to society.[31]

A "*tiyu* for society" would thus train the entire social body, suppressing any behavioral aberrations in Chinese society.

The social trainers in China's universities and educational organizations did not treat the masses as a single entity; rather, they realized that different programs would be needed to reach each segment of mass society. As the Education Department advised, "For the masses of the peasant, worker, and merchant communities, all manner of methods should be used, at any time and any place, to get people interested, attentive, and motivated toward *tiyu*."[32]

Cheng Dengke, a Chongqing native educated at the Reichshochschule für Leibesübungen (German National Sports Institute), envisioned a Citizens' Tiyu Office (Guomin tiyu shu) with eighteen separate departments *(chu)* to execute all the functions needed to spread *tiyu* throughout society.[33] Wang Geng saw the need for a separate women and children's area at athletic grounds, since "women's and children's capacity for exercise and interest in exercise is different from that of adult men. . . . [The area] should have lots of plants and flowers, since women and children all love flowers, and this will make them happy to come exercise."[34] In 1935 treatises on mass *tiyu*, two writers published independently nearly identical schemes for the classification of programs for mass *tiyu* work:

1. Classification by age: young children, children, youth, adult, elderly
2. Classification by organizational unit: individual, family, school, society, military/police, party, nation
3. Classification by profession: farmer, worker, merchant, student, military/police, bureaucrat
4. Classification by sex: male, female[35]

One of the writers then listed fifteen different types of locations where steps to promote mass *tiyu* would have to be taken, including mass athletic grounds; public pools and rinks; public exercise rooms; sunbathing facilities; village teahouses; park exercise areas; women and children's exercise areas; children's playgrounds; school, military, police, factory, store, and hospital physical fitness departments; union exercise facilities; and martial arts academies.[36] China's mass *tiyu* experts, conscious of the diversity of their nation's population, thus sought to deliver a regime of discipline and health appropriate to both each individual subject and the nation as a whole.

One of the greatest areas of concern was the Chinese farming village and, as one Anqing *tiyu* activist described them, "the remote and backward village schools, where no one ever even mouths the two words 'physical education.'"[37] In the village schools where *tiyu* was taught, as another writer pointed out, teachers did not understand the principles of *tiyu* and hygiene and did not take their young students' psychology into account when selecting activities for instruction.[38] A student at Shanghai's East Asia Physical Education School wrote in 1935 to the editors of the *Chin Fen Sports Monthly* on the defects of village youths' bodies: their shirts off, they looked the picture of healthy beauty *(jiankang mei)*, but in truth their muscles were not agile or flexible, since the motions of their work were so heavy and repetitive.[39] It was clear to this Shanghai student that the modern gymnastics and corrective exercises he suggested for these village youth would be more beneficial to their bodies than the undisciplined movements of their daily precapitalist tasks.

Another problem, as Suzhou Agricultural School P.E. Instructor Chu Jianhong explained, was that peasants made up 85 percent of China's population but were simply like "loose sand," not understanding the spirit of solidarity and struggle or the virtues of courage and sacrifice. In 1935, Chu introduced a village *tiyu* program, centered on a village-level public athletic grounds, that would give peasants the chance to have healthy and developed bodies; imbue *(guanshu)* peasants with hygiene knowledge; cultivate the habit of entertainment through sports and games; cultivate a spirit of cooperation, solidarity, chivalry, courage, and initiative; promote peasant societal interaction; and destroy dangerous class consciousness among the people. The project would be funded by tobacco and alcohol taxes, county mass education funds, and proceeds from showing *tiyu*-related films and selling *tiyu* stamps and photos. Village *tiyu* work would include compiling a detailed survey of each village resident's sex, age, hobbies, and activities; organizing teams and competitions; holding women's and children's health competitions; collecting peasants' opinions; and holding regular health and hygiene inspections.[40]

An important administrative innovation designed to measure this spread of *tiyu* among the masses was the Physical Culture Experimental Zone (Tiyu shiyanqu), born of the need "to investigate the individual histories of people who come to exercise."[41] The Education Department's 1932 plan for citizens' *tiyu* required that every provincial and municipal education department establish such a program. P.E. experts would be sent to experimental centers all around China, where they would be assisted by *tiyu* advisors from each county; representatives from Mass Education and Peasant Education Institutes; security, hygiene, and police departments; and public athletic grounds managers. Funded by provincial or municipal education departments, a center would hold seasonal athletic meets, run sports leagues, teach approved scientific martial arts forms, lead morning calisthenics for merchants, distribute *tiyu* publications, hold *tiyu* expositions, carry out local health inspections, and even hold annual health contests for men, women, and children. Keeping careful track of the personal particulars of participants in these *tiyu* activities, a center could then use these aggregate profiles to work to spread *tiyu* knowledge in the entire province.[42] Besides this number crunching, mass surveillance, using the state's security forces, was the key to the state's mass *tiyu* program. Whereas 1920s liberal democratic *tiyu* relied on the self-disciplining capacity of the Chinese citizenry, the Guomindang sought to centralize this process, bringing functions of disciplining and classification back within the state's reach.

One place where these efforts were carried out very conscientiously was the Jiangxi Provincial Athletic Grounds in Nanchang, center of Chiang Kai-shek's New Life Movement. This movement aimed to improve everyday habits and customs in order to transform what Chiang saw as the disorganized Chinese masses into a cohesive, politically and nationally conscious middle class. At these grounds, a Research Division was established to investigate and compile statistics on *tiyu* participants' personal and family life conditions. Some 627,324 participants registered at the grounds in 1934, and questionnaires were distributed among the citizens who came to play and work out. The Research Division compiled statistics on the participants, classifying them by *jie* (occupation) (Table 5). Statistics were also compiled for participation in different activities on the grounds; the favorite was basketball, with at least ten thousand Nanchang residents playing every month.[43]

Private institutions followed the state's lead on mass *tiyu*. In 1933, the Nankai School's *tiyu* director Zhang Jiwu boasted that his school rejected the "commercialism" and "professionalism" of individualistic Western sports like tennis and track and field and moved toward trends of "proletarianism" and "athletics for the masses" in team sports like volleyball.[44]

TABLE 5. Jiangxi Athletic Grounds
Participation by Occupation *(Jie)*, 1934

Occupation	Number	Percentage
Students	243,744	38.85
Military/police	121,872	19.43
Children	91,404	14.57
Merchants	50,202	8.00
Bureaucrats	33,351	5.32
Women	22,815	3.64
Workers	21,351	3.40
Other	42,585	6.79
Total	627,324	100.00

This trend had begun even earlier at Nankai, when the school instituted mandatory physical standards testing for all male students. Nankai authorities spurred their students' performances by printing in the school paper the best and worst scorers in all four testing events. In 1931, students could admire their peer Liu Sijiu, who scored top marks in the one-hundred-meter dash and long jump, and scorn weaklings like Wu Weizhen, who finished with the lowest long jump (6'7") and shotput (10'0") marks. In 1932, last-place finishers like Meng Zhuang (21.5 seconds in the one-hundred-meter dash) were derided in the *Nankai Weekly* as "worse than grade school girls."[45] The task of spreading ideas of physical fitness, even within elite institutions, was tackled with equal coerciveness, as peer pressure and print media impressed standards of normality on individuals of all classes and backgrounds.

MASS *TIYU* FOR THE WOMEN OF CHINA

Women were another target population for the men charged with designing China's new *minzu*-centric mass physical culture. By the 1930s, however, a cadre of female *tiyu* experts had emerged who sought to add their particular expertise to that of the men in charge. Fan Hong describes this trend as giving women in the 1930s "an enhanced opportunity to free their bodies further through exercise."[46] I would suggest, however, that tropes of "opportunity" or "freedom" are inadequate to describe the intense body discipline that *tiyu*-active women were asked, and chose, to undertake in the 1930s mass *tiyu* movement.

In Chapter 4, I described how the male managers of Chinese physical culture tried, relatively consistently, to restrict women's physical culture to domestic, traditionally female spheres of society. By the 1930s, programs suggested by men were no longer so uniform, now varying from the embarrassingly reactionary to the benevolently paternalistic. The notorious eugenicist Pan Guangdan publicly addressed the "exercise fever" sweeping through women's communities in Shanghai, opining that women should not be encouraged to exercise at all. Participation in activities like tennis, cycling, or basketball was too dangerous in terms of women's reproductive health and threatened his ideal "more-sons-and-grandsons" *(duo zi duo sun zhuyi)* China.[47] Wu Yunrui, the American-educated head of the Education Department's Sports Standards Research group, impressed by what he learned on a fact-finding tour through Great Britain, France, and Germany, became an ardent supporter of women's *tiyu* programs, but hardly out of any progressive motives. In 1935 he wrote:

> Women's physical fitness is very important in terms of managing the household and the family. The woman's responsibilities in the household are cooking and cleaning. The former requires preparing three meals a day; if this presents too heavy of a burden, then there is no way that one can succeed at it. In addition to the three meals, there is also the cleaning and sweeping and tidying up, which can easily exhaust the spirit and fatigue the body. Again, if the body is weak, then there is no way to succeed in these tasks.[48]

Many authors premised their ideas for women's fitness programs on what they saw as basic scientifically defined differences between female and male bodies. One argument for girls' lack of physical strength was based on the brand-new discipline of physiopsychology.[49] Another used essentialist "science" to directly challenge a feminist notion that equality between the sexes implied identical physical expectations for men and women:

> This type of theory [of equality between the sexes] only brings great harm to our nation's women. . . . So-called "male-female equality" does not mean that women must do whatever men do. This is not equality; in fact it is inequality. For example [this is like saying that] if women can give birth, equality can only be achieved if men give birth too. So-called equality [must recognize that] women have a heavier biological responsibility. . . .
> For the sake of distorting the true meaning of male-female equality,

women's participation in men's sports has resulted in quite a few tragedies that make one want to weep in sorrow. Women's biological in-
heritance, their physiology and anatomy are different from men's; we
should not have women participating in the same kinds of competition
as men. . . . [T]he price is a biological tragedy.[50]

The nature of women's involvement in 1930s *tiyu* was a transformation of
this realm; male specialists' apprehensions about this innovation only
confirmed the special role that all observers agreed women could play in a
Chinese nation-race with a highly developed physical culture.

Cheng Dengke seemed to understand just how unique, liminal, and powerful women's position in the physical culture community was. In 1935 he
wrote an open letter to his new physical culture "comrades" (*tongzhi*), that
year's graduates of Central University's Physical Education Department.
He made ten requests of the graduates as a group but made eight more points
specifically to the women graduates about their new responsibilities as "female *tiyu* comrades":

(1) New female *tiyu* comrades, you must understand clearly—women
are the mothers of citizens. If the [female] body is deficient in any
way, this will affect the physiques of our citizens and will directly
determine the fate of our nation—survival or extinction. . . .

(2) . . . [Y]ou are the mothers of New China, and all our eyes are on the
women of our nation. . . .

(3) . . . [Y]ou are the engineers who will build the New Woman. . . .

(4) . . . [Y]ou are the needle in the compass of women's health and
fitness. . . .

(5) . . . [Y]ou are the nurses and caretakers of women. . . .

(6) . . . [Y]ou are the models and teachers of hygiene. . . .

(7) . . . [Y]ou are the heroes and leaders of the women of New China. . . .

(8) . . . [T]he Oriental skin-as-white-as-paper sickly beauty is not really
beautiful. Using makeup to add color only ends up making one lose
one's true face; it makes one uglier, not more beautiful.[51]

These were the expectations confronting female "*tiyu* comrades" as they
entered this crucial realm of the Chinese nation-state in (male-defined)
crisis.

By the 1930s a new group of female physical education experts had
emerged who used their scientific and specialist educations to create their own
justifications and conditions for a women's physical culture. Xiang Xianggao, one of these experts, wrote in the *Republican Daily News* in 1929 on
the history of women's physical fitness and its relation to their position in

society. Xiang cited late-nineteenth-century archeological discoveries proving that ancient societies were controlled by women—until men began training their bodies. "[Men] practiced running, wrestling and fighting, throwing and leaping. As a result their physiques became stronger by the day, and this spelled the elimination of female [dominance] *(nüxing taotai)*."[52] Xiang understood physical fitness as a way for women to "retake" a role in Chinese society. She cited, as proof of women's decline in societies all over the world, the fact that skulls of Stone Age women averaged 2,200 to 2,400 cubic centimeters in volume, as compared to an average of just 1,338 cubic centimeters for modern women. Xiang wrote:

> I dare say, if women want to be rid of all the layers of oppression and to take back our natural women's rights, we must revive our inherent abilities. . . . The women's abilities of which I speak are not simply the abilities to be a virtuous wife and doting mother, but the ability to be a strong and fit member of society. . . . Physical training should follow more radical suggestions—and not the light and easy, cultured and refined dance, or the soft and tender, leisurely and slow calisthenics. Only then will we be able to get things done. We should learn the skills of track and field, the warlike courage of martial arts, the team spirit of ball sports, and the strength and vitality of other outdoor activities. . . . Fellow women! If you want to know your future, from this day on, look to your physical fitness![53]

The theme of women's participation in competitive sports was not new in China, although more and more female *tiyu* experts, led by women like Xiang, were themselves defining the significance for the nation of women's bodily endeavors.

In 1933, a group of five highly educated professional women (magazine editors, artists, and designers) published a two-part piece on physical fitness for the modern working woman, stating: "We are all in very prestigious professions—which means that we must use our gray matter (as much as we have) in carrying out our work every day. This causes unending strain and injury to the capacities of our mind and spirit, and no matter what, we never have the slightest chance to engage in any work for the health of our own bodies."[54] These women's solution was to shun the fashionable tennis, golf, swimming, and horseback riding of the rich and, ignoring the comments of confused neighbors, to take crash courses in acrobatics and martial arts. After the training was completed, the women ridiculed the traditions that kept women away from vigorous physical exercise, and they described how their newfound vitality gave them even more of an advantage in competing with men to earn their "daily bread" *(meiri de mianbao)*.[55]

Women also tried to take control of narratives of women's physical culture by reappropriating the popular discourse on menstruation and exercise. The possible dangers to women's reproductive health that could be incurred by jarring exercise during menstrual periods had constituted the bedrock of male discourse on women's *tiyu* since the 1920s. By the 1930s, however, female *tiyu* experts began to reform the menstruation-exercise debate on their own terms. One woman writer, in two articles published in the *Chin Fen Sports Monthly*, used statistics on Chinese, Japanese, and European women's menstruation and referred to nine close-up drawings of disembodied, cross-sectioned pelvic bones, vaginas, and uteri—formerly the territory of male *tiyu* experts.[56] Her findings were not radical in themselves: she concluded that "[w]omen must not do the same exercises as men, and married women especially must not do the same exercises as virgin women, or else physiological harm will be done."[57] However, her assertion that different categories of women were suited to different types of exercise and her call for "those of us responsible for guiding women's *tiyu* in the near future [to] perform and compile similar investigations and statistics"[58] made it clear who would define this important realm of study.

In 1931, an author in *Modern Home* wrote on the recent progress in women's physical culture, also seeking to define the realm in female terms. She raised the question of physical difference, seeing the difference as liberating rather than restrictive, as male *tiyu* experts had seen it for decades. Declaring, "[W]omen's souls are different from men's," she addressed the contentious subject of soccer's appropriateness for women. Her viewpoint was simple—we women are the "masters of our minds and bodies," and have no use for "[t]he fierce, intense struggles on the soccer field . . . [that] have no true significance and cannot satisfy our true wishes. [Soccer] is a rough and violent sport that can only exhaust us and cannot interest us."[59]

Zhang Huilan, the American-educated director of the Hebei Provincial Women's Normal College P.E. Department, also contributed to this female-centered approach by discussing the uses of science and looking at different divisions of women's physical culture. Zhang advocated frequent physical examinations for students so that their P.E. instructors could better understand their physical condition.[60] This knowledge would also be used to help divide physical education classes into sections, using "physical ability and general health" as the criteria. Whereas Jinling Women's College and Central University, both in Nanjing, simply had all the women in the school exercise at the same time, Hebei Women's Normal divided its classes not only by year but by three or four skill levels as well.[61] Thus Zhang described the field of women's *tiyu* as a complicated one requiring detailed sci-

entific knowledge and planning; its direction was not a task that careless instructors could perform without detailed preparation.

This appropriation of the women's *tiyu* agenda was an idea that seemed
to appeal to women in the reading audience as well; in 1934 a female *Chin
Fen Sports Monthly* reader wrote in with her detailed four-point program
for constructing a women's physical culture to help "revive the nation-race."
This goal would be accomplished best, she wrote, by training more female
tiyu instructors, providing specialized higher-level training for standout athletes, spreading women's *tiyu* to the larger population, and paying close attention to the effects of physical exercise on women's physiological health.[62]

Academic women were not the only ones with an agenda for *tiyu*. Women
workers could also use *tiyu* to challenge the oppressive conditions of modern factory discipline. In 1934, an author in the Shanghai YWCA's *Young
Women's Monthly* wrote on inequalities in many factory settings, where
women were paid less than men and often lost their jobs if they took ma-
ternity leave. She also made an appeal based on "modern *tiyu* principles"
for more rest and break times during work hours so that working women
could take time for deep breathing exercises or calisthenics routines that
would allow them to recover from their exhaustion.[63]

Still, the narrative of women's *tiyu* was not always one of dramatic "liberation" and unflagging "progress." More accurately, women's physical culture presented what Christina Gilmartin, in describing women's participation in the 1920s Communist movement, has called a "complex dynamic of
agency and compliance." In other words, women's "agency was counter-
balanced by their compliance to subtle forms of patriarchal controls"[64]—an
apt description of the ways in which the women's *tiyu* movement, which
developed at the same time, also was much more complex than the emancipatory discourse often used to describe it.

This dynamic can be seen in a short 1931 article in *Life Weekly*, by a
Shanghai woman named Dai Mengqin, on "the way to build a healthy body
and a healthy nation" and her conversion to a healthy, exercise-filled life.
Dai opened her piece by providing "historical background" to explain the
weakness of Chinese women throughout time immemorial: "Our nation's
women have always sat around, just keeping an eye on the home and not
being accustomed to movement. Except for women working in the fields,
they were practically all just Lin Daiyu [the delicate and sentimental pro-
tagonist of *The Dream of the Red Chamber*], possessing beautiful features
but lacking a healthy body."

Dai confessed that she personally had exacerbated the problems of this
sorry heritage by ignoring her husband's enthusiasm for exercise and his sug-

gestions that she take part as well. Not until she examined some of the "Healthy Beauty" pictorials often featured in *Life Weekly* did she see the light:

> I started to understand that a body's features and look are not unchangeable, that one can use one's own power to change oneself. My soul was extremely moved. That night I went to a bookstore and bought an American sports magazine, and after reading through it I realized that my interest was growing even stronger. I decided that I would learn how to exercise. The next day I bought a swimsuit and came back home to put it on before a mirror. I looked like a woman with a healthy body, but upon closer examination I noticed some major faults: (1) I had too much body fat, (2) my thighs were too thick, (3) my chest was too skinny, (4) my arms were a bit too large.

Determined to correct these faults, Dai began practicing sixteen types of exercise that her husband taught her. She explained how she always took this exercise while "examining myself in the mirror. The me in the mirror is my companion and also my strict teacher."[65]

Dai was a woman with many of the freedoms that a modern narrative of progress and liberation would reify: she was literate, sophisticated, modern-and open-minded; she participated in the "public sphere" of the modern media; she had purchasing power; and she sought to gain control over her body. But her program for strengthening China via women's physical fitness was still predicated on Western and Chinese males' ideals of beauty, control of the media, and general scientific authority. Dai's exercises in the mirror were her way of surveilling her own contributions to strengthening the nation. Yet they also made her a perfect example of the "self-conscious subject of self-knowledge," ever *grateful* for the chance to watch the "me in the mirror" disciplining, regulating, evaluating, and normalizing her own body.

Women were not the only ones worried about how their bodies conformed to official and popular standards of health and beauty. In its June 1935 issue, the "Readers' Counsel" of the *Chin Fen Sports Monthly* addressed letters from a Tianjin woman and a Shanghai man who were both concerned with the same problem—that their thighs were growing thicker and stouter as they intensified their track and field training regimens.[66] It is clear that 1930s programs to bring *tiyu* to the masses and promulgate standards for health, fitness, and physical ability placed both men and women in new quandaries unique to modernity. However, for all the efforts made by women to claim the space of women's *tiyu* as their own and to use the cause of women's physical fitness to stake new claims in society, women were still disproportionately blamed for their lack of attention to physical fitness and were stereotypically described in terms of a history of weakness and sloth. The powerful

Shanghai media transmitted these pressures to the masses, whom the state hoped to reach with its message of health and strength, and defined women as a special "problem" of the general mass *tiyu* program.

MASS *TIYU* AND THE SEARCH FOR A NATIONAL PASTIME

One theme developed in the drive to create a physical culture for the masses was the importance of identifying a national pastime that could appeal to the Chinese people as it strengthened and united them. Perhaps the first suggestion along these lines was made by Chen Lifu, the University of Pittsburgh–educated confidant of Chiang Kai-shek. In a 1933 essay, Chen described the importance of a "National Sport" (typeset in English, then translated as *guomin de yundong*) in uniting and strengthening citizenries in, and thus determining the rise of, Greece, America, Britain, and Japan.[67] Chen was eager to develop a national sport for China but insisted on several conditions: it could not be track and field, any ball sport, or any other activity falling under the categories of "aristocratic or gentry class sport."[68] He also argued that "[i]n today's China, with its trouble within and danger from without, the modern and fashionable exercises that contain much of the *play element*, but include very little *educational value*, are just not very suitable."[69] Chen also insisted that a national sport would have to cultivate virtues of teamwork and the spirit of struggle and to be "productionized" *(shengchanhua)*, allowing "the power of exercise to be used for production work."[70]

A year later, the physical education expert Wu Cheng addressed the same subject: "Each nation in the world has proceeded from the inherent nature of its people to establish one or several national sports *(guomin yundong)* in which the entire population can immerse itself, maintaining the health and fitness of the entire nation, like Britain's soccer, America's baseball, and Germany's handball and gymnastics." Wu suggested swimming as China's national sport. Most sports were "foreign goods," wrote Wu, but swimming hailed from ancient China, as proved by the line "Southerners are fond of swimming" *(nanren shan yong)* in an ancient history. And with all China's rivers, there would be no need to build "aristocratized, Westernized" pools or other equipment to strengthen and build the courage of the Chinese people.[71]

The "national game" was a common trope in writings of the early 1930s, reflecting both new ideas of the role of sports in bringing together Chinese athlete-citizens and new anxieties about the national strength and status of China's Asian neighbors. Some authors could confidently refer to soccer as

the Chinese "national game" *(guoji, guomin bisai)*.[72] But talk of other nations' national sports could be frustrating, like the discussion in 1934, after
the Far Eastern Games, about Japanese prowess in their "national game" of
baseball.[73] Or it could be even downright threatening, like the *Chin Fen
Sports Monthly*'s decision to report in its "Overseas Sports" column the
puppet Manchurian Athletic Association's nomination of soccer as their
official "national game."[74]

In 1935, an opportunity came to settle on a national pastime for China
once and for all. In a promotion to mark a subscription drive, Shanghai's
Chin Fen Sports Monthly announced a contest open to all subscribers submitting essays on the question, "Which type of game or sport should our
nation take as its national pastime *(guomin youxi)*?"[75]

Five months later, the contest results were announced. Five physical education experts read the 3,476 essays received. Soccer received 915 votes and
basketball 825 votes; these sports were named the two Chinese national pastimes. Martial arts were third with 309 votes, followed by volleyball, swimming, shuttlecock, jump rope, mini-soccer, track and field, gymnastics, boxing, ping-pong, tai chi calisthenics *(taijicao)*, calisthenics, fencing, acrobatics,
footraces in full military gear, military games, handball, health calisthenics,
tai chi *(taijiquan)*, marathon, racewalking, war games, boat races, home construction, target shooting, dance, and labor. All 3,476 participants won prizes,
most receiving book coupons valued at one *yuan*. Twenty-seven received
sporting goods equipment, three won free accounting classes by mail, nineteen won coveted enrollments at one of Shanghai's five *tiyu* academies, and
the two grand prize winners earned cash prizes of fifty *yuan* (U.S.$15).[76]

The two co-champions also had their essays published in *Chin Fen*. Huang
Jianxing, from Wuzhou, Guangxi, told why soccer was the most appropriate sport to serve as China's national pastime. Not only was the game invented by the Yellow Emperor himself, and not only were soccer games the
hallmark of physical culture in the heyday of China's Tang dynasty, but the
game was now known around the world to cultivate solidarity and a cooperative spirit in its participants.[77] Soccer's unique status as a Chinese game
that also had been developed by other modern nations of the West thus made
it the perfect choice. Zhuang Wenchao of the Jimei School in Xiamen based
his advocacy of basketball as the Chinese national game on arguments from
physiology and evolutionary science. He chose basketball over soccer because
the latter was already taken as a national sport (by Britain) and because soccer's popularity was limited in scope to the Hong Kong-Guangdong region.
In contrast, Zhuang described participation in basketball as a nationwide and
unifying phenomenon.[78]

The *Chin Fen* editor Shao Rugan explained in the same issue the larger importance of this national pastime question. It was true that this contest had been used as "a type of *tiyu*-psychological exam" to indicate the preferences of the magazine's readers. But, Shao continued, the implementation of soccer or basketball, or both, as China's national pastime would be an important step in stimulating the development of modern physical culture in China. He appealed to the *tiyu* community for participation in further discussions on the subject and hoped that once a consensus was reached the central government could formally decree an official Chinese national game.[79]

The search for a national pastime represented one extreme of the quest, so popular during this Nanjing Decade, for a physical culture that would turn the Chinese populace from a "sheet of loose sand" into a single strong and able national body. The editors and most readers of Shanghai's *Chin Fen Sports Monthly* still believed in the virtues of Anglo-American competitive sports. These forms, though criticized by many in the 1930s *tiyu* world, encouraged the qualities of sportsmanship and citizenship so valuable to the Chinese nation. (And, as the prize packages illustrated, these sports maintained the ties to the capitalist ethic that had inspired the rise of modern *tiyu* in the first place.)

The experts and activists who hoped to create a mass *tiyu* out of the exclusive, bourgeois Anglo-American sports saw no contradiction between these forms and the goal of creating a Chinese physical culture that could be spread to all Chinese people. If these endeavors could just be made more affordable and available for China's working and farming populations, "national pastimes" like soccer or basketball would be perfect both for cultivating notions of collective struggle and sacrifice in the Chinese masses and for developing a stronger athletic tradition and deeper talent pool that would be reflected in international competitions. However, adapting exclusive team sports for mass purposes had less ideological appeal than instituting fascist models of *tiyu* linking Chinese citizens' bodies to the needs of both modern industry and national defense.

MASS *TIYU* AND RATIONAL LABOR FOR SOCIETY

The human body is an active machine, the most complex machine in the world.

WU YUNRUI, "Tiyu kexuehua"
[The scientization of physical culture] (1935)

Production, in China with its weak nation and poor people, is naturally of paramount importance. . . . The most important factors in production are capital, land, and labor, and everyone knows that of these, labor is the most important. . . . The source of labor is the human body—without strong bodies there of course could be no powerful labor for production, agriculture, or handicrafts work. To increase efficiency one especially needs healthy bodies. In the great enterprises of Europe and America, for the sake of rationalization, the health of all workers is especially emphasized. Workers are supervised not only during working hours but even during rest time. Equipment and counseling are provided so that their bodies can stay healthy.

MENG GUANGPENG, "'Tiyu' yu 'Xin shenghuo'"
["Physical culture" and "New Life"] (1936)

These excerpts from the mid-1930s demonstrate clearly an important element of the drive toward a mass *tiyu*, namely the crucial link between the healthy body and a strong labor force, mentioned in many 1930s prescriptions for a mass physical culture. The latter author, a member of the Hubei Province Party-Government-Military-Scholastic Physical Culture Promotion Society (a New Life Movement organization), took as his model "the radical nations like Nazi Germany, Fascist Italy, and Bolshevik Soviet Russia, which, in the ever-worsening international climate, have included military affairs in their physical education, with citizens everywhere strictly trained."[80]

The topic of the healthy individual body and production was crucial in the fiercely nationalistic atmosphere of mid-1930s China, just as in Mussolini's Italy, where the Fascist regime emphasized the beauty of harmonious production for national interests.[81] Another member of the Hubei New Life group, in an article on the national economy and the revival of the Chinese nation-race, wrote that China needed strong bodies to work in its munitions, transportation, steel, pharmaceutical, and textile industries; to produce its traditional handicrafts; and to tend its agricultural fields.[82] And Wu Yunrui ingeniously explained that physical fitness was beneficial not only for production but also for workers, since increased work efficiency would result in higher paychecks for piece-work.[83]

Of great concern in this regard were the short life spans of Chinese people in comparison with those of Japanese and Westerners. In an article on "the frightening waste of Chinese lives" and the need for mass *tiyu*, one author wrote on expensive investment of creating a "useful element in society":

After birth, to raise and educate an individual takes on the average twenty years' time. During these twenty years, the entire society must expend a certain amount of energy and money to reach this goal. In other words, the entire society must invest twenty years in each individual to finally receive any interest—the individual's contributions to society. . . . If one's life is long, then society can reap much interest, but if not, then very little.[84]

The author then supplied statistics that placed the Chinese average life span at thirty years, in contrast with Australian, American, British, French, German, and Japanese life spans of forty-three to fifty-five years. If the first fifteen years of life counted as an investment period, for Chinese the payoff period in which an individual could contribute to society was only fifteen years, whereas Westerners and Japanese could serve their society for twenty-eight to forty years.[85] These contrasts became most striking when the author converted loss of life into financial terms. China's yearly death rate, according to these numbers, stood at 3 percent; the author forecast a yearly cost to China's economy of three hundred million *yuan* (U.S.$122,000,000). He estimated that this sum could pay *annually* for seventy thousand *li* (twenty-one thousand miles) of asphalt roads, six hundred water purification plants, eight hundred factories, thirty thousand *li* (nine thousand miles) of railroads, five thousand modern hospitals, one thousand universities, and one hundred thousand elementary schools.[86] Only the lack of citizens' physical education stood between China and this astounding level of productivity.

The concept of a "national physique" *(minzu tige)* introduced by activists promoting mass-based physical culture thus allowed many in the *tiyu* community to imagine the benefits to national production that a strong Chinese citizenry could provide. Visions of a newly strengthened and revitalized Chinese national body devoting all its energy to the national economy were part of the Guomindang's fascist vision for Chinese industry and society. Physical culture planners thus designed *tiyu* programs that would reproduce on Chinese bodies, via modern bodily motions taught to and demonstrated before Chinese citizens, the fascist ideals of a unified nation-race and disciplined state-controlled industry.

THE GEOGRAPHICAL EXPANSION OF MODERN PHYSICAL CULTURE

The spread of *tiyu* personnel throughout China was another key to the Guomindang's goal of creating a unified *minzu* body out of individuals from disparate conditions all over China. The Guomindang state handed down all manner of legislation and directives to encourage local attention to national *tiyu* programs. But these ambitious plans depended on a nationwide cadre of dedicated physical culture agents who, once educated in the coastal urban institutes of *tiyu*, could take knowledge of this discipline and theory back to their home regions for the state.

The most successful component of this policy was the Education Department–sponsored Summer Physical Education School, held annually beginning in 1933 for elementary and junior high school teachers from all over China.[87] The Nanjing Summer School encouraged P.E. instructors in each province to come to the capital for high-level exposure to physical education theory, science, and practice. Letters written by Summer School alumni and published in Shanghai's *Chin Fen Sports Monthly* offer information as to enrollment trends. The 131 graduates who supplied data on their place of residence and employment situation came from urban and rural areas in eighteen provinces.[88] They took back to their hometowns and cities the knowledge they had gained from an intense six-week, thirty-five-hour-week curriculum.[89]

That May and June, Tianjin's *Sporting Weekly* published two opinion pieces on the Nanjing Summer School. The journal's editors praised the central government's steps to spread *tiyu* knowledge throughout China but complained that the program would be of limited use as long as provinces like Hebei and Guangdong insisted on holding their own summer programs. They stated that individual provincial work "would never equal [the results of] the whole nation uniting under a single plan, centering efforts in a suitable location."[90]

Yu Zizhen, an elementary *tiyu* teacher, the leading *tiyu* activist of Anhui province, and a graduate of Shanghai's East Asia P.E. School, did not agree with this centralism. Yu ridiculed the notion that the average *tiyu* instructor earning forty to fifty *yuan* (U.S.$10–13) a month would have the resources or the time for a six-week stay in the nation's capital. On this basis, but still not questioning the central government's primacy, Yu recommended that Nanjing fund similar *tiyu* summer schools in each province.[91] The long-term compromise result of this debate on central versus local distribution of central *tiyu* knowledge can be seen in the Education Department's Normal School Tiyu Instructors' Summer Training Class program for 1937. Identical versions of this three-month session were to be held in Nanjing, Beiping, Guangzhou, and Wuchang so that every *tiyu* instructor from each of China's 815 normal schools would supposedly be able to participate.[92] The Wuchang session was canceled, but more than three hundred normal schools sent *tiyu* instructors to the other three training class locations just before China erupted in total war with Japan.[93]

Just as effective in training *tiyu* specialists for work in their hometowns all across China were the leading specialized physical education training schools in the Jiangnan area. The Physical Education Department at Nanjing's Central University (formerly Southeastern University and before that Nanjing Higher Normal School) was one. Some 150 P.E. majors graduated in the department's first nine classes from 1917 to 1930. The majority of these students were Jiangnan locals, but seventeen provinces were represented among Central University's alumni.[94]

This distribution of specialized *tiyu* instructors, a process begun long before the national-level programs described above, was especially important to the development of modern *tiyu* in inland China. An example can be seen in a list, compiled by *tiyu* scholar Wang Qihua, of fifteen physical education instructors who returned from study in China's larger cities to teach in the poor inland province of Guizhou in the late 1920s and 1930s. Seven graduated from Shanghai's East Asia Physical Education School, two from the Shanghai P.E. School, two from Nanjing's Central University P.E. Department, one from Suzhou's Zhongshan P.E. School, one from Beijing Women's Higher Normal, and one from National Wuchang Higher Normal. (Predictably, the only martial arts instructor of the bunch had the least glamorous credentials, having graduated from Qinyang Wushu School in Henan.)[95] Thus, a generation after the systematic introduction of modern physical education theory was begun in China's prosperous coastal regions, the Jiangnan region served as a major conduit for the spread of this theory back into the once-remote interior of China, now increasingly exposed to modernizing, nation-building exercise regimens.

MASS SPORT AND THE COMMUNIST MOVEMENT

A final important site of the 1930s promotion of a Chinese mass physical culture was the Chinese Communist Party's (CCP's) Soviet base movement throughout China. *Tiyu* was a primary element of the modern revolutionary education that the CCP worked to spread via educational, military, governmental, and youth organizations. By the late 1920s and 1930s, every political movement had to be active in the domain of physical culture to establish its credibility as a force for strength and order in a modern China. The CCP was no exception and from an early date linked itself closely to the cult of the strong and disciplined body and nation via its "red physical culture" *(chise tiyu, hongse tiyu)* movement.

The Communists, vanguard for a New China, defined their "red physical culture" as the polar opposite of the Nationalists' supposedly feudal, bourgeois, treaty-port urban athletic culture. In fact, to this day, laudatory accounts of Communist physical culture attempt to isolate uniquely "socialist" characteristics distinguishing it from dominant contemporary Nationalist *tiyu* forms and marking real progress and innovation in the field of Chinese physical culture. For example, Fan Hong writes of "red *tiyu*" that "[i]ts emancipatory role to date has not been adequately recorded."[96] Yet any cursory examination of the red *tiyu* movement in CCP base and border areas shows that Communist physical culture was not at all a radical departure from proven Chinese means of propagating this modern form of bodily discipline and knowledge. Consequently, apart from explaining a few of the main differences between dominant Nationalist and Communist *tiyu* programs, I do not spend much time here describing what many have supposed to be a revolutionarily unique program of training China's masses.

Official party statistics claim that in 1934, there were 3,052 Lenin Elementary Schools offering instruction in 2,232 Soviet-controlled villages in Jiangxi, Fujian, and Guangdong. The elementary school physical education curriculum included morning calisthenics as well as P.E. class three times a week, where students were led in more calisthenics, running, stone throwing, games, and expressive singing and dancing.[97] Programs like this were important in that they brought modern physical education instruction to areas that otherwise would not have experienced it. The content, however, was far from uniquely Communist and in fact differed little from the standard "calisthenics and games" model of elementary P.E. taught for decades in Republican schools. Records from the Sichuan-Shaanxi Border Soviet from 1932 to 1935 show that middle school students there, in addition to learning skills of soccer, basketball, and gymnastics, practiced with bayonets, swords, target shooting, emergency drill, and hand grenade throwing.[98] Communist historians are accurate in pointing out how programs like these differed from the traditional Anglo-American sports popular in Nationalist China but seldom mention that they originated in the Nationalist "militarized *tiyu*" programs popular in the 1930s (and described below).

Schools held large athletic meets much like those held in Nationalist areas, with few meaningful innovations. A four-day School Athletic Meet in Taiba District, Shanghang County, brought together some 486 students competing in several track and field events, including the three-student four-legged race and the fully armed footrace. As in the bourgeois model, however, prizes—including silver and bronze medals, ribbons, Communist International flags, and five-starred CCP flags—were awarded to top finishers.[99]

Like the Nationalists, leaders and propagandists of the Communist movement could imagine social progress in terms of images and metaphors of sports. A 1934 issue of the newspaper *Red China*, now on display at the

Longyan Revolutionary Museum in western Fujian, had on its front page a picture captioned "Great Leaps and Bounds by Changting County." The drawing portrayed an athlete in a dark tank top and shorts, with white characters spelling "Changting" stenciled across his chest, long-jumping past hashmarks signifying Red Army recruiting goals.[100] Government leaders were quite fond of discussing the red *tiyu* movement, but their efforts in these base areas had few viable consequences. For example, the Chinese Soviet Republic Red Tiyu Committee, formed in Ruijin in June 1933 and headed by Provisional Central Government Vice Chairman Xiang Ying, listed, among its initial goals, "representing the hundreds and thousands of masses, to join the Red Sports International [operated by the Comintern] and under this leadership to oppose the reformist Lucerne Sports International [an arm of the Socialist International] and China's local bourgeois physical culture organizations and to institute collective and red *tiyu* activities for the workers, peasants, youth, and toiling masses of the Soviet base areas."[101] Despite these ambitious plans, however, the committee held only one small meet (an International Youth Day competition in Ruijin on 2 September 1933) and was eventually broken up when the Guomindang began its Fifth Bandit Suppression campaign in mid-1934.

Finally, sports and physical culture were spread throughout the Red Army by means of the "Club" *(Julebu)* and "Lenin Room" *(Liening shi)* systems, which administered educational, cultural, and recreational programs within the army. *Tiyu* was one division of these organizations, which also included programs in literacy, wall poster writing, art, and music.[102] The Red Army held many sports meets that included competitors drawn from local student, worker, and peasant populations. For example, the Red Army Political Department held a May Sports Meet in Tingzhou, Fujian, that brought students and police together with army personnel for competitions in basketball, volleyball, ping-pong, track and field, martial arts, and the ubiquitous grenade throw.[103]

Whereas the Nationalist military structure had made no real contribution to the modern *tiyu* movement in Nationalist China, the CCP military was an important component of the red *tiyu* movement. The CCP's fighting mission, whether in opposition to rural landlords or Japanese imperialists, decreed that a sports movement under their direction would be understood as part of the military mission. However, the physical culture of the Red Army, as approved by faithful students of New Culture modern *tiyu* like Mao Zedong and Zhu De, would never depart too radically from the models dominant in Nationalist China. The contribution of the CCP and its Red Army to red *tiyu* was not a fundamental or revolutionary alteration of its content but rather a new geographical and institutional source of its dissemination.

JUSTIFYING THE MILITARIZATION
OF CHINESE PHYSICAL CULTURE

In 1984, Cheng Dengke, one of the leading Guomindang proponents of a "militarization of physical culture" *(tiyu junshihua)*, remembered and revoiced a disturbing admiration for 1930s Germany and its efforts in the cause of physical culture:

> After their defeat in the first European war, the Germans were able to develop and foster their spirit of self-strengthening and independence through physical education for the nation. . . . No matter how difficult it was, they never stopped striving for and promoting the cause of physical culture, and no matter how depleted their finances, they continued to find ways to increase *tiyu* funding and improve [*tiyu*] facilities of all types. The Germans' success in their movement to revive the race can only be described as the just reward for their physical culture efforts.[104]

Four years' study at Berlin's Reichshochschule für Leibesübungen, which qualified him to the position of Professor of Physical Education at Nanjing's Central University upon his 1933 return to China, convinced Cheng of the need to restore discipline and military spirit to the Chinese masses via physical education. He recalled his work promoting a militarized *tiyu* as a necessary effort to show his community how

> Chinese *tiyu* was going down the wrong road. For decades, it headed down the road of aristocratic *tiyu*, depriving the common people of sport and exercise, just telling them to stand aside and watch as the aristocrats participated in sport. . . . People were told to throw away the innate national-essence *tiyu* and to give all they had to promote foreign sports, to use foreign goods, and to follow the new tides of international sport. . . . The only way out for our nation's physical culture was to use compulsory *tiyu* to implement a physical culturization *(tiyuhua)* of the entire populace.[105]

Coming from the fascist order and discipline of the German National Sports Institute, Cheng was horrified by the state of Chinese physical culture and saw as his mission the introduction of German-style physical culture to the Chinese *tiyu* community. He wrote in 1934 that 80 percent of that community was corrupt and rotten *(fuhua)*, "truly obstacles in the path of our physical education, our public enemies."[106] There was no choice but to start over in a new fascist *minzu*-centric direction. Indeed, Cheng's 1945 *Essen-*

tial History of World Sport identified 1933, the year of his return from Germany, as the beginning of a new militarized era of Chinese *tiyu* history.[107]

After 1933, a new cadre of physical culture activists who saw their task as crucial to the progress of the Nationalist revolution, a new state reach into provincial affairs, and a new wave of anti-Japanese nationalism all combined to afford a new opportunity for implementing militarized *tiyu*. One of the activists was Liu Shenzhan, from Fuling County in southeastern Sichuan, who graduated from the Zhejiang Physical Education School in 1923 and returned to establish the Southwestern P.E. School in Chengdu in 1925. After a decade of *tiyu* work in Sichuan, Liu published a book entitled *The Tiyu Revolution* (1933), perhaps the decade's most strident call for a physical culture by, of, and for the Chinese nation-race.

Liu's book, beginning with excerpts from Sun Yat-sen and Chiang Kai-shek on the role of physical education in the national cause, presented *tiyu* as the key to the success of the Nationalist revolution. A physical culture revolution was just one of the many smaller movements—a literary revolution, an arts revolution, a technological revolution—that would be necessary for the success of the whole. But *tiyu* preceded all—"if we are all to become revolutionaries, we first need to receive a revolutionary and ideologized *(zhuyihua)* physical culture training." Its definition could be neither too restrictive nor too inclusive:

> To promote a Chinese *tiyu* now, we absolutely cannot continue saying that martial arts are unscientific and therefore should be seen as worthless. We also cannot say that since track and field and ball sports are foreign, we must reject them. We cannot say that *tiyu* is track and field and ball sports, thereby establishing a definition for *tiyu* as "Western." And we must not say that since martial arts are "Chinese" they can be set apart from *tiyu*. I support the promotion of martial arts and their development into a Chinese national-racial *tiyu* suitable for the national condition and the nature of the citizenry *(guominxing)*. As for track meets and ball games—Western sports—we must learn from their strong points and not just swallow them whole, trying to use them without a full understanding. . . . [T]he most important criteria are (1) *tiyu* and national-racial *(minzu)* consciousness, (2) *tiyu* and *minzu* nature, (3) *tiyu* and *minzu* spirit, (4) *tiyu* and *minzu* confidence, (5) *tiyu* and *minzu* struggle.[108]

Chu Minyi, Secretary of the Executive Yuan and one of China's highest-profile advocates of modern *tiyu*, would have agreed with these sentiments. Chu wrote in 1934 that *tiyu* should focus not so much on the individual body as on the entire "Chinese *minzu*," or what he alternately called the *guozu*, "nation-race." Using his customarily self-conscious "scientific" approach, he argued that only through programs that promoted fitness of this nation-race as a whole could the technological progress essential for national power be achieved:

> Take, for example, a truck that can haul a load of one thousand or even ten thousand pounds. Of course the strength of one person will not be able to move it, and perhaps the strength of a hundred or even a thousand people might not be able to move it. But one small engine can move it and get it going. Thus, we can see that making the individual still bigger and stronger will be of no use at all.[109]

Similarly, in explaining the political implications of his program for a *tiyu* revolution, Liu recalled Sun Yat-sen's 1924 words on the importance of "corporate," or institutional, and not individual freedom in the success of the Nationalist revolution.[110] Liu stated simply that the result of the revolution would be "*minzu* freedom" and not "individual freedom":

> Now on the calisthenics grounds, roll call is scattered and confused, and after roll call the students just sneak away as they wish! . . . Athletes attend lectures wearing their clogs, wander through the streets and alleys outside the school gates, and wear their clothes and caps at crooked and odd angles. . . . Isn't this the education of a doomed nation? These problems spring from the liberal "natural movement" sports *tiyu*, because people don't understand the true meaning of freedom. They confuse freedom with leisurely aimlessness, liveliness, and relaxation of any discipline. The only thing to do is to institute strict military education.[111]

Liu's visions of a fascist physical culture for China also included the need for a strong individual leader whom all could follow. He wrote in 1934, "For *tiyu* comrades to be able to truly unite with faith and dedication, and to become powerful, we still need a brilliant, able, wise, and experienced leader."[112] And for those who might question the use of the term *fascist* in describing this culture, it is worth seeing what Liu revealed as the main goal of the revolutionary national-racial sporting struggle to which he was so committed: "If our *minzu* rises up, besides shutting off the entrance of foreign control and oppression, we can also be the controllers *(tongzhizhe)* and oppressors *(yapozhe)*."[113]

THE FOREIGN FASCIST INFLUENCE ON CHINESE *TIYU*

This envy of the "oppressors" and "controllers" of the world was a defining element of the militarized *tiyu* vision. Liu Shenzhan explained how *bushidō*, the way of the warrior, was the key link between physical culture and the Japanese national-racial spirit, as was the "iron-blooded spirit" for the Germans. He concluded that China needed to develop through physical culture a "martial spirit, a moral spirit of devotion, duty, respect and trust, propriety, justice, honesty, and shame," embodied by the knight-errant tradition in China's past.[114]

Liu and others made clear associations between the recent industrial and national successes of the German, Japanese, and Italian nation-races and their success in tuning modern physical education programs to unique racial qualities summoned up from their national pasts. The key to this success was revealed as an understanding of the true *guoqing* (national condition) of one's country. Most dictionaries gloss the character *qing* as pertaining to the fleeting or ephemeral—situation, condition, sentiment. But this is not how the term *guoqing* (national condition) was understood or used in the 1930s discourse of a *minzu*-centric physical culture. The *guoqing* was the unconditional, essentialist nature of the nation that, if packaged in *tiyu* and distributed to the masses, would provide successes like those of the Yamato or Teutonic races.

In 1935, Liu, then serving as the *tiyu* inspector of Sichuan Province, cited his knowledge of German philosophy in describing how an understanding of the *guoqing* would make possible the creation of a new physical culture: "What I call for is the creation of an entirely new *tiyu*. New physical culturists must create a single unified body of the Chinese citizenry, where all citizens making up this body understand the same goals—of saving the nation and revitalizing the nation-race—in their hearts and minds."[115] Indeed, the German devotion to the national physical culture enterprise through even the most adverse circumstances was much admired in the Chinese *tiyu* world of the 1930s. Cheng Dengke, writing on the German use of concepts of race and nation strengthening in elementary school physical education, wrote, "From the circumstances shared by China and Germany, which have both been oppressed by the powers and their treaties, and whose economies are in straitened condition, we especially know the importance of elementary school physical education."[116] The Nazis, for all their sporting conquests, disgusted many Chinese with their racial supremacism and their reign of terror inside and outside Germany. However, the dozens of articles published in China on German physical culture by German-educated *tiyu* planners like Cheng still allowed this model to achieve great currency throughout the Chinese *tiyu* community.

There was also great admiration for Mussolini and the recent Italian advances in fascist physical culture. For example, one popular publication featured four photos of "Mussolini's sporting life," portraying Il Duce fencing, doing farm labor, riding a horse, and riding a motorcycle, the author opining that "a politician should do his utmost to serve as a great example in order to make strong and fit persons of his citizens."[117] The journal *Chinese Architecture* went out of its way to feature pictures of Rome's new Mussolini Stadium, praising its design, budget, and utility.[118]

Japanese *taiiku* was once again seen as a model with great bearing on the future of Chinese *tiyu*. With the 1910s ascendance of the Anglo-American model of sports *tiyu*, the Japanese model had been relegated to the sidelines. In the 1920s *tiyu* activists and educators maintained a connection with Japan mostly in the realm of high-level competitive sports—the biennial Far Eastern Championship Games or private team tours of Japan. In the 1930s, however, Japan's national, industrial, and military successes were seen as self-evidently related to their recent international sporting triumphs.[119] This again made the Japanese *taiiku* model very appealing, even if, ironically, the Chinese would appropriate it as part of their defense against the Japanese enemy. Chu Minyi explained, in a preface to the Chinese translation of a Japanese-language *Physical Education and Anatomy,* how Japan's strength as a nation was due to its *bushidō* tradition, the spirit of the "Yamato soul," and their recent achievements in science. Chu, clearly placing his hopes for China in essentialist pan-Asian regionalism, saw that these preconditions for national strength were within the reach of a China sharing so many traditions with its Japanese "friends" *(bibang).*[120]

All facets of the Japanese physical culture enterprise were cited as examples for Chinese *tiyu* promoters to follow. One author praised Japanese media conglomerates for their sponsorship of large competitions and tournaments.[121] An elementary school *tiyu* instructor from Linchuan County, Jiangxi, praised Japan's "3M-ism" (Man, Money, Munitions) plan for national defense and patronizingly explained, "The Japanese understand fully the implications of the short stature of the Yamato race, and this is the reason for their special emphasis on *tiyu.*"[122] In 1936, the *tiyu* expert Ruan Weicun wrote an article using tables and graphs to trace the evolution of Japanese physiques since the Meiji era, concluding, "[T]he stones from their mountain can be used [by us] to mine jade."[123] Zhou Weizhuo, P.E. director of the Hebei Provincial Zhengding High School, led a group of eight Beiping Normal University students on a *tiyu* inspection tour to Japan in 1935. There they met with several physical education experts and toured dozens of physical education schools and facilities.[124]

Not every Chinese physical educator was as enthralled with Japan. Anhui elementary *tiyu* instructor Yu Zizhen in 1932 outlined an "Anti-Japan Expressive Calisthenics" performed to the song "Stab at Japan," the first verse of which went,

> Comrades, take your guns and swords,
> Prepare them well, prepare them well.
> Stab at Japan, stab at Japan,
> Smash and destroy the den of the dwarf slaves.
> Capture the Japanese, get them alive,
> And kill the thieves down to the last dog.
> Don't fear the dwarf slaves, as proud and arrogant as they may be,
> Don't fear the dwarf slaves, as proud and arrogant as they may be.[125]

Hu Tong, a like-minded instructor at Dongtanxiang Elementary School in Nanchang, Jiangxi, designed ten "patriotic games," the main theme of which was armed anti-Japanese resistance. Hu hoped that these games could allow students "to keep [this resistance] firmly in mind, by combining recreation with the stimulation of the children's determination to wipe away the shame and save the nation." Games like "Defeat Japan," "Boycott Japanese Goods," "Root out the Traitor," and "The People of Shanghai Flee Calamity" allowed Hu's students, by throwing balls and swinging sticks, to act out and come to share their teacher's generation's dreams of repelling the Japanese imperialists.[126] But despite these aspirations, the Japanese example of creating a strong nation-race through scientific and thorough physical training, like that of the Germans and the Italians, was seen as extremely relevant to the workings of the Chinese *tiyu* community.

IMPLEMENTING THE MILITARIZATION OF CHINESE PHYSICAL CULTURE

Militarized physical culture *(junshi tiyu)* arrived at the forefront of national *tiyu* debate during the early 1930s, due to an intense wave of Japanese imperialist activity from 1931 to 1933, the presence of a new qualified and committed cadre of fascist-leaning *tiyu* experts, and the Guomindang's further consolidation of national rule. This category of *tiyu*, narrow as it might seem, included many different visions of the connections between war, military necessity, and modern physical culture. Yet all the programs for a militarized *tiyu* shared a similar goal—a unifying Han martial spirit that could protect the borders of the nation-race.

In China in the 1930s, it was never too soon to begin physically training children for the inevitable prospects of war. In a piece on German elementary school physical education, Cheng Dengke concluded that "the foundations of strengthening the nation and strengthening the race, guarding against humiliation and wiping away the nation's shame, have to be laid in elementary education."[127] Chen Kuisheng, P.E. director at the Hunan Provincial First Normal School, wrote in 1933 that in this era China needed an elementary school physical education curriculum that was "completely militarized (wuhua)," incorporating all the movements that would be needed in time of war—running, jumping, climbing, throwing, wrestling, swimming, policing, and scouting.[128]

Adults were not exempt from militarized tiyu training. In December 1934, the Executive Yuan approved a plan for "The Use of Military and Police Force to Assist in Mass Physical Culture Programs to Tiyu-ize the People." Under this program, all citizens would be divided into groups by age (fifteen to twenty-four years old, twenty-five to thirty-four, thirty-five and up) and once a week would receive training for two hours in one or more of the following: martial arts, calisthenics for health (jianshencao), basketball, volleyball, target practice, and gymnastics. Besides tiyu-izing the people and working toward Sun Yat-sen's goal of a military power of the masses, this program would allow the public to "connect emotionally" (ganqing lianluo) with the military personnel who enforced this mandatory sport.[129] These fascist state-run tiyu programs were implemented as part of the New Life Movement in Jiangxi Province, where the CCP posed a grave threat to Guomindang rule. By 1934, a one-year Citizen Training program had been instituted in Nanchang, with mandatory weekly participation for one individual from each of the provincial capital's 51,105 households.[130] Pictures in Sweat and Blood Monthly from the Yaohua Tiyu Experimental Center show adults in military uniforms, scholarly gowns, and padded work clothes all participating in mass morning calisthenics.[131]

Another genre of militarized tiyu consisted of military-themed variations on the standard Anglo-American sports model. For example, in 1936, the Jiangxi Province Party-Government-Military-Scholastic Tiyu Promotion Society[132] proudly unveiled its new "fully armed pentathlon" (wuzhuang wu xiang yundong). This new event, using standard track and field scoring methods, consisted of five events—two-hundred-meter dash, long jump, 175-meter obstacle course, grenade throwing, and 3.5-kilometer run—all performed while in full military uniform and strapped with a rifle and bayonet, 120 bullets, and two grenades![133] This new pentathlon would have pleased critic Edward Y. K. Kwong, who in 1936 called competitive sports a "purposeless and often useless luxury" and wrote:

If it is expected that the new system of sports will train men to be at the same time sportsmen and soldiers, then the only sensible thing is to include in the list of sporting events items found in military training. Now military education includes training for discipline, intelligence, endurance, mobility (especially in mass formation) and the art of killing. All these things can be learned in the sport or athletic field.[134]

Representatives of the Eighteenth Army weighed in with their own suggestions for activities that brought the fun of team sports to the art of killing, publishing detailed rules for military *tiyu* competitions in stealth movement, fencing, grenade throwing, footraces, and target shooting.[135] And in 1937, an author from the Guangzhou Branch of the Central Military Institute published the rules of a game called *"military-ball" (junshiqiu)*, a combination of basketball, rugby, and American football that was easy and economical to teach and could "cultivate military virtues of courage, agility, activity, and cooperation."[136]

The area of most contention over militarizing *tiyu* was that of physical education for middle school and university students. This endeavor was led by that dedicated student of German youth training, Cheng Dengke, whose trademark terse prose, always punctuated with extremely detailed lists, tables, and charts, could be found in virtually every journal in Chinese educational publishing. Cheng wrote that Chinese youth were "the treasures of the nation, the lifeline of the *minzu*," and saw their militarized *tiyu* training as essential in this age of struggle. He wrote often on youth training in other nations, describing to Chinese readers the utility of training designed by the British and American Boy Scouts, Hitler Youth in Germany, French labor service organizations, the Italian Balila, and the Soviet Young Pioneers.[137] His conclusion was that the Chinese youth training should be a mixture of four components: (1) competitive sports, which would breed organization, bravery, and a sense of dealing with the enemy; (2) Boy Scout training, which would provide education in military, citizenship, and party affairs; (3) military training; and (4) political training to cultivate in Chinese youth a spirit like that of the Ottoman "iron-blood-ism" or Japanese *bushidō*.[138] This four-pronged plan designed by Cheng, incorporating the seemingly opposed philosophies of Anglo-American team sports and fascist-style political and martial training, soon became the standard form for militarized *tiyu* training for the youth of China.

In one of his most important articles, Cheng prefaced his discussion of militarized *tiyu* training by tracing the "true *tiyu* spirit" of the Chinese nation through time. He began with prehistoric figures like the Yellow Emperor (who discovered archery in the year 2697 B.C.E.) and his sometimes-

TABLE 6. Cheng Dengke's 1936 Program
for Militarized Physical Education

Basic Training	Advanced Training
Martial arts	Footraces and swimming in full military gear
Calisthenics	Jumping over ditches
Gymnastics	Hauling ammunition
Militarized ball sports	Target shooting
Wrestling	Hand grenade throwing
Weightlifting	Gymnastics
Mat exercises	Mat exercise
Boxing	Obstacle course
Track & field	Ball sports and martial arts
Swimming	Bicycling
Target shooting	Map reading
Singing	Surveying
	Equestrian training
	Applied surveying and statistics
	Rowing

archenemy Chi You, lord of warfare, and continued through heroic, dynastic, "antibarbarian" warriors like the Song dynasty martyr Yue Fei and the Ming general Shi Kefa.[139] It would not be enough, as some advised, to merely "strengthen the body to save the nation *(jianshen jiuguo)*"; Cheng also hoped that a militarized *tiyu* training could "produce a single entity from military training and *tiyu* . . . [and] teach students to see the sports field as a playground and as a battlefield" (Table 6).[140]

Militarized *tiyu* training had been implemented in many areas of China by the time full-scale war broke out in 1937. In 1933, the central government passed a regulation requiring each school to register its military training curriculum with local military authorities and to invite military authorities to inspect its student troops monthly.[141] A 1937 issue of the *Educational Review* included pictures of two youth training centers. Students in the Provincial Chuzhou Junior High School Youth League (Zhejiang) took part in archery, marching band, bicycling, anti–poison gas training, target shooting, and wrestling. Students in the "Emergency Period Physical Training" program at the Provincial Nanchang First Middle School trained in archery, rope and wall climbing, and weightlifting (using large rocks).[142] In 1933, the Provincial Education Department in remote Qinghai sponsored a "Summer Military Training Camp," where hundreds of students trained in Boy Scout and calisthenics drills.[143]

Many of China's universities had provided military training since the early 1930s. At National Qingdao University in 1931, of sixty-two mandatory credits, eight were in *tiyu* class and six were in military training *(junxun)*.[144] In 1935, the Henan Provincial University student body was organized into a Henan Provincial University Military Training Squad with three levels of command. Military-style orders or commands were used all day long at the university to mark the beginning and end of classes, study hall, and rest periods, "in order to militarize student life and discipline [students'] actions and movements." This military discipline included mandatory calisthenics every morning at 6:35. Physical inspections *(tige jiancha)* were held twice a year, and the university reserved the right to expel any students with "malignant diseases."[145] And in 1936, of Guangxi University's fifty-two faculty members, seven were military training instructors, with fifteen of eighty-one "life snapshots" in the school yearbook dedicated to students' military training.[146]

With the growing realization that a war would have to be fought soon against the ever-encroaching Japanese imperialists, it is easy to understand how militarized *tiyu* training won such currency in China. However, many in the *tiyu* world still saw great drawbacks to these militaristic models and were unabashed in their appreciation of Western bourgeois and cosmopolitan sporting traditions. One of the first challenges to Cheng Dengke and militarized *tiyu* came in 1935 from Central University P.E. Professor Fang Wanbang. Fang, a native of Minhou County, Fujian, graduated from the Beijing Normal University P.E. Department in 1919 at age twenty-six. After teaching for several years in Taiyuan, Shenyang, Changsha, Fuzhou, and Xiamen, Fang began graduate study in physical education at Columbia University.[147] After returning to China in the early 1930s, his Columbia master's degree and the publication of his 271-page *Principles of Physical Education*[148] instantly made him a major figure in the national *tiyu* community.

Fang's critique came within the context of his discussion, published in the *Educational Review,* of the ten greatest problems facing the Chinese *tiyu* community at the time. In the article, he used ideas, probably absorbed at Columbia, to explain how a *tiyu* curriculum should allow youth to experiment, be socialized, and pick up lessons about life in general. He opposed the militarization of *tiyu* because the scientific nature of modern warfare made skills learned in military-style *tiyu* training obsolete and because the true goals of physical education were the health of the individual and the revival of the nation-race, not military strength.[149]

This challenge to militaristic *tiyu* produced a nine-page rebuttal by Cheng Dengke in the pages of *Physical Education Quarterly*. In a polite but forceful piece, Cheng described how the militarization of *tiyu* was simply necessary for a China "riddled with so many hundreds of holes and so many thousands of sores, it is hard to know where to begin treatment." Cheng covered all his bases, justifying the militaristic *tiyu* program by briefly describing similar preparations in eighteen European nations but also reminding readers that the inherently *(guyou)* Chinese physical culture rather than European-American sports (often unsuitable to the Chinese context) should serve as the basis of *tiyu* programs in China.[150]

Despite Cheng's attempt to nip this debate in the bud, Fang's critique of militarized *tiyu* emboldened other *tiyu* activists to question the militaristic position. Zhang Jiwu of Nankai University wrote on the Cheng-Fang debate, siding with Cheng by citing Columbia's W. L. Nash: "Do not bow to authoritarianism, do not worship military force and narrow patriotism."[151] Lin Liru, writing in the *Educational Review*, expressed his doubts about the militarized program and its "superstitious faith in strict training," pointing out that "militarized physical culture" by its very nature was un-*tiyu (fei tiyu)* and counter to the principles of *tiyu (fan tiyu)*.[152] Wu Yunrui, educated in anatomy and physiology at the University of Chicago and in physical education at Columbia University,[153] contributed a piece on this question to the *Physical Education Quarterly* in 1937. Wu stressed the psychological uses of physical education in training the individual to be "a good element *(lianghao fenzi)* in society" and opposed the teaching of "autocratic" "military training that only upholds imperialism and the plundering of others' land."[154]

In this debate, perhaps the most ironic contribution came from Liu Xuesong, a native of Bishan County, Sichuan. Liu first studied physical education at the West China Union University in Chengdu in the early 1920s. He was a varsity standout in soccer and track and field but never emerged from the shadow of the school's most famous athlete, dentistry major Cheng Dengke. For decades, Cheng's and Liu's *tiyu* careers would parallel each other in telling ways. Cheng was offered a scholarship to study physical education at Springfield College in Massachusetts, but he refused it and in 1920 tested into the Southeastern University P.E. Department in Nanjing.[155] Liu left Chengdu soon after Cheng, receiving a YMCA scholarship to study at Soochow University.[156] Cheng graduated from Southeastern in 1925 and taught physical education at Shanghai's East Asia P.E. School and Patriotic Girls' School before leaving for Berlin in 1929. Liu graduated from Soochow in 1927 and taught at the YMCA-run Qingxin Girls' Middle School in Shanghai before leaving for the United States, courtesy of a YMCA scholarship, in 1929. In 1933, the same year that Cheng returned from Berlin, Snowpine Liu (his English name a direct translation of the Chinese) returned to China with master's degrees in P.E. and general education from Springfield College and the University of Southern California.

Liu was never as proficient a physical education activist as Cheng, but in this debate on militarized *tiyu* there was little doubt where he stood. In the same issue of *Physical Education Quarterly* as the Wu Yunrui article above, Liu also opposed the Cheng plan to "unite" the traditions of sports, Boy Scout paramilitary training, and martial arts. He allowed that all three disciplines were meant to train the body-mind *(shenxin)* but found their methods of training, administration, and organization so dissimilar as to make the effort utterly impractical. Finally, Liu doubted that martial arts, which had always been practiced for personal self-defense, could be meaningfully combined with *tiyu*, "the finest tool for training human socialization *(qunxing)*."[157]

These exchanges, known as the "*yang-tu* (foreign vs. Chinese) debate," opposing the uses of Western-style sports *tiyu* to those of traditional Chinese martial arts, illustrated clearly the divisions in the *tiyu* community of the time. On one side were the German-trained and Guomindang faithful, like Cheng Dengke, Liu Shenzhan, and Wu Cheng, who saw hope for China in the order and discipline of the Nazi youth training regimen and transformed what were once progressive ideas of a "mass *tiyu*" into the terms of a ruthless sporting militarism. For these specialists, the terrifying rise of Germany in the 1930s only proved physical culture's utility to a Chinese nation-race in recovering and fine-tuning the national essence. On the other side were the American-educated P.E. specialists like Fang Wanbang, Wu Yunrui, and Liu Xuesong, who, in times of national crisis, saw more value in "scientific" or "democratic" models of a strong nation based on strong and self-disciplining individual citizens. For them, *tiyu* remained the "body cultivation" of its origins, providing a spectrum of psychological and socializing influences on youth of any nationality. *Tiyu* was thus a crucial site where concerned Chinese of all political backgrounds could contest meanings of a modern Chinese nation.

CONCLUSION

During the Nanjing Decade, debates like those surrounding *tiyu* marked other social and political realms, as Chinese writers, artists, educators, and progressive political figures attempted to present more liberal models of the society and nation that questioned the totalizing "New Life" visions propagated by the Guomindang state. Although many of these movements were brutally suppressed, the liberals of the *tiyu* world enjoyed a unique space from which they could criticize official fascist models: the power of the Olympic movement and the prestige of its international ideals of teamwork, fair play, and free competition demanded that Chinese *tiyu* experts defending Chinese participation in "Western" forms of sport be taken seriously. Chapter 6 describes the competitive sports movement that became the most powerful expression of these cosmopolitan sporting objectives.

PLATE 1. Organizers of the Pure Martial Athletic Association (Jingwu tiyuhui), 1920. Chen Tiesheng is seated on the right, Yao Chanbo is on his side on the right, Chen Gongzhe is standing on the right, and Lu Weichang is standing on the left. Chen Tiesheng, ed., *Jingwu benji*, 57.

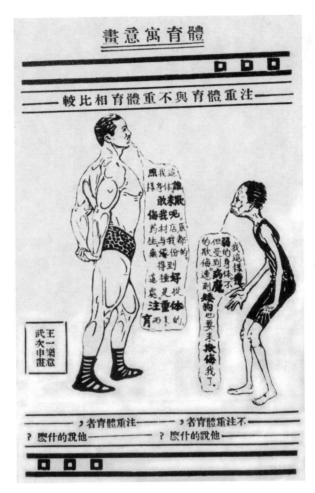

PLATE 2. "The Moral of Physical Culture: A Comparison of Emphasizing and Ignoring Physical Culture," illustration inside the front cover of Wang Huaiqi's 1929 book *National Humiliation Commemorative Calisthenics*. The decrepit man on the right, whose words are written vertically (in the traditional style), says, "Not only does a weak body like mine suffer the humiliating curse of disease, but I am bullied by the [Japanese] dwarfs." The musclebound superman on the left, whose words are written left to right in the modern convention, replies, "With a body like mine, who would dare to try to push me around?" Wang Huaiqi, *Guochi jinian ticao*.

PLATE 3.   Zhang Suhui (from Shandong), champion eighty-meter hurdler at the Fifteenth North China Games, Ji'nan, 1931. *Di shiwu jie Huabei yundonghui.*

PLATE 4.   The Beiping women's four-hundred-meter relay team at the Fifteenth North China Games, Ji'nan, 1931. *Di shiwu jie Huabei yundonghui.*

射

箭

PLATE 5.   Female and male champions of the 1933 Qingdao Municipal Archery Competition. Qingdao shi tiyu xiejinhui, eds., *Liang zhounian gongzuo zongbaogao.*

PLATE 6.   Olympic pole vaulter Fu Baolu, here competing for Shanghai at the Fifth National Games in Nanjing, 1933. Fu was later killed while flying with Claire Chennault's Flying Tigers during the Anti-Japanese War. Ershier nian Quanguo yundong dahui choubei weiyuanhui, *Ershier nian Quanguo yundong dahui zongbaogao shu.*

PLATE 7.   National champion sprinter Sun Guiyun (from Harbin), pictured in the "Sweaters" section of the *National Athletic Meet Special 1933. Minguo ershier nian Quanguo yundonghui zhuankan.*

PLATE 8. Yang Xiuqiong ("The Beautiful Mermaid," at far left) and the Chinese women's swimming team, Tenth Far Eastern Championship Games, 1934. *Renyan zhoukan* 16 (26 May 1934), front cover.

PLATE 9. Swimmer Yang Xiuqiong, Li Sen ("The Sprinting Queen," from Hunan), and officials from the 1936 Chinese Olympic delegation. *Chuxi Di shiyi jie Shijie yundonghui,* third page of photos.

PLATE 10. Members of the 1936 Chinese Olympic men's track and field, swimming, racewalking, and cycling teams. (Fu Baolu is on the far right in the front
row, Liu Changchun is third from the right in the middle row, Dr. Ma Yuehan
is seated third from the left in the middle row, and Howard Wing is standing
on the far left.) *Chuxi Di shiyi jie Shijie yundonghui,* sixth page of photos.

PLATE 11. The Chinese Olympic delegation leaves the Berlin train station after
their arrival on 23 July 1936. *Chuxi Di shiyi jie Shijie yundonghui,* Section 1, 25.

PLATE 12.   1936 Olympic sprinters Jesse Owens and Cheng Jinguan, training
in Berlin, July 1936. Photo courtesy of Cheng Jinguan.

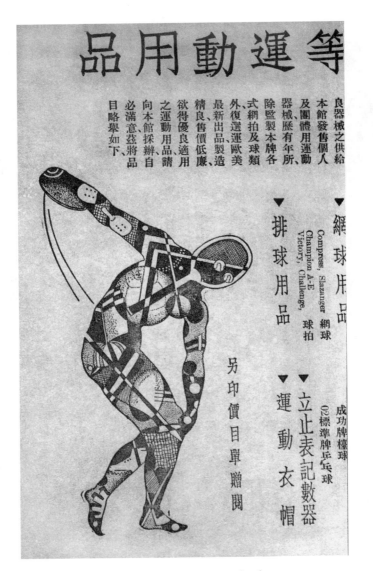

PLATE 13. Commercial Press sporting goods advertisement, 1937.

6   Elite Competitive Sport in the 1930s

China has never produced an earthshaking scientist or author or explorer . . . not even a talented athlete for the Olympics! When you think about it, how could anyone respect us?

LAO SHE, *Ma and Son* (1935)

This agonized outcry, voiced in novelist Lao She's chronicle of British scorn for China and its degraded manhood, reveals much about the authority that the international Olympic movement—and its power to classify the general worth of any nation on earth—carried among the urban Chinese population. During the 1930s, many in China's physical culture community worked to distinguish an elite sphere of competitive sports from the mass *tiyu* mission described earlier, marking it as a form of physical culture less accessible to the masses, requiring time and capital not available to any but the most privileged. Yet the power of the Olympic movement, and its promise as a site for exhibiting the true face and physique of modern China, ensured competitive sport's continued relevance in the contentious world of *tiyu*. Even the most vociferous critic of elite sport had to admit that only success in the visible realm of competitive sport could ultimately produce the images of a strong and healthy China that belonged in the world of respected modern nations.

It was difficult to draw a sharp line between mass and elite or productive and consumptive sports, as these two realms intersected over many different areas. The national quality of high-level competitive sports depended on the presence of a large crowd representing the "masses" in whose name these spectacles were produced. Modern sport's very premise was the familiar myth that any athlete, starting on the hardwood floors of Shanghai's finest gyms, or on ramshackle athletic grounds in backward Guizhou, could achieve success with enough skill and effort. In fact, the relationship between mass and elite modes actually represented a feedback system in which only the interest and participation of the "masses" could validate competitive sports, and successes of "elite" athletes and teams were necessary to shape mass *tiyu* efforts.

The realm of international competition and glory was the factor that allowed competitive sports, criticized throughout the 1930s as "trophy-ism" and "moneybag sports," to maintain their status as a crucial aspect of Chinese physical culture under the revolutionary Nationalist regime. While high-level competitive sports were an option for only a small minority of China's population, these endeavors clearly had more potential to win the respect of the world's powers than did a "fully armed two-hundred-meter dash" competition or any of the other mass *tiyu* programs so fashionable in the 1930s.

This chapter follows the trajectory of elite-level competitive sporting events, not in absolutely chronological fashion, but in order of scale, visibility, and imagined value to the sporting Chinese nation. I begin with provincial-level and regional meets held in locales from the cosmopolitan Lower Yangtze, to the Jiangxi-Hunan-Guangdong border region, to far Dihua during the 1930s. Next I discuss the venue in which only the finest regional and provincial athletes could hope to compete—the National Games projects of 1931, 1933, and 1935. Competitors who excelled at this national level could expect to be honored by selection to China's delegation to the Far Eastern Championship Games; I describe here the events of the games of 1930 and 1934. The last section of this chapter is devoted to the greatest privilege for any of these athletes—to represent China in the Olympic Games, a tradition begun at Los Angeles in 1932 and continued in Berlin in 1936.

THE WINDS OF SPORT: PROVINCIAL AND REGIONAL MEETS

> Guizhou . . . [as] a feudal tribe *(fengjian buluo)* has no real politics
> to speak of. . . . Under these conditions, no one cares if this tribe
> has any sort of duty to perform for the nation and race. Fortu-
> nately, today our chance to rise from the dead and come back to
> life has begun to take shape.
>
> "Quanyun bimu zhi ci," [On the closing of the Provincial Games],
> *Guizhou Morning Post* (1935)

The 1930s saw the institutionalization of the provincial-level athletic meet all over China. Although several Chinese provinces put on large provincial meets in the early years of the Republic and even the late Qing, this institution was standardized during the 1930s as provincial meets became more subject to national schedules, norms, and agendas.

Province-level meets of the 1930s also heralded a new level of inclusion of the Chinese people in the national enterprise of competitive sport. Meets became larger in scope. Women's events were now included, and meets attracted teams from farther reaches of the provinces than ever before. Perhaps most significantly, by the mid-1930s many provincial meets were now theoretically extended beyond student-athletes to "average citizens" as teams were drawn up to represent counties and cities rather than schools of that province.

Zhejiang held its third provincial meet in Hangzhou in 1930, featuring 518 male and female athletes on forty-nine municipal and school teams competing in track and field, soccer, basketball, volleyball, and tennis. Promoters of the meet were sufficiently impressed with the modern, inclusive nature of these games to bill them as the "First Zhejiang Provincial Games," officially erasing the significance of two earlier efforts sponsored by previous regimes.[1] Jiangsu's 1930 provincial meet was likewise labeled the "First Jiangsu Provincial Games," marking the meet as an altogether different enterprise from the six provincial meets held between 1914 and 1921.[2] The Guizhou Games of 1935, seen as such a great step for that province, were not its first meet either. But the two provincial meets held in 1927 and 1928 during the reign of warlord Zhou Xicheng, a time when the "winds of sport had not yet blown over the entire province,"[3] were now dismissed as being "who knows how many thousands of miles away from the true meaning of the athletic meet."[4]

The 1930s saw the spread of this institution to other poor inland provinces where the state and capitalist structures necessary to the spread of the modern *tiyu* were being put into place. In 1931 Chahar Province, today part of Inner Mongolia, held a small-scale Provincial Games at the new Provincial Athletic Grounds at Zhangjiakou. Three years later, Chahar held its 1934 High School Autumn Games at these same grounds featuring 182 athletes, 133 male and 49 female, from nine schools in the greater capital region. In addition to these student contests, track and field competitions were held in a "Society Division," which included athletes from the Twenty-Ninth Army, the Provincial Construction Department, and the Lower Garden Train Station.[5] The meet's Publicity Section produced eighteen slogans emphasizing a new mass *tiyu* orientation, including:

"Our citizens' lack of vigor and fitness is an omen heralding the extinction of the nation-race!"

"Only by advocating *tiyu* can we carefully root out the old customs of weakness!"

"To achieve male-female equality, we must first make men's and women's *tiyu* equal!"[6]

The same autumn, the Guomindang held a Southern Jiangxi Military-Citizenry United Athletic Meet in Dayu in the Jiangxi-Hunan-Guangdong border region, just to the southwest of the Jiangxi Provincial Soviet Government. The timing of the meet was notable: it was held in October 1934, just following the Jiangxi climax of Chiang Kai-shek's successful fifth Communist extermination campaign. This celebratory meet brought together 370 civilian athletes from six southern Jiangxi counties and 554 soldier-athletes from seven different divisions and brigades stationed there. Meet planners hoped that the sporting engagement would "allow the military and the citizenry to be together forever . . . forever united under a single cause—completing our present tasks of reconstruction and exterminating the [Communist] bandits."[7]

The meet featured a spectacular demonstration by famed strongman Tan Wenbiao and the South Asia Acrobatic Squad, whose feats were captured in photographs published in the official meet report. In one scene, one performer rides a bicycle over another's stomach. Another picture shows shirtless strongman Tan using his teeth to pull an automobile with four performers standing on its sideboards. And in the most breathtaking of all the demonstrations, the same auto, weighted down even more by the four acrobats, drives over a wooden ramp balancing only on Tan's torso. Tan and his squad seem truly to have earned the large banner reading "Extraordinary, Unlike Any Other" *(chulei bacui)* presented to them by Yu Hanmou, meet chairman and commanding officer of the First Guangdong Army.[8]

The spectacle provided by these demonstrations and the skillful planning of the other competitions, provided by a team of twenty-four *tiyu* experts from Guangdong Province, could hardly hide the fact that these Southern Jiangxi Games, like many other provincial-level athletic meets, were designed with explicitly political meanings in mind. Chen Jitang, a Guangdong warlord and co-honorary chairman of the Southern Jiangxi Games, explained his views of the importance of physical culture: "Today we must use bloody warfare and hand-to-hand combat to resist humiliation at the hands of the foreigners, while using material and spiritual force to wipe out the bandit scourge *(suqing feihuo)*. If we do not have strong and healthy physiques and a firm and resolute spirit, then I ask, how will we be able to carry out our responsibilities to save the nation?"[9] These Southern Jiangxi Games were clearly part of the Guomindang's Communist extermination campaign, which Chiang Kai-shek described as "70 percent politics plus 30 percent military affairs." *Tiyu*, featured in the anti-Communist New Cultural Movement promoted in Jiangxi, could be applied in both of these domains.[10] The Guomindang elites considered the Nationalist spectacle of the games invaluable for their cause—no other provincial-level meet was blessed with championship prizes donated by the likes of Chiang Kai-shek and the Central Executive Committee member Hu Hanmin, who both sent large silver *ding* cauldrons, and the Central Military Commission member Li Zongren, who sent a hand-painted scroll to Dayu.[11]

Other provincial meets were also part of the general program of consolidating a Pax Guomindang in areas rocked by rebellion and unrest. Months after Chiang's fifth Communist suppression campaign was extended into Guizhou, the Guizhou Games were held in this bandit-infested land. Provincial Chairman Wu Zhongxin was praised for his decision to hold the meet and "bestow rest and recreation on the people, as we handle the remnants of the bandits' uprisings."[12] Shortly afterward, a hastily arranged Yunnan Provincial Games was held simultaneously in Kunming and ten other cities throughout the province on 25 December 1935. The official reason given for the meet was to commemorate the twentieth anniversary of the 1915 Yunnan Uprising (*Huguo yundong*) against Yuan Shikai, but the recent extension of Chiang's fifth suppression campaign into Yunnan was a more likely reason.[13] Hung-Mao Tien has described how Guomindang anti-Communist campaigns allowed for the extension of Nanjing-designed administrative reforms, political education programs, and plans for interprovincial cooperation into "Bandit Suppression Zones."[14] The same is true of physical culture, as the extension of the central state into these provinces had great implications for the modernizing and nationalizing realm of *tiyu*.

The staging of athletic events was also employed in Guomindang campaigns against northern warlords. Months after Feng Yuxiang's failed rebellion in Chahar, Provincial Chairman Song Zheyuan was hailed as a visionary for holding that province's 1934 meet:

> Our Chahar is a land on the far frontier, and our provincial government was established later than others. In the field of physical culture, everyone has waited for someone else to begin planning. Now Chairman Song has taken charge of the administration of this land, working to address the accumulated ravages of warlords and their troops. [These games are] an act of government to bestow rest and recreation on the people, as we work to look after and allow people rest from their hardships.[15]

Chahar's participation in national affairs like *tiyu* under Song's rule reflects the extent to which this warlord was willing to submit to Nanjing authority, especially after Chiang Kai-shek's courting and financial subsidizing of his loyalty.[16]

Besides explicit political motivations for engaging provincial populations in the participation and consumption of competitive sports, there were more *tiyu*-specific factors behind the planning of province-level meets. By the 1930s, these competitions were almost always held shortly before National Games, functioning as selection meets for the national contest. For example, at the Guizhou Games on 7–9 September 1935, eight men out of 343 participants were selected to represent Guizhou at the National Games scheduled to begin on 10 October.[17] That same week, besides other provincial meets held in Fujian and Jiangsu, Xinjiang held its first Provincial Games on 9 September at the Anti-Imperialist Military School in Dihua (Urumqi). Nearly one thousand students participated in these games, and eleven of them were selected to take part in track and field, swimming, and *guoshu* events at the National Games the next month.[18]

Athletes from all over the nation could take pride in the knowledge that even in the most distant corners of the nation their fellow Chinese athletes were engaging in the same strenuous sporting endeavors. Indeed, they were going through the same motions, for provincial games across the nation consisted of the same exact set of men's and women's competitions—track and field, volleyball, basketball, martial arts, tennis, baseball/softball, swimming, and soccer—as the official set of competitions of the National Games, that all-important center around which the universe of Chinese *tiyu* now revolved.

By the 1930s, the provincial meets were one of the main points of intersection between the realms of mass *tiyu* and high-level competitive sport. Too inclusive to provide the greatest thrills of elite competition, and too reliant on exclusive bourgeois forms to be truly popular, they still were an arena where athletic competitions had real correlations with the health and fitness of local populations. Provincial meets addressed local concerns and particularities while still remaining relevant to national and nation-building enterprises in ways that no other types of competition could. Even the choice of honorary meet chairman, nearly always the chairman of that provincial government, accomplished this end. Each of these figures brought to the meets prestige owing to his association with national political movements but probably hoped to profit in specifically local arenas from his sponsorship of the games. Most provincial meets received little national publicity but played an important role in supporting the national system of competitive sport in the 1930s.

For the provinces that did not hold provincial games, this level of competition was replaced by regional meets such as the North China Games, Northwest Games, and Central China Games. The largest of these was the North China Games (Huabei yundonghui), convened eighteen times between 1913 and 1934. Whereas the first fourteen Huabei Games (1913–29) were run by YMCA organizations and warlord governments, and participation was restricted to student teams, the last four (1931–34) were held in ways that symbolized the importance of North China in Nationalist affairs.[19] For many northerners, these games took the place of the provincial meets in representing and creating specifically "northern" sentiments and needs within the national enterprise of physical culture.

The first highly publicized North China meet was the Fourteenth Games, held in Shenyang in 1929, in a spectacular thirty-thousand-seat stadium built on the Northeastern University campus by the militarist sports enthusiast and new Guomindang team player Zhang Xueliang. Zhang was already well-known for his patronage of sport,[20] but he further thrilled all present by personally entering the long jump competition at the North China Games.[21]

It was also at the Fourteenth Games that a young Dong Hanwen, then a star player on the Northeastern University High School soccer team, fell in love with the glory and the beauty of track and field. Sitting in the living room of his longtime friend Li Shiming's Taipei rest home apartment in June 1996, Dong remembered attending this meet with a group of curious fellow students. The triple gold medal performance of the Dalian sprinter Liu Changchun (including new national records in the one-hundred- and four-hundred-meter dashes) so inspired Dong and his friends that they all immediately went out and bought track spikes. He and his friends began regular training—but at night, so that no one would laugh at their irregular running forms. The famed Liu was a student at Northeastern University, but Dong did not dare to bother this national figure with his questions on track technicalities. Li, a lesser-known Northeastern student-athlete also on the Liaoning provincial team, seemed more approachable. Dong asked the elder Li to be his track mentor, beginning a sporting friendship that would last for more than seventy years.[22]

These meets also allowed northern fans to imagine and create regional ties with true national consequence. The Fifteenth Huabei Games, held in Ji'nan in May 1931 with 990 competing athletes from sixteen northern provinces and cities, featured all the trappings of a fully Nationalist enterprise. Dozens of Guomindang figures like Chiang Kai-shek, He Yingqin, and Song Ziwen sent calligraphy inscriptions to commemorate the events. The games' opening ceremonies featured the playing of the party anthem, bows to the Guomindang flag and Sun Yat-sen's portrait, the reading of Sun's last will and testament, a speech by a personal envoy sent by Chiang, the chant "Long live the North China Games! Long live the Chinese Nationalist Party!

Long live the Republic of China! Long live the Chinese nation-race!" and the swearing of an "Athlete's Oath" *(yundongyuan shici)* pledging respect to the late Sun's writings on physical culture and the rules of the meet.[23] The games clearly posed opportunities to express national concerns. One commentator saw hope in the sporting progress exhibited at Ji'nan in terms of training the "three powers"—physical power, mental power, and the power of solidarity—that were the "marrow of the nation-race."[24] A Beiping commentator writing on the Eighteenth Huabei Games, held in 1934 in Tianjin, was critical of the current status of North China *tiyu* and its monopoly in the hands of the "leisured, moneyed" *(youxian youqian)* classes; he expressed concern about the health of the larger population and China's ability to wash away the stain of the "Sick Man of East Asia" epithet.[25]

Participation in the Huabei Games also could serve as a meaningful protest against the Japanese presence in northern China. Ex-stars Dong and Li shared stories of their trip from Dalian to Tianjin to join the Eighteenth Huabei Games, which have gone down in Chinese *tiyu* history for the movingly anti-Japanese nationalist content of the opening ceremonies.[26] Dong and Li actually experienced Japanese oppression firsthand on their way to the games, for they and two teammates were arrested in Dalian and then in Shenyang. Their crime? Being standout members of the Liaoning Province track team, whose participation could only confirm and dramatize the province's martyred status. Fortunately for the four athletes and their team, Li's connections in the Japanese sports community in Liaoning were extensive enough that the athletes were able to gain release and go on to Tianjin, but the nationalist pride and scars of this experience still remain.[27]

Other regional athletic meets like the Central China Games (Huazhong yundonghui)[28] and the Northwest Games (Xibei yundonghui)[29] also gave provincial locales rare opportunities to bring together competitors from specific regions of China, asserting the vitality of local or regional athletics while addressing and conforming to national concerns and standards. Some of these meets attracted great attention, particularly the Huabei Games of the 1930s; one observer wrote, "[W]hen the 17th annual North China Athletic Meet was in progress at Tsingtao, the reported imminent outbreak of warfare in Chahar, the predicted failure of the World Economic Conference and even the scorching heat were all forgotten; and instead readers in North China, especially Tientsin and Peiping, turned their eyes to the sports pages. Papers with sport supplements sold like 'hot cakes.'"[30] The record-setting performances of superstars like Liu Changchun and Sun Guiyun, the influence of famed national figures like Zhang Xueliang and Zhang Boling, and the tremendous amounts of money spent to put on these meets[31] made the North China Games gala events significant not only to this endangered region but to the newly united Chinese nation.

THE STAR-CROSSED 1931 NATIONAL GAMES

In the 1930s, China's National Games (Quanguo yundong dahui) became the center of the ever-expanding universe of China's physical culture. These spectacles, planned as biennial events, were strange brews of celebratory nationalism, Guomindang political hype and swagger, media overkill, lavish commercialism, and tense antagonism between regional *tiyu* cliques. Starting with the fifth national meet, scheduled to begin on 10 October 1931, the *tiyu* community came to expect from this ritual drama, teamwork, and individual achievements that could fulfill the great promise their field held for a national future.

The Fourth National Games, held in Hangzhou in 1930 and described in Chapter 5, did not satisfy the Guomindang *tiyu* establishment, who knew the party had more to offer the physical culture world. Just days after the completion of the Fourth Games, a Planning Committee met to organize the 1931 National Games, to be held at Nanjing.

Chief among these plans was the decision, handed down in April 1930 by the National Affairs Conference (Guowu huiyi), to build a Central Stadium (Zhongyang tiyuchang) on some 165 acres (one thousand *mu*) in Nanjing's Purple and Gold Mountains, just four miles southeast of the new and majestic Sun Yat-sen Memorial.[32] Liping Wang has described the Guomindang's work to nationalize this large eastern suburb, transforming it into a sacred Nationalist/Sunist space. Designed to become a focal point of the capital, this new Nationalist center also was a direct spatial expression of Chiang Kai-shek's will to capture Sun's revolutionary legacy for his own use.[33] And in this competitive age, what better way to commemorate the father of the Chinese nation-state than with a grand Central Stadium, a monument to the productive promise and consumptive excesses of modern sport? Built by the Jitai Engineering Firm at an expense of 1,433,900 *yuan* (U.S.$449,000) and completed in May 1931,[34] this monument to sport, Sun Yat-sen, and Guomindang grandeur included seven separate facilities, for track and field, soccer, martial arts, swimming, baseball, basketball, tennis, and volleyball competitions, which could seat a combined total of sixty-four thousand spectators, as well as a horse-race track and a polo field. The facility even included dormitories, built under the stands, to accommodate up to 2,700 visiting athletes and coaches.[35]

Today the stadium grounds serve as the Nanjing Institute of Physical Education campus, and the stadium itself is a practice facility. Its front is now freckled with garish red and gold signs proclaiming the institute as a "Civilized Work Unit" and recognizing the stadium's status as an official Nanjing historical relic. The track stadium houses a new synthetic track, built in 1995 at a cost of one million *renminbi* (U.S.$118,000), but its grandstands are now partially blocked by large trees growing inside the stadium. Surrounding facilities built in 1931 are in various stages of decay and neglect. At the time, however, there was nothing like the Central Stadium in China or in the whole of East Asia. One architecture critic of the era wrote that stadium construction was "[t]remendous in scale, imposing in its layout, incorporating the Chinese architectural spirit while meeting the needs of the present era. It will wake up our citizenry, preserving the national essence while it transforms old into new. There is no doubt that it will carry out the new mission of Chinese architecture . . . [and] revitalize Oriental architecture."[36]

One key issue for the Games Planning Committee was the composition of an official meet anthem. In February 1931, the committee member Du Tingxiu asked the Education Department for assistance in the matter. They responded by placing an advertisement in Nanjing's *Central Daily* and Shanghai's *Republican Daily News*, asking budding songwriters to submit lyrics of sixty to one hundred words, "composed to encourage citizens' physical culture, bring out the sporting spirit, and elaborate on the significance of competition." The ad announced that a winning meet song would be selected in April, with the winning composer receiving prizes of one hundred *yuan* (U.S.$31) and some National Games souvenirs.[37] More than sixty entries came in by the deadline. Of these, the finest entries were submitted by young composers Liu Qingxu and Zhan Tianlang, whose lyrics were merged into one single anthem that went:

> How beautiful, brilliant the Games, how the warriors run and dance!
> Those who capture the trophies also win the hearts of the multitudes.
> Soldiers! Going all out, all the way, exhibiting your vitality and your strength,
> We all march forward! March on! March on!
> On this day the games are won and lost, but we must live this spirit every day.
> The dignity, the composure, the spirit and elation!
> Joy for the winners, but no regret for the defeated.
> Soldiers! Have courage and virtue, know ritual and bearing.
> Jubilation for all! Jubilation! Jubilation!
> Exalting the martial spirit, improving the health of the nation-race.[38]

Planning for these 1931 National Games continued smoothly into September, just weeks before the grand opening of the meet, until rumors began to circulate that flooding in several provinces that fall might force postponement of the meet. One writer for the journal *Athletic China* hoped that this would not be the case, taking issue with those who would see the National Games as mere "hopping and skipping tricks" unimportant in a time of national crisis:

> Rescuing people from flooding is a mission, but strengthening the nation and the race is also a mission. On the surface it might seem that flood rescue work is an emergency now. But who is to say that strengthening the nation is not even more important than flood rescue? . . . Here's a mischievous suggestion: "Let those who are enthusiastic and sincere about flood rescue go do their flood rescue work, and let those enthusiastic and sincere about hopping and skipping hop and skip to their hearts' content." . . . China is a great land with rich resources and an abundant population, and there are enough people to carry out all types of enterprise. . . . And the might of this nation may even succeed in scaring off a few red empires as well.[39]

Despite the flooding, the games were still on, and athletes started to make their way to Nanjing. After two months on the road, traveling from northwestern Xinjiang through Kazakhstan and Siberia, Xinjiang's three-man martial arts delegation to the games reached Manzhouli in September and were preparing to make the trip south to Nanjing.[40] The Singapore delegation was already in Hong Kong.[41] Indeed, anticipation was building for this celebration, which would bring healthy athletes from all corners of China[42] to the stadium at Zijinshan, nestled in the heart of Guomindang China's most sacred suburb, on the twentieth anniversary of the Wuchang uprising.

The machinery of Japanese imperialism, however, would render all this work, travel, and hope for naught. The September 18th Incident at Mukden and the beginning of full-scale Japanese invasion of the Northeast meant, among other things, that the 1931 Games would never occur. The sporting bureaucracy recovered from this stunning attack quickly. At a National Tiyu Conference held in 1932, it was decided that the Fifth Games would be rescheduled for 1933, on the same historic date (10 October) and at the same hallowed location (Nanjing Central Stadium). A 1933 National Games Planning Committee was established, and the equipment, prizes, signs, furniture, office supplies, and printed materials that had been prepared for the 1931 Games were inventoried and handed over to the new committee. China's *tiyu* planners probably hoped that there would still be some of that Nationalist magic left at the bottom of the prize cauldron and silver cup donated by Chiang Kai-shek and Chen Guofu when the National Games arrived two years later.[43]

THE NATION-RACE IS STILL UNITED:
THE 1933 NATIONAL GAMES

> Since the September 18th Incident at Shenyang two years back,
> Manchuria and Rehe have fallen in turn into the hands of the
> enemy. Thirty million of our compatriots have lost the protection
> of the motherland and now groan under the enemy's iron heel.
> Many are killed, others are trampled, living a life not meant for
> humans, tasting the suffering of the subjugated nation. . . . If we
> want to have a people to fight national humiliation and save the
> nation-race from extinction, we must first have strong and fit
> bodies. But in what kind of shape are our population's bodies?
> Our vitality extinguished, the streets full of the diseased, in this
> vast universe, who will summon the soul of *tiyu*?
>
> SHAO RUGAN, "Di wu jie Quanguo yundong dahui
> yu minzu fuxing" [The Fifth National Games
> and the revitalization of the nation-race] (1933)

Shao Rugan, *tiyu* director of the Shanghai Education Department, captured in this passage the importance placed by so many observers on the Fifth National Games, held in Nanjing in October 1933. Not only was it the first national meet planned by Guomindang officials from beginning to end, the first competition held at Nanjing's famed Central Stadium, and the first meet to attract substantial delegations from the majority of China's provinces, but its staging so soon after the Japanese invasion of Shenyang in September 1931 and attack on Shanghai in January 1932 made it a cherished statement of the Chinese will to stand up to the Japanese enemy.

The long-awaited opening ceremonies, held on 10 October, packed Central Stadium with fifty thousand fans (fifteen thousand over capacity) by 9:00 A.M. Spectators crammed into any possible cranny, including the press box, to the dismay of many reporters. Crowds of some sixty thousand milled around outside, and many tried repeatedly to jump fences and outrun Boy Scout guards to gain access to the main event.[44] Spectators who ventured out to the Zijinshan area for the meet became stars in their own right, as the other subjects of this great Nationalist undertaking. As long as they behaved themselves, they served as the "masses" whose presence was required to justify this endeavor—at the same time both the pool from which China's athletic talent was drawn and the less-talented ordinary people who could only watch and dream of skills like those possessed by the national-class athletes. They were the subjects of the national project to train Chinese citizens to be good consumers and disciplined spectators—to view and understand properly and become rationally involved in the nationalizing enterprise taking place before them.

The opening ceremonies provided sporting thrills rarely surpassed in the Republican era. But little of that excitement came from the stilted speeches given by Games Chairman Wang Shijie and honorary vice chairmen like Wang Jingwei, Sun Ke, and Dai Jitao, or from the telegram from Chiang Kai-shek, read by Military Aide Xiao Qin, which stated in part,

> All types of sporting competitions require a type of discipline. Cultivating our nation's virtues of propriety, justice, honesty, and a sense of shame, while at the same time setting a good example for the younger generation, has much to do with sport as well. Zhongzheng [referring to Chiang himself] is now engaged in battle in Jiangxi Province and thus does not have the opportunity to attend the games. I hope that our National Games athletes understand these principles.[45]

Tellingly, Chiang's typical attempt to position the games as part of his vendetta against Communist "bandit" bases in Jiangxi was at sharp odds with the anti-Japanese sentiments on the minds of the fifty thousand people in Central Stadium that day.

The moving moments of that morning came not with ideologically freighted speeches but with the spectacles that allowed the crowd to envision the making of the nation right before them. Following the now-customary airplane flyover and colored leaflet drop into the stadium, teams from each province and locale, marching behind their own banners, began their procession around the track. First out of the tunnel and onto the track was the Xinjiang delegation of nine men competing in track and field, swimming, and martial arts.

The inclusion for the first time of Xinjiang athletes in the National Games served as an appropriate symbol for the new Nationalist inclusiveness of the meet. This far-off frontier province had long been imagined as simply unsuited to the modern realm of sport. In 1931, an author passed on a story testifying to the impossibility of promoting modern sports in Xinjiang. He reported that suspicious postal authorities there, ignorant of what the "tennis rackets" and "tennis balls" itemized in a bill of lading for a shipment from Harbin were, and assuming that this notation must have been "the secret code of some reactionary clique," seized the shipment and interrogated the addressee as to the true contents of his sporting goods cache.[46] Xinjiang's participation in these National Games thus said much about the efforts of the people of this region to work toward national goals.

Other distant locales sending teams to the National Games for the first time included Qinghai Province, who sent one coach and four track athletes to the games. (Among these athletes was Wang Tingzhang, a star sprinter who also planned to stay in Nanjing after the games to enroll in the Academia Sinica Meteorology Training Institute.) The Qinghai squad left Xining on 11 September but were delayed by rain for several days. The team's decision to walk one leg of the journey was an unfortunate one, as they were robbed by bandits apparently unaware of the prestige of their victims. The Qinghai delegation's slot in the athletes' procession remained unfilled, as the team did not arrive in Nanjing until 9 November, three weeks after the games were over.[47]

Some 2,259 athletes represented twenty-five provinces, six municipalities, and Philippine and Indonesian Chinese communities in the meet,[48] making the National Games one of the few sites where healthy, patriotic youth from all over China could mingle in a truly national environment. I have written elsewhere on notions of a sporting Greater China that made it possible to imagine "national" ties—by this time, the only type that mattered—between Republican citizens and their long-lost overseas sojourners. During the 1920s and 1930s, this trend of Southeast Asian "*Huaqiao*" (Overseas Chinese) participation was an encouraging element of the Chinese sporting scene.[49]

Yet the greatest cheers came for the athletes representing the northeastern provinces now occupied by the Japanese invaders. These "athletes in exile" (*liuwang xuanshou*), most of whom now studied in Beiping, marched last in the opening procession. When they emerged from the tunnel, many "in tears, feeling deeply moved," and joined the procession, the response from the crowd was deafening. As they marched with their banners, the name of their respective provinces stenciled over outline maps of each province in dramatic black and white, many in the stands joined them in crying tears of sorrow and joy. No less a figure than General Li Du, commanding general of the Northeast National Salvation Army, was noted as "weeping silently" as his fellow exiled northeasterners filed solemnly past the VIP section.[50] Another eyewitness was moved to write, "Is the Northeast done for *(wang le)*? No, the Northeast is not done for!"[51] After the emotional procession, a representative of the northeastern athletes read an appeal to the crowd:

> Entering this august and majestic stadium brings to our minds the
> horseshoe-shaped stadium at Beiling [the Zhang Xueliang-built
> Northeastern University stadium in Shenyang]. . . . We sincerely
> declare, the trophy we in our hearts most want to struggle for is the

recovery of our five northeastern provinces and their colors on the map! . . . After the closing ceremonies, all here have homes to which they can return, while we must drift from place to place. . . . Finally, we ardently hope and sincerely pray that the next National Games of the Republic of China will be held at Shenyang's Beiling Stadium and that the next trophy of the National Games of the Republic of China will be the recovery of the Northeast territories![52]

This ritualistic appearance by Chinese sons and daughters of the occupied Northeast was the highlight of the games, assuring many patriots, more than any Guomindang officials' speeches could, that there was a strong and united China with whom the Japanese would have to contend. As an observer later wrote, "Our nation's territory has been shattered, but at these National Games we could see that China is still whole and is still ours. With representatives from the occupied Northeast, from Xinjiang in the Northwest, and Yunnan in the far Southwest, China is still whole, and the *minzu* is still united!"[53] Chiang Kai-shek may have envisioned the games as part and parcel of his latest Communist-suppression scheme. However, it was clear to anyone actually at Central Stadium that the Japanese were the true enemy for the sons and daughters of China to fight. The anti-Japanese nationalism brought to the games by the Northeast athletes—and quickly spread among the Nanjing fans—marked an amazing, effective, and safe way for China's *tiyu* community to register its discontent with Nanjing's muddled policies toward the Japanese imperialist machine.

The games themselves provided no letdown to the rousing opening ceremonies. One highlight was the mass demonstration of "tai chi calisthenics" *(taijicao,* a simple three-minute routine based on basic motions of *taijiquan),* led by Chu Minyi, Secretary of the Executive Yuan and National Games vice chairman. Performed by some two thousand children from forty-one Nanjing elementary schools, this newest of Chinese sports was a fantastic hit with the crowd. Every track and field and swimming record from the last national meet of 1930 was broken in Nanjing. Including martial arts, basketball, soccer, volleyball, tennis, baseball, and softball, 263 competitions were held over ten days, with the Shanghai men's and women's teams taking home the overall championships. This first National Games appearance of *guoshu* martial arts, featuring eighteen men's and two women's events, as well as several demonstrations by Chu Minyi, was heralded as a great success (Table 7).

The fan favorite Liu Changchun, the Liaoning sprinter, won two gold medals, broke two national records, and continued to please longtime fans. New national stars were born as well. Qian Xingsu, a sprinter from Jiading,

TABLE 7. 1933 Fifth National Games Results,
Men's and Women's Events

Men's Event	1st Place	2nd Place	3rd Place	4th Place
Track & field	Shanghai	Beiping	Hebei	Liaoning
All-around	Shanghai	Beiping	Guangdong	Nanjing
Swimming	Guangdong	Hong Kong	Liaoning	Shanghai
Basketball	Hebei	Shanghai	Nanjing	Guangdong
Soccer	Shanghai	Guangdong	Hebei	Hong Kong
Volleyball	Shanghai	Guangdong	Zhejiang	Hong Kong
Baseball	Guangdong	Hebei	Hong Kong	Beiping
Tennis	Shanghai	Sichuan	Batavia	Hebei
Guoshu	Beiping	Henan	Qingdao	Shandong

Women's Event	1st Place	2nd Place	3rd Place	4th Place
Track & field	Shanghai	Guangdong	Shandong	Henan
Swimming	Hong Kong	Guangdong	Qingdao	Liaoning
Basketball	Shanghai	Guangdong	Hebei	Beiping
Volleyball	Shanghai	Beiping	Guangdong	Hong Kong
Softball	Guangdong	Shanghai	Beiping	Nanjing
Tennis	Shanxi	Sichuan	Beiping	Shanghai
Guoshu	Nanjing	Zhejiang		

Jiangsu, was well-known in Shanghai sports circles, having burst onto the scene with a surprising second-place finish to her "blue-eyed blond-haired" opponent in the 1931 Shanghai International Meet.[54] Here in Nanjing, Qian gained national attention for the first time by winning three gold medals and a silver and capturing women's overall track and field honors.[55]

The brightest of all new stars, however, known as "the Beautiful Mermaid," or "Miss China," was the fifteen-year-old Hong Kong swimmer Yang Xiuqiong, who attained superstar status with her record-setting sweep of all four women's swim events in Nanjing. Few were immune to Yang's demure beauty and charm; the omnipresent Chu Minyi scandalized the political and sports worlds when he personally served Yang as carriage driver on a scenic tour for two around the capital.[56] This was the beginning of a public life that made young Yang by far the best-known athlete in 1930s China. Her youthful charm and beauty put her on the covers of dozens of magazines and also made her the subject of endless marriage rumors. Just days after her triumph at Nanjing, the Hong Kong press was reporting that Yang would soon become the eighth wife of Chen Baiyuan, chief consultant of the Guangxi Bank. Yang also soon became an unofficial government spokeswoman of sorts, putting on swimming demonstrations at New Life Movement–related events in Nanchang, Xiamen, and Nanjing, as the Guomindang attempted to break down the boundaries between elite competitive sport and mass physical fitness programs.[57]

Games planners also attempted to match this sporting excellence with record-setting heights of ideological orthodoxy. All athletes not competing the morning of the sixth day of the meet, 15 October, were required to gather at 6:00 A.M. to walk, led by—who else—Chu Minyi, to the Sun Yat-sen Memorial north of Central Stadium. Turnout was disappointing, however; organizers had to resort to making noisy loudspeaker announcements to rouse the sleepy heirs of Sun's last will and testament. Finally leaving the stadium at 7:00 A.M., some six hundred athletes followed Chu up Zijinshan to the memorial. There, athletes laid wreaths, sang the Guomindang party anthem, recited Sun's final testament (in which Sun had called on his comrades to continue awakening and uniting the people of China), inspected the inner chamber of the memorial, and posed for photos on the memorial steps.[58]

The games also served as a coming-out for the new sports media. In all, 679 media passes were distributed to reporters and photographers (including eight for the American Associated Press and one for Tokyo's *Nichinichi Shinbun*). After the completion of the ten-day meet, the Publicity Department of the Games Planning Committee did a survey of newspapers in eight cities around China—Nanjing, Shanghai, Tianjin, Xuzhou, Zhengzhou, Jiujiang, Anqing, and Hankou—and found 1,281 articles totaling 219,595 characters in length written on the games at the capital.[59]

Photography was an equally important medium of the National Games publicity blitz. Photos of national leaders in attendance, posed male and female champions, and action shots were part of any games publication worth purchasing. National Games pictorials flourished as well. One number, published by Shanghai's Era Books, featured a foldout page of shots of the Hong Kong swimming darling Yang Xiuqiong. One photo taken from Yang's back showed her standing in her swimsuit before a male media horde. Similar shots were taken of sprinter extraordinaire Liu Changchun standing before the media, and of Li Lili—who was not even a real athlete but would soon play one in the film *Sports Queen (Tiyu huanghou)*—being photographed by another pack of reporters as she trained with coach Wang Jingxi. This same pictorial took the primacy of the photographic to an extreme, even featuring several snapshots of photographers taking pictures of unseen subjects.[60]

However, not all observers were satisfied with the National Games. The mainstream media, their circulations and revenue fattened by the games, soon cast them aside. But the specialized *tiyu* press continued to mull over the meet, elaborating on aspects of the enterprise that would have to be rectified at the next games. Instances of unsportsmanlike conduct by games participants were the main target of criticism. Several incidents in particular gave many pause about the condition of sports in China. The Guangdong basketball team refused to finish their game versus Shanghai after reserves and coaches brawled with opposition players and officials when several questionable calls by a Shanghai-based referee went against them.[61] Liaoning soccer left wing Li Bailian, losing his quarterfinal match to the Shanghai side 6–0, came up swinging when a Shanghai fullback slide-tackled him after a whistle. A referee tried to restrain Li, but the angry player had to be hauled off by military police as fans poured onto the Central Stadium field to join the fighting.[62] Other brawls took place between the Guangdong and Hebei baseball teams, and even between groundskeepers and meet officials over the condition of the track for the men's two-hundred-meter dash finals.[63] The "savage beating" given a Central Political Academy student by a platoon commander of the 88th Division in the stands at a *guoshu* competition also attracted much attention.[64] And the Jiangsu long-distance runner Jin Zhongkang was criticized for not coming clean after "winning" the ten-kilometer race by only running nineteen laps (instead of twenty) around the Central Stadium track.[65] One author took these events as proof of unhealthy trends in the Chinese sports world and took the chance to write at length on the difference between sportsmanship and "dirty play."[66] Another offered a psychological analysis, sprinkled with English terminology like "latent attention" and "psychology of testimony," to identify these unsportsmanlike incidents as signs of a Chinese nation-race "drowning in disillusionment."[67]

Other *tiyu* commentators weighed in with critiques of the spectacular new Central Stadium. Wu Yunrui cited German sports scientist Carl Diem in taking stadium architects to task for technical problems like bleacher and track dimensions and the layout and design of sandpits.[68] Others, like Chu Minyi, tackled much larger philosophical issues:

> On the surface [Central Stadium] is certainly grand and imposing, the greatest in East Asia. But speaking practically and directly, no one goes there to exercise. Foreigners might see this stadium and praise its magnificence and the great amount of money spent on it. But what if a for-

eigner were to ask for statistics on how many athletes trained at this stadium every year? There would be nothing we could say. A stadium this big, and no one going to exercise there—it is just a showcase, truly a fine joke. Only wanting the superficial, ignoring the practical—having this stadium is just the same as not having one at all.

Let's make a comparison with eating. . . . We all know that eating is done to replenish the energy our body uses, so there is no need to spend lots of money—vegetables and tofu are fine and provide just as much nourishment as anything else.[69]

Chu's metaphors of mass physical fitness and individual nutrition clearly fit with popular Guomindang images of "national physiques." Although Chu was vice chairman of the National Games, he was also the chief Guomindang spokesman for a mass *tiyu,* and his practical concerns over making physical training available to the masses conflicted with his responsibility to provide for the material and symbolic needs of elite events like the National Games.

Others followed this line of critique as well. One author denounced the Guomindang *tiyu* establishment for spending "gargantuan sums" *(juzi)* on this meet—total meet expenses amounted to 123,434 *yuan* (U.S.$38,100)—writing that "the means of the people have been squandered by government spending, as this autumn, the bodies of the starved clog the avenues."[70] Another activist wrote, "There was one thing most regrettable about these games, something that laid the greatest possible shame on our nation's *tiyu* community! And this is that looking at the games program, one had doubts as to whether this was actually a meet run by foreigners! Where has our national-racial spirit, the sport of our national essence [i.e., martial arts], gone? . . . It's all the leisured, moneyed people's favorite [Western-style] 'games of a subjugated nation' *(wangguo wanyi)!*"[71]

This concern for the health of the Chinese masses and nation, and the Fifth National Games' failure to address it, persisted among commentators for months after the games were adjourned. Some, anxious about China's future, hoped to correct possibly inauspicious terminology that might bode ill for the nation. The intellectual Luo Jialun, who served as a vice chairman of the games, hoped that when describing the breaking of national records, sportswriters would abstain from using the unlucky-sounding abbreviated phrase *po quanguo* (literally, "break the entire nation"), instead using the more propitious expression *quanguo xin* (literally, "new for the entire nation").[72]

The modern sporting narrative, used skillfully by Guomindang bureaucrats, emphasized the national inclusiveness of a meet that attracted Chinese athletes from thousands of miles in all directions to this hallowed Nationalist shrine in the Purple and Gold Mountains. Wide media coverage and appearances by top Guomindang leaders only confirmed, for this narrative at least, the unifying and empowering spectacle of healthy Chinese youth engaging in healthy competition in Western sports and also in the indigenous martial arts. And the numerous records set in Nanjing signified much more about national progress than could a day's worth of speeches by Sun Ke and Wang Jingwei.

Yet try as they did to assert that national competitions like these would have a trickle-down effect on the larger Chinese population, spurring them on to greater and greater fitness achievements, National Games publicists and Guomindang spokesmen lost ground to the activists who called for a truly mass *tiyu*. The games, now a biennial affair,[73] were in many ways a brilliant creation of national drama and will. But the hollowness of the concept that they somehow expressed the spirit of the nation as a whole, revealed with the repeated thumping by critics advocating a mass *tiyu*, made them in some ways as tragic as the games of 1931 that were never played. The international meets in which Chinese athletes participated in the 1930s—namely the Far East Championship Games and the Olympics—never provided the pure drama that China's National Games did during the 1930s. However, these international meets, by giving proof of the results of national *tiyu* programs, could resolve (or at least render moot) the contradictions between a mass *tiyu* that could strengthen the Chinese people and elite competitive sports that perhaps only distracted the masses while emptying their wallets.

THE FAR EASTERN CHAMPIONSHIP GAMES

The Far Eastern Championship Games (FECG) provided, after the National Games, the next ascending level of competition and national significance. The site of Chinese athletes' first participation in international sport (in 1913), the Far Eastern Games presented a bittersweet opportunity for Chinese athletes to set their athletic talent against the best of East Asia ten times between 1913 and 1934. For two decades, these games allowed China to ascend the venerated stage of international sporting competition, contributing to what one author in 1930 called a "foundation of the friendship between the five hundred million people of East Asia."[74] Unfortunately, participation in these international competitions was a dubious honor, as it usually resulted in the Chinese varsity champions getting their clocks cleaned by the Olympic-caliber Japanese athletes whom the Chinese hoped so passionately to defeat.[75]

The first Far Eastern meet of the 1930s came just weeks after the Fourth National Games at Hangzhou in April 1930. Some 150 athletes from the National Games were selected to try out for the Chinese Far Eastern team later that month in Shanghai. They were joined there by the Honolulu Chinese Baseball Team, who paid their own way to Shanghai to make their regular appearance representing China in the games.[76] In Shanghai, the athletes trained for a month, competed in exhibitions against top foreign YMCA and police teams, and were feted in banquets sponsored by newspapers and government officials.[77] Finally, on 15 May the squad of 115 athletes boarded the Japanese postal ship *Daiakan* setting sail for Kobe and eventually the Ninth FECG at Tokyo.[78] One of these competitors was Cheng Jinguan, then an eighteen-year-old studying at Dongwu High School in Suzhou. In conversations some sixty-seven years later, Cheng described this trip to me as an unbelievable chance to represent his country before the judgmental gaze of China's Asian neighbors and rivals.

The games got underway on 24 May in Tokyo's Meiji Shrine Outer Garden before sixty thousand fans. Minister of Education Tanaka Ryūzō read a speech on behalf of Games Chairman Prince Chichibu, welcoming athletes from China, the Philippines, and India to the games.[79] Over the next eight days, 520,000 fans came to watch eight different competitions; Japan won five outright and tied the Chinese for the soccer championship.[80] The Honolulu Chinese Baseball Team's threat to take gold was neutralized by the Japanese, who countered with their own Hawaiian ringer, a star pitcher named Kobayashi. The Chinese delegation took home only one outright championship, in nine-man volleyball. The track and field category was a blowout: the Japanese earned 131.5 points; the Filipinos, 32.5 points; the Chinese, 1 point; and the Indians, 0 points.

When remembering these games decades later in 1997, what stood out most in eighty-six-year-old Cheng Jinguan's mind was the humiliation of "having a population of four hundred million people and winning only one bronze medal in track and field."[81] The Chinese team returned home to few heroes' welcomes. Some face was saved for the athletes as observers blasted the unfairness of Japanese referees and the dirty play of Japanese athletes that left their Chinese and Filipino opponents "grasping their wrists in anger."[82] However, many critics wanted answers for the Chinese delegation's poor performance. One author demanded to know how "the Republic of China, with its three thousand years of culture and history, 34,403,740 square miles of fertile land, and population of 474 million, could be defeated, sent away crying, by a tiny nation of three islands! This is not only a shame—it is pathetic!"[83] Even the normally staid *Educational Review* joined in, commenting that the team's failure was due to "individual selfishness and the lack of any cooperative effort—it is due to this fault that [the team] managed to finish even behind Sun Shan [the legendary last-place finisher on the imperial exam]."[84]

Few observers on the *tiyu* scene could have been pleased with the Chinese performance at the games. The official goal of participation in these international competitions was to share in an international spirit of sportsmanship and fair play and by doing so to stimulate an interest in sports and fitness among the Chinese masses. But no one wanted to be the nice guy who finished last, especially when the Japanese were making off with all the honors. In 1930, the mass *tiyu* critique was not developed enough to capitalize on the Far Eastern failure and blast the sports system that spent a small fortune to send 115 college students abroad for weeks of fun and travel. But disastrous performances like these gave advocates of *tiyu* for the masses much ammunition for their arguments in later years.

The next Far Eastern meet, the tenth such affair, was planned for May 1934 in Manila. This switch to a quadrennial schedule posed the Far Eastern Games as a junior-level Olympics; in fact, Olympic rules were adopted for all Far Eastern competitions in the late 1920s. The Far Eastern Games adhered to Olympic tradition in other ways as well; by that spring, ominous political rumblings threatened to cancel the meet altogether. On 13 March, Japanese representatives paid a visit to Wang Zhengting, the Far Eastern Athletic Association vice chairman and Chinese Far Eastern team leader, in his office in Shanghai's French Concession. There, they floated the idea of letting Manzhouguo, the Manchurian puppet regime established by the Japanese in 1932, participate in the Tenth Games. Wang declared that there was "no room for discussion and nothing to discuss, and [the delegation] silently departed."[85]

The issue was far from resolved, however. On 9 April, the Japanese raised the Manzhouguo question again at a Standing Committee meeting in Shanghai, and debate continued the next morning in the Huamao Hotel on Nanjing Road. The Japanese proposal to allow Manzhouguo athletes to participate in an unofficial "demonstration" capacity got nowhere, and both Chinese and Japanese delegations threatened to pull out of the games. Ultimately, Dr. Tan, the Filipino representative to this meeting, concluded that a strict reading of Article 3 of the Far Eastern Games constitution, which required unanimous approval for the admittance of new members, did not allow for the entry of Manzhouguo over Chinese objections. The meeting finally broke up on the 11th, with the Japanese threat to withdraw still valid, as was the Philippine Amateur Athletic Federation's constitutional stand.[86]

Tryouts for the Chinese delegation to the Manila meet began in mid-April, with athletes coming to Shanghai from Beiping, Tianjin, Shanxi, Hubei, Hebei, Nanjing, Guangdong, Hong Kong, and even Singapore and Indonesia for the chance to make the Chinese squad. Competition was fierce as selected government *tiyu* officials warred over the composition of each team.[87] Some star athletes worked out ways of ensuring they would be selected. The Shanghai native Cheng Jinguan related to me, with a boyish grin, a plan designed by him and the Liaoning star Liu Changchun, the two top Chinese sprinters of the time.[88] The two friendly rivals simply agreed before the selection meet that Liu would let Cheng win the one-hundred-meter dash and Cheng would let Liu win the two-hundred-meter dash—this way both stars, sure to finish first and second in the sprints anyway, would secure spots on the track team and transcend the notorious regional favoritism of the selection officials.[89] For these athletes, who understood their efforts in explicitly national terms, it was easy to solve the problems of regionalism that threatened to rend China asunder.

After a warm-up meet against the expatriate Western Track and Field Club, in which the Chinese athletes won all thirteen events,[90] the Chinese team left Shanghai aboard the American ship *Jackson*, transferring in Hong Kong onto the *McKinley*. Cheng Jinguan, whose memories of his sporting trips abroad are rife with feelings of Chinese national humiliation, interrupted his story of this trip to emphasize the irony of a Chinese national team taking American ships to an international meet, "not like now, when we have our own airplanes."[91] But the events of their arrival in Manila only irritated Cheng even more.

The team was honored by a tremendous welcome at Pier Seven by some seven or eight thousand members of Manila's Chinese population—as one observer wrote, "the activity and human tide seemed to set the entire great structure of the pier itself in motion." A procession of more than two hundred cars paraded the athletes through the Manila streets in "the warmest welcome these skies have ever seen."[92] However, what remained foremost in Cheng's memory was not this rowdy welcome but a quiet episode taking place in the Philippines customs division that day. One Chinese athlete brought in his bags a small package of Chinese soil—a common charm to solve the problem of "disagreeing with the new environment" (*shui tu bufu*, literally "unease with the water and soil"). Manila customs officials, no doubt conditioned by the stories that the Chinese found so ignominious, assumed that the packaged soil was opium and immediately detained the offending athlete. Cheng's polished English allowed him to intervene on the part of his teammate, explaining this Chinese folk custom to the customs agents, who finally released the athlete. But the encounter left an impression on Cheng that he still carried at the age of eighty-six—a complicated mixture of anger, at foreigners who had such low opinions of the Chinese, and shame, for being a member of a nation and race whose customs and superstitions made it so easy for foreigners to equate China with weakness and indulgence.

This memory of Chinese weakness is not the only one that pained Cheng for decades. After talking for a while, Cheng offered to tell me yet another "ridiculous story" *(xiaohua)* about the Manila Games. Manuel Luis Quezon, president of the new Philippine Commonwealth, gave a long speech at the meet's opening ceremonies, orating for so long that a Chinese marathoner fainted in the Manila heat. Cheng would not confirm the name of this runner for me, saying he did not want to embarrass any of his old teammates; he meant only to underscore just how weak Chinese bodies, even those of its best marathoners, were at the time.[93]

The games themselves, held at Manila's new Rizal Stadium, offered no tremendous surprises for Chinese observers. Again the team captured just one title,[94] in soccer, to three each for Japan and the Philippines and none for the Indonesian squad in their inaugural Far Eastern appearance.[95] That the soccer team beat Japan 4–3 to clinch the title was a welcome relief for Chinese fans, who were dying for victories in what the *New York Times* called the "Sino-Japanese sports 'war.'"[96] The Chinese basketball team finished in second place to the Philippines, but the 48–47 win over Japan that clinched the silver medal was as sweet as any championship; Tang Baokun was carried off on the shoulders of the exhilarated crowd after he won the contest with a last-second free throw.[97] The games also featured the usual brawls and broils, as violence broke out at the Chinese-Filipino soccer and basketball games and during the Japanese-Filipino demonstration boxing match.[98]

Yet happenings after the end of competition became the real story of the Far Eastern Games. On 19 May, regularly scheduled FECG administrative meetings to plan the next games, scheduled for Shanghai in 1938, began. The first session of the meeting saw several routine changes made—adding boxing, target shooting, and water polo and making women's swimming and volleyball official competition events.[99] Good feelings ceased quickly, though, as Japanese representatives returned to the issue of Manzhouguo joining the Far Eastern Athletic Association. This time, they were better prepared. Where before they had somehow counted on persuading the Chinese to allow Manzhouguo participation, their new approach combined clever constitutional interpretation and old-fashioned imperialist intimidation. Japanese delegates proposed to use Article 10 of the Far Eastern Games code, which required a two-thirds majority to alter the constitution, to remove the unanimity clause of Article 3.[100] Now China's vote was no longer required to achieve Manzhouguo membership. Indonesian representatives had left for home before the meetings began, leaving only the Chinese, Filipinos, and Japanese—who insisted that this qualified as a valid meeting, since three of four participants were in attendance.[101]

Some convincing gunboat diplomacy during the course of the games also helped the Japanese delegates to ensure Philippine cooperation. The Japanese Consul to Manila changed the mood of a banquet held for Japanese and Filipino officials when he thundered at the hosts, "Japan has sent some 170-plus athletes to join these games, and this is a joyous occasion. But if we were to send 170-plus battleships, how would you feel then? . . . If the Philippines want to remain independent it had best maintain friendly relations with its Japanese neighbor!"[102] When Filipino delegates were still unwilling to side with Japan, the Japanese delegates threatened to file the ultimate sporting protest by committing mass *harakiri* in the lobby of the Manila Hotel if their requests went unheeded by the hosts.[103] Against the wishes of the Manila sporting public and press,[104] Filipino delegates were convinced to go along with the Japanese scheme. When Chinese delegates walked out of the meeting, the two remaining Far Eastern countries declared the FEAA dissolved and instantly founded a new Amateur Athletic Association of the Orient.[105]

The Chinese delegates returned to Shanghai to explain their side of the story to a sympathetic public, beginning with a large press conference at the New Asia Hotel. Delegates took the sportsmanlike high road, explaining that they had withdrawn from the offensive meetings only to "preserve the glorious and pure traditions of athletic competition."[106] It was announced that China would still prepare as usual for the next Far Eastern meet, scheduled for Shanghai in 1938, and that CNAAF Secretary William Sung had already filed an appeal with the International Olympic Committee over the incident.[107] Chinese observers also saw a chance to contrast the independent, high-minded Chinese diplomatic spirit with the weaker-willed approach of the Philippine delegation. One author scorned the Philippine decision to use the Far Eastern Games as "a tool to win Japanese favors."[108] Another wrote, "It is true that the Philippines are about to get their independence, but after all they are a weak nation and should side with China instead of serving as a vassal of Japan whose ambition knows no bounds."[109]

Many saw in these events darker consequences, however. One author wailed, "Weak nations have no foreign diplomacy! We have even failed in sports diplomacy!"[110] Many hoped for ways to keep up Chinese morale in the face of this latest humiliation. A *Shenbao* article urged that May 20th, the anniversary of this treacherous Japanese-Philippine conspiracy, be formally observed in the future. Suggesting that this violation of Chinese sovereignty ranked with those of May Fourths and May Thirtieths past, the author hoped that all public athletic grounds in China would hang their flags at half-mast on this day and that all sporting activities would be suspended to commemorate this "humiliation of the *tiyu* community." He hoped that future National Games could be held on the same day as the "so-called East Asia Meet," awarding special prizes to athletes who managed to surpass East Asian marks and even subsidizing participation by China's smaller Asian allies. Finally, he asked that one sentence be added to the official National Games oath: "I vow to wipe away the humiliation suffered by our elders on 20 May of the twenty-third year of the Republic of China."[111]

The Far Eastern Games of 1930 and 1934, the final acts of a ten-round production that had begun in 1913, provided the Chinese *tiyu* community with the international perspective so valuable to forming conceptions of a sporting Chinese nation. With the Japanese presence growing daily in the affairs of the Chinese nation and in the minds of its people, the 1930s meets also provided rare opportunities for Chinese underdogs to triumph over the reviled Japanese imperialists. Unfortunately for the Chinese *tiyu* community, Japanese sporting superiority and years of world-class experience in Olympic competition ensured that this did not happen often.

Cheng Jinguan's emotions in experiencing and remembering his participation in the Far Eastern meets—a mixture of pride in his role as a pathbreaker for Chinese sport, grief at the affronts suffered by his countrymen abroad, and shame at the mediocre performances consistently turned in by his team— were probably not unique among athletes and interested spectators of his day. Each time the Far Eastern Games were held, ships carried proud and optimistic delegations to Tokyo or Manila, only to return to Chinese shores weighted down much more heavily by nationalist shame and guilt than by any championship cargo of medals or trophies.[112] As Chinese sportsmen's first connection to the thrills and complexities (and the national-racial hatred and violence) of international competition, the Far Eastern Games holds a special place in the history of modern Chinese *tiyu*. But the games' legacy as a promising investment that always disappointed, never paying the expected dividends of sporting superiority in East Asia, is what lives on in the hearts of elderly athletes and observers who understood *tiyu* as an important part of the twentieth-century Chinese national narrative.

LIKE A FISHERMAN IN A PEACH-BLOSSOM HAVEN:
LIU CHANGCHUN AND THE 1932 OLYMPIC GAMES

"If a people wants to pursue freedom and equality in today's world where the weak serve as meat on which the strong can dine, they first must train strong and fit bodies."[113] So wrote Wang Zhengting, Chinese foreign minister and CNAAF president, in 1930 on the significance of the Olympic Games. Wang, who in 1922 was named China's first representative to the International Olympic Committee, contributed these comments to the preface of a volume written by a young physical education expert named Song Ruhai. Two years earlier, Song had the honor of serving as the first Chinese Olympic participant, when he was an official observer at the Amsterdam Games of 1928. Now, after two years of research and reflection on this journey, Song put out a volume on these and past Olympics, introducing Chinese sports fans to the customs, symbolism, and history of the modern Olympic Games.

The contribution of Song's volume was not its content, most of which was translated and pasted together from foreign sources, but rather the ingenious transcriptive device with which he introduced the Olympics to Chinese readers. He semiphonetically rendered *Olympiad* as *Wo neng bi ya* (literally, "I can compete!"), a phrase that he felt "carries great significance. It means that we can all participate in these events and competitions."[114]

Two years later, China made its inaugural Olympic appearance in the 1932 Games at Los Angeles. By this, their tenth incarnation, the modern Olympics had become a powerful symbol of national accomplishment, strength, and will to participate in the international community called by the Olympics' founder Pierre de Coubertin the "republic of muscles."[115] The official decision to join the Olympic Games represented the ultimate test of an ambitious, if somewhat self-doubting, Chinese sporting community. On an Olympic stage, the stakes were more than merely the reputation of China's basketball, soccer, swimming, and track and field programs. The Chinese citizens who saw their Olympic representatives off to the West and followed their performances via the mainstream print media all knew that their nation, its race and its people, would be held up to scrutiny on the playing fields of Los Angeles.

China's entry into this grand company of nations was made by a single pioneer venturing out West—a twenty-two-year-old fruitpicker's son, sprinter Liu Changchun. Liu's rise to national fame began at age fourteen, when he won the one-hundred- and four-hundred-meter sprints at a Japanese-run Kantōshū Track Meet held in his native Dalian, a Japanese-controlled northeastern port city. As a youth, Liu was a soccer enthusiast, joining in games with Japanese youngsters in his spare time from work as an apprentice in a glass factory and as a city bus ticket taker. The Northeastern University soccer team, touring Dalian in 1927, discovered the seventeen-year-old talent. Liu returned with the team to the provincial capital at Shenyang, where he was enrolled in the Northeastern Prep School and given free tuition and board, courtesy of famed sportsman and university president Zhang Xueliang. Liu flourished at Northeastern, entering the university in 1929 and profiting greatly from the school's commitment to sports excellence. As a favorite of Zhang's, Liu enjoyed a thirty-*yuan* (U.S.$16) monthly stipend from the president. Zhang's hiring of a German ex–world champion to coach track at Northeastern and his frequent sponsorship of meets pitting his athletes against Japanese, French, and German track stars allowed Liu to progress further. In a stretch of six months, Liu made his name in the Chinese sports world, winning two silver medals at an October 1929 Japanese-German-Chinese meet in Shenyang and then winning three golds in his historic performance at the 1930 National Games in Hangzhou.[116]

During the 1932 countdown to the Olympic Games, the CNAAF, China's official sports body, announced on 25 May that they had no plans to send a team to Los Angeles that July.[117] However, the Japanese announcement, just four days later, that Liu and fellow Dalian runner Yu Xiwei would be representing the puppet Manzhouguo state in the Olympics sent the Chinese *tiyu* community into a rage.[118] One commentator issued a bold challenge to the Nanjing government, linking its very credibility to this issue of Olympic participation. Addressing the fact that Japan, with a population of some seventy million, was sending a delegation of more than two hundred athletes to Los Angeles, while "the great Chinese nation of four hundred million" could only afford to send an official observer, he commented, "Quite an interesting contrast. . . . The Education Department says it is because of shortages of time and money. The CNAAF says there isn't any talent. These are not real reasons. . . . What a mysterious nation we are. The people devote everything we have to the nation, but the nation sure doesn't do anything to give us people any hope at all."[119]

The galling prospect of China's most famed sports star running for Olympic gold under the flag of the Manzhouguo puppet government was quickly resolved. Liu himself made a statement for Tianjin's daily *Dagongbao*, vowing, "I am of the Chinese race, a descendant of the Yellow Emperor. I am Chinese and will not represent the bogus Manzhouguo at the Tenth Olympiad."[120] He also vowed that he had never made any contact with sporting personnel from the puppet regime, assuring his public that "I still have a conscience, my hot blood still flows—how could I betray the nation and serve others like a horse or cow?"[121]

Weeks later, the relief that Liu would not be representing Manzhouguo turned to pure Olympic joy. In a dramatic graduation ceremony of the Northeastern University Physical Education Department on 1 July, Zhang Xueliang grabbed the national sporting spotlight. He announced that he would be donating eight thousand *yuan* (U.S.$2,500) for Liu and Yu to run for China in the Olympics, with Northeastern instructor Song Junfu accompanying the two as coach and translator.[122] While national sports officials, with the funds now collected, crowed about the importance of joining the sacred Olympic Games, the small Olympic team prepared to depart for California. After a quick meeting with Beiping Mayor Zhou Dawen, who presented Liu with a new suit for the great occasion,[123] Liu and Coach Song left Beiping for Shanghai on 2 July, while sports officials tried to get in touch with Yu Xiwei in Dalian. By the 4th, Liu was in Shanghai, training in public sessions, being feted in Olympic banquets, and even making a slapdash two-day film at the Chinese Stadium.[124] Yu, on the other hand, was nowhere to be found. Japanese authorities still hoped to coax him to represent the puppet state. Their veiled threats, along with the policy of informal house arrest applied to Yu and other Northeastern stars they feared would join the Chinese team, convinced Yu to ignore the Chinese Olympic call and stay in Dalian for the sake of his family's safety.[125]

After a ceremony at Xinguan Pier where CNAAF President Wang presented Liu with the Chinese national flag, Liu and Song boarded the *President Wilson* on 8 July for two weeks at sea. While on board ship, Song wrote several letters back to Shanghai, informing the sporting public that Liu woke up every morning at 4:00 for calisthenics and was able to eat Chinese meals prepared especially for him. The handful of other Chinese passengers on board, all students, included a thirteen-year-old sports fanatic who impressed Liu and Song with his collection of sports pictures and clippings that he took abroad with him.[126] All was well until the ship made its first stop, in Kobe. There, a crowd of Japanese reporters boarded the *Wilson* to interview Liu but asked if he was representing Manzhouguo. An infuriated Song wrote how he sent them away after "I declared strictly and firmly that the two of us represent the great Republic of China." The Japanese taunting was not over, however, as the next day Liu and Song received a telegram from the Japanese Athletic Association wishing the "Manzhouguo representatives" good luck in the Olympics.[127]

Liu and Song arrived in Los Angeles on 29 July, just one day before the games were scheduled to begin, and were greeted by dozens of excited Chinese Californians. A car with police motorcycle escorts, sirens wailing, immediately took the Olympians to the Chinese Chamber of Commerce, where the two lodged. After a morning press conference the next day, Liu was taken by police escort, followed by five busloads of Chinese American fans, to the Los Angeles Coliseum for the opening ceremonies. There, Liu and Song were joined by four Chinese sports officials already in the United States in the Olympic procession, where China marched eighth of fifty-one nations. Despite promising starts in his two races, the one-hundred- and two-hundred-meter sprint heats, Liu placed fifth and fourth, respectively, and was quickly eliminated from competition in both events.[128]

Liu devoted the rest of his stay to viewing many of the Olympic competitions (which he described in great detail in his diary), hobnobbing with members of the Chinese community and even Hollywood stars, and reflecting on the significance of his Olympic voyage. He recorded in his diary how fans would approach him at the games or on the street, asking if he was a Japanese athlete. When Liu answered that he in fact was Chinese, he accurately read in their reactions the curious, condescending, and complicated feelings Americans had for the Chinese people: "The people react by crying out in surprise. Or they say, 'Here's an athlete representing the four hundred million Chinese,' and then I get surrounded. It's as if they have found some dirty fisherman in their peach-blossom haven—they all ask, 'You're the Chinese representative?' Then they will pat me on the shoulder, saying, "Fine, fine, just great—but it's really too bad that China couldn't send more athletes.'"[129] Besides the personal encouragement that Liu gained from his many acquaintances in Los Angeles, he was greatly impressed by the sympathy for China's plight shown by Americans and athletes from other Olympic nations:

> I have paid attention to the attitudes of Americans since I got to the States, and everywhere I go they make me feel as though they really do sympathize with China. It's the same with [athletes from] the smaller nations—especially during meals, when there are more opportunities [to chat]. They don't say anything explicitly, but with athletes from all nations, it's in the sound of their voice when they say, "Japan . . ." with a bitter laugh. As far as I can tell, almost every nation sympathizes with us. . . . Have even I made some contribution? Have even I made some contribution?[130]

David Welky has written on the Japanese delegation to these 1932 Olympic Games and the threat that this well-conditioned team of nearly 250 athletes posed to American notions of athletic superiority. While the American media tried to dismiss the Japanese Olympians as "little brown men" or the "brown-skinned wonders" of the games,[131] the charming novelty posed by the stoic Liu Changchun's one-man Chinese squad provoked no such racial fear or insults from his American hosts.

Liu's failure to win any medals during his Olympic travels was treated with more leniency than earlier Far Eastern Games disappointments had been. Sports commentators were simply more realistic about these Olympics, explaining that Liu went to Los Angeles not with the goal of winning medals but rather to learn from athletes of other nations so that he could spread this knowledge throughout China. One asked how anyone could expect the Chinese to win any Olympic medals competing against athletes from fifty nations when they could not even compete among three Asian nations in the Far Eastern Games.[132] But Chinese Olympic participation was seen as a great step in establishing a foothold in the community of modern nations. Hao Gengsheng and other officials had explained earlier that a Chinese Olympic appearance was necessary to maintain a respectable position in the world and to offset the effects of Manzhouguo possibly sending a team.[133] But the response Liu received in Los Angeles made the trip seem even more worthwhile:

> This was our nation's first time participating [in the Olympics], being listed as one of the fifty nations. And the flag of the white sun on the blue sky fluttered over the Coliseum alongside the flags of the world's nations for the first time. This has profound significance for our nation . . . On 31 July, when Liu Changchun ran his one-hundred-meter heat, the audience responded with a startlingly intense welcome, with applause that roared like thunder. . . . The fact that our nation's participation could leave the spectators with this kind of impression is very satisfying.[134]

TRAINING AS OTHERS TRAINED IN THE 1936 OLYMPIC GAMES

Given the satisfaction that the 1932 Olympics afforded the Chinese sporting community, it was certain that plans for the next Olympics would not be postponed so late. Official planning for the 1936 Games at Berlin began in October 1934.[135] One innovation designed to meet both the training and bureaucratic needs of a modern Olympic team was the two-month Qingdao Summer Training Camp, held at Shandong University in July-August 1935.[136] The CNAAF paid for transportation, room, and board for athletes it invited or who were recommended by regional sporting bodies. The session was also open to confident competitors able to pay their own way plus five hundred *yuan* (U.S.$200) to cover the costs of training. These were significant costs, for the CNAAF had enlisted the services of four top-notch German coaches to supplement the work of the top *tiyu* names in China, including the camp director Song Junfu, the assistant director and track coach Ma Yuehan, the basketball coach Dong Shouyi, and the martial arts coach Chu Minyi.

This training camp seemed to evoke Shenyang sprinter Dong Hanwen's dearest sporting memories. In conversations with me in Taipei in 1995–96, Dong often reminisced about the sporting camaraderie he enjoyed with his fellow Chinese athletes in Qingdao—both in training and in outsmarting their German coaches by climbing out their dormitory windows after curfew to take in the Qingdao nightlife. For Dong, who barely missed qualifying for the Olympic track team, the training camp represented the best and worst of Chinese sport during the 1930s. He spoke to me at length about the "purity" and sportsmanship in friendships between Chinese athletes of the day, answering me with quizzical, almost disbelieving, looks when I asked if regionalist identity ever entered into these competitions. Once I asked if he had felt the same competing against Guangzhou natives as he did running against a fellow northeasterner. Dong answered with a stern lecture on the attitude of the "sportsman" (using English for this term), maintaining that "athletes do not worry about politics or personal business, just victory."

On other occasions, however, Dong talked about the regional favoritism that plagued the whole selection process. The Olympic team was selected so that North and South would be evenly represented, in order to satisfy the bull-headed Olympic planners who cared about such matters. Dong remembers the "behind-the-scenes" *(neimu)* corruption of southerners like Ma Yuehan, who worked to weight the track team more heavily in favor of southern athletes. Other authors describe the dirty dealings of the northerner Dong Shouyi, who loaded his basketball team with Beiping and Tianjin players.[137] (The sociologist Olga Lang, in her *Chinese Family and Society*, cited this same Olympic selection process as a revealing example of nepotism in 1930s China.)[138] However, by remembering such regionalism as merely another brand of Republican-era official "corruption," Dong has been able to keep intact the memories of pure and sportsmanlike conduct among athletes dedicated to the Chinese nation.

The sprinter Li Shiming, another Liaoning native, was also left off the 1936 Olympic team. This was a particularly egregious example of regional favoritism, but it does not intrude on Dong and Li's reflections about their sporting careers. The Qingdao training camp was designed to assemble the backbone of the Olympic delegation to Berlin without having to rely on unreliable one-time records at the 1935 National Games. Training camp guidelines explained that an athlete would be automatically selected to the Olympic track team if he or she broke a national record in 1935, had broken a national record at an officially sanctioned meet since 1933, or reached official standards listed for each track and field event.[139] Li fit the final qualification, meeting standards in two events by finishing a four-hundred-meter trial in 53.2 seconds on 15 July and running eight hundred meters in 2:03.3 on 27 July. The *Chin Fen Sports Monthly* even listed his time in the eight hundred meters as the "second most valuable achievement of the training camp," including a picture of Li celebrating his record with Coaches Ma and Wilhelm Ludwig.[140] Li later improved his time in the eight hundred meters to a national record of 2:01.9 in a May 1936 meet in Wuxi,[141] and the official government report of the 1936 Games shows that Li qualified for the Olympics once more at a Qinghua University training camp in May 1936, running the four hundred meters in 52.2 seconds.[142] Despite these several world-class performances, Li was never allowed to join the Olympic team.

For Li, despite his world-class athletic prowess, was guilty of a grave crime against the Chinese nation. As early as 1932, he had joined track teams organized in Liaoning under the new pro-Japan Manzhouguo puppet regime. In 1933 and 1934, he represented his hometown Fengtian in the Second and Third Manzhouguo National Games, held in the new capital Xinjing.[143] As noted above, Manzhouguo's nationalizing physical culture project began almost just as soon as the state was established.[144] Many of Northeast China's finest athletes, who along with their fans were condemned in the Chinese press as "slaves of a conquered nation" *(wangguo nu)*,[145] chose nonetheless to compete in meets and competitions sponsored by the new regime.

Li, a veteran of several Japanese-run sporting organizations in Dalian in the 1920s, studied and played baseball in Japan for three years before returning to his native Liaoning in 1931. That fall, he would have represented Liaoning Province in the Republic of China National Games if they had not been postponed due to the Japanese invasion of Manchuria in September. He decided to continue his athletic career under the new Manzhouguo regime for three years before finally leaving home for Northeastern University in Beiping and the "athletes in exile" groups active there.[146]

Today, Li is only willing to describe his Manzhouguo career as "bad . . . just really bad." Those officials choosing the Olympic team in 1936 agreed, obviously giving little thought to the real-life choices made by people living in these areas—virtually sacrificed by the Nanjing state to the Japanese— and labeling Li as a simple traitor. Even his eventual choice to leave his

Northeast home to compete for his Chinese motherland in the Olympics was insufficient to wash away the nationalist repugnance at his Manzhouguo contamination. For these reasons, when the Olympic team left for Berlin, they were without China's finest middle-distance runner.

Final selections were made in pressure-filled training sessions in Shanghai in May-June 1936. The track and field, basketball, weightlifting, and *guoshu* teams, which were assembled after months of practices and competitions, but other Chinese teams came about through different circumstances. The Chinese soccer team was put together solely from Hong Kong Soccer Association teams.[147] They came to Shanghai for a 30 April game against a Nanjing-Shanghai all-star team and a match before twenty thousand fans against the Shanghai Foreign All-Stars and then immediately left for Southeast Asia. There they played an Olympic fundraiser exhibition schedule of twenty-seven games in sixty-two days in Vietnam, Singapore, Indonesia, Burma, Malaya, and Siam before meeting the rest of the Olympic team in Bangkok in July.[148] China's four-member boxing team came from the ranks of Henan Provincial Chairman Shang Qiyu's 32nd Army; Shang paid for the boxers' Olympic trip and five months of intensive training in Shanghai beforehand.[149] Chinese Olympic officials were also ecstatic to hear that Howard Wing (He Haohua), a Dutch cyclist of Chinese ancestry, had refused the requests of the Dutch Olympic Committee in order to be able to ride for his Chinese motherland.[150]

The team's Olympic voyage began on the morning of 23 June, when all fifty-five athletes (not including the soccer team or cyclist Wing) and twenty-nine sports officials met at the Shanghai North Station in their official dress uniforms—dark suits and ties for the men and white *qipao* dresses for the women. They boarded a 6:55 train for Nanjing, arriving in the capital at 2:00 P.M. A bus took them first to the Sun Yat-sen Memorial, where a quick ceremony was performed, then to the Officers' Moral Endeavor Association *(Lizhishe)* for tea, and then to Chiang Kai-shek's Zijinshan home for a short lecture by Chiang and a flag presentation ceremony. After they returned to Shanghai that night, there were two more days of banquets, the largest held by the German Consul in Shanghai at the Daguangming Theater. The athletes and officials, joined by a large "Olympic inspection group," several reporters, and a group of diehard sports fans paying their own way to cheer on their team in Berlin, boarded the Italian steamship *Conte Verde* at noon of 26 June. They were sent off with a musical farewell performed by bands from the Shanghai Municipal Government and Shanghai Garrison Command and a flyover by two aircraft sent by the Chinese Aviation Association.[151]

The Olympians were on board the *Conte Verde* for twenty-five days, making stops in Hong Kong, Singapore, Kuala Lumpur, Bangkok, Bombay, Massawa, and Suez before reaching Venice on 20 July. Each stop in Southeast Asia brought fabulous welcomes from the Chinese populations there and allowed the Olympic enterprise to foster transnational "Greater China" ethnic pride. In Singapore, more than a thousand local Chinese residents greeted the team, taking the Olympians in ten cars on a tour of Singapore and then to a banquet hosted by Consul Diao Zuoqian. Huge crowds also attended a basketball scrimmage between the Chinese Olympians and the Singapore All-Stars, followed by a demonstration by the nine-person martial arts team.[152]

Yet the long trip at sea was not meant to be a pleasure cruise for the Olympians. A regimen was designed to prepare the team physically, mentally, and linguistically for their important tasks. The athletes' days began with mandatory morning calisthenics from 7:00 to 7:30 and then specific training exercises from 8:00 to 9:00 on deck, which often gathered gawking crowds of Western tourists. After lunch, lectures were scheduled every day from 1:00 to 2:00, followed by one hour of German class and one more hour of physical training.[153] Singing and dancing practice occupied after-dinner free time for many members as they prepared for a "China Night" program to be held later in the trip.[154] Unfortunately, these plans did not last long. By the first week of the trip, athletes and coaches alike became violently seasick almost daily. Sprinter Cheng Jinguan remembers conditions getting worse on the ten-day leg of the trip from Bombay to Italy, so bad that few of the Olympians could even hold food down, let alone train or study German, by the end of the trip.[155]

After their ship finally docked in the middle of the night on 20–21 July, the weary athletes were greeted in the *Conte Verde*'s concert hall by representatives of the Chinese and German Consuls to Italy and of Chinese student associations in Germany and Italy. At 3:00 A.M., they finally were allowed to get off the boat for Venice's Continental Hotel. After a day's rest, the team left for Munich. Arriving at 7:00 P.M., they were welcomed by Chinese and German representatives and whisked off by the mayor to visit the site of Hitler's Putsch before their 11:00 train for Berlin that same night.[156]

The team's arrival in Berlin was memorable for all involved. Arriving in the Olympic host city on 23 July, the team was greeted by three hundred Chinese residents and students, all chanting, "Long live the Republic of China" and waving Chinese flags that local restaurants had sold before the team arrived. The celebratory ceremony inside the train station included speeches by Cheng Tianfang, the Chinese ambassador to Germany, the German International Olympic Committee member Dr. Ritter V. Hart, and the Chinese Olympic delegation leader Shen Siliang, who concluded his speech with a ringing call (repeated three times), "Long live the Republic of China! Long live Germany!"

Li Huitang, soccer team captain, carried the Chinese flag as the team marched smartly out of the station—so smartly that one Berlin paper noted the Chinese team as "these Olympics' most orderly delegation."[157] This was also the proudest moment of the whole Olympics for Cheng Jinguan, who remembers the crowds of Berliners who came to the train station out of great curiosity. The march out of the train station was a great victory for Cheng, as the Olympians were finally able to convince these "foreigners" of the truth about the Chinese people. As Cheng recalls it, "They thought that Chinese men wore little hats and Chinese women had little bound feet, but we came out wearing Western suits!"[158]

This sense of Chinese ascendancy to a new level of international recognition is expressed in numerous Chinese historical sources and memories of the 1936 Olympics. Shen Siliang remarked after the games were over, "During the Olympics, the Chinese flag was on all the stands, and on the streets it was plainly seen, with those of other nations. The sight of our delegation, marching in orderly array, training as others trained, participating in games, was all good propaganda. At least other people are now aware we are a nation to be counted."[159] Some Chinese observers were critical of this approach, calling the government simply vain to spend 170,000 *yuan* (U.S.$51,300)[160] to send "some athletes who will suffice . . . just so that the flag of the white sun on the blue sky can flap above the Berlin Olympic Stadium."[161] But Shen rejected this utilitarian critique, asking the Chinese sports world to abandon pure economics for the grandeur of the Olympics and its world-recognized symbols: "The achievement of international recognition alone is worth millions to us as a nation and more than justifies the amount spent on the tour. . . . I believe [the athletes] have accomplished more for China than several ambassadors could have achieved in years."[162] For those who saw currency in international symbols, the Olympians' arrival in Berlin was itself a Chinese triumph.

The particular circumstances of the 1936 Olympics contributed to the sense of victory. The Chinese athletes were well aware of recent events in Germany, and even if envying in many ways the military strength of the revitalized German *Volk*, many felt "great discomfort" at the racial policies of their Nazi hosts. Indeed, a photo taken as the team marched out of the Berlin train station on 23 July shows the athletes looking coolly straight ahead, perhaps having mixed emotions about the smart *Sieg Heil* salutes accorded them by the workers, sailors, and officials who crowded along the walkway.[163] In the opening ceremonies held days later, the Chinese were one of the few teams not to salute Germany's number one sports fan, Adolf Hitler, with the *Sieg Heil;* a photo shows the team passing in front of Hitler's viewing stand holding their Olympic hats over their hearts with their right hands.[164] Cheng Jinguan remembers the "absolutely fascist" atmosphere of these ceremonies—the Luftwaffe airplanes and zeppelin soaring over the stadium and the roar of the German audience for Hitler as he took his seat. Cheng told me proudly that he and his teammates never stood for the Nazi flag, although they did stand for the German national flag, as "respect for other country's flags is just part of the Olympic spirit."[165]

The accomplishments of American sports hero Jesse Owens also provided the Chinese team with the inspiration that even in the fierce modern world, the racial underdog could indeed triumph. After the games, one Chinese progressive praised Owens's quadruple-gold efforts, proclaiming that his performance had "destroyed the poisonous myth of white supremacy."[166] Another asked defiantly, "Now who says the colored races *(youse renzhong)* are inferior to the white race?"[167]

Owens's involvement in these games was also personally significant for Cheng Jinguan, who befriended the American champion during training sessions. Cheng's smooth Soochow University English was more than sufficient to chat with Owens and ask for technical training and running tips. The Olympic friendship was captured for posterity in a snapshot of Owens, the very picture of the relaxed and confident sportsman, clad in his USA sweatsuit, with one arm around and the other clasping the hand of a stiff Cheng in sweater, tie, and slacks. This photo, determinedly preserved by Cheng through the Cultural Revolution,[168] has become a treasured artifact of Chinese Olympic history. In October 1996, Suzhou postal authorities released a limited edition commemorative envelope featuring a reproduction of this picture to mark the hundredth anniversary of the modern Olympic movement and the sixtieth anniversary of China's participation in the Berlin Games. The different Olympic triumphs of both these men, Owens and Cheng, were events of great significance for the Chinese sports world, providing the sorely needed proof that there was hope for oppressed peoples, African Americans and Chinese alike.

It was fortunate that the Chinese athletes could take home with them this type of victory, as there were few others. The results of the actual games confirmed for many Chinese that their nation was still unable, as one critic put it, "to produce men like Jesse Owens."[169] The long trip aboard the *Conte*

Verde had sapped the Chinese athletes of their strength. Long shots for Olympic honors to begin with, they turned in yet another disappointing performance. Of the nineteen track athletes in Berlin, only pole-vaulter Fu Baolu managed to advance past initial trials and into actual medal competition. But even Fu, ill the day of his event, was quickly eliminated with a top mark of 3.80 meters, a full twenty-five centimeters off his personal best of 4.05 meters.

Cheng Jinguan's Olympic hopes were dimmed for different reasons. Cheng's best event was the 440-meter hurdles. He was well known in China for his unorthodox hurdling style, in which he folded his rear leg inside, under his groin, rather than to the outside. But when the team arrived in Berlin, team leader and CNAAF Secretary Shen Siliang pulled Cheng aside to inform him that he would not run the hurdles in Berlin. When a confused Cheng asked why, Shen answered, "Not only does no one else in China use your hurdling style, but no one else in the world does. When the winners cross the finish line, you will still have thirty to forty meters left to go, and you will lose face for China [with the strange style]." A disheartened Cheng joined several sprinting competitions instead but was quickly eliminated from all of them with disappointing times that he attributes to the rough month at sea.[170]

China's other entries provided little to cheer about either. The soccer team, even more spent after their whirlwind trip of South Asia, lost to Britain 2–0 after a gutsy performance before a crowd that included Dai Jitao, Ambassador Cheng, and six hundred Chinese fans. The basketball team managed to win one game in the consolation bracket against the French but lost decisively to Japan, Peru, and Brazil.[171] China's best Olympic hope, Dutch cyclist Howard Wing, crashed on his fifth lap around the Berlin velodrome, ending his medal hopes.[172]

One of the few bright spots of these Olympics came with the demonstrations performed by the nine-member (six men, three women) *guoshu* team, selected after extensive tryouts at Shanghai like the others. In a significant self-Orientalizing gesture, the martial arts team was sent with the official Olympic team to share the wonders of China's "ancient *tiyu*" with the modern sporting fans of Europe and the world. During the trip to Germany, *guoshu* demonstrations were a large part of the shows put on for the Singapore Chinese and the "Olympic Evening" and "China Night" variety shows performed aboard the *Conte Verde*. In Germany before the games began, the group performed before Hamburg audiences at an International Concert, an International Boxing Exhibition, and an International

Sport Carnival, and then before Berlin crowds at a military camp and an International Sport Research Camp.[173] As another way of promoting the Chinese native martial arts, the CNAAF made a German-language film of Chu Minyi demonstrating tai chi calisthenics, *taijiquan*, shuttlecock, and archery, especially for entry in the Olympic Sport and Physical Education Film Contest to be held in Berlin.[174]

The biggest moment came on 9 August, when the martial arts squad put on a one-hour demonstration in the Olympic stadium before some thirty thousand fans. Chu's tai chi calisthenics, designed to synthesize the most useful elements of the ancient *taijiquan* and modern calisthenics, served as an appropriate opening to the performance. The martial artists, and the state that sponsored them, hoped to give the sports fans of Berlin and the world an understanding of the glories of traditional Chinese culture—but more specifically the fact that this Chinese culture could be modified and modernized and made to fit the twentieth-century world. It is doubtful that the nuances of the exotic Chinese movements they watched were apparent to the Berlin crowd, but it was an impressive spectacle nonetheless, for which "applause reverberated up to the heavens."[175] This sign of approval from the German people must have come as a great relief for the entire Chinese team, although many probably wished the Olympic crowd might have afforded the same welcome to Chinese athletes participating in actual Olympic events.

Of all the indignities that the team suffered in Berlin, the defeat of Chinese boxing standout Jin Guidi was particularly galling for the Chinese sporting community, as it captured in perfect microcosm the weakness of China's position in the 1930s world order. Middleweight Jin, fighting Briton Dick Shrimpton on 11 August, got off to a good start, punishing especially Shrimpton's jaw. After Jin delivered a quick left-right combination, the Briton got Jin into a clinch. As the referee separated the two boxers, Shrimpton, with a "terrifying charge," delivered a left upper-arm blow to Jin's head that put him down for the ten count. A side judge quickly intervened, ruling that Shrimpton's charge had come before the referee had finished separating them. He disqualified Shrimpton and awarded Jin the victory. However, the next day, an Olympic boxing rules committee decided that Shrimpton's infraction was not serious enough to warrant disqualification and named the Briton the winner by knockout. The Chinese delegation argued the point but did not issue an official protest, instead electing to have Jin carry the Chinese flag during the Olympic closing ceremonies as a more understated show of objection.[176]

Commenting days later, the foreign sporting press in Shanghai, perhaps even relieved by the decision that kept Olympic gold in white fists, praised the Chinese Olympians for

> accept[ing] without murmur the judges' reversal of their own earlier decision against the Briton. . . . Pettiness and a lack of spirit would have prompted the Chinese to protest the second decision and demand that the bout be refought. . . . But [Jin Guidi] and the entire Chinese delegation chose the course of honor.
>
> This one incident has covered China's athletic representatives with glory. They are bringing back intact the laurel they wore with them to the Olympic Games—the spirit of genuine sportsmanship.[177]

Chinese observers back home, on the other hand, were hardly as delighted by the capricious discarding of one of their very few Olympic triumphs. Many contrasted the Chinese acceptance of this wrongful defeat with the actions of the Peruvian soccer team, who, after a bad call against them, charged onto the field to argue with referees and then withdrew from their game against Austria. One writer lamented, "Just as our territory is always being invaded, this is not anything new or curious. China is always being bullied, and our tolerance is even greater than that of the Peruvians! Some have said, in exaggeration, that this event illustrates the Chinese penchant for generosity—'Oh, it doesn't matter, it's all right!' Ah Q–style Chinese are really too plentiful to count."[178]

The theme of failure dominated the post-Olympics evaluations delivered by members of the Chinese *tiyu* community. It may seem odd that supporters of the Chinese team could turn on the team so viciously as to write, "How badly they have failed, all the world knows."[179] Conditioned by ideologies of fair play and "It's how you play the game," it is easy for us to pretend to ignore the other strain of sporting ideology, which decrees that nice guys finish last. Few Chinese fans, desperate for any sign of success on the world stage, seem to have suffered from any such sportsmanlike qualms. They wanted to win. Any victory would have done—any true victory, that is. The Chinese soccer team's pride at their strong showing in their 2–0 loss to Britain was again derisively dismissed as mere "Ah Q–style self-consolation."[180]

Track star Cheng Jinguan remembered well the humiliation of representing a population of four hundred million but not being able to garner any Olympic laurels at all. He remembers Shanghai newspapers mocking the team's "goose egg" *(yadan)* in the points column, or, as another wrote, their failure "to salvage even half a bronze medal!"[181] China's Olympic athletes were raked over the coals for their failure. One journalist opined not only that their techniques were "lacking in scientific quality" but that team members were "too corrupt and truly in need of reform *(gexin)*. Some say that among students, the athletes and ballplayers mostly do not study, but enjoy making girlfriends and other bad habits."[182] A concerned educator suggested that the Chinese athletes' failure was due to their "lack of spiritual discipline."[183] Another simply dismissed them as "bad [i.e., arrogant] winners," "cajoled into thinking themselves tin gods by an indulgent public."[184]

One point on which almost all seemed to agree was the idea that the still-sickly, weak Chinese body was truly to blame. Head Olympic delegate Shen Siliang, upon returning to Shanghai, simply remarked, "[Chinese] physiques are underdeveloped *(luohou)* and just not fit enough to compete with others." A Shanxi observer found several factors that contributed to the Olympic "failure"—Chinese high death rates and short life spans, traditional anti-physical ideology, and even the legacy of the weak Qing state.[185] Seven years later, one prominent eugenicist still asserted that this Olympic failure proved the Chinese national body to be a "weary, humpbacked cripple."[186]

The standard for comparison was clearly the hated Japanese. Even before the Olympics began, one author had warned the sporting public, "There are no Chinese among the heroes on the international athletic stage! The success of our Eastern neighbors' heroes on the international athletic stage is a fine example of endurance of hardship and self-motivation for our Chinese athletes!"[187] After Japan's triumphs at Berlin—eighteen medals, eighth-most overall—Chinese sports enthusiasts were in awe of Japanese progress. One author wondered, "Their physique is no better than ours; they are usually shorter in height. There are 101 things that can be said to be similar between these two nationalities. Why are they so far ahead of us?"[188] Xie Siyan proclaimed their example the most suitable for Chinese reference, citing in particular Japanese self-discipline, their deep understanding of physical education and the body, and the pride that Japanese P.E. instructors took in their work.[189]

The Japanese athletes' outstanding performance before the eyes of the sporting world clearly made the Chinese "failure" in Berlin that much more unpalatable and portentous. As a result, concerned Chinese saw no choice but to get back to the basics of building a strong Chinese body and delivering the mass *tiyu* programs described in Chapter 5. Their goals were quite different from those of activists who saw mass *tiyu* as the opposite of, and a solution to, the ills brought on by China's emphasis on competitive sports. Yet the faith in "mass-izing" physical education (making it more accessible to the masses) as a cure-all was the same. For those who immediately began working toward a stronger Chinese delegation for the 1940 Olympic

Games to be held at Tokyo, "mass sports" would be the key to transforming and creating Chinese bodies that could win honors for their motherland on the most international of international stages.

Foreign observers in China clearly did not understand the national significance of this Olympic entry for the Chinese sporting public. In a remarkable move that erased the Western role in introducing the sports cult of victory to China in the first place, Westerners made sportsmanlike graciousness the only allowable reaction to the outcomes of the recent games. They saw Chinese fans' criticism of their nation's delegates after the Olympic losses as "ignorant," explaining to them that the goals of the Chinese Olympic team merely were "to display the utmost sportsmanship under all circumstances, and thus impress the civilized world with the fact that in China the athletes are taught and understand what sportsmanship really is."[190] Unsurprisingly, few Chinese observers bought this defeatist line of reasoning, instead choosing to be honest about the simple failure of pampered Olympians to give the Chinese nation a return on the considerable resources invested in their sport. The "goose eggs" next to China's name in the 1932 and 1936 medal tallies were not acceptable to a sporting community who for years now had been chanting, "We can compete!"

CONCLUSION

Perhaps the most interesting interpretation of the 1936 Olympic "failure" was offered in the Nanjing journal *Xikang-Tibet Vanguard*. The author, who—judging from his surname Chang—was probably not Han Chinese, was himself an athlete who had competed for Xikang Province in the Sixth National Games of 1935. Chang capitalized on post-Olympic feelings of weakness and shame among the Chinese sporting public to make an incisive statement about the status of people from China's western border areas. He related the pregames hopes of border-area athletes that their performance in Shanghai would give the "China proper" *(neidiren)* majority a "good impression" of the border peoples. But after they were defeated by superior athletes like Liu Changchun, "The average person's evaluation went something like 'The border areas are making no progress; everything about them is just backward.' Their discriminating attitude was only strengthened, and our weaknesses were only proven to be true."[191] He continued,

> If we open our eyes just a little wider, we can see clearly that border
> athletes participating in the National Games and Chinese athletes par
> ticipating in the Olympic Games are actually in identical situations. It's

the same tragic one-act play, acting out the same truths and the same emotions. . . . Foreigners look down on Chinese as low and weak, and Chinese *(neidiren)* see people from the border regions as worthless—is there any difference here? Foreigners assume that everything in China is backward, and Chinese assume that everything in the border regions is crude and uncivilized—is there any difference here either?[192]

Perhaps most important, this rejection of Han hegemony in China did not even bring into question the field of modern competitive sport. The plateaus of Xikang and Tibet were among the last regions to be exposed to China's modern *tiyu*, a cultural enterprise that more accurately represented the hopes and aspirations of urban coastal China than those of the far western population. This author, a proud competitor for his home Xikang province, scarcely questioned this mode by which he hoped to liberate Xikang and the border regions from the double oppression of Han dominance within China and imperialist dominance on an international level. For China's physical culture, from the mass *tiyu* of the county athletic grounds, to the provincial- and regional-level athletic meets, to the National Games explosions of patriotic sentiment, to the pressure of international competition presented by the Far Eastern Games and the Olympics, had become a firm part of the multilayered senses of identity shared by millions of Chinese. National Games triumphs in the sacred Purple and Gold Mountains and international defeats suffered in Manila boardrooms and on Berlin fields alike contributed to the complicated sense of nation that competitive sport created for the Chinese. Provincial pride, regional rivalries, and nationalist shame and passion were all equal parts of this creation.

The mass *tiyu* so fashionable in the 1930s among party stalwarts and fascist activists constituted an important practical link between physical exercise and the strong bodies needed to protect the Chinese nation from acts of invasion and denigration. Elite-level competitive sports were at the other end of the spectrum of symbols and representations. In competitive sports, national *face* was ultimately much more important than the "national body" to which the mass *tiyu* aspired. In the 1930s, the threat of war and the need for strong battleworthy bodies was every bit as real as the diplomatic need for foreign nations to see China as "a nation to be counted." The elderly ex-stars whom I have met, and assuredly their male and female teammates, believed that their sporting efforts could bring a better day for the Chinese nation. Mass *tiyu* activists worked at a local level to train a generation of self-respecting, clean-living, Japan-hating, patriotic Chinese. The functions of these groups were complementary, and both were crucial to how Chinese in the 1930s envisioned their race, nation, and global status. The charisma and skill of these athletes helped make sports appealing on the popular level, facilitating the work of mass *tiyu* activists. And the high-level meets where the athletes flourished were just as dependent on some sort of (middle-class) "mass" interest that, via ticket sales and newspaper circulations, supplied a justification and foundation for these athletes' dreams of glory.

The onset of total war with Japan just one year after the Berlin Olympics rendered competitive sports useless for a decade. But their "hopping and skipping tricks" continued to be an important part of the mass *tiyu* programs flourishing during the long and lean war years. Gold and silver medals were hardly the point anymore as the Japanese invader threatened to bring the Chinese nation to its knees. But in the postwar years, and even more in the early efforts of the People's Republic of China to gain international respect and recognition, competitive sports would return and validate the efforts of the men and women athletes of this earlier era.

7   From Martial Arts to National Skills

The Construction of a Modern Indigenous Physical Culture, 1912–37

> It is our nation's original cultural calisthenics. It is a psychologically suitable form of specialized exercise. It brings one hundred benefits and is without a single harm. It is spread by men, not taught by spirits. Masters disseminate it via educational methods, not by blind mechanical obedience. It can be described exactly and justly by written and spoken language. It is a military force that can be used to maintain peace and order and an appropriate form of self-defense. It is artful and technical, not laborious and based solely on power. The recent New Thought and New Tide are roaring in. . . . How can we not begin by transforming the physiques of our countrymen?
>
> SIR STRENGTH (Qiang Gong),
> Chinese Wushu Association of Shanghai, 1921

The martial arts, the most famed and supposedly authentic genre of Chinese physical culture, which so far have seldom been mentioned in this study, were influenced in Republican-era China by many of the same factors that shaped the sporting and calisthenics modes discussed in the past several chapters. Those hoping to promote the martial arts were forced to rationalize, shape, and explain them and elaborate just what they had to do with the modern nation-state. Stigmatized as backward, feudal, and superstitious, martial arts in the early Republican period seemed as destined for the garbage bin of history as *tiyu* sports were for everlasting prominence. Agents of foreign physical culture faced much less resistance from the forces of urban, literate, commercial China than martial artists did. Yet it is clear today that the martial arts have survived, and famously. This chapter explores the Republican-era campaign, undertaken by individual urban martial artists, private organizations, and the state itself, to make the seemingly threatening and mysterious world of martial arts safe for a new China.

MARTIAL ARTS IN THE LATE QING

In the late Qing and early Republic, government officials, educators, intellectuals, and foreign missionaries worked for a new modern physical culture for China—some proposing militaristic systems based on German and Japanese models, others favoring an emphasis on Anglo-American competitive sports. Whatever their differences here, however, these modern parties shared one thing—their almost complete neglect of native Chinese martial arts as a viable form of Chinese *tiyu*.

Scholar Lin Boyuan has described the rapid transformations occurring in the diverse world of martial arts during the latter decades of the Qing. Itinerants pushed by rural poverty into cities like Tianjin, Qingdao, Ji'nan, and Shenyang included many martial arts performer-instructors. Workers moving into cities also brought with them their penchant for martial arts study and play. In dozens of Guangzhou factories, workers set up *wuguan* martial arts schools, hiring itinerant martial arts instructors *(quanshi)* to teach their skills.[1]

Despite this continued popular attention to martial arts, the agents of a modern *tiyu* "body cultivation" for China had little use for this indigenous body of knowledge. Few of the new government-run academies included any martial arts in their curriculum. Even if some were interested in including martial arts in their physical education, the 1904 decree calling for military drill to be taught in all academies strained most schools' resources too much to allow them to provide this instruction as well. The independent physical education associations founded in the late years of the Qing also ignored martial arts as an area of study. The first modern organization to emphasize training in the indigenous martial arts, Shanghai's Pure Martial Calisthenics School (Jingwu ticao xuexiao; hereafter referred to as the Pure Martial School), was founded only in 1910, years after dozens of physical education, sports, and military drill organizations had begun popping up all over coastal urban China.[2]

Around 1910, however, much of the popular disregard for Chinese martial arts was reversed, perhaps as a rush of anti-Manchu sentiment made the consciously "Chinese" martial arts seem like a useful anti-Qing weapon. Once-disparate bands of itinerant performers and teachers, suddenly exposed in China's cities to *wushu* schools and artists from other regions, began to mature and coalesce into a "community" of martial artists. This new community, inspired by trends of patriotic concern and faith in the people as an agent of positive change, also partook of the late Qing movement to form public associations uniting urban residents with similar interests and concerns. These simultaneous changes created a brand new institution in Chinese cities—the public martial arts organization—which became a commonplace landmark in urban China by the early Republic, a space for mostly middle-class, concerned citizens to live out a martial vision of the nation-state. The first and most monumental of these bodies was Shanghai's Pure Martial Calisthenics School,[3] formed in 1910, which in April 1916 changed its name to the Pure Martial Athletic Association (Jingwu tiyuhui; hereafter referred to as the Pure Martial Association). Several other different organizations—from Tianjin's Chinese Warriors *(Wushi)* Association in 1911, to Shanghai's Martial Arts *(Quanshu)* Research Society the same year, to Beijing's Swordsmanship Research Society in 1912—soon followed, up and down China's urban coast.

The lore of the Pure Martial School's founding is well known among martial arts enthusiasts. Martial arts expert Huo Yuanjia left Tianjin in 1907 for Shanghai, where he quickly became renowned for his penchant for flattening Japanese *ronin*, Russian rascals, and foreign rogues in general. In 1909–10, a barnstorming muscleman (Russian or English, depending on which version of the story one hears) was stirring up trouble in Shanghai's brothels and other places of vice. He publicly claimed that the whole of China could provide no competition for his strength and fighting abilities, and he pledged to "flatten any Sick Man of East Asia *(Dong Ya bingfu)*" who dared challenge him. Unable to bear this display of disrespect, the Tongmenghui revolutionaries Chen Qimei and Nong Jinsun urged the well-known Huo to bring an end to this humiliation. Huo recruited his star pupil Liu Zhensheng to fight this particular bully in a great showdown at his new boxing arena on Jing'ansi Road. But after spying on Liu's training sessions, the Russian fled in fear of the Pure Martial prowess he saw there.

Having achieved this glorious victory, Huo and Tongmenghui figures like Chen and Song Jiaoren set about establishing a school that could produce more Chinese citizens possessing the skills and the will to crush the foreign reprobates and lowlifes defiling China's cities.[4] The Pure Martial Calisthenics School was soon founded in the Zhabei district of Shanghai, in the extra rooms of a house belonging to a Wang family living near the Shanghai-Nanjing Railroad water tower.[5] Ten weeks later, though, Huo died suddenly. Although many contend Huo died of a lung ailment, likely tuberculosis, popular Pure Martial lore holds that Huo was poisoned by a Japanese Dr. Akino, who, like many of his countrymen, clearly feared the rise of a strong Chinese martial arts community.[6]

Regardless of how much of the Pure Martial creation myth one believes, the founding of the Pure Martial School marked the beginning of a new era for the indigenous martial arts. Recent Chinese martial arts action films seem to locate this break as a moment when native *wushu* experts found the ability and inspiration to pound into submission sneering, bad-Mandarin-speaking Japanese and Western bullies. This popular theme is not totally a latter-day invention, as records exist of such showdowns between young martial arts virtuosos and expatriate foreign fighters. For example, Liu Baichuan, a major figure in the physical culture world of the 1920s and 1930s, defeated a 250-pound Russian strongman in a great bout held at the Pure Martial Association ring in Shanghai in 1916. News of this victory was carried in Tianjin's *Dagongbao* and several Southeast Asian newspapers and even reached Sun Yat-sen in Japan, where he penned a scroll reading "Martial Spirit" *(shangwu jingshen)* for Liu.[7]

Yet the new era ushered in by the founding of the Pure Martial School was more than this. In the first decade of the new Republic, the *wushu* community would begin to give their martial culture a modern, scientific, and national packaging. Martial artists worked to dissociate their domain from the humiliating legacy of the Boxer Uprising or Boxer Rebellion, the 1900 spasm of anti-Western nationalism led by members of martial-religious cults. They also set out to define martial arts as an indigenous brand of physical culture just as useful and important as the modern sports and exercises of foreign origin. New and appropriate terms were used to refer to the diverse field of martial arts as a more unified body of knowledge. The skills and arts passed on for centuries in China had previously been referred to as *quanyong* (fists of valor), *wuyi* (martial arts), *jiji* (skills of assault), *shoubo* (hand combat), or *jiyong* (skills of valor).[8] Martial artists of the 1910s used terms like *wushu* (martial skills), *quanshu* (skills of the fists), or *guoji* (national skills) as they crafted forms that would make more sense in China's Republican age.

HYBRID GAMES: MARTIAL ARTS IN THE EARLY REPUBLIC

When I look at our nation's martial arts *(guoji)*, deep feelings well up inside me. Why? Boxing and wrestling both existed in ancient China but are also the root of [modern] physical culture. . . . If the conservatives were to add the new movements of Swedish and German calisthenics to their boxing and wrestling, and if the reformers would add the old movements of Chinese boxing and wrestling to their calisthenics, then both sides could compromise and create a new spirit combining the old and the new. . . . In ancient times martial arts were used to kill people, while today they are used to educate people.

FAN JUN, "Duiyu guoji zhi ganyan"
[Thoughts and words in martial arts] (1918)

These thoughts on martial arts, expressed by Nanjing Higher Normal School student Fan Jun, are representative of arguments of China's martial arts community in the first decade of the Republic.[9] Caricatured as hopelessly old-fashioned, 1910s martial artists nevertheless worked tirelessly to carve out a place for the martial arts tradition that they knew could someday serve as a basis for a Chinese and modern physical culture. Many worked to show that *wushu* could be integrated into the new culture of modernity and science. However, this is where *wushu* met the most resistance, for New Culture modernists guarded jealously their realm of ideas and practices that would succeed in making a new and strong China.

Members of the martial arts community agreed that the old ways—passed down orally, scattered among numerous clashing traditions and schools, irrational, and un-national as they were—had to be changed if martial arts were to remain a vital part of a modern Chinese culture. One solution to this problem was to group martial arts with competitive sports. The chief architect of this strategy was the Pure Martial Association. By showing Pure Martial films and putting on demonstrations at schools around the country, the association spread quickly, with branches in Shaoxing, Guangzhou, Foshan, Shantou, Xiamen, and Hankou by 1919. Southeast Asian Chinese also opened several branches in locales like Selangor, Kuala Lumpur, Saigon, Penang, and Jakarta by 1920. But this expansion had its costs. The Pure Martial message had to be diluted before it made much sense to urban Chinese of the early Republic; the association achieved its larger success only after holding classes and competitions in un-martial sports like soccer, basketball, track and field, bicycle racing, table tennis, billiards, hiking, and roller skating.[10] The association's annual graduation day performances, a tradition that began in 1912, were called "athletic meets" *(yundonghui)*.[11] And in a telling demonstration of the thin line between Pure Martial arts and sports, a 1916 National Day celebration included a "hybrid game" that was "played" with all manner of martial arts and sporting equipment, from tennis rackets and baseball mitts to spears and swords.[12]

Other activists envisioned similar strategies for creating a more popular martial arts. One author urged that martial arts *(quanyi)* be made into a sports event, with competitions of all sizes sponsored by gentry members. He also felt that a "national hero-worship" could be created if China's news media were to take a page from their Japanese counterparts, who helped the growth of *sumō* wrestling with their daily standings and rankings.[13] An author writing for *New Youth* in 1916 felt that "no team sport played by students anywhere in the nation is as competitive as wrestling, jūdō, or fencing."[14]

Forces of urban capitalism saw the fusion of martial arts with modern physical culture as a good marketing opportunity. The June 1917 *Chinese Educational Review* carried a Commercial Press advertisement dominated by a drawing of happy short-haired boys in school uniforms holding signs that spelled out, "Strengthen the nation, strengthen the race," selling seven books on sports and four on martial arts. By July 1918, the Commercial Press had enough martial arts titles in print to warrant a separate martial arts advertisement for thirteen titles under the heading "national-essence physical culture" *(guocui tiyu)*.[15]

A more logical, if not quite as fashionable, strategy for martial arts activists was to promote their specialty as an integral part of the military-themed calisthenics and drill so popular in the late Qing and early Republic. The above-quoted student Fan Jun suggested a "hybrid" of Swedish-German drill and Chinese martial arts as the key to a new era of martial physical culture. Another author saw martial arts as important elements of a new "training-ism" *(duanlian zhuyi)* to replace the more explicitly militarist education of the late Qing. The new philosophy of physical education would provide a "total and complete development of people's minds and instincts, sharpening the emotions and consciousness." Instructors' use of tough language like "You're not a real man" or "You're not a true citizen of our nation," paired with a consciousness that "if I do not kill the enemy, I will be killed by the enemy," would allow martial arts to truly train the nascent nation.[16]

Others worked to craft martial arts into more modern, user-friendly calisthenic forms. As early as 1913, Jiading author Xu Yuxin did this in a book on Chinese boxing *(quanshu)*. A preface to the book explained how boxing techniques that in former times had been passed on orally from father to son easily "died out"; in contrast, Japan took a modern approach to its "national (martial) arts" *(guoji)* and integrated indigenous Japanese forms into modern military drill regimens for the sake of strengthening the nation and race.[17] Xu's book contained one-hundred-plus pages of detailed descriptions of the stances and motions of Chinese boxing as well as thirty-six photos of the author (in modern military uniform) demonstrating these movements. Xu provided other innovations as well, explaining:

> Our nation's boxing had no oral commands in the old days, so the order was extremely hard to remember, and the movements were just as difficult to keep in proper time. So in this book, the movements and their order are noted by calisthenics-style oral commands. . . . Martial arts routines are not inherently divided into segments. This book follows the *ticao* convention of dividing the movements into several segments

for ease of learning. For teaching, this also makes it easier to isolate each segment. After one is familiar with all the segments, they can be connected front to back.[18]

Other martial artists followed similar synchronizing impulses. Wang Huaiqi, later to become one of the biggest names in Chinese physical education, in 1915 published a routine called "*batuanjin* calisthenics," a "simplified" version of the ancient Chinese stretching exercise *baduanjin*.[19] Such "hybridizing," popular during the New Culture Movement of the 1910s, was yet another approach to reforming ancient Chinese arts for urbanites concerned about training their bodies and their nation.

Including martial arts instruction in school curricula was considered an equally important means to this end. A Jiangsu educator writing in 1914 gave a defensive answer to his own rhetorical question, "Are martial arts *(jiji)* suitable for classroom instruction?"

[Martial arts] are absolutely genuine skills, containing nothing faked [i.e., no staged tricks]. It is only that over the last century or so, those who have studied them have not been suited to the task and have used all the wrong methods. So now society has chosen to adopt an attitude that slights and despises [martial arts], seeing them as the lowest and most undignified arts around. False rumors beget still more false rumors, and the once-great national [martial] arts have become so scarce they are on the edge of extinction. . . . Every school is now concerned about physical education, each one working to allow its students to have healthy bodies. That is why they should enlist in their curricula every type of exercise and game that would strengthen students and make them healthy. . . . Today, there is no unified effort to include our nation's ancient martial arts in classroom instruction. Still, these skills would definitely allow students to develop true physical fitness.[20]

Xu Yibing, one of the early leaders of China's physical education community, petitioned the Education Department in Beijing that instruction in Chinese martial arts, "the most noble and lofty form of exercise . . . the most ancient and finest form of calisthenics,"[21] be added to the curricula of all China's schools. In April 1915, Beijing's Physical Education Research Society introduced the resolution "Requesting the Promotion of Ancient Chinese *Wushu* as a Required Course" at the First National Education Conference in Beijing. The society's logic that martial arts was "a form proving that we do not have to imitate others" was irresistible, and the motion was approved.[22]

One fascinating example of this integration of martial arts into the educational system can be seen in the "Boxing Team" (their English for *Ji-*

jibu) formed at Nanyang University in 1912 by school president Tang Weizhi. Legend had it that Tang formed the team after discovering a student skilled in "southern fists" (nanquan) who halted a foreign professor's accelerating motorcycle with his bare hands.[23] A picture of the club in its first year shows twenty-four members in black long-sleeved shirts reading "NY Boxer" in white English lettering across the front, each frozen in a different swordsman pose.[24] Their use of the term *Boxer*, and the modern masculinity and nationalism that this implies, is fascinating. By calling themselves "Boxers," these college men could both appeal to the legitimacy of the Western sport of boxing and, simultaneously, confront the history of the rural and superstitious martial arts on their own terms: if arrogant foreigners wanted to label the Chinese as ignorant "Boxers," then here were the Boxers of the new Republic, educated, cosmopolitan, and ready to engage in the world of modern men and their nations. Nanyang University's annual athletic meet featured a martial arts competition for the first time in 1915, and two years later, "endless praise" was lavished upon the dozens of martial arts demonstrations performed at the school's twentieth anniversary celebrations.[25]

To make martial arts an acceptable pastime for citizens of the new Republic, the ancient skills had to be shown to be conducive to new modern ways. The Pure Martial Association called the movement the "new martialization" and followed the slogan "Scientize martial arts, and spread them to the millions." Scientization required purging the martial arts of superstitious relics like "spirit fists" (shenquan) or "divine swords" (jianxian)[26] and called for other conspicuously modern touches. For example, the association opened its own photography studio on Nanjing Road and was thus able to include thirty photos in its 1918 book *Pure Martial [Association]* and 440 photos in the 1920 volume *Record of the Pure Martial [Association]*.[27] The Pure Martial Association also hoped to keep in step with the movement for gender equality. A Women's Department was established in 1917 with female *wushu* standout Chen Shichao as director. By the next year, Pure Martial students were teaching martial arts in seven women's schools across Shanghai.[28]

Martial arts enthusiasts began to explain their favorite techniques in the authoritative terms of Western science. When Huang Xing, publisher of Changsha's *Tiyu Weekly*, promoted meditation as a native Chinese and "tranquil" form of exercise, a sporting friend retorted that this "stillness" would only turn China into a "Daoist Buddhist nation" like India, Tibet, and Mongolia.[29] No small challenge, this threat that the Han race would devolve and follow the example of once-great peoples whose (supposedly) de-

bilitating and meek religious traditions had transformed them into the ultimate laughingstocks of the modern age, feminized non-nations. Huang explained that his advocacy of meditation was merely part of his greater advocacy of *tiyu* in general, part of his conviction that strong and healthy
bodies were needed to live "the life of an evolved people":

> Have those with the ability to jump, run, throw and climb completely
> achieved all the abilities needed in life?. . . . We can see that human life
> is governed by something different. This something is especially devel-
> oped, and what is it? In the past, Chinese doctrines spoke of the heart
> (*xin*); today, speaking with scientific accuracy, we know it as the brain.
> *Tiyu*, in the very first place, was supposed to be about helping the brain
> to develop. So our advocacy of tranquil exercise takes as its main goal
> the clear and alert brain.[30]

But not everyone bought this presentation of martial arts as an acceptable part of the new scientific culture and thought. *Wushu* was far too easy
a target for the May Fourth generation, for it seemed to be everything that
these modern men wanted China not to be. It had been part of the old "closed
China" and traced no heritage to the modern West. Despite the recent attempt to tailor martial arts to the forms of modern physical culture, at heart
it was still unquantifiable and unscientific. It belonged to the wandering
jianghu (itinerants of the countryside), not to the enlightened classes of urban China. It left no written records that could be spread among the masses.
The field was heir to a legacy of secrecy and division, clearly the exact opposite of what was needed to unify the nation. Indeed, little about *wushu*
seemed to suit the needs of the modern nation-building project.

When in 1918 members of the Fourth National Education Conference
at Shanghai called for schools to promote *wushu* education throughout
China,[31] they were rebuked by Lu Xun's "Random Thoughts" in the October 1918 *New Youth*:

> There are many now who actively support and advocate boxing.
> Remember, this was advocated in the past, but then it was pushed by
> Manchu kings and princes; now it's Republican educators. . . . These
> educators take these old ways, "passed down from a mystic woman
> of the highest heavens or some such, to the Yellow Emperor, and then
> to some nuns," now called "new martial arts" or "Chinese calisthen-
> ics," and tell youngsters to practice. . . . Some say that the efficacy of
> Chinese people learning Western calisthenics cannot yet be seen, so we
> have no choice but to teach our own nation's calisthenics (or boxing).
> But I think that if you pick up foreign hammers or batons and begin
> exercising your arms and legs, this will have some "efficacy" in terms
> of muscle development. How could you not see it? Apparently we now

have to switch to "Wusong Slipping out of Handcuffs" or some other [martial arts] tricks. I suppose this is due to Chinese people being physiologically different from foreigners. . . . We have seen all this before, in 1900. That time it ended in the total destruction of our reputation. We will have to see what happens this time around.[32]

Lu Xun's sarcastic association of a *wushu* curriculum with the disastrous Boxer Uprising of 1900 was designed to show the utter irrelevancy of martial arts to the national tasks at hand. However, the new martial artists of China's cities were more literate and urbane than Lu Xun had supposed. Four months later, *New Youth* published a rebuttal by Chen Tiesheng, one of the pillars of the Pure Martial Association in Shanghai.[33] Chen could not quietly stand by while Lu Xun rudely dismissed the entire *wushu* tradition; a reporter by trade, he had the literary talents to go toe to toe with China's foremost cultural critic.

Chen began his article with a strong parry: "Who is this Mr. Lu Xun? I've never heard of him; he must be a youngster. This guy's mind seems to be filled with a few misconceptions—managing to confuse Boxer bandits *(quanfei)* with the martial arts *(jijishu)*."[34] Aware of the opportunity that this *New Youth*–sanctioned bout afforded his cause, Chen explained the inadequacy of Lu Xun's critiques. He made a clear distinction between the "unregulated bestial dances," sorcery, and supernaturalism *(guidao zhuyi)* of the "Boxer bandits" and the humanism *(rendao zhuyi)* celebrated by true martial artists. For those *New Youth* readers who could not endorse any culture not connected to the progressive West, Chen even noted the recent American publication of a book on northern Chinese martial arts and described "boxing" (in English) as a perfectly normal pastime in the West. Finally, he closed his piece with a quick knockout combination that turned the tables on his modernist foes, calling Lu Xun "simply a foreign Boxer bandit through and through" and taunting *New Youth*'s editors by claiming that they would be just like the Manchu Qing dynasty if they "shelved and did not publish" his article.[35]

Chen Tiesheng's defense did little to change the modernists' instinctive distrust of the martial arts, however. A year later in *New Youth*, the journal's founder Chen Duxiu panned educator Ma Liang's program for a "New Chinese Martial Arts": "We have already had enough of the 1900 'Spirit Boxers,' but now we are supposed to teach Commander Ma's martial arts in school. Do not once more allow the 'extraordinary feats of strength, chaos and spirits,' of which even Confucius did not speak [because of their supernatural content], to come and 'deceive the next generation.'"[36] Chen, like

Lu Xun, hoped to effect a massive forgetting of this mystical aspect of China's cultural heritage.

Yet these famed iconoclasts' biting anti-*wushu* criticisms probably did less harm than the uniformly short shrift given *wushu* by many modern chroniclers of Chinese physical culture. The martial arts were diverse and inexact (and therefore nonsensical in the modern nation); perhaps it never occurred to these modernizers that there even remained a *wushu* to ignore. Only seven pages of Guo Xifen's 1919 outline of the history of Chinese *tiyu* covered post-Ming martial arts.[37] The YMCA *tiyu* coordinator Hao Geng-sheng, in his *Physical Education in China*, limited his discussion of modern martial arts to a passing reference to Pure Martial legend Huo Yuanjia. His twenty-eight-page chapter on "Chinese Games" ignored martial arts completely, seeing the Chinese *tiyu* tradition instead as embodied in games like kite flying, Squirrel Holes, and Catch the Puppies.[38]

Modernists like Guo and Hao wrote *wushu* out of existence, actively denying and forgetting the martial arts, as they remembered the new Western-style *tiyu* into Chinese history. For many, the martial arts were simply too "Chinese" (or in other words, too backward) and too unquantifiable to play an important role in the physical culture of the new Chinese nation. Thus martial arts activists' efforts to depict their skills as indispensable constituents of Chinese education, sport, or modernity in general often met great resistance. However, the continuing influence of the May Fourth Movement in the early 1920s would bring surprising new life to the field, as martial artists employed clever and far-seeing tactics to remake martial arts into an integral element of modern Chinese physical culture.

THE PURE MARTIAL ERA, 1920–27

In the 1920s, public figures from all over the political spectrum worked to promote modern martial arts. Warlord Feng Yuxiang cleverly exploited the contradictions of May Fourth anti-*wushu* thought when he thundered in a 1927 speech:

> I don't oppose playing ball in the least, but I do oppose this feverish consumption of foreigners' goods. This is exercise, but it is the exercise of the gents and ladies of the leisured classes. If you want to exercise your body, is a blade not enough? Is a sword routine not enough? Are wrestling or boxing not enough? Of China's eighteen types of martial arts, not one is incapable of drenching our entire bodies in sweat, stimulating all the body's blood, tendons, and bones. You say those activities

are old-fashioned, but you don't even know that the Western sport of track and field is all left over from the Greek and Roman eras. . . . Now it is all just about blindly following the West, . . . and when you think about it this is really our greatest national shame.[39]

Communist Party member and social activist Yun Daiying saw martial arts as a key to spreading his progressive social philosophy in the Chinese countryside. In two different articles, Yun recommended that idealistic students "going down to the people" during school vacations teach martial arts to rural youth or join in already-existing martial arts groups. He saw *wushu* as perfect for rural youth, since it was a form valued in traditional Chinese culture and could be practiced at night so as not to interfere in farm work. Yun pointed out that through activities like martial arts, "We can be around them and get to know them every day, and this will make them feel much more interested [in our political work]."[40]

Yet the parties who did the most to promote a modernized and modernizing martial arts were Shanghai organizations, particularly the Pure Martial Association. The story of martial arts in the 1920s is not simply the story of the Pure Martial Association, but the organization's story shows just how versatile these arts, their practitioners, and their promoters had become by the 1920s. The audacity of their proselytizing can be seen in this 1920 statement from Pure Martial leader Lu Weichang:

> Confucianism is based on the principle of self-control. Buddhism is based on the principle of equality. And Christianity is based on the principle of brotherhood. Self-control, equality, brotherhood—the spirit of Confucius, Buddha, and Jesus. Today one sees that Pure Martial members are the ones able to bring these ideas together harmoniously and thoroughly. And this cannot be refuted.[41]

Indeed, the 1920s Pure Martial mission was nothing less than the conversion of China and all the world's Chinese people to the doctrine of "Pure Martial–ism."

The Pure Martial Association worked in many ways to achieve martial arts' ascendance to "the international sporting stage."[42] One strategy was to privilege the written text and its role in a modern *wushu*. Pure Martial leaders cultivated important links to powerful political figures and showed a commercial acumen that disproved once and for all the image of martial artists as itinerant stragglers unfit for modern life. The Pure Martial Association cemented this success by reaching out to two important groups that were somewhat ignored by the mainstream *tiyu* community—women and Overseas Chinese in Southeast Asia—who energized the state of Pure Martial affairs and in the latter case sustained the Pure Martial enterprise when other pillars of support crumbled.

Perhaps the most important motto at the Pure Martial Association head-quarters in Shanghai was, "Without letters *(wen)*, the effort to spread [martial arts] far and wide is futile."[43] The ancient martial arts tradition of oral transmission among a select few was the most crucial aspect of the modernist portrayal of *wushu* as a premodern and irrelevant culture. Thus the Pure Martial Association understood better than any other physical culture enterprise the importance of written knowledge in spreading their craft. The association's literary era began in 1916, with Chen Tiesheng's illustrated articles in the *Students' Magazine* on Dragon Pond boxing, Bodhidharma swords, and five-tiger spears.[44] The organization's real push came with the 1920 publication of *Record of the Pure Martial*, a three-hundred-page commemoration of their ten years of teaching *wushu*. This volume began with a long essay by editor Chen Tiesheng, fresh from his *New Youth* debate with Lu Xun the year before, on the "Great Pure Martial–ism." Chen introduced the principles of health, wisdom, morality, and equality that made the Pure Martial Association such a great force for peace and progress in Asia.[45]

Later, Chen described his "martial library," listing thirty books published over the last decade and defying the popular conception of martial arts as crude sport for illiterate rustics.[46] Dozens of essays, 440 photos, and pages of charts combined to tell forcefully the story of the first Pure Martial decade. The association continued its mission of putting martial arts knowledge in writing by starting its own journal, *the Pure Martial Magazine (Jingwu za-zhi)*, in 1922, published by its own Pure Martial Printing Company after 1923.[47] In 1924 the association opened up its own library containing numerous books, magazines, and newspapers in Chinese and English.[48] And by 1921 the association could impress possible converts with a five-reel film, featuring segments on diverse Pure Martial activities like women's martial arts, Mandarin instruction, ping-pong, Beijing opera, gymnastics, archery, and workers' martial arts instruction, and closing with an inspiring scene of the association flag fluttering proudly over a backdrop of the planet Earth.[49]

The Pure Martial Association also sought to spread its influence by associating with leading Chinese political figures. The second article of the association's constitution declared that members "were not allowed to become involved in politics," but no observer would have failed to notice the frequency with which political leaders praised the association. In 1916, the revolutionary hero Wang Jingwei contributed a preface to Chen Tiesheng's book *Dragon Pond Boxing.*[50] The same year, Sun Yat-sen attended a Pure Martial boxing exhibition and proclaimed, "The martial arts are our China's national essence. . . . I deeply hope that young students, soldiers, and compatriots of all walks of life will all pay close attention to this."[51] The 1920 *Record of the Pure Martial* was graced with a preface by Sun, who saw martial arts as an important contribution of the Chinese people to world peace.[52] To this same volume, the Sunist-Marxist activist Hu Hanmin contributed an inscription that read, "Use the scientific method to spread the artistic spirit."[53]

Still, Pure Martial editor Chen Tiesheng continued to claim that "the Pure Martial Association does not carry the stench of politics." His justification was simple—Sun's advocacy of martial arts in his *Pure Martial* preface was simply that of "a very learned medical doctor . . . providing specific scientific proof for the uses [of martial arts]." When Pure Martial Association representatives, on a 1923 trip to Beijing, presented association materials to President Li Yuanhong, this was not a political act either—for Li was also honorary chairman of the Tianjin YMCA, and was this not an enterprise funded solely by Chinese?[54] For an organization that mythically traced its origins back to the revolutionary Tongmenghui, the Pure Martial Association spent considerable effort trying to distance its martial arts work from the "stench" of politics in China's messy warlord era. However, the shrewd use of connections with lofty figures in the Chinese political scene necessarily tied the association's fate closely to shifts in the Chinese political world.

Another basis of the Pure Martial Association's success was sharp commercial acumen. If martial arts had traditionally served as an avenue of advance for rural youth excluded from market networks and commercial connections, the modern *wushu*, as presented by the Pure Martial Association, was intimately tied to urban commercialization. The origin myths about roving *wushu* master Huo Yuanjia never address the fact that the tremendous later growth of the association was made possible only by the financial resources of three of its earliest bourgeois graduates—Lu Weichang, Chen Gongzhe, and Yao Chanbo. Lu and Chen, whose families hailed from Guangdong Province, were both highly educated, English-speaking hardware store owners. Yao, a Jiangsu native who followed his father into the dye business, befriended this Cantonese pair at the association.[55] The trio of aspiring martial artists were so successful financially, and such close friends after two years training together, that they became known as "the Three Corporations" *(san gongsi)*, a name alluding to Shanghai's three largest department stores of the day (Wing On, Sincere, and Xinxin).[56] For the next decade, the Pure Martial Association was supported not only by the tireless efforts of these three to spread the Pure Martial word but also by the proceeds of their investments in a Watson's soda pop factory, the Hexing Photo Studio, the

Central Printing Company, the Yufan Iron Mines, and a venture importing textile spindles from England.[57]

Besides the business enterprises of these association leaders, other Pure Martial practices reveal the extent to which the association depended on Shanghai capital. The *Pure Martial Magazine* was funded by advertisements from the Liantai Flood and Fire Insurance Company, the Nanyang Brothers Tobacco Company, Girl Brand Fruit Syrup and Face Cream, Watson's, and the Zhang Yu Brewery of Shandong, among other sponsors.[58] The Shanghai Pure Martial Association held elaborate fundraisers, where teams "representing" China's ancient capital cities competed to collect contributions from individuals who would then be awarded honorary Pure Martial titles corresponding to the size of their donations.[59] The Pure Martial Association sought out any way in which it could promote itself as a uniquely Chinese capitalist organization. In late 1924, it announced its line of "new-style" New Year's cards, which sold for 0.36 *yuan* (US$0.28) each or 3.89 *yuan* for a pack of twelve.[60] Representatives from Shanghai dazzled the crowds at the Eighth National Goods Exposition, held in Hangzhou in June 1924, with three days of martial arts (*guocao*, literally "national calisthenics") demonstrations.[61]

Like the competitive sports that rode their association with China's new commercialism and capitalism to physical cultural supremacy in the 1920s, the martial arts of the Pure Martial Association spread through China with these strong winds at their back. Modern firms estimated that advertisements placed in *wushu* publications would pay off as well as those in the mainstream sporting press, and the association's identification with the nationalistic capitalism of the national-goods movement provided more proof that martial arts participation was beneficial to the Chinese nation and economy.

If the Pure Martial Association drew on strategies of team sports promoters to attract followers, it also held two trump cards that allowed it to surpass sports in many ways. First, the association and its arts fundamentally were much more accepting of women's participation than were sporting organizations. In addition to its mission of building the body and psyche of the new Chinese man, the association seemed to be a refreshingly equal-opportunity provider of modern strength and confidence. Although the association could spout scientific jargon with the best of the sports activists, a difference was that here the authority of science was never directed against women and the dangers to women of practicing the Pure Martial arts. Instead, the Pure Martial Association's Women's Department, formed in 1917 by Chen Shichao (the sister of Chen Gongzhe), became an integral part of the Pure Martial movement. Reformers who had seen martial arts

as inextricably bound up with feudal Chinese society had to have been impressed by the association's promotion of women's martial arts, an effort
that far surpassed that of 1920s sports activists.

The 1920 *Record of the Pure Martial* volume featured thoughts by some
female members on the role of women in martial arts. Emboldened by newfound strength that came from her participation in the Pure Martial Association, Huang Wanxiang ridiculed the boors who felt that physical exercise was a domain for men, calling them "ignorant and arrogant men proud
of their seven-foot height [in Chinese measure], but never realizing that
this came from their mothers."[62] Another female member, answering those
who would use talk of scientific "differences" between the sexes to exclude
women from certain areas of physical culture, stated simply,

> We are both round-skulled and square footed, and both richly naturally
> endowed. How could there be distinctions between male and female?
> If women are weaker, it is probably because of the imperial system of
> favoring men over women. But the democratic era is not like the old
> days—men and women are equal, and all can handle and take responsi-
> bility for any undertaking. . . . We can wait no longer to begin this work
> for women's physical fitness.[63]

The main Pure Martial spokesman Chen Tiesheng also encouraged women's
participation in martial arts, stating that "women are the mothers of citizens, and tiger mothers will not beget dog sons," a play on the old cliché that
brave "tiger" fathers would not beget laggard or weak-willed "dog" sons.
Chen even rectified Chinese paradigms of physical beauty, continuing, "The
beautiful women of our [nation] are those who can capture martial arts championships. Compared to these women, those in skirts that end two feet off
the ground, in stunning and seductive outfits, slender and curvaceous and
fluttering in the wind, are simply worthless devil women *(muyecha)*."[64] Thus
the modern reintroduction of martial arts to Chinese society took place without the exclusion of women that plagued the "modern" sports of the West.
The heritage of women's participation in martial arts—long dramatized by
wudan martial heroines and since made famous in the West as the "woman
warrior"—is one reason for this unique position.[65] However, perhaps more
important in this case, the martial artists' conscious embrace of selected aspects of a "Chinese essence" allowed them to circumvent less desirable side
effects of *tiyu*'s often-chauvinistic modernism, like the ease with which competitive sport was so commonly mapped as a male province. *Wushu*'s position gave martial artists a unique perspective from which they could skillfully point out the contradictions in the May Fourth faith in modern
democracy as offering equal opportunity to all Chinese citizens.

The final element of the Pure Martial Association's appeal throughout China—allowing it to reach a peak of fifty-two branch organizations—was its work to spread martial arts and the doctrine of "Pure Martial–ism" beyond the borders of the Republic to a Greater China that included millions of sojourners in Southeast Asia.[66] This extension southward to the Chinese of Malaya, Indonesia, Cambodia, Vietnam, and Siam was instrumental in creating the powerful image of the Pure Martial Association as a repository of truly Chinese arts and skills, capable of transcending Republican borders.

The Pure Martial Association's first venture into Southeast Asia began when the appropriately named Huang Qiangya (Strong Asia), a Shanghai reporter and Pure Martial member, went to work for the Kuala Lumpur Chinese newspaper *Yiqunbao* in 1919 and found there a group of Chinese youth who enjoyed practicing martial arts with him. Soon after, Luo Xiaoao, director of the Guangzhou Pure Martial Association, traveled to the Malayan peninsula, teaching martial arts and spreading the association's message.[67] The Malayan Chinese could not get enough. Letters poured into the offices of the central office of the Pure Martial Association in Shanghai, requesting copies of the association's constitution and regulations and asking that representatives be sent to help found association branches in these Overseas Chinese communities.

The amazing demand gave rise to the celebrated trip of the "Five Special Ambassadors"—five of the association's top names, including Luo, the Shanghai leader Chen Gongzhe and the Shanghai women's director Chen Shichao—to Nanyang in the summer of 1920, visiting Malaya, Indonesia, and Vietnam. Besides their valuable *wushu* knowledge, the ambassadors took with them more than three thousand feet of Pure Martial film to assist them in passing on what they called their "national-essence calisthenics" (*guocui ticao*). Their cargo also included bundles of Pure Martial publications to sell to their Nanyang patrons.[68] The moneymaking possibilities of the new martial arts could also be turned toward nationalist ends. The highlight of this trip was a two-night benefit performance given by the ambassadors before some ten thousand spectators in Singapore, with proceeds going to benefit flood victims in China.[69] With the counseling and coaching of the ambassadors and the enthusiastic support of local Chinese who offered their homes and gardens as office and exercise space, four branches were operating in Malaya by 1921—Selangor, Singapore, and Kampar Associations, and a Selangor Women's Pure Martial Association.[70]

The Pure Martial Association quickly became as serious about its Southeast Asia operations as it was about its new branches in Jiangnan, Guangdong, Hubei, and Jiangxi. Huo Dong'ge, the second son of Pure Martial founder Huo Yuanjia, left his work at the Guangzhou Pure Martial Association in 1923 to take his teachings to Surabaya, Indonesia. Able to converse in Cantonese after working in Guangzhou, Huo soon created kung-fu fever in Surabaya by holding demonstrations (sponsored by the Nanyang Brothers Tobacco Company) of "Huo Family Boxing" and "Eight Drunken Masters" and teaching martial arts in local schools. This led to the founding of the Surabaya Pure Martial branch in 1924, followed by a similar success in Jakarta the next year.

During the 1920s, twenty-two other Pure Martial ambassadors (including three women) would be sent to spread *wushu* in the Chinese communities of Malaya, Indonesia, Cambodia, and Siam.[71] Prominent Central Association leaders from Shanghai also ventured to Southeast Asia to inspect local facilities and put on still more martial arts demonstrations for the adoring fans there. In December 1924, a Seremban crowd of some seven or eight hundred *wushu* aficionados gathered in the Yijing Movie Theater to welcome Pure Martial messengers Lu Weichang and Luo Xiaoao. Lu and Luo treated the audience to a demonstration of their skills and also to Pure Martial films and a slide show as they explained the association's modernized martial arts.[72] When Lu returned to Shanghai, he spoke about conditions in several Southeast Asian branch organizations, trying to express to local Pure Martial personnel the great enthusiasm shared by the Chinese there for the Pure Martial Association. Perhaps the most telling anecdote concerned the precocious Chinese marketing schemes in Southeast Asia: "The two words *Pure Martial (Jingwu)*! One could say that they truly stir deep feelings within people there. In every locale in Southeast Asia, they love to use the Pure Martial emblem. So the businessmen there all add the two words *Pure Martial* to their goods—like Pure Martial hats, Pure Martial shoes, Pure Martial firecrackers, etc. Everyone seems to love [buying these items], and it is great for business too."[73]

The Pure Martial Association's extension to the overseas Chinese community in Southeast Asia speaks directly to another difference between martial arts and other modes of modern physical culture. The sports *tiyu* as learned from the West was all about the modern nation-state—with its emphasis on competition between nations, the accumulation of points and scores, its set and clearly defined spatial and temporal boundaries. Participation in modern sport was meant to recreate in every contest, for every participant, the experience of living in the modern nation-state. The association's martial arts that its messengers brought to the Chinese of Southeast Asia shared none of these constraints. Joining in the association's *wushu* allowed anyone, anywhere, the chance to finally relearn what it was like to be Chinese. The techniques and movements of *wushu*, having survived Manchu prohibitions and Republican ridicule, were a perfect resilient match for these sojourners, with their long and often thankless service to China from abroad. The martial arts, supposedly ancient and timeless, extended perfectly to this boundless imaginary realm called Greater China.

The Pure Martial Association achieved its greatest currency throughout China and beyond in the first half of the 1920s, at the same time that the Anglo-American sports were beginning to sweep across the consciousness of Chinese urban youth. Surprisingly, the antifeudal, antitraditional legacy of the May Fourth Movement did very little to slow the advance of the Pure Martial message. The Pure Martial Association came to dominate the Chinese martial arts world during these years, thanks in part to policies that borrowed heavily from the Western-themed *tiyu*—namely, association with modern science, a literate citizenry, and rising urban commercial forces. The association also explicitly associated martial arts with modern sports, crediting its sports activities as the nutritious "rice and bread" that fueled its growth.[74] In fact, one important moment for the Pure Martial movement in the 1920s was the inclusion in China's 1924 National Games of three days of martial arts *(guocao)* demonstrations before the Wuchang crowds.[75] In another telling instance, the Manila Pure Martial basketball team captured the 1928 Philippines basketball championship.[76]

Yet the architects of the Pure Martial movement were more than mere imitators of successful Western strategies. Their strategies of emphasizing written texts, forming alliances with famed political leaders, uniquely welcoming women's participation in the world of modern martial arts, and energetically pursuing a Southeast Asian Chinese following allowed the Pure Martial Association to succeed impressively in promoting a *wushu* product long dismissed as moribund by many modernists. A drawing in the 1920 *Record of the Pure Martial* shows a *wushu* practitioner holding a heavy Pure Martial shield atop a platform that is supported by pillars marked "press," "political circles," "merchant community," "scholarly community," "military community," and "women's community."[77] These diverse connections and means of support served the Pure Martial Association well during the first half of the 1920s.

However, the association soon learned the hard way the fate of those who became dependent on political ties in those unstable times. In 1924, the association was riding high, fresh off its performance at the National Games at Wuchang and its establishment of new Southeast Asia branch associations in Ipoh and Sumatra. However, when Nie Yuntai, a key co-investor on the association's spindle-import venture, went broke, the three main investment and management partners of the association, Lu Weichang, Chen Gongzhe, and Yao Chanbo, lost their fortunes as well.[78] After this embarrassment, Chen, a charter association member, left the organization to "retire to study," working on the *Zhuangzi* (a Daoist classic) for years with scholars Zhang Taiyan and Chen Zhenggong.[79]

Two years later, Chen attempted to make a spectacular comeback for himself and the Pure Martial Association. When Chiang Kai-shek's Northern Expedition reached Nanjing in 1926, Chen intensively lobbied Guomindang power holders, citing his personal friendships with such Sunist luminaries as Hu Hanmin, Wang Jingwei, Liao Zhongkai, and Zhu Zhixin and asking that subsidies from the new Guomindang government be used to create a new National Pure Martial Association. These were the wrong names to drop with Chiang by this time, however, and plans were already underway within the Guomindang for Commander Zhang Zhijiang to found a national martial arts organization of his own.[80] The loss of this all-important financial and political support was too much for the association to withstand. The Pure Martial Association survived, but mostly in Southeast Asia, and in China it was never dominant again. In the age of the Guomindang national government at Nanjing, martial arts, now called *guoshu* (national arts), would be usurped from this private Pure Martial realm and enlisted in official Guomindang state programs for the survival of the Chinese nation and race. Yet the Pure Martial Association's work in reshaping the martial arts into an acceptably modern, sporting, and worthwhile enterprise is what made the Guomindang *guoshu* experiment possible at all.

GLAD TIDINGS FOR HUMANITY: THE STATE *GUOSHU* PROJECT DURING THE NANJING DECADE, 1928–37

If the story of pre-1928 *wushu* is best narrated by a history of the Pure Martial Association, the history of modern martial arts during the Nanjing Decade can only be written as a history of the state *guoshu* project embodied by the Central Guoshu Academy (Zhongyang guoshuguan). If the Pure Martial Association dominated pre-1928 *wushu*, the state *guoshu* project defined Guomindang-era martial arts. As described in Chapter 5, the Nationalist state announced its leadership of the sports realm with the 1930 National Games, but its claim to the martial arts realm began two years earlier, in 1928, as it pulled once-autonomous martial arts practitioners into its nationalizing endeavors.

The origins of the Guoshuguan are in keeping with the political maneuvering by which Chiang Kai-shek's Guomindang achieved national power in 1928. In 1927, Feng Yuxiang sent Zhang Zhijiang, commander of Feng's Northwest Army and former military governor *(dutong)* of Suiyuan Province, to Nanjing to serve as his official liaison to Chiang after agreeing to throw his support behind the Generalissimo. Zhang was a fanatic practitioner of martial arts who credited this exercise with his earlier recovery from a period of partial lower-body paralysis. In Nanjing, he teamed with Li Jinglin, former warlord of Tianjin, and Zhang Shusheng, a military underling from his days in Chahar, to propose that the newly ascended Guomindang subsidize a new national martial arts organization.[81] With the support of Nanjing heavyweights like He Yingqin, Kong Xiangxi, Yu Youren, and Cai Yuanpei,[82] the Guoshu Research Academy (Guoshu yanjiuguan) was established in March 1928 by National Government Decree #174, which also named Zhang the academy's director.[83] Interestingly, the new academy was first housed in a small Nanjing church[84] until the Executive Yuan's extremely generous support (ten thousand *yuan*, or U.S.$6,400, a month) enabled Zhang to move the operations into a larger facility.

The academy was originally organized into two schools *(men)* teaching the Wudang and Shaolin styles. This arrangement was short-lived, however, as the devotees of these historically rival schools were unable and unwilling to put centuries-old differences behind them in the name of the new academy's mission. Before long, the leaders of these two schools were literally at each other's throats. The academy's two executive directors—Gao Zhendong, a Wudang school master of *xingyi*, or mind/form boxing (an art based on the postures and motions of the dragon, tiger, monkey, hawk, snake, and other animals), and Wang Ziping, an expert in Shaolin's Dragon Pond boxing and wrestling—quickly resorted to furious battle to settle administrative disagreements. The teaching directors from each school, Liu Yinhu (a Wudang *taijiquan* expert) and Ma Yufu (another Shaolin wrestler) also attacked each other with bamboo spears in another savage fight.[85]

These conditions were clearly unacceptable for a body dedicated to erasing the factionalism that had given martial arts such a bad name in this Republican age. By July 1928, the two-school setup was abolished; new team-oriented personnel were brought in to head the new Teaching, Publishing, and General Affairs Divisions; and the name of the organization was changed to the Central Guoshu Academy. Only this centralizing project could resolve the factionalism that threatened to tear the new "national arts" movement apart. The accomplished figures recruited to stabilize the foundering Guoshuguan enterprise, like educator Ma Liang and Japan-educated lawyer Tang Hao,[86] were men unlikely to fall prey to the temptation—now so discredited—of factional enmity. The task facing them was to turn the young Guoshuguan into a truly national movement involving citizens all over China in the ancient "national arts" in the name of explicitly national causes. As academy officials said in the July announcement of their new body:

> Standing in the twentieth-century arena, where if one does not compete one cannot survive, we beseech the Chinese people, how can we avoid the disrespect of others? . . . *Guoshu* is not something in which one is constrained by financial status—it can be popularized *(pingminhua)*. It doesn't matter if one is old or young, poor or rich, male or female, and it doesn't depend on how many people are present, or how much space or time one has available—it can be practiced anywhere.[87]

Official Guoshuguan rhetoric presented a picture of a "leveled" China united by participation in this new national realm, without the least regard to social, economic, or geographical hierarchies that operated in the Nanjing Decade. This was indeed part of the imagination of *guoshu* as a "national realm." As Daniel Segal and Richard Handler have explained, for *guoshu* to be an attractive national concept, these citizens' "hierarchical differentiation," as in the nation itself, "had to be placed under erasure."[88] The truth, of course, is that the national martial arts were mostly designed for, and marketed to, an urban bourgeoisie with its own unique reasons for delving into this celebrated, yet dangerous and mysterious, Chinese martial tradition.

As for *guoshu*, the official name used to encompass all 161 known types of Chinese martial arts (the Guomindang tried to count![89]), little is known about the term's origins. Wu Wenzhong, grandfather of the study of modern Chinese *tiyu* history, explains that the term was meant to be shorthand for *Zhongguo wushu* (Chinese martial arts). He remembers that at the time many wanted a new designation that followed the Nanjing Decade trend by including the word *national,* but *guowu* (national martial) "did not sound ideal." The answer was thus *guoshu,* a term meaning simply "national skills"[90]—a typically bureaucratic and nationalist solution to this crucial linguistic and ideological question.

In 1929, a *Hubao* reporter put things differently, as he explained the qualifications necessary for being known as a specifically "national" entity:

> The *guo* ["nation"] in *guojia* ["nation-state"] must not be used lightly. It must be used only to refer to the things that belong specifically to our nation and not to things copied from others. These things can be said to belong to the nation (like "national music" or "national currency"). And as for the character *shu* ["skill"], it refers to technique *(jishu).* Every kind of technique must have its own particular charac-

teristics and must carry some benefit to the human body, spirit, and knowledge to be worth passing on. So are our nation's martial arts worthy of calling a *shu?* And are they worthy of being called a *guoshu?*[91]

Despite these concerns, the transition from older terms to the new, uniformly used *guoshu* seems never to have been a topic of much debate. As one commentator put it in 1930, "What in the past was called *quanyi, guoji, guocao,* and *wushu*—they're all the same thing [as *guoshu*]."[92] Now that all names were properly and acceptably rectified, it was time for the Guoshuguan to do its work in spreading these all-important national skills.

The Guomindang's project to bring *guoshu* to China's four hundred million people can be divided into two parts: the activities directly relating to the Central Guoshu Academy and its hundreds of nationwide branches and the mass publicity work done, if not directly for the Guoshuguan, by martial arts educators and activists associated with the academy. Here, I will first describe the work of the Guoshuguan in creating Chinese citizens with proficiency, or even teaching credentials, in these ancient but relevant "national arts."

Guoshuguan Work: Teachings and Competitions

By February 1929, the Guoshuguan had formulated and published its design for national domination of the Chinese martial arts world. A series of "Organizational Outlines"—for the central Guoshuguan, provincial-, municipal-, and county-level academy branches, and district- or village-level *guoshu* societies—issued forth from Nanjing, each document describing the standards for funding and administrative arrangement expected of all local branches.[93]

The mission began slowly but surely. Representatives of the Central Academy in Nanjing teamed with local party officials and martial arts masters to found some thirty branches in Anhui, Jiangsu, Gansu, Chahar, Shandong, Shanxi, Fujian, Suiyuan, Henan, and Sichuan Provinces and in the cities Beiping, Nanjing, Shanghai, Qingdao, and Tianjin by 1931.[94] Growth quickened with Guomindang consolidation of power in the provinces. By 1933, there were more than three hundred branch academies operating in twenty-four provinces and municipalities.[95] By 1934 Henan boasted thirty-nine county-level Guoshuguan, Sichuan Province forty-one, and Jiangxi thirty, and by 1936 Shandong could list seventy-six county branches (along with twenty-nine municipal sub-branches in capital Ji'nan).[96]

The central Guoshuguan in Nanjing operated two types of programs. Sixty students, most sent by their home provincial governments, were ac-

TABLE 8. Winter 1934 Men's and Women's Course Schedules,
Central Guoshuguan (Instruction Section)

Men			
Boxing	3 hrs	Chinese	2
Bayonets	2.5	Physiology & hygiene	1
Taijiquan	1	Guoshu history	1
Mantis-fists	1.5	Party principles	1
Xingyi	3	Geography	1
Ape-back cudgels	1	Mathematics	2
Short-sword fencing	1	Military studies	1
Wrestling	9	History	2
Fencing	4.5	Sun Yat-sen study	2
Bagua	1.5		
Military drill	3		

Plus: Saturday afternoon field trips
Saturday evening and Sunday morning lectures on scholarship and morality

Women			
Three-power swords	4.5 hrs	Chinese	2
Six-direction spears	2	Physiology & hygiene	1
Taijiquan	1	Guoshu history	1
Pushing-hands	1	Party principles	1
Xingyi	2	Geography	1
Ape-back cudgels	3	Mathematics	2
Bayi boxing	1	Military studies	1
Bagua	3	History	2
Military drill	3	Sun Yat-sen study	2
Independent review	10.5		

Plus: Saturday afternoon field trips
Sunday morning lectures on morality

cepted to the Instruction Section each term. Graduates acquired three years of instruction in several styles of martial arts and several academic topics, living in Guoshuguan dormitories and taking forty-four hours of courses each week (Table 8). The Training Section provided free *guoshu* and academic instruction to youths not accepted into the degree program (Table 9).[97]

TABLE 9. Fall 1935 Men's and Women's Course Schedules, Central Guoshuguan (Training Section)

Men

Boxing	4.5 hrs	Chinese	2
Bayonets	1	Physiology & anatomy	1
Pushing-hands	1	Guoshu history	1
Wrestling	4	Party principles	1
Chinese boxing	7.5	History & geography	1
Weaponry	6.5	Mathematics	1
Archery	1	Military studies	1
Practice with partner	1	Music	2
Team sports	1	First aid	1
Military drill	2	Physical education outline	1
Gymnastics	1	Lectures	1
Sun Yat-sen study	1.5		

Plus: Saturday afternoon field trips and scientific lectures

Women

Chinese boxing	12 hrs	Chinese	2
Weaponry	10.5	Physiology & anatomy	1
Taijiquan & pushing-hands	1	Guoshu history	1
Archery	1	Party principles	1
Practice with partner	2	History & geography	1
Team sports	1	Mathematics	1
Calisthenics	1	Military studies	1
Music	2		
First aid	2		
Physical education outline	1		
Lectures	1		
Drawing	1		
Sun Yat-sen study	1.5		

Plus: Saturday afternoon field trips and scientific lectures

Male and female students at the academy trained in *guoshu* according to curricula that were distinct in predictable ways. Men's and women's programs featured similar proportions of boxing to weapons forms (swords, spears, cudgels); Nanjing's *guoshu* heroines were by no means getting off easy. Still, several forms (e.g., mantis boxing, bayonet training, wrestling) were practiced only by male *guoshu* students, and the women of the academy spent more time with "softer" arts like pushing-hands. Academy women also spent 10 ½ hours each week practicing these forms under their teachers' individual supervision, while the men's program was positioned strictly within the realm of head-to-head competition.[98]

Pedagogical ideals aside, however, the Nanjing state *guoshu* bureaucracy seemed to make little effort to continue the gender equality that the Pure Martial Association had initiated. In 1934, citing "immoral" relations between male teachers and female students at his affiliated Central Guoshu and Physical Education School, Academy Director Zhang Zhijiang stopped admitting women to the institution altogether. An irate Ms. Qiu Shan blasted Zhang in the pages of the *World Daily* "Women's Column" for his crude solution to the sexual harassment plaguing the school, pointing out sardonically, "Women are once again being sent back into the kitchen. . . . Instead of ending women's enrollments, why doesn't [Zhang] end men's enrollments?" However, this logical argument found little acceptance among *guoshu* leaders, many of whom were exclusively concerned with the project of making China more "masculine." Even Tian Zhenfeng, editor of the radical Ji'nan martial arts journal *Seek Truth* and persistent critic of the Central Academy, had to agree with Zhang's measures, reminding readers that in the end, women still did belong in the kitchen. What upstanding Chinese martial arts devotee, he asked, would rather hire some "dirty cook" to prepare his dinner instead of his own wife?[99] Committed *guoshu* activists were working hard to save the nation and its martial arts by transforming them for the modern era, and they had to transmit this knowledge to those who could truly administer it—the men of China.

If the academy in some ways was united by this common masculinist ideology, the material conditions in each local-level academy still differed greatly. The provincial academy in Ji'nan, Shandong, received yearly funding of thirty thousand *yuan* (U.S.$9,900) in the early 1930s, as opposed to 2,400 *yuan* (U.S.$800) a year for the Suiyuan Province branch in Guihua.[100] Instructors in academy branches were allowed to teach their local martial arts specialties. The majority of the curriculum, however, was constant across the nation. All academy students would study an official curriculum of the standard tai chi, mind/form boxing, eight-trigram boxing *(bagua)*, and wrestling styles. Unlike the rural unlearned martial artists of the premodern age, academy students also had to master a scientific and nationalist educational curriculum consisting of Guomindang Party principles, Chinese, *guoshu* history, physiology, hygiene, history, geography, and history of national humiliation.

This instruction was meant to make modern martial arts practitioners well-rounded citizens as skilled in the *wen* cultural disciplines as they were in the many *wu* martial styles that made up the modern *guoshu*. In the martial arts part of the curriculum, at least, students were taught by the very best. Indeed, this was one of the keys to the success of the Guoshuguan—the academy's ability to attract famed martial arts masters like Wang Ziping, Li Jinglin, and Sun Lutang to teach bright and talented young *guoshu* pupils from all over China.[101] Another example was Sun Diyun, a tai chi and *qigong* sage known as "the Buddha with the Iron Shoulders." Sun had taught for the warlord Sun Chuanfang in Nanjing and various Sichuan warlords for years in the 1920s and early 1930s before retiring to Gansu's Mt. Kongtong to study Buddhist scriptures. A call from Zhang Zhijiang to Gansu Provincial Governor Shao Yuanchong ended this retirement, however. Sun soon made his way back to the capital to compensate for his past work for regional warlords by joining the nation-minded academy faculty.[102]

Just as important, local Guoshuguan branches were successful in attracting martial arts masters who had been famed for their talents long before Director Zhang even conceived the academy. With the advent of the Guoshuguan, these traditional local arts and skills were finally being granted a place of honor on the nationalist Chinese stage; it is easy to imagine many of these masters' enthusiasm in putting their arts to such worthy and important use. For example, the Taigu County (Shanxi Province) Academy was established by Bu Xuekuan, a fifty-nine-year-old master of mind/form boxing. Bu began studying these *xingyi* arts in the 1890s and had trained local disciples in these Shanxi native forms for twenty years.[103] The willingness of masters like Bu to work for the state's rationalized martial arts apparatus gave instant local legitimacy to the academy system and its hundreds of branches. At the same time, their presence allowed state Guoshuguan functionaries to present each academy enterprise as a truly local manifestation of and contribution to the national cause.

Association with the new academy structure could also supply one more layer of state backing and prestige for local authorities. One telling example of the convenient relationship between the academy and local power structures can be seen in the case of Gansu's first Guoshuguan, established in Zhangye County, nestled against the Longshou Mountains. Ma Fengtu, a county magistrate and martial arts aficionado, established the academy in 1929 and soon was able to score great victories for both the causes of Zhangye local pride and Chinese *guoshu* when some two hundred of his righteous Guoshuguan pupils took on and defeated a band of three hundred horse bandits who were ravaging the area in 1930.[104]

Besides the training of local cadres of upright, nationally minded, *guoshu*-proficient citizens, the Guoshuguan was charged with managing the system of county-level, provincial, and national *guoshu* exams announced in 1927. The Nationalist exam combined elements of the imperial military exam of the Ming and Qing dynasties, traditional local martial arts contests and festivals *(leitai)*, and modern sporting competition. Like the imperial martial exam, the *guoshu* exam consisted of physical and academic testing, although the trope of the martial expert equally trained in the letters was much more crucial in the Republican era. Where imperial-era military examinees had only to memorize passages from three military classics, the successful modern candidate now had to demonstrate proficiency in the Three People's Principles, written Chinese, mathematics, geography, history, *guoshu* history, physiology, and hygiene.[105]

The old martial exam required candidates to demonstrate archery ability and to perform three feats of strength—bending a rigid bow into the shape of a full moon, brandishing a heavy halberd and swinging it around one's body, and lifting a stone block at least one Chinese foot off the ground.[106] However, the modern *guoshu* exam required examinees to prove a great breadth of skills in three of four martial arts fields (boxing, wrestling, fencing, spears), first with individual demonstrations and then in three rounds of actual bouts with other examinees. Staying true to tradition, successful *guoshu* exam candidates were awarded titles as they progressed from county ("hero," *zhuangshi*) to provincial ("warrior," *wushi*) to national exam status. And in a form that recalled both the Olympic-style customs of sporting competition and the old imperial exams, special awards were reserved for the top three performers in each event.

The First National Guoshu Exam was held in the Nanjing Municipal Stadium from 15 to 19 October 1928, just days after the Nationalist government was officially inaugurated in the old Ming capital. Some four hundred eager martial arts practitioners, many from as far away as Taiyuan or Fuzhou, came to China's new first city for this hastily arranged exam. After a three-day round of individual performances, a pool of some two hundred participants was selected to advance to direct competition. Each match followed a best-of-five-rounds format, and the competitions were organized in the modern single-elimination bracket system. On the last day of the exam, seventeen top-three finishers were crowned with the title *guoshi* (national warrior) in this proud culmination of the prestigious national examination and competitive sports traditions.[107] The presence of the Beiping martial arts masters Sun Lutang and Sun Cunzhou and the Guomindang leaders Feng Yuxiang (who gave an address on the 18th), He Yingqin, and Dai Jitao (who presented prizes to the champions) dramatized the proceedings even further.[108]

The Second National Guoshu Exam was held in Nanjing's Central Guoshuguan from 20 to 30 October 1933, its opening day overlapping with the last day of the Fifth National Games, which was awarded the prestigious 10 October National Day starting date. Although no one ever admitted it, the exam could have been scheduled only at this time to take advantage of the fact that hundreds of the nation's top martial artists were in Nanjing anyway for the National Games. The 219 *guoshu* stars who represented sixteen provinces and municipalities in the National Games stayed in the capital for the exam and were reinforced by 210 more examinees who had advanced from the local and provincial exams but had not been selected to provincial National Games teams.[109]

Besides their martial arts skills, these 429 martial heroes shared one other characteristic—they were all men. I have described above the difficulty that the Guoshuguan had in imagining their modern martial arts as a domain friendly or relevant to the women of China. Other high-profile martial arts competitions of the day, like the 1929 Zhejiang Guoshu Fair or the 1933/1935 National Games *guoshu* contests, prominently included and celebrated the martial arts heroines of the new age. It is possible that paternalistic Nationalist planners saw the long competition process as simply too grueling for women to endure. Or it may have been that, as opposed to the academy classroom where the presence of women was permitted, the challenge and promise of this national and nationalizing exam could be trusted only to the real men of Han.

The *guoshu* stars found a different, more rationalized exam than their predecessors after regulations were revised in 1931. Competitors were classified in five weight classes, ranging from lightweight (less than 133 pounds) to heavyweight (more than 182 pounds). The individual performance segment, decidedly unfit for the modern era of competition, was eliminated. No more could examinees advance purely on the basis of subjective judgment. Now round-robin competitions were held in each weight class in all four competitions—boxing, wrestling, fencing, and spears. Detailed regulations were issued for all four events, clearly outlining rules for scoring and penalties. Finally, consistent penalties could be handed out to unsportsmanlike boxers who hit or kicked their opponents while they were down, wrestlers who poked their adversaries in the eyes or throat, fencers who parried at their opponents' backs or lower bodies, or spearmen who used their hands to grab or deflect their opponents' weapons. Taking a page from international boxing rules, matches in all events consisted of three three-minute rounds.[110]

The National Guoshu Exam posed two important challenges to its academy organizers. They needed to redefine it as a more modern, competition-friendly, and rationalized form to compete with Western-styled *tiyu* in these heady sporting times. But at the same time they needed to bring out a "national essence" in the exam to differentiate it from the sporting-style competition featured at the National Games. This explains the odd character of the Second (and last) National Guoshu Exam,[111] in which elements of imperial-era martial exams and traditional local boxing festivals were combined to convey both the essence of the nation-state and the character of its symbiotic alter ego, sports *tiyu*.

Not only did the academy's exam system fail to captivate a national public of physical culture spectators, but the academy apparatus itself was shut out of several local sites of martial arts practice in China. This was due in part to politics; the influence of Nanjing's Guoshuguan could extend only as far as the Nationalist Party's own dominion. The northern province of Shanxi was known as "the birthplace of *guoshu*." Under the rule of warlord Yan Xishan, however, there was little room for the Nationalists' Academy, even in this densest and most promising of martial arts markets. In Shanxi in the 1930s more than 560 registered martial arts organizations—like the Shanxi Guoshu Promotion Association, the Taiyuan Guoshu Reform Research Society, and the Yangquan Miners' Wushu Squad—were operating independently of the provincial academy network.[112] Independent organizations' use of the state's official term *guoshu* was telling; the prestige afforded by the term was clearly important to these activists, even if association with the Nanjing state was not.

In the southeast coastal city of Xiamen, too, martial artists remained much more oriented toward their overseas compatriots in Southeast Asia than toward Nanjing. The Pure Martial Association in the city's Sun Yat-sen Park thrived into the 1930s, publishing its own Pure Martial journal. The Singapore industrialist and Overseas Chinese leader Tan Kah Kee (Chen Jiageng) organized Southern Fujian Province Guoshu Squad fundraising tours of Malayan Chinese communities throughout the 1930s.[113] Tenuous Nationalist control over China's southwestern provinces is also reflected in the absence of any academy presence there during the Nanjing decade. During the 1930s, martial arts practitioners there ignored the Guoshuguan system, instead organizing groups like the Yunnan Guoshu Squad, sponsored by the Kunming Municipal Cultural Center, and the Gallant Martial Society, sponsored by the Jiangxi Fellow-Provincials' Guild in Kunming. In fact, the first Guoshuguan to open in Kunming was the Central Academy itself, when it was based there for two years in 1938–40 during its move west from Nanjing with the national government.[114]

Far-off provinces under warlord rule hardly provided all of the state academy's competition. Even in Guanyintang Town, in the very shadows of Shanghai and the powerful state presence there, underground radicals and peasant movement organizers put together their own martial arts society that mocked Nationalist claims to cultural/political hegemony in China.[115] Thus there were many enthusiasts at the geographical and ideological margins of Guomindang China who were able to pursue their martial interests without falling under the purview of the Guoshuguan organization, even if they did hijack the Nationalists' *guoshu* terminology for their own nationalistic purposes.

Most Nationalist agents were probably accustomed to the immense difficulty of penetrating rural and decidedly unmodern martial arts networks. But their failure to extend academy domination over urban *guoshu* organizations in key areas like Shanxi or Fujian—and the discouraging implications for the Guoshuguan project of nationalizing the martial arts—could only have been much more frustrating. Because of the academy's limited success, most national-scale *guoshu* work would have to be done by organizers and activists working independently of the academy. In the next section, I will describe ideological and political work, done mostly outside the formal Guoshuguan system, to spread the national martial arts and doctrines of this "national-essence physical culture" to citizens all over China.

Ideologies of Modern Guoshu

A Central Guoshu Academy was required, all understood, because *guoshu* was a body of arts and knowledge dedicated to building and unifying the new nation and supremely appropriate to the "national condition" *(guoqing)*. As a state manifestation of the national martial arts, the Guoshuguan structure would seem to have left little ideological room for debate or challenge. Yet the discourses of pragmatic state building and ideological nationalism were harder to combine than leading *guoshu* architects assumed.

The Chinese martial arts world that *guoshu* leaders hoped to dominate and define was an extremely complicated jumble of local and regional styles, schools, factions, and rivalries. It was composed of diverse traditional or superstitious (and by definition, un-national and unmodern) understandings of the workings and meanings of martial arts. The Nanjing state and its Guoshuguan thus needed to construct and disseminate an official and coherent ideology situating *guoshu* as a scientifically and rationally based native Chinese sport. In the 1930s, an intensely committed cadre of *guoshu* activists soon met this need, creating an influential new realm of "national arts" literature and propaganda to spread the word throughout China's martial arts and physical culture communities.

The most diverse and compelling arguments for the relevance of *guoshu* to a modern, unified, and uniquely Chinese Republic often came from independent activists and educators who, if perhaps associated with the Guoshuguan, had other means of making their voices heard. Many martial artists who saw deficiencies in the academy project worked to buttress the state's *guoshu* program. This section examines these activists and their efforts to make the martial arts a truly useful element of modern Chinese culture by nationalizing the old martial arts, unifying them into a newly constructed sport based on a cosmopolitan scientific rationality, and asserting *guoshu*'s worth as a part of a modern physical culture.

The first problem with which the *guoshu* community had to come to terms was the feudal, superstitious legacy of martial arts that still remained in the minds of many. This legacy was a historical problem, many explained, and not an inherent weakness of martial arts itself. Wu Zhiqing, leader of the Chinese Wushu Association of Shanghai during the 1920s, implicated members of all ranks of society in the decline of the arts:

> In the past, our nation's *wushu* had a glorious history, illustrating
> the noble spirit of brotherhood and righteous courage inherent in our
> people. . . . Unfortunately it declined in later years, with the emphasis
> on letters and the neglect of the martial virtues that still lay deep in
> the hearts of the people. Officials and gentlemen arrogantly felt that
> to study boxing, rolling up one's sleeves and courageously baring one's
> arms, was not fit for people of learning and instead preferred to remain
> weak literati without the strength to bind a chicken. This was the re-
> fined attitude they insisted on, so our nation's *wushu* went into deeper
> decline by the day. And then the European wind began to blow east, the
> new learning began to develop, and the average sportsman figured that
> the track and ball sports from the West made our nation's *wushu* look
> like a bowl of mud rice and dirt broth, not even condescending to look
> at it. It continued to decline, without a hope of being restored or reju-
> venated. The only ones spreading it were the so-called "medicine huck-
> sters," the people creating ruckuses in the market and blocking the
> streets with their cursed displays.[116]

Wu's *Outline of Guoshu Theory* also included a chapter called "How *Guoshu* Was Ruined," where he catalogued the many reasons for the decline of martial arts over the centuries. Martial arts were never openly discussed, and petty factions kept their skills secret. The terminology of martial arts was too abstruse and obscure for the masses to understand. All Chinese rulers after Qin Shihuang used the examination system to control the minds of the Chinese people and make them neglect their bodies. Governments, especially the hated Qing, opposed the private ownership of any weapons or the exercise of any martial skills that could be used against them. The *wushu* world was dominated by "the supernatural," "sorcery," and "occult talk in total darkness." At the same time, the nature of the Chinese people worked against them, as their inborn benevolence *(ren'ai)* led them to see only struggle in the martial arts and to miss the point that peace is the very goal of *wushu*.[117]

The "Boxer bandits," whose 1900 uprising brought on the imperialist ravages of the Eight-Nation Allied Expedition, continued to be a popular target of those tracing the degeneration of martial arts into superstitious, self-destructive mumbo-jumbo.[118] The Boxers were despised for their reckless superstition that endangered the nation at a crucial historical moment, and the antiscientific spirit of "supernaturalists" like them became a specific archenemy of the new *guoshu* reformers.[119] In 1934, the initial article of the radical new martial arts journal *Seek Truth* lambasted backward *wushu* schools that "cling to factional views, siding only with their own and attacking all others, and cultivating slavish bigotry in all who enter. They are always bragging about themselves but never teach their secrets to others, selling their bunkum to the fools who come to study with them, flaunting their artifice and dazzling all with their mystery and wonder."[120] *Guoshu* activists were now out to prove that their arts were, as one author explained, "one of the basic elements of the new civilization, a science in its own right."[121] They took every opportunity to display *guoshu* in the most scholarly way. The *Seek Truth* faction singled out Beiping as a city plagued with "one-fist, one-kick, tiger-punching, dragon-kicking styles that confuse and mislead and modern martial arts organizations that can still never abandon the feudal imitate-the-teacher-and-pass-it-on structure." To remedy these ills, concerned martial arts activists formed a North China Guoshu Research Association in 1933.[122]

In the 1930s, all responsible *guoshu* advocates had to develop an effective answer to the argument that their arts were "unscientific." This charge had been made most concisely by track and field expert Xie Siyan, who once joked that the martial arts were designed and taught by "those who can't even read the character *ding* (丁) [one of the easiest possible characters]."[123] The damning legacy of the martial arts' association with the crackpot mysticism of feudal hermits simply had to be repudiated for the guoshu to flourish.

Liu Shenzhan, a committed and dogmatic Guomindang agent, addressed this question in his 1933 book *The Physical Culture Revolution*:

> If one wants to speak about "scientific" or "unscientific," we should first be clear about the origin of the term *science*. The term *science* naturally is foreign, although ancient China also had similar terms like *zhizhi* (pursuit of knowledge) and *gewu* (investigation at the source).
>
> I feel that when Chinese trust foreign talk about "science" and suppose that their own nation's things are "unscientific," this is a basic sign of the loss of self-confidence. China has had several thousand years of civilization; isn't this civilization the crystallization of "science"? For example, Chinese palaces, homes, towers, pavilions, bridges, and other edifices are all built according to the principles of geometry, physics, etc. . . . Let us go back to *guoshu*. Why is *guoshu* unscientific? We cannot dismiss the whole of *guoshu* as unscientific, just because it has a few faults, and neglect *guoshu*'s value. Why are all *guoshu* practitioners broad-shouldered and strong, rarely falling ill and living long lives? The most amazing aspects of *guoshu*—long fists and short fists, the fists and the feet, left and right, high and low, horsemanship and archery—every single one of these uses geometry, physics, mechanics, and such, so they are just as scientific as track and field or ball sports. Those who criticize *guoshu* as unscientific simply have never studied it, so how can they blindly criticize it?[124]

Liu's argument not only removed the formidable realm of "science" from the foreign and placed it back in Chinese history, language, and culture but also located *guoshu* squarely in the center of this Chinese scientific tradition, deftly rendering invalid the cursed equation "*guoshu* = Chinese = unscientific" that had stood for so long.

Defining a scientific *guoshu* was a task that headed Wu Zhiqing's agenda as well. His 1931 book *A Scientized Guoshu* was a presentation of seven martial arts routines, supplemented with forty-eight photographic plates that would allow the reader "to understand at a single glance, with no difficulties standing in the way," and accompanied by explanations of these different movements' physiological, psychological, and educational uses.[125] Wu's 1935 *Outline of Guoshu Theory* devoted parts of three chapters to the relationship between *guoshu* and different scientific theories and disciplines, from Einstein's theory of relativity to the findings of Darwin, from essential biological differences between southern and northern Chinese to "natural values" of mathematics.[126]

Besides merely identifying *guoshu* with the precise, tested, and socially accepted theories of science, Wu criticized those who would privilege the modern over the ancient in criticizing *guoshu*:

> Most peoples that had ancient cultures do not have written records [of these cultures]. But a lack of written records does not imply a lack of history. Rather, it is just that written records only came later as these cultures developed. And it is also true that before the advent of written records, plenty of things could have been recorded, even though they were not recorded. This was so in China; this situation was quite common and included [among unrecorded items] martial arts.[127]

In other words, *wushu* was not to be blamed for not leaving all its methods and truths to posterity in the form of written records. Instead, it was the fault of modernists who, blinded by the cult of science, accepted as valid and worthwhile only literate cultures.

Wu's "scientized *guoshu*" thus involved two different ideas: that guoshu was inherently a body of practice and knowledge based on scientific principles and that it had to be reintroduced into the scientific mainstream that had ignored and scorned it for so long. Martial arts, far from being backward and superstitious, were in fact progressive and rational, even though the arbiters of progress and rationality were too biased to understand this fact.

Other martial arts activists felt that the case for a scientific *guoshu* had not been made strong enough. One author decried tai chi's lack of a technical terminology *(shuyu),* something he felt was requisite to any "specialized discipline," and thus undertook to design both vernacular Chinese and English terms for all seventy-two steps of the tai chi routine. Some of the "scientific" English terms chosen ("Frictional Force" and "Neutral equilibrium") worked better than others ("2 humeruses are drawn like a stiff bow" or "The highest Part of the Head is Hanged by thought").[128] Yet this attempt to deliver tai chi from its unwritten limbo into a bilingual cosmopolitan future says much about the modernist pressures facing the 1930s *guoshu* movement.[129]

What was the ultimate goal of all this effort to highlight scientific and rational aspects of the Chinese martial arts? If some wanted some modern recognition of these ancient skills, and others hoped to give *guoshu* a rightful place in the physical culture hierarchy, others had much more grandiose plans. Chu Minyi, the French-educated Secretary of the Executive Yuan of the Republic of China, was one of the greatest advocates for a rational new *guoshu*. In 1928, in the earliest days of the state *guoshu* movement, Chu wrote at length about traditional martial artists' lack of scientific understanding and about the glorious rewards awaiting those who properly reformed *guoshu* for a new cosmopolitan world:

> In the past, *guoshu* and physical fitness were two totally unrelated entities. Those who practiced martial arts in the past took martial capability as their only goal, never even uttering the words *physical fitness*. They were even more ignorant about physiology, hygiene, mechanics, and psychology, branches of science that are closely linked to *guoshu*. So the practice of these martial arts resulted in bodily harm. . . .
>
> Now we know that Chinese boxing styles are the finest of all the *guoshu* and provide even and healthy physical development. We can scientize them now, using the methods of science to do this research— but how do we do it? It requires paying attention to mechanics and psychology, looking into physiology and hygiene, setting down rules and methods, and explaining them with sound theory. . . . This type of *guoshu* will be a scientific *guoshu* that suits the needs of physical fitness.
>
> . . . Our goals in working to promote *guoshu* are to gather together all those who excel in martial arts and all of the finest points of martial arts. Then we can give this organized, systematized, scholarly, and methodological *guoshu* to all the people of the world. . . . Spreading Chinese *guoshu* to the entire world will mean glad tidings for humanity.[130]

The drive to scientize *guoshu* could lead, in the most optimistic scenarios, to a Chinese starring role in international science and culture. Yet the Chinese *guoshu* community had another mission with implications more relevant to the survival of their nation. This was the effort to "unify" the martial arts under the new nationalizing *guoshu* rubric. Besides the Guoshuguan's bureaucratic and statist work to gain centralizing control over the many and diverse Chinese martial arts, this drive for unification was meaningful to *guoshu* activists for nationalist reasons.

Guoshu was imagined to be more than just martial arts. It was literally a body of "national skills" that could preserve the nation in its time of crisis. The fascistic mass *tiyu* described above was thought to produce a unified "*minzu* body," a nation-race taught to move as one in compulsory paramilitary training. Elite-level competitive sport sought to strengthen the nation by presenting a sportsmanlike and united China to the sporting world. *Guoshu*, meanwhile, provided a third model of a nationalized physical culture—one that could accomplish modern goals of national unification and self-strengthening via the teaching and practice of specifically Chinese arts and movements. In the end, mass *tiyu* and competitive sports advocates had to admit that their programs for Chinese strength depended on Italian, German, Japanese, British, and American inventions. Only the *guoshu* community could make a rhetorical claim to Chinese purity and to a direct correspondence between the fate of their "national arts" and the nation itself.

Guoshu proponents imagined this correlation in all sorts of ways. Some looked back into recent history and saw the lack of a unified *guoshu* as the key factor allowing the oppression and misery recently inflicted on the Chinese by Manchu rulers, warlords, foreign imperialists, and bandit gangs.[131] Others, like Wu Zhiqing, hoped that a reformed, united *guoshu* would reintroduce the concept of "risk" to the Chinese people, most of whom "die in their hometowns, never taking a step out of the village gates. If they go to a city or a big port even once, they think they're Columbus discovering the New World. Or if they travel on a train or steamship a few times, they think they're Lindbergh crossing the Atlantic. This is not only pathetic but also ridiculous." Wu hoped that a new openness to risk would carry over into China's task of reunifying the motherland, giving rise to adventurers who would replant the Chinese flag in Tibetan and Mongolian territories lost during the recent centuries of Chinese weakness and apprehension.[132]

In one essay perhaps meant to be read on several different political levels, an author longed for a wise "*guoshu* leader" who, like Liu Bei of the Three Kingdoms era, would surround himself with capable (martial arts) masters of all schools in order to truly unify the fractious *guoshu*.[133] Tian Zhenfeng, publisher of Ji'nan's *Seek Truth*, wrote a piece on cooperation between *guoshu* factions in which he directly related this enterprise to the very survival of China's four hundred million people.[134] And Chu Minyi, ever the dreamer, wrote in the inaugural essay for the journal *Guoshu Unification Monthly* that only a "unified" *guoshu* that was "scientized, particularized, and common-ized [i.e., made more common throughout society]" would be able to achieve a Chinese martial arts influence that was "internationalized, globalized, and humanized throughout the universe."[135]

Perhaps the most urgent call for *guoshu* unification came again from the pages of *Seek Truth*, where adherence to guoshu in its currently factionalized and divided state was compared to "falling in love with a beautiful woman with syphilis, infecting your own body and eventually your descendants with syphilis—making the same mistakes again and again until the whole race is destroyed!"[136] A *guoshu* that was cured by the related processes of "scientization" and unification would by definition create a strong China, comfortable and confident in its modern use of its ancient heritage. But a *guoshu* contaminated with premodern superstition and factionalism could only pass on this bane to a tragic and doomed Chinese body politic.

The martial arts narrative of the 1930s was based on the idea that only a properly unified *guoshu* could be a nationally unifying *guoshu*. Only a martial arts rationalized and honed to its Chinese martial essence could be a technology grand enough to achieve, via the force and rhythm of its human motions, the goals of the Nationalist revolution. And the rational and unified *guoshu*, once constructed, would have to be disseminated throughout society for martial arts to transcend their traditional secretive mode and to become somatic tributes to the unity and martial spirit of the Chinese nation.

Despite the claims to a national purity that often accompanied the promotion of this perfected *guoshu*, the martial arts seemed to flourish most when combined with the foreign calisthenics and sports forms that many hoped *guoshu* could eventually replace. The state Guoshuguan apparatus hoped to establish martial arts as an independent form of physical culture worthwhile in its own right but also understood the legacy of the Pure Martial Association and its important strategy of mixing the martial arts with more modern pastimes like soccer, ping-pong, and roller skating.

The trappings of competitive sports were crucial to *guoshu*'s survival in the Nanjing Decade. The greatest public celebrations of the martial arts could only come with competitions like the *guoshu* exams or the *guoshu* events at the National Games. *Guoshu* was also a featured competitive event in almost any municipal-, provincial-, or regional-level meet in the 1930s. In 1929, martial arts received great publicity with the two-week Zhejiang Guoshu Fair held in Hangzhou. The genre won great acclaim when Wang Ziqing, grand champion of the meet, showed the true "lofty character of the *guoshu* community" by electing to share his five-thousand-*yuan* prize money (U.S.\$2,750) with the twenty-five other finalists who had reached the meet's last stage of competition.[137]

The feeling of unity and equality that could be produced by even the fiercest one-on-one competition now was clearly of great value to the modern martial arts community. Even the radical Tian Zhenfeng of *Seek Truth*, known to curse and even wish violence on prima donna "athletes" taking part in Western-style sports,[138] envisioned 1930s *guoshu* in terms of modern-style competitions. Tian speculated about why the circular and piercing movements of the spear arts *(qiangshu)* were more appropriate for competition judging than the more strictly lateral and vertical motions of the cudgel arts *(gunshu)*.[139] Eventually, the Central Guoshu Academy itself was forced to connect its martial arts realm with larger physical culture trends. In 1935, a new Central Guoshu and Physical Education Research Association was founded, with the Guoshuguan founder Zhang Zhijiang, the Guomindang officials Sun Ke, Yu Youren, and Niu Yongjian, and the physical culture specialists Wu Yunrui, Cheng Dengke, and Hao Gengsheng among its trustees.[140]

Guoshu also fit perfectly in the plans of several mass *tiyu* planners and activists. Wang Geng suggested the use of traveling martial arts teams not only to publicize the new *guoshu* but also to spread awareness of modern ideas of hygiene and physical fitness. One demonstration that he described, held before some four hundred people in Zhenjiang, Jiangsu, interspersed boxing and fencing routines with speeches on health, literacy, and education.[141] Cheng Dengke, foremost of the German-returned planners of a militarized *tiyu*, saw a curriculum combining activities like *guoshu*, calisthenics, gymnastics, military-themed "ball wars," and wrestling as the best way of creating a "revolutionary physical culture" where "the sports field is an amusement park and a battlefield."[142] And Zhang Zhijiang borrowed phrases from the mass *tiyu* movement when he talked about plans to "health-ize" and "warrior-ize" the Chinese masses, using martial arts to "train four hundred million iron Hans with eight hundred million steel arms."[143]

The most outstanding example of the trends of *guoshu* integration into the dominant *tiyu* forms was a new form of exercise introduced by political figure and martial arts master Chu Minyi. This form, called *taijicao* (tai chi calisthenics), combined elements of the ancient *taijiquan* with modern *ticao* calisthenics. Chu described in his 1933 book *Tai Chi Calisthenics Instructions and Commands* the reasoning behind this innovation. Whereas Western-style calisthenics were too angular and rigid and not physiologically beneficial, tai chi calisthenics were based on natural and smooth circular movements. And whereas traditional tai chi was simply too difficult for any but the most dedicated martial artist to master, tai chi calisthenics were pleasingly easy to learn and practice.

Chu's standard tai chi calisthenics routine consisted of six segments, exercising the wrists, hands and lower arms, shoulders and upper arms, feet and legs, chest and back, and finally the entire body. The first four segments consisted of four movements, the fifth and sixth segments of two movements each. Each movement was repeated four times and was counted off, "1–2, 3–4, 4–3, 2–1." Most convenient of all for the busy bourgeoisie and schoolchildren for whom the *taijicao* was designed, the entire vigorous routine would take just three minutes.[144]

The movements of tai chi calisthenics were introduced to the public by a great demonstration held during the 1933 National Games. There, two thousand Nanjing elementary school students dressed in white shirts and shorts followed their leader Chu, who directed the performance while perched atop two stacked tables. This triumphant demonstration was the result of six months' planning by Chu, who recruited Nanjing teachers willing to involve their students in this creation of a new "national calisthenics" *(guocao)*.[145]

Chu Minyi's tai chi calisthenics were perhaps the most publicized form of the new rational, easy-to-learn *guoshu* that could now be classified as a valid form of physical culture. Chu, the holder of a medical doctorate earned in France in the 1920s, designed this exercise to embody the modern and scientific Chinese Republic, not the feudal and unenlightened Chinese imperium. The mysticism of *taijiquan* was replaced by the simple routine of the tai chi calisthenics, its conflicting schools by one simple form and founder, its enigmatic terminology by easy-to-follow numbered orders, and the tranquil hush of its ancient movements by a jaunty series of calls and counts.

These modifications to tai chi exemplified a significant trend in China's modern martial arts community. In the past, *taijiquan* and martial arts in general had been a domain, a set of skills, and a marker of a dispossessed and marginalized rural populace. But such associations grated on educated, cosmopolitan martial artists like Chu. Chu took his task of creating a modern tai chi exercise very seriously, endlessly employing metaphors of the workings of electric fans, steamboats, and automobiles to demonstrate the superior efficiency of his tai chi calisthenics.[146] His conscious and conspicuous attempts to link the martial arts world to the realm of industry and labor discipline had other results as well. In transmitting his vision of a scientized and unified guoshu, Chu consistently assumed martial arts practitioners of his era to be members of the urban professional class (rather than, as formerly, the rural poor), and always portrayed these arts as inculcating bourgeois virtues in the people who performed them. The subjects of this discourse, the Chinese urbanites serving as the audience of this state project, sought to "re-Sinify" themselves as they made the martial arts safe for polite modern participation.

Chatterjee's work on the late-nineteenth-century Bengali middle-class "nationalist elite" offers an important analogue to Chu's "tai chi calisthenics" project and to the Nationalist *guoshu* project in general. Subordinated to a British colonial elite, the Bengali middle class turned to authentic Indian religion to represent an "Eastern" spirituality that the European colonial project could never encompass. This appropriation of the timeless "authentic" or "popular" Indian tradition, however, also required sanitizing "all marks of vulgarity, coarseness, localism, and sectarian identity" that by definition made up these cultural forms. Thus this elite project of "nationalizing" a middle class, of imbuing it with a national consciousness, in order to define it vis-à-vis the colonial power fundamentally altered and normalized on elite terms the most powerful forms of popular culture.[147]

A similar process unfolded in 1930s China as urbanites turned to the supposed "familiarity" of Chinese "traditions" like martial arts. China's martial arts were in no way relevant to the social, economic, or cultural conditions of the 1930s; they had to be made so. If the *guoshu* was to be a rational manifestation of the national essence, of what it meant to be Chinese, then nationalist elites were not about to locate this Chinese "essence" in laughable and crude peasant mysticism. China's middle classes needed a sanitized, rationally structured version of this cultural domain.

This class-specific viewpoint certainly comes out in Chu's addresses when he explains that tai chi calisthenics have been especially designed for members of the middle classes:

> People are just like machines. If a machine is not used it will rust;
> if people do not move they also will deteriorate. The intellectual class
> consists of people who all use their brainpower but never exercise.
> This is why most of them are so physically weak. Students at voca-
> tional schools, peasant schools, work-study students, are always mov-
> ing their bodies, so they do not need any more exercise. But it is
> among those studying letters or the law that physical exercise needs
> to be promoted.[148]

To confirm Chu's focus on the middle classes, one need only look at the illustrations in his book *Tai Chi Calisthenics Instructions and Commands* (see Figure 1), where the sweater- and plus-fours-clad martial arts instructor guiding readers through the routine looks more like a natty golf pro than a conveyor of China's ancient martial heritage.[149]

Chu was as tireless in promoting his invention as he had been in condensing the many and diverse old forms into the new *taijicao*. More than five hundred students graduated from Chu's Taijicao Lecture Seminar held in the summer of 1934. That same year, Chu collaborated with the Department of Education to establish a Taijicao Research Institute and a Taijicao Course-by-Mail Institute. The latter, open to any physical education teacher or enthusiast, consisted of correspondence on tai chi calisthenics theory and

Figure 1. "Outward leg rotations," fourth movement, fourth segment of Chu Minyi's 1933 tai chi calisthenics. Chu Minyi, *Taijicao zhi shuoming ji kouling*, 26.

details by mail (for a two-*yuan* fee, or U.S.$0.72), reinforced by free consultation with any of the three-hundred-plus alumni of Chu's Nanjing program now teaching all over China.[150]

Chu translated his program into English and French, calling it "Circular Exercise" or "Exercise Circalaire [*sic*]" so as not to scare off potential followers with antiquated *taiji* terminology.[151] He presented it at the Belgian Centennial Exposition, where "European and American educators and physical education specialists agreed that it was a new discovery for international physical education."[152] Tai chi calisthenics were featured in the film, made especially for entry in the 1936 Olympic Sports and Physical Education Film Contest, of Chu Minyi himself demonstrating "our nation's ancient *tiyu* styles" for the international sporting audience that would gather in Berlin that year.[153] The *taijicao* also served as the opening to the performance put on by China's nine-member *guoshu* team (hand-picked by Chu) at the Berlin Olympiad before thirty thousand fans, whose applause for the act "reverberated up to the heavens."

Coming from a man who had written of the "glad tidings for humanity" to be achieved by a modernized *guoshu*, Chu's flair for the international should not be surprising. He understood international acceptance of China's national arts as both the validation of *guoshu*'s scientific worth and the supreme proof that China belonged in, and could contribute to, the modern world. Chu saw himself as a true Chinese visionary. He rooted himself in the Chinese martial tradition, often growing his hair and beard long in an ancient sagely style or challenging Mongol princes to horse races in Nanjing's Central Stadium.[154] But no one who ever saw Chu posed shirtless and flexing in *Young Companion* or *Modern Student*,[155] or his martial arts–themed inventions like the *Taiji*-ball or the *Taiji*-baton devices,[156] would ever have doubted his devotion to a modern China at home in the new scientific and rational world order.

Chu's career in the *guoshu* movement was marked by this struggle between the uniquely Chinese and the scientifically international, between a national essence and a cosmopolitan common sense. Yet his starry-eyed idealism led Chu and his *taijicao* to a sorry fate. In 1939, he joined the "peace movement" led by his brother-in-law Wang Jingwei, taking several top posts in Wang's pro-Japan puppet Nanjing government. Chu's *taijicao* became the official "citizen's calisthenics" *(guomin ticao)* of the new regime, and a great Citizen's Calisthenics Meet was held in 1941 to mark the anniversary of the national government's "relocation" to Nanjing.[157] The end of the war, however, brought Chu the fate that awaited many who worked in this regime for peace and Pan-Asianism under the Japanese. Chu was arrested, imprisoned in Suzhou, and sentenced to death in 1946. The death sentence was soon carried out, but only, legend has it, after Chu performed one last serene and dignified *taijiquan* routine before the eyes of his stunned executioners.

CONCLUSION

I'm a fighter
Use kung fu each time I can
Not that I like it
Not that it's really what I am
Where does the line between
Defended
And defensive
Stand *!*
SCOTT MILLER, "Top Dollar Survivalist Hardware,"
1996 (The Loud Family, *Interbabe Concern*)

The story of the martial arts in Republican China was complicated. Whereas the orthodox forms of modern physical culture came to China via foreign agents and processes, *wushu* came to urban locales via the late Qing exodus of itinerant rural job seekers to large cities. While May Fourth modernists hoped to relegate the martial arts to the feudal past, literate and patriotic *wushu* aficionados built a new future for their arts based on modern ideas of the nation, science, and sexual equality. When the martial arts were dismissed as hopelessly Chinese and fatally particular, the Pure Martial Association created a martial arts dynasty by mixing their *wushu* with Western sports and hobbies (such as roller skating and photography) and by vigorously disseminating their message to sojourners in Southeast Asia starving for a culture both Chinese and martially potent. When the Nanjing Guomindang state attempted to craft these arts into national arts manifesting a purely national essence, practical *guoshu* promoters soon found that the martial arts were most accessible to young Chinese when served with equal portions of modern competition and physical education philosophy. And when the Guomindang *tiyu* apparatus realized the value of *guoshu* as a supplementary Orientalizing counterpart to the sports of the Western-dominated Olympic movement, sending a *guoshu* demonstration team to the 1936 Berlin Olympiad, they were discouraged that this only real Chinese triumph of the whole games was understood by the world as an impressive but ultimately meaningless demonstration.

In recent decades, martial arts has profited from a self-Orientalizing agenda—the exact opposite of the rigorously and untiringly modern approach of agents like the Pure Martial Association and the Central Guoshu Academy. "New Age" trends in the West, combined with searches for Chinese precapitalist "authenticity" throughout Greater China, have created a space for invented traditions of a timeless "martial arts" to flourish. However, the onset of total war in 1937 brought great trepidation to the martial arts community. No less an authority than Sun Yat-sen had insisted that martial arts were crucial in "the decisive last five minutes [of a battle] over the last five feet of ground."[158] That he might have been wrong, that martial arts might not be enough to stop the Japanese invaders, was now a chilling possibility.

8 *Tiyu* through Wartime and "Liberation"

During the summer of 1937, China's *tiyu* elites engaged in feverish planning for the Seventh National Games, set to begin at the Central Stadium in Nanjing's Purple and Gold Mountains on 10 October. With a budget of three hundred thousand *yuan* (U.S.$90,000),[1] there was much political pressure to make these games something more than just another exercise in Western-style sports and "trophy-ism." Indeed, new martial-themed demonstration events were to include the modern pentathlon, polo, the fully armed five-kilometer race, grenade throwing, and Western-style boxing.[2]

Once again, the hope of holding a Nanjing National Games was shattered by the eruption that July of the eight-year war against Japan. This war, and the three more years of civil war that followed, obviously had great implications for Chinese physical culture. From Chongqing in the Southwest to Yan'an in the Northwest, from Xinjing in the Northeast to Nanjing, to Taipei off the southeastern coast, various Chinese regimes, Nationalist, Communist, and otherwise, crafted new modes of physical culture in order to promote notions of popular participation and acceptance.[3] Yet none of these different *tiyu* movements ever departed radically from the established fundamentals and traditions of modern Chinese physical culture. The "Liberating" 1950s importation of Soviet Russian models of training, bureaucracy, and socialist education brought important changes to sports and physical culture under the new Communist regime. However, until that moment, the established modern *tiyu* structure was so logical and powerful that few in the 1930s and 1940s could imagine changing it in drastic or meaningful ways.

TIYU IN THE NATIONALIST TERRITORIES, 1937–45

("Get up, get up!" every morning a comrade would blow his
whistle and shout.)
The sky
In April
Is blue;
The park
In the north
Is blue;
On a blue morning, in a blue world, amidst a blue war,
In the morning
We do calisthenics.

> T'IEN CHIEN, "In the Morning We Do Calisthenics" (1937?),
> in Julia C. Lin, *Modern Chinese Poetry: An Introduction*

The tragedies of war did not stop the pursuit of the *tiyu* enterprise in Nationalist China. Agents of the *tiyu* project, retreating west and finally set-
tling in the provisional capital of Chongqing, continued and intensified the
Nationalist physical culture programs to reach and teach all China's citizens through the powerful motions and disciplines of *tiyu*. For participants
in Nationalist areas of China, *tiyu* became an important way of living and
creating the wartime experience and further developed Nanjing Decade
trends of mass and militarized physical culture that would later be found in
the *tiyu* of the early People's Republic of China (PRC; 1949–).

By 1939, two years after hostilities began, thirty-four of China's 108 institutions of higher learning had been uprooted and made grueling long-
distance treks inland.[4] These mobile institutions included many physical education schools and departments, whose members were able to bring their
science to the inland and southwestern communities that hosted their efforts. When educational elites migrated to southwestern cities like Zunyi,
Guilin, Kunming, and Chongqing, they imagined and included the populations of those cities into a national community in unprecedented ways, discovering that people they had previously dismissed as unknown "provin-
cials" or "natives" in exotic locales were able to discipline themselves as
healthy citizens, just as their coastal compatriots had done for decades now.
Although these cities were familiar with *tiyu* by the late 1930s, the wartime
newcomers worked to develop the physical culture enterprise there to levels of saturation rivaling China's coastal cities.

Then these agents of modernity expanded their disciplines to even more
remote provincial reaches. In 1941, after Japanese forces occupied Vietnam,

the Yunnan-Guizhou Pacification Office sent an army engineering corps to Malipo County on the Vietnam border to destroy roads and bridges that would make a Vietnam-Yunnan crossing more practical for Japanese troops. The corps' accomplishments in Malipo also included planning and executing a massive three-day Anti-Japanese National Salvation Athletic Meet in Shuidongping Village, which drew more than three thousand fans.[5] The sporting movement thus created an even wider nexus of personal discipline and national identity that allowed southwesterners to experience their nation and their role in it in ways they had never known.

The arrival of the Central Government at the provisional capital at Chongqing brought to this secluded and damp "Mountain City" the units of the Nationalist *tiyu* bureaucracy that had led the competitive sports, mass and militarized *tiyu*, school physical education, and martial arts movements of the Nanjing Decade. During wartime, these institutions found their goals and activities converging much more than ever before. When the 1940 Tokyo Olympics were canceled and this worldwide sporting stage mercifully dismantled, elite competitive sports in China lost almost any justification whatsoever. Likewise, total war rendered obsolete the militarized *tiyu* dreams of the fascist wing of the Nanjing *tiyu* movement,[6] as even the most militaristic exercises prescribed in Chongqing could be of pathetically little use against the Japanese war machine. Wartime physical culture now adopted an emphasis on a well-rounded and healthy sports program for the masses who would lead and live in a postwar Nationalist China.

National and municipal *tiyu* bodies prepared and published physical education standards and curricula, investigated the fitness of Chongqing students, and sponsored a wide range of sporting activities for the people of Chongqing. Memorable Chongqing events included a Capture-the-Traitor Mountain Climbing Competition on 9 June 1940, with dozens of youth racing to the top of a mountain to "capture" lifesize paper effigies of pro-Japan Nanjing collaborators, and a January 1940 Provisional Capital Tiyu Parade, with over ten thousand participants putting on mobile demonstrations of martial arts, group calisthenics, cycling, track and field, basketball, and even billiards played on moving wheeled tables.[7] The most important mass *tiyu* achievement of the *tiyu* bureaucracy in Chongqing was the establishment in 1942 of 9 September as a national holiday, Sports Day *(Tiyu jie)*, to be a festival of physical activities for all—from martial arts to mountain climbing, swimming to rowing, weightlifting to ball games. In Chongqing, where the holiday was celebrated most conspicuously, more than two thousand Chongqing citizen-athletes took part in a great thirty-three-day athletic meet.[8]

Events like these Sports Day festivities demonstrate the new concentration on the physical fitness of the "masses," which now took on more importance than national "face" and Olympic prestige, national essence and martial arts, or national strength and militarized *tiyu*. Thus the Guomindang regime's attention to the bodies and minds of the local southwestern populations in many ways disproves the caricature of its wartime rule as the last pathetic acts of a corrupt and exploitative governmental farce and gives the lie to notions of 1937 as the end of Republican history. The "Liberation" delivered by the Communists just years later was hardly as original or "New" as advertised; by 1949 Chinese people in Chongqing and other areas of the wartime Nationalist realm had been educated and trained for years in self-consciously "mass" forms of culture like those described here.

"RED *TIYU*" AND THE COMMUNIST MOVEMENT

As described briefly in Chapter 5, the Chinese Communist Party also worked to ground its reputation and credentials in the cult of the strong and disciplined body and nation via its red *tiyu* movement. The CCP's sporting endeavor, begun in southern China, continued throughout the Long March,[9] and in 1937 a Soviet Physical Culture and Sports Committee was formed under the command of Zhu De, Lin Boqu, and Xu Teli.[10] The CCP obviously lacked the great resources spent by the Nationalist central government on great competitive sports meets, societies, and publications. The *tiyu* role of Shaan-Gan-Ning government bodies consisted mostly of crafting and disseminating catchy *tiyu* slogans like Mao Zedong's "Train the body well, fight Japan thoroughly" and Zhu's "Hitting a ball is also hitting thought,"[11] both clever if not entirely original examples of linking the wartime struggle to the *tiyu* project. Physical culture in the Communist base camps, before and during the Anti-Japanese War, also helps us to understand the CCP as a thoroughly modern *part of,* not just a revolutionary and utter *exception to,* a greater Republican-era Chinese milieu.

The Communist Party defined their red *tiyu* as a fundamental alternative to the athletic culture promoted by the Nationalist regime. Still, these bitter enemies shared more in this realm than they could have admitted. Red *tiyu* emphasis on "the masses"—as in the simultaneous disciplined motions of group calisthenics[12] that were used to impose a "popular" image upon authoritarian culture—was not uniquely red but a relic of the Japanese drill models imported into China in the 1890s. The CCP media's assertions that the cheering squad *(laladui)* was a revolutionary and productive mode of sports spectatorship[13] and that the bourgeois notion of sportsmanship *(yundong daode)* was a uniquely revolutionary feeling[14] were similarly empty (if inspiring) claims.

Communist writers often condemned Nationalist sport as decadent and hopelessly "trophy-ist" *(jinbiao zhuyi)*, full of athletes who competed not for the sake of the nation or race but merely for the trophies they could collect. Yet these denunciations rang hollow, especially since public and official write-ups of every CCP meet included detailed accounts of what prizes were donated by whom and awarded to which winners. Money, championship banners, athletic shoes, sporting goods, clothing, stationery, comic books, teas, medicines, personal effects and hygiene items, rugs, paintings, wood carvings, and porcelain were all among the prizes that Shaan-Gan-Ning's best athletes took home after successful sporting performances.[15]

Party propagandists talked a red game, but they offered few challenges to the sporting ideology that swept the modern world in the twentieth century. CCP physical culture did not represent any fundamental shift in the field. Nor was it a far-seeing red *tiyu* revolution that foreshadowed later PRC world sporting dominance. Instead, it represented merely a series of necessary and practical variations on a strong and almost hegemonic modern *tiyu* theme.

PHYSICAL CULTURE IN THE CIVIL WAR PERIOD, 1945–48

The glory of the 1945 victory in the Eight Years' War of Resistance allowed the Chinese *tiyu* community to fantasize about the future of their discipline and their nation. On 7 September, before relocating to Nanjing, members of the China National Amateur Athletic Federation resolved to apply to the International Olympic Committee to host the XVth Olympic Games in 1952.[16] Indeed, physical culture, as a P.E. coach at Guilin Middle School wrote in 1947, seemed the only real way to build a national community and allow "the nation and race to throw off once and for all this danger of [national] extinction."[17] On the theme of liberation through sport, the *New Fujian Daily* columnist (and former star athlete) Chen Zhang'e concluded an essay in 1948 on the triumphs of African American stars Jesse Owens and Joe Louis with a classical and melodramatic flourish: "Alas! The black slaves have been liberated, but what of the yellow slaves?"[18]

Soon, however, notions of a peace dividend, betrayed by the advent of Guomindang-Communist civil warfare, gave way to a new right-wing siege mentality in Nationalist-ruled areas. Physical culture became one more element of the desperate attempts to rebuild a Nationalist China and to shelter the citizenry from harmful Communist, liberal, or even slightly democratic ideologies. Notions of *tiyu* discipline and "social control"[19] not addressed in decades emerged during these civil war years. The militarist Cheng Qian, honorary chairman of the Ninth Hubei Provincial Games in 1947, reflected on competitive sports in a tellingly distressed fashion:

> There is so little justice or fairness in society of which to speak. The result is that there is no right or wrong. People take pride in destroying order and disrupting discipline. Observing rules and abiding laws is seen as stupid and weak. . . . If one wants to make China independent and strong, then all our citizens must heartily awake, thoroughly reform, wipe out habits of vanity, perfunctoriness, deception, and selfishness, and honor the virtues of justice, determination, responsibility, and respect for law. Today's games are the touchstone for these virtues.[20]

Yet Nationalist physical culture functionaries ultimately could not safeguard the supposed purity of the *tiyu* realm. Relentless civil war–era inflation made it increasingly difficult to maintain a respectable *tiyu* movement. A letter from He Zhiliang, director of the Mass Education Center in Toksun County, Xinjiang, informed provincial authorities in Dihua that even his six-hundred-some-billion-*yuan* budget would not be sufficient to sponsor a October Tenth County Track Meet.[21] Worst of all were the moments when the joy of sporting competition gave way to terror and brutality. At the October Tenth Basketball Tourney in Luoping County, eastern Yunnan, the Banqiao Merchants began to dominate their game against the Stray Bullets, a team from the local military encampment. Armed troops from the Bullets' unit did their part to prevent this loss, taking to the court and bashing the Merchants' heads and torsos with their weapons.[22]

The "Retrocession" *(Guangfu)* of Taiwan to Guomindang rule in late 1945 created another important site for physical culture to serve as an agent of Nationalist Chinese hegemony. Taiwan, a Japanese colony for fifty years, looked, sounded, and felt much more like enemy territory than "an inseparable piece of the Chinese motherland" when *tiyu* agents arrived to help ease Taiwan's masses, confused and disoriented by the "slave life" they had led for half a century,[23] back into polite Chinese society.

Chief among issues on this *tiyu* agenda was the promotion of baseball.[24] This game, imported into Taiwan in the earliest years of the colonial period, carried a Japanese/colonial stigma so distinctive that only the rarest of Guomindang-fearing administrators could even accept the presence of a baseball team on their campus.[25] However, at the same time, state agents involved in Retrocession efforts realized what a valuable exception baseball could be to the rule of suppressing colonial culture in Taiwan. Officially endorsing baseball soon became one method of appropriating this sport for Nationalist purposes, even though Taiwan was clearly the only region of China with any real baseball tradition. The Taiwan Provincial Games, held annually on 25 October to mark Retrocession anniversaries, became another central arena of a physical culture aimed at transforming the Taiwanese into good Nationalists. Crucial enough to merit the occasional presence of Chiang Kai-shek and Song Meiling, the games gave "New Taiwan's new heroes" an opportunity to perform in a completely saturated Nationalist environment, surrounded by national and party flags, anthems, photos, insignia, and iconography.[26]

The Nationalists' last significant *tiyu* project on the Chinese mainland was the preparation of a delegation to the XIVth Olympic Games in London. It is a tribute to the resilience of the Nationalist sporting community that many individuals had high hopes for these games; as one writer noted in desperate hope,

> China's taking part in the Olympic Games shows that, despite chaos and hardship due to warfare and animosity among political parties and cliques, the Chinese common people are at heart united by brotherly love and harbor no grudge against one another. . . . They have the ability to cooperate and stand together upon any question which affects the honor, prestige and reputation of their country.[27]

The raging civil war placed obvious financial constraints on this mission; when the central government was only able to contribute a mere five billion *yuan* (U.S.$2,500), the CNAAF turned to several wealthy Shanghai and Singapore sports fans, who made sizable contributions in exchange for official "advisor" status, and the Olympic basketball and soccer teams departed on pregames tours of Southeast Asia to raise one last cache of badly needed funds.[28]

The delegation, consisting of thirty-two athletes and twenty managers, advisors, secretaries, and assistants, hauled with it tons of food for all the Chinese athletes' meals in a final attempt to pinch *yuan*. The team was well received in London, honored by invitations into Londoners' homes and a royal reception at Buckingham Palace, but once again finished the games with no medals—as one government report described it, a "disastrous failure."[29] More humiliating, however, was the fiasco that took place after the games, when Olympic officials realized that they did not have enough money to pay for the delegation's return plane tickets. The team was reduced to selling their leftover food and asking for small donations from

British well-wishers before they could purchase the tickets and bring to an end yet another Olympic adventure,[30] perhaps unknowingly providing a very appropriate conclusion to the factionalism, corruption, and blundering that seemed to characterize much of the thirty-eight-year Republican interregnum.

AFTER 1949

The PRC sporting era began on 22 October 1949, just three weeks after the dramatic founding of the new state, when a great "mass-ized . . . collectivized . . . politicized . . . nationalized" Beijing Municipal Athletic Meet attracted over thirty thousand participants and spectators to the Temple of Agriculture Stadium. Four days later, the new All-China Athletic Federation was formed out of the ashes of the old Republican CNAAF.[31]

The 1950s importation of Soviet models of training, bureaucracy, and socialist education, combined with the party's unprecedented reach into local life, allowed the PRC *tiyu* project to take Chinese sport to breadths, lengths, and depths never reached during the Republican era. Yet great continuity still existed between Nationalist and Communist conceptions of physical culture. The connections between the modern, competitive nation-state (itself a recent historical invention whose logic few questioned) and a self-disciplining, healthy populace were not in the broad range of categories that the CCP sought to change with their grand revolution.

The physical culture and sporting project developed during the Republic had problems. It lacked credibility on the elite level of competitive sport, having never produced a world champion or Olympic medal of any kind. It was insufficient on the mass level as well, as large segments of China's urban and rural populations had still never benefited from these new games and exercises. Many of those who were lucky enough to participate in this new domain were doing so with positively unsocialist attitudes, as they joined in sport for sport's sake, or worse, for the sake of glory and material gain. But few of modern *tiyu*'s founding principles would ever be seriously interrogated by the new masters of China. Official 1950s programs to "rediscover, systematize, and raise standards" of martial arts and to hold large-scale *wushu* competitions with the aim of popularizing these "traditional" forms would not have offended even the most dogmatic of Guomindang martial arts advocates.[32] Likewise, early 1950s work to organize the "Ready for Labor and Defense of the Motherland Physical Culture System"[33] could only have made the old 1930s-era advocates of fascist-style militarized *tiyu* proud. And the internationalist platitudes of sport were quickly put to surreal use by the new regime during the Korean War, when Chinese People's Volunteer forces organized and publicized an "Inter Camp Olympics" for United Nations POWs at Pyuktong in November 1952.[34]

Even the most bourgeois of Nationalist-era sports, basketball, could be transformed into a powerful and convincing site for the everyday practice of Communist ideology. In periods of great political radicalism, such as the late 1950s and the Cultural Revolution, the popular game—once defiled by Guomindang-era capitalism and corruption—had incontestably revolutionary credentials. Xie Jin's 1957 film *Woman Basketball Player No. 5* showed how hardworking and selfless (female) players and (male) coaches remade the once-bourgeois game into the embodiment of Communist sportsmanship and will.[35] In 1962, *New Sport* published pictures of a Beijing night-soil carriers' work unit engaged in a healthy basketball game with high school students, representing the possibility of basketball hosting a revolutionary alliance unthinkable in Old China.[36] And Liang Heng, in his memoir *Son of the Revolution,* discussed the great emphasis placed on, and the shocking amount of material and bureaucratic resources devoted to, factory and regional basketball teams even during the Cultural Revolution.[37] The recent globalizing and commodifying influences of Michael Jordan and his NBA have altered the terms in which basketball is understood in China, but—witness the nationalist mania surrounding the success of Yao Ming in the NBA—the game's century-old role as an important marker of national progress and status has remained constant.[38]

Sports and physical culture under the Republic of China (ROC) regime have also remained an important priority since its 1949 relocation to Taiwan. Nationalist-Communist fighting on the mainland had hardly ceased when the war turned to another vitally important battleground: the Olympic Games. Beginning in 1951, two Chinese Olympic Committees—one representing the Taipei Nationalist regime[39] and encouraged by International Olympic Committee Chairman Avery Brundage, the other representing Beijing and aided by the Soviet Union—began making their respective cases for their exclusive right to represent "China" at the 1952 Helsinki Games.[40]

The International Olympic Committee, long before formulating its "Olympic model" that in 1981 recognized the ROC only as "Chinese Taipei" (Zhonghua Taibei),[41] in July 1952 ruled to allow both Chinese teams to join the games. The ROC's representative Hao Gengsheng declared that his athletes would never compete in the same arena as Chinese Communist athletes and announced the ROC's withdrawal from the 1952 Olympics. The coast was now clear for the PRC delegation, who also refused to recognize an Olympic regime that included the old ROC renegades. After ensuring that Taiwan would not send a team, the PRC team left Beijing six days after the games had begun in Helsinki. Premier Zhou Enlai dismissed any who would quibble over such minor details, declaring, "Raising the five-starred red [PRC] flag at the Olympic Games is in itself the victory." The PRC flag was raised, and one Chinese male swimmer was able to join a backstroke preliminary race, before the games ended.[42] This small victory preserved intact one of the bases of the modern Chinese *tiyu* project, the understanding of inclusion in the sporting rituals of the world community as a fundamental victory for a Chinese nation entering the ranks of modernity.

The PRC-ROC battle for Chinese sporting legitimacy continued for the better part of three decades, although it usually could be characterized more by "worse" than by "better." At the 1956 Melbourne Olympiad, which the ROC joined and the PRC boycotted, an agent working for the PRC pulled off a switch in the Olympic Village flags department. The intended result, the raising of the PRC's red flag on the ROC ("Formosa China") delegation's arrival, stunned and shocked the free sporting world.[43]

In the most daring chapter of this cross-Straits Olympic skullduggery, PRC intelligence agents enticed two traitorous teammates of Taiwanese legend C. K. Yang (Yang Chuanguang) to drug him before the 1964 Tokyo Olympic decathlon. Ma Jingshan and Chen Jue earned the right to defect back to their beloved mainland by spiking Yang's orange juice just days before the competition and thus preventing Yang, the world-record holder at the time and *Sports Illustrated*'s reigning "World's Best Athlete," from embarrassing the Communist regime with a sure gold-medal effort.[44] This sporting dispute was so bitter not only because both sides wanted desperately to be recognized as the sole sporting representatives of "China" but also because the two sides held deep and similar faiths in the significance of the Olympic movement and competitive sporting competition for the health and future of their nations.

The most visible area of Taiwan's *tiyu* endeavor has of course been Little League baseball, a realm that allowed Taiwanese to walk a tightrope between memories of Japanese colonialism and the realities of Guomindang-American hegemony in Taiwan. In a tremendous run perhaps unmatched in the history of international sport, Taiwanese teams won ten Little League World Series titles between 1969 and 1981 and sixteen between 1969 and 1995. This success brought a desperately appreciated sense of victory to Taiwan in a time when its most important ally, the United States, was gradually distancing itself from the island in favor of forming ties to the PRC. It also allowed complicated national-racial tensions and negotiations to be played out between "native Taiwanese," "provincial outsider," and Aborigine populations (as many of these top baseball teams were made up of Aboriginal youth from eastern Taiwan).[45]

In this way, baseball, despite the colonial legacy it represented, carried on the most important of modern Chinese *tiyu* traditions. The young players from eastern and southern Taiwan perhaps had no idea of the century-long heritage that their efforts represented—as their sport became one more realm designed perfectly for teaching, learning, and living what it meant to be a fit and active citizen, at all times keeping firmly in mind the interests, status, and boundaries of one's Chinese nation-state home.

CONCLUSION

Although it is possible to draw historical *tiyu* connections between youth in 1890s Qing military academies and the young Aborigine baseball stars of 1990s eastern Taiwan, the "body cultivation" project that spans this century was designed for a world that few Chinese of today could recognize. Fears of national-racial extinction are as antiquated as assumptions of PRC power and status are commonsensical. China and its sporting project now stand on top of a world order that seemed merciless and threatening one hundred years, or even fifty years, ago. One wonders if *tiyu* remains an extraordinarily charged symbol of China's status in the world, despite or *because* of the incredible changes that have taken place there and all over the world over the last century.

China's modern physical culture originated largely in the German-Swedish-Japanese drill programs that sought to inculcate physical discipline and constant mental awareness in their participating subjects under the command of a single strong leader—characteristics seen as necessary for the population of a nation facing imperialist aggression. The Anglo-American sports *tiyu* soon brought a different focus to physical culture, that of teamwork and sportsmanship. Sports were rational and modern with their measurements, race times, physical and behavioral boundaries, rules and regulations, theories of free movement and "natural" motions, and celebrations of the modern masculine national and personal ideal. As sports *tiyu* became the dominant form in Chinese physical culture, it provided the grounds for make-believe Darwinist struggles that could cultivate the competitive instinct so necessary for survival in the modern world and condition team members in the ideology of "friendly struggle" and "fair competition" under which capitalism justified its global expansion. Finally, sports *tiyu* created a new modern subject—the paying fan with different layered and intersecting regional and national loyalties.

The next stage in the development of *tiyu* was the model—proposed by Chinese reformers and Western missionaries alike—of a liberal democratic physical culture. Winning currency in the postwar, post–May Fourth 1920s, the *tiyu* community believed that this mode of exertion and training would be instrumental in creating responsible, self-disciplining modern citizens who would take care of their bodies in the interest of the national community. Also during this period, rationalizing forms of athletic training and organization and disciplining practices like physical fitness exams and health inspections, developed by Western physical educators, became part of the Chinese physical culture agenda. Perhaps less obvious, however, was the phenomenon of an "intercultural zone" of contact between Westerner and Other, where both sides were able to immerse themselves in the realm of *tiyu* as a way of escaping from the histories of Western imperialism and violence in China.

From 1924 to 1928, imperialist brutalities in China, the growing Guomindang nationalist movement, and events within the physical culture world itself gave rise to a more stridently nationalistic form of *tiyu*. This nationalism was also directly implicated in programs for physical culture for women, who were advised to cast aside the passivity that crippled them physically and mentally and to take responsibility for shaping bodies that could produce the next generation of healthy, strong Chinese citizens. Whereas previous authors have seen the extension of the *tiyu* gaze to women as a type of liberation, I have shown here that little was liberatory about a discipline that used Western science and the male dominance of the Chinese media to create ideals of a physically fit "mother of citizens."

The Nanjing Decade, dating to the establishment of the Nationalist regime there in 1928, saw the Guomindang's explicit efforts to change the focus of physical culture from the individual nation-minded citizen to the united *minzu* nation-race. The official 1930s *tiyu* agenda, followed by many loyal educators, called for the creation of a "*tiyu* for the masses," in which a proper scientific physical training would allow all Chinese to become efficient members of the production force and of the new muscular "*minzu* body." Mass *tiyu* consisted of militarized, politically correct curricula presenting China's youth with systematic mixtures of team sports, military training, and Boy or Girl Scout training. Alongside these efforts, however, Chinese sports teams of elite athletes were garnering national attention as they represented the nation on international stages such as the Far Eastern Championship Games and the Olympics. The prestigious realm of competitive sport forced the *tiyu* community to question the very basis of the national project to cultivate a new Chinese national body. Indeed, many in the Guomindang were reluctant to devote scarce resources to athletic events that clearly brought little to the Chinese masses whom modern *tiyu* was supposed to benefit. These contradictions between the Guomindang's focus on a mass militarized national-racial training and their obligation to enter the world of commercialized international sport highlighted political tensions in China in general, as concerned Chinese (who may have thought of themselves only as sports fans) contested meanings of a modern Chinese nation.

Chinese martial arts during the Nanjing Decade, but also as early as the 1910s, also were fundamentally affected by the nationalizing, modernizing trends described above. In the early Republic, *wushu*, so steeped in oral and feudal tradition, was seen as too Chinese, too backward, to be of any use in the modern age. In the 1920s, however, activists from Shanghai to Beijing worked to remake martial arts into a "native physical culture"; intensive organizational and publishing efforts allowed the new *wushu* to become accepted as a modern form of physical endeavor. Then, in 1928, one of the new Nanjing regime's first cultural measures was the establishment of a Central Guoshu Academy, which soon worked to enlist local martial arts traditions and leaders, impose its new scientific and national curricula on these branches, and hold national martial arts competitions to rival the excitement, splendor, and spiritual and strategic significance of nationwide athletic meets.

EPILOGUE: BEIJING, 2008

It is significant that exactly a century after Tianjin YMCA missionaries asked their students, "When will China be able to invite all the world to come to Peking for an International Olympic contest?" the Games of the XXIX Olympiad will take place in Beijing. One measure of the lasting resonance of the missionaries' challenging questions can be seen in their inclusion in the celebratory volume *Beijing 2008*, published just weeks after the IOC's official acceptance of Beijing's bid.[46]

That the year 2008 also marks the eightieth anniversary of the establishment of Nanjing's Central Guoshu Academy is also significant for the critical role that martial arts symbolism played in the official bid for these games. The Beijing 2008 Olympic Games Bid Committee, founded in 1999, used explicitly self-Orientalizing terminology and logic—with China's traditional "graceful" and "harmonious" martial arts at its center—to convince the world of the PRC capital's relevance to the twenty-first century:

> By hosting the [2008 Olympic] Games, Beijing and China will be further opened to the world. . . . The concept we have proposed for Beijing as a host city of the 2008 Olympic Games may be summed up in these words: Harmony between man and nature; blend of sport and culture; essential application of rapidly developing information technologies. The [Beijing 2008 Olympic bid] emblem resembles a person doing "taiji" [tai chi], symbolizing gracefulness, harmony, vitality and mobility as well as unity, cooperation, exchange and development.[47]

The martyred martial artist Chu Minyi and his *guoshu* comrades would surely take great pride in the emblem of the successful Beijing 2008 Olympic Games bid, knowing that this momentous achievement for the Chinese nation was accomplished in part through the symbolism and science of China's own martial arts. As the Bid Committee's Web site explained about the official logo, "The star shapes a person doing 'taiji' shadow boxing, referring to the essence of China's traditional sports culture, which are Smoothness, harmony, vitality and mobility [sic]."[48] Even the very origins of the *taiji*-star were meant to represent a modern cosmopolitan China; the committee was careful to explain that "members decided the emblem and slogan in a vote by raised hands" and that they "received enthusiastic response from all sectors in China, including Hong Kong, Macao and Taiwan [sic]."[49]

Surely, only a China truly liberated from its self-conscious fears of the feudal, hooligan nature of the martial arts could now take tai chi "shadow boxing" as an emblem of a harmonious and vital sporting nation. The decision to stake the success of Beijing's Olympic bid on the image of tai chi is perhaps the most important illustration that the martial arts, for an entire century, have been much more appropriate to the worlds of commerce and marketing than to any real sort of national defense. For all the caustic attacks on premodern and prenational martial artists, it was actually those shameless hucksters "blocking the streets with their cursed displays" who understood the real secret of martial arts all along.

The range of ideas and promises attributed to Beijing's hosting of the Olympics is astounding. The Beijing 2008 enterprise—which is supported by 94.6 percent of the population, according to the (strategically used) public opinion polls[50]—seems to be functioning at present as a giant magnet to which the filings of decades of broken PRC promises can adhere. Officially, the games are being sold as the "Green Olympics, Hi-tech Olympics and

People's Olympics." Commitment to improved human rights standards, higher living standards, environmental progress, cleaner air, faster infrastructure development, new communications and sewage treatment facilities, unification with Taiwan, and even cleaner public toilets are all among the more specific guarantees issued with regard to the Olympic project.[51]

Yet the Beijing 2008 authorities are keeping some of their movement's greatest plans to themselves, or at least to the Chinese-speaking world. The official English-language motto of the 2008 Games is "New Beijing, Great Olympics," which does not quite correspond with the Chinese motto that accompanies it—"*xin Beijing, xin Aoyun*," or "New Beijing, *New* Olympics." The point of this Beijing Olympic movement surely is much greater than the official pothole-fixing impulse described above (and greater than the odd logic of the admission that only the "openness" that comes with the Olympic project, and not the CCP's six-decade-old "Liberatory" commitment, will force the PRC regime into recognizing more progressive human rights policies). The dream that two weeks in Beijing in 2008 can fashion a "new" Olympics—that China is now powerful enough to remake the Olympic experience itself—is more truly in the hearts of the 94 percent of Beijing's citizens who would like to volunteer to work at the games.

Few in the Republican-era *tiyu* community could dream in this way of a Chinese-led sporting reformation. Those who could, like Chu Minyi, imagined the Chinese people bringing "glad tidings to humanity" via their own essentialized and unique martial arts. More typical was the pride of being included at all in the "republic of muscles"—being able to shake hands with Jesse Owens, or to witness the ROC flag flying alongside those of the world's nations for the first time—after having been on the edge of national-racial extinction for so long.

Today, the medals won and records set by Chinese athletes in Olympic and other international competitions are understood as unquestionable proof of China's superpower status in the world and of the ruling Chinese Communist Party's hegemony within the PRC. The Republican-era goose eggs earned by the Chinese delegations to the 1932, 1936, and 1948 Olympic Games have become a dead-on caricature of the inadequacies and weakness of "Old China." These failures serve as a perfect metonym for the pre-Liberation agonies and defeats that China suffered at the hands of the powerful imperialist nations of the world, who, not coincidentally, no longer dare to perpetrate these aggressions on the citizens of New China.

Such pre-1949 sporting misfortunes are now scorned by a twenty-first-century China, fiercely nationalistic and proudly materialistic, where might is as right as weakness and defeat are laughable and pathetic. As Xie Jin, director of the 1997 sado-Darwinist blockbuster film *The Opium War*, trumpeted endlessly while promoting his work, "The weak and backward just have to accept their beatings" *(luohou jiu yao aida)*. Weak and backward nations do not host the Olympic Games—witness the epochal qualities attributed to the 1964 Olympic moment in standard narratives of Japan's postwar redevelopment. Beijing 2008 will probably take on similar significance in the narratives of the reform era. Gallup China, itself an artifact of these very same reformist trends, in fact found that "among those questioned, elderly residents showed the strongest desire to see Beijing win the bid, hoping they could see the Games come to their city before they died. 'Some senior people said they would exercise and build up their bodies in order to live until the day when the Games are staged in Beijing.'"[52] Clearly, the Olympics will mean many different things to the athletes, fans, and citizens of China in 2008 than they did in 1932 when sprinter Liu Changchun saw himself as a "dirty fisherman in the [Los Angeles Olympic] peach-blossom haven." Yet one factor will be the same—the intense desire of all Chinese involved in the world of physical culture to use their muscles, training, skills, and consumer power to make China truly again "a nation to be counted."

Notes

CHAPTER 1. INTRODUCTION

1. Wu Tingfang, *America through the Spectacles of an Oriental Diplomat* (New York: Frederick A. Stokes, 1914; reprint, Taipei: Ch'eng-wen Publishing, 1968), 257–58 (page citations are to the reprint edition).

2. Wu Tingfang, *America*, 217–22.

3. *Annual Reports of the Foreign Secretaries of the International Committee, October 1, 1909 to September 30, 1910* (New York: International Committee, YMCA, 1910), 192. *Annual Reports of the Foreign Secretaries of the International Committee, October 1, 1907 to September 30, 1908* (New York: International Committee, YMCA, 1908), 163, contains the same questions with slightly different wording.

4. *Annual Reports of the Foreign Secretaries of the International Committee, October 1, 1909 to September 30, 1910*, 192. Zhang Boling, founder of the Nankai Middle School, a great *tiyu* enthusiast and a close friend of Robertson, also wrote in 1907–8 in the YMCA publication *Tientsin Young Men* on his dream of a Chinese Olympic team. Chih-Kang Wu, "The Influence of the YMCA on the Development of Physical Education in China" (Ph.D. diss., University of Michigan, 1956), 106.

5. Qiwu [Xu Yibing], "Jinggao jiaoyujie," *Tiyujie* 1 (1st day, 3d lunar month [20 April], 1909), 1–2.

6. Beijing Organizing Committee for the Games of the XXIX Olympiad, "Olympics 2008: Our Vision," retrieved 7 January 2003 from www.beijing-2008 .org/eolympic/xay/xay_index.htm.

7. "Athletics," *Tientsin Young Men* 5.6 (23 March 1906), 1. The several misspellings and missed punctuation are the original author's.

8. Phillip Whitten, "Strong-Arm Tactic," *New Republic*, 17 November 1997, 12.

9. Y. Y. Hsuh, "The Far Eastern Olympic Games," *Tiyu huikan* 1 (June 1925), 2.

10. Accounts of limited scope include Jonathan Kolatch, *Sports, Politics and*

Ideology in China (New York: Jonathan David Publishers, 1972), which concentrates on explicit ties between official ideology and Chinese sport; Wu, "The Influence of the YMCA," which privileges Western missionary contributions to sport in China as the central aspect of its development; and Gael Graham, "Exercising Control: Sports and Physical Education in American Protestant Mission Schools in China, 1880–1930," *Signs: Journal of Women in Culture and Society* 20.1 (Autumn 1994), 23–48, which analyzes missionary writings in order to understand the rise of Chinese student nationalism.

11. Fan Hong, *Footbinding, Feminism and Freedom: The Liberation of Women's Bodies in Modern China* (Portland, Ore.: Frank Cass, 1997), 12.

12. Andrew Morris, "'To Make the 400 Million Move': The Late Qing Dynasty Origins of Modern Chinese Sport and Physical Culture," *Comparative Studies in Society and History* 42.4 (October 2000), 883–88.

13. Joan Judge, "Citizens or Mothers of Citizens? Gender and the Meaning of Modern Chinese Citizenship," in *Changing Meanings of Citizenship in Modern China*, ed. Merle Goldman and Elizabeth J. Perry (Cambridge, Mass.: Harvard University Press, 2002), 24.

14. Susan Brownell, *Training the Body for China: Sports in the Moral Order of the People's Republic* (Chicago: University of Chicago Press, 1995), 10–13, 67–98.

15. Brownell, *Training the Body for China*, 80–92.

16. James Riordan, *Sport in Soviet Society: Development of Sport and Physical Education in Russia and the USSR* (New York: Cambridge University Press, 1977), 63–65, 43–44.

17. Douglas R. Reynolds, *China, 1898–1912: The Xinzheng Revolution and Japan* (Cambridge, Mass.: Council on East Asian Studies, Harvard University, 1993); Lydia H. Liu, *Translingual Practice: Literature, National Culture, and Translated Modernity—China, 1900–1937* (Stanford, Calif.: Stanford University Press, 1995).

18. *Undō*, like *bunka* (Chinese *wenhua*) or *seiji (zhengzhi)*, is a term restored (with modern meanings) by Meiji-era Japanese from ancient Chinese usage. Gao Mingkai and Liu Zhengyan, *Xiandai Hanyu wailaici yanjiu* (Beijing: Wenxue geming chubanshe, 1958), 83–88.

19. P. L. Cuyler, *Sumo: From Rite to Sport* (New York: Weatherhill, 1979), 96–100.

20. Kevin Gray Carr, "Making Way: War, Philosophy, and Sport in Japanese *Jūdō*," *Journal of Sport History* 20.2 (Summer 1993), 175–80.

21. The very earliest calisthenics instruction in Chinese schools was carried out under the auspices of Western missionary education, possibly as early as the 1870s. The earliest known Chinese school to feature such instruction was Kang Youwei's Wanmu caotang, founded in Guangzhou in 1891. Jung-Pang Lo, ed., *K'ang Yu-Wei: A Biography and a Symposium* (Tucson: University of Arizona Press, 1967), 3; Qu Lihe, *Qingmo Minchu minzu zhuyi jiaoyu sichao* (Taibei: Zhonghua wenhua fuxing yundong tuixing weiyuanhui, 1984), 99.

22. Xiao Chong, "Qingmo Sichuan liu Ri xuesheng yu Sichuan jindai tiyu," *Sichuan tiyu shiliao* 17 (August 1986), 32–36.

23. Lin Mingyi, "Qingmo xuexiao tiyu," *Shida tiyu*, no. 31 (1990), 21–22; Paul J. Bailey, *Reform the People: Changing Attitudes towards Popular Education in Early Twentieth-Century China* (Edinburgh: Edinburgh University Press, 1990), 31–34; Lu-Dzai Djung, *A History of Democratic Education in Modern China* (Shanghai: Commercial Press, 1934), 46–48. These edicts were closely followed; even the few government-run schools in Tibet, such as the Zangwen Chuanxisuo and the Hanwen Chuanxisuo, included *ticao* as part of their curricula by 1907. Yang Wanyou, "Jindai Xizang chuangban xuexiao tiyu gaikuang," *Tiyu wenshi* 52 (November 1991), 27–28.

24. Charles Hodge Corbett, *Shantung Christian University (Cheeloo)* (New York: United Board for Christian Colleges in China, 1955), 75–76.

25. G. G. Tan [Chen Zhang'e], "Chinese Origins of Diverse Types of Modern Ball Games," *China Today* 2.10 (October 1959), 75.

26. For a more complete treatment of this point, see Andrew Morris, "Cultivating the National Body: A History of Physical Culture in Republican China" (Ph.D. diss., University of California, San Diego, 1998), 33–46.

27. For example, see Gu Shiquan, *Zhongguo tiyu shi (xia ce—jindai bufen)* (Beijing: Beijing tiyu xueyuan chubanshe, 1989), 4–5.

28. Qiao Keqin and Guan Wenming, *Zhongguo tiyu sixiangshi* (Lanzhou: Gansu minzu chubanshe, 1993),169–71; Guojia tiwei tiyu wenshi gongzuo weiyuanhui and Zhongguo tiyushi xuehui, eds., *Zhongguo jindai tiyushi* (Beijing: Beijing tiyu xueyuan chubanshe, 1989), 51. My own, less nationalistically defined, estimate locates the earliest entry of concepts of modern physical culture into China with the 1860s–70s entry of military calisthenics into various Qing armies. Li Ning, "Wan Qing jundui bianlian yu jindai tiyu chuanbo," *Tiyu wenshi* 7 (June 1984), 7; Qiao Keqin, "Gansu jindai tiyu dashi jilüe (1840–1949)," *Gansu tiyu shiliao* 9 (March 1987), 7, 24; Guojia tiweiand Zhongguo tiyushi xuehui, *Zhongguo jindai tiyushi*, 53.

29. Hsu I-hsiung, "Zhongguo jindai minzu zhuyi tiyu sixiang zhi tezhi," *Tiyu xuebao* 12 (December 1990), 15.

30. Private conversations with Japanese scholars Munakata Tatsuya, Inoue Akio, and Abe Ikuo, 1995–96.

31. However, Chinese scholars preferring to find Anglo-American roots to their *tiyu* have ignored this obvious Japanese connection. In the 1920s and 1930s a myth was born that *tiyu* was a contraction of the longer phrase *shenti jiaoyu*, translating as "physical education" (in its institutional sense); this mistake has unfortunately survived to the present day. Luo Yidong, *Tiyuxue* (1924; reprint, Shanghai: Zhonghua shuju, 1931), 1; Wang Geng, "Tiyu zhi kexue de yanjiu," *Xiandai xuesheng* 3.1 (October 1933), 1.

32. Earlier, several military academies founded in the 1880s–90s in Tianjin, Guangzhou, Fuzhou, Shanghai, Hubei, and Nanjing hired German, French, Japanese, and British officers to teach military calisthenics and gymnastics. Guojia tiwei and Zhongguo tiyushi xuehui, *Zhongguo jindai tiyushi*, 54–55; Li Ning,

"Wan Qing jundui bianlian," 8; Wu Wenzhong, *Zhongguo tiyu fazhan shi* (Taibei: Guoli jiaoyu ziliaoguan, 1981), 67; *Hubei wuxue* (n.p., 1900).

33. Zhang Tianbai, "Guanyu Zhongguo ticao xuexiao yi xie qingkuang de shizheng," *Tiyu wenshi* 49 (May 1991), 62.

34. Tony Bennett, "The Exhibitionary Complex," in *Culture/Power/History: A Reader in Contemporary Social Theory*, ed. Nicholas B. Dirks, Geoff Eley, and Sherry B. Ortner (Princeton, N.J.: Princeton University Press, 1994), 137.

35. Li Houcheng, "Sichuan di yi ci yundonghui," *Sichuan tiyu shiliao* 14 (August 1985), 32–33.

36. The Guilin meet included 990 students from thirty-nine schools. Rao Kai, "Guangxi zui zao de yi ci shengji yundonghui," *Guangxi tiyu shiliao* 9 (April 1985), 15–16. The Chishui meet included two hundred–plus students from four schools. Xie Zunxiu and Tan Zhiyong, "Chishui lishi shang de di yi ci yundonghui," *Guizhou tiyu* 84 (June 1982), 35.

37. "Yundonghui lei zhi," *Jiaoyu zazhi* 2.11 (10th day, 11th lunar month [11 December], 1910), 93.

38. "Ji Shanghai ge xiao yundonghui," *Jiaoyu zazhi* 3.5 (10th day, 5th lunar month [6 June], 1911), 41.

39. Mao Anjun [Andrew Morris], "1909–1919 nian *Jiaoyu zazhi* tiyu wenzhang fenxi de chubu," *Tiyu xuebao* 21 (June 1996), 49–53.

40. The Quanguo xuexiao qufendui di yi ci tiyu tongmenghui was organized by M. J. Exner, physical director of the Shanghai YMCA, Zhejiang-Jiangsu Governor-General Duan-fang, his successor Zhang Renjun, and the industrialist Zhang Jian. The meet was mostly managed by YMCA personnel, but YMCA and exposition organizers combined to form a sixteen-man national committee, "equally divided between Chinese and foreign members," to make all final decisions. H. A. Moran, "The Nanking Meet: The First National Athletic Sports in China," personal report to YMCA, 24 December 1910; Hao Gengsheng, *Hao Gengsheng huiyilu* (Taibei: Zhuanji wenxue chubanshe, 1969), 21; Wu Wenzhong, *Zhongguo tiyu fazhan shi*, 77.

41. For more on what came to be called China's "First National Games," see Morris, "'To Make the 400 Million Move,'" 894–98.

42. "China Is Getting Athletic," *Association Men* 36 (March 1911), 243.

43. Fong F. Sec, "The First National Athletic Meet," *China's Young Men* 6.1 (January 1911), 30.

44. *Annual Reports of the Foreign Secretaries of the International Committee, October 1, 1909 to September 30, 1910*, 176.

45. [Untitled article in Chinese], *Tientsin Young Men* 9.15 (2 July 1910), 4; "North China Interscholastic Athletic Records," *Tientsin Young Men* 9.15 (2 July 1910), 4; "The Autumn and Spring Athletic Program," *Tientsin Young Men* 9.20 (8 October 1910), 2.

46. Moran, "The Nanking Meet"; *Annual Reports of the Foreign Secretaries of the International Committee, October 1, 1909 to September 30, 1910*, 176; Wang Zhenya, *Jiu Zhongguo tiyu jianwen* (Beijing: Renmin tiyu chubanshe, 1987), 136.

47. Neil Lazarus, *Nationalism and Cultural Practice in the Postcolonial World* (New York: Cambridge University Press, 1999), 6.

48. Theodor W. Adorno, *Minima Moralia: Reflections from Damaged Life,* trans. E. F. N. Jephcott (London: Verso, 1978), 52, quoted in Lazarus, *Nationalism and Cultural Practice,* 1.

49. Lazarus, *Nationalism and Cultural Practice,* 3.

50. Gregory Jusdanis, *The Necessary Nation* (Princeton, N.J.: Princeton University Press, 2001), 5–7.

51. Joan Judge, *Print and Politics: "Shibao" and the Culture of Reform in Late Qing China* (Stanford, Calif.: Stanford University Press, 1996), 22.

52. David Strand, "Citizens in the Audience and at the Podium," in Goldman and Perry, *Changing Meanings of Citizenship,* 52.

53. Leo Ou-fan Lee, *Shanghai Modern: The Flowering of a New Urban Culture In China, 1930–1945* (Cambridge, Mass.: Harvard University Press, 1999), 58.

CHAPTER 2. "NOW THE FUN
OF EXERCISE CAN BE REALIZED"

Parts of this chapter were originally published in Andrew Morris, "Mastery without Enmity: Athletics, Modernity and the Nation in Early Republican China," *Republican China* 22.2 (April 1997), 3–39.

1. *St. John's University 1879–1929* (Shanghai: St. John's University Alumni Association, 1929; reprint, Taipei: n.p., 1972), 59 (page citation is to reprint edition).

2. "Quanguo lianhe yundong dahui," *Jiaoyu zazhi* 6.3 (15 June 1914), 35. Soon, however, this 1914 meet was being recognized as the "Second National Games," as the 1924 national meet in Wuchang was called the Third National Games (Di san ci quanguo yundong dahui).

3. "Physical Training," *China's Young Men* 9.6 (June 1914), 166.

4. *Di qi jie quanguo yundonghui jinian shouce* (Shanghai: Shenbaoguan, 1948).

5. Susan Brownell, *Training the Body for China: Sports in the Moral Order of the People's Republic* (Chicago: University of Chicago Press, 1995), 130–31.

6. Takashi Fujitani brought to my attention this idea of a new type of national geography.

7. "Physical Training," 166–67.

8. "Physical Training," 167.

9. Francis E. Wilber Photo Album, vol. 2, YMCA Archives, University of Minnesota, St. Paul.

10. Opening speech by W. Cameron Forbes, president of the First Far Eastern Championship Games, quoted in Chih-Kang Wu, "The Influence of the YMCA on the Development of Physical Education in China" (Ph.D. diss., University of Michigan, 1956), 132–33.

11. Regino R. Ylanan and Carmen Wilson Ylanan, *The History and Development of Physical Education and Sports in the Philippines* (Quezon City: University of the Philippines Press, 1974), 53, 68; Celia Bocobo-Olivar, *History of Physical Education in the Philippines* (Quezon City: University of the Philippines Press, 1972), 71; Gunsun Hoh [Hao Gengsheng], *Physical Education in China* (Shanghai: Commercial Press, 1926), 96–97; Wu, "The Influence of the YMCA," 130–33.

12. Malay and Siam were also invited to join the first Far Eastern Games but never did. *Annual Reports of the Foreign Secretaries of the International Committee, October 1, 1911 to September 30, 1912* (New York: International Committee YMCA, 1912), 630–31.

13. The Far Eastern Olympic Association's overture drew a quick response from many in the International Olympic Committee (IOC), who also saw the Olympic movement as an integral part of the world nation-state system. American IOC representatives sent a congratulatory wreath to the association in 1912 on the occasion of the upcoming First Far Eastern Games. However, the association's use of the term *Olympic* was not approved by the IOC, who were much more generous with their ideals than with their registered trademarks. Ruan Weicun, *Yuandong yundonghui lishi yu chengji* (Shanghai: Qinfen shuju, 1933), 6; Wu Wenzhong, *Zhongguo jin bai nian tiyu shi* (Taibei: Taiwan shangwu yinshuguan, 1967), 93.

14. *Annual Reports of the Foreign Secretaries of the International Committee, October 1, 1911 to September 30, 1912*, 630.

15. China's three official administrative representatives to the First Far Eastern Games were Alfred Swan and Francis Wilber of the Shanghai and Guangzhou YMCAs and Dr. Arthur Shoemaker of Qinghua University.

16. "The New Olympian," *Philippines Free Press* 7.5 (1 February 1913), 1.

17. "P. I. Victors in First Orient Olympics," *Manila Times*, 10 February 1913, 9.

18. Attendance was 155,058 over seven days at the first games in Manila. "Huge Throngs Visit Fiesta: Nearly 160,000 in 7 Days Pay for Admission," *Manila Times*, 8 February 1913, 1.

19. The team was made up of a northern section (nine athletes from Qinghua and Beijing Universities in Beijing), a central section (nine athletes from Nanjing's Jinling University, Shanghai's Nanyang and St. John's Universities and the Shanghai YMCA), and a southern section (eighteen athletes from Guangzhou's Nanwu School, the Guangzhou YMCA, Hong Kong University, and Hong Kong's Nanhua Sports Association). "Dongya yundonghui di yi ci dahui ji," *Zhenxiang huabao* 17 (1 March 1913), 1.

20. The Chinese team did not enter the baseball, tennis, or cycling events.

21. "China's Record in Olympiad Is Good," *Manila Times*, 5 February 1913, 9.

22. "Dongya yundonghui di yi ci dahui ji," 2.

23. "Chinese Object to Local Team: Soccer Protest Brings up Difficult Decision," *Manila Times*, 5 February 1913, 8.

24. "The Olympic Protests," *Manila Times*, 6 February 1913, 4.

25. Frank Dikötter, *The Discourse of Race in Modern China* (Stanford, Calif.: Stanford University Press, 1992), 97–115.

26. "Open Meet Is Next on Card: Week-End Will See Final Decision Made," *Manila Times*, 7 February 1913, 5.

27. "Governor General Opens Olympiad," *Manila Times*, 1 February 1913, 5.

28. *Annual Reports of the Foreign Secretaries of the International Committee, October 1, 1912 to September 30, 1913* (New York: International Committee YMCA, 1913), 298, 473.

29. "The Far Eastern Olympic Games," *North-China Daily News*, 17 May 1915, 8. See also "Yuandong yundonghui di yi ri bisai jishi," *Shenbao*, 16 May 1915, 10. Both reports erred slightly on Yang's identity. The *Daily News* referred to Yang as "Foreign Minister," while *Shenbao* called him "Yang Xiaochuan," misprinting his alternate name Shaochuan.

30. "Yuandong yundonghui jishi," *Shenbao*, 13 May 1915, 10; "Far Eastern Olympic Games," *North-China Daily News*, 14 May 1915, 8.

31. "The Far Eastern Championship Games," *China's Young Men* 10.9 (15 May 1915), 367.

32. *Annual Reports of the Foreign Secretaries of the International Committee, October 1, 1913 to September 30, 1914* (New York: International Committee YMCA, 1914), 73.

33. J. Wong-Quincey [Wang Wenxian], "The Far Eastern Championship Games," *China's Young Men* 10.10 (15 June 1915), 429; "Yuandong yundonghui di san ri bisai jishi," *Shenbao*, 18 May 1915, 10.

34. Hoh, *Physical Education in China*, 97; Wong-Quincey, "The Far Eastern Championship Games," 426.

35. Wong-Quincey, "The Far Eastern Championship Games," 429.

36. J. H. Crocker, "100,000 People at the Far Eastern Championship Games," *Association Men* 40 (August 1915), 565.

37. Crocker, "100,000 People," 565.

38. Quoted in Jonathan Kolatch, *Sports, Politics and Ideology in China* (New York: Jonathan David Publishers, 1972), 57.

39. Francis E. Wilber, Letter to "Dearest Folkses," 21 May 1915, YMCA Archives, University of Minnesota, St. Paul.

40. Wilber, Letter to "Dearest Folkses."

41. Wong-Quincey, "The Far Eastern Championship Games," 427.

42. "Far Eastern Olympic Games," *North-China Daily News*, 19 May 1915, 8.

43. Wong-Quincey, "The Far Eastern Championship Games," 430.

44. Of China's thirty-four track and field athletes, twenty-seven were college students. "The Far Eastern Olympic Games," *North-China Daily News*, 17 May 1915, 8.

45. "Yuandong yundonghui di yi ri bisai jishi," 10; Advertisement, *North-China Daily News*, 13 May 1915, 1.

46. "Yuandong yundonghui di si ri bisai jishi," *Shenbao,* 20 May 1915, 10; "The Far Eastern Olympic Games," *North-China Daily News,* 20 May 1915, 8.

47. "Zhongguo yundongjia yousheng qingzhu yu zhi," *Shenbao,* 22 May 1915, 10; Jeffrey N. Wasserstrom, *Student Protests in Twentieth-Century China: The View from Shanghai* (Stanford, Calif.: Stanford University Press, 1991), 39.

48. Shi Likang, "Yuandong yundonghui zai Shanghai jiqi yingxiang," *Shanghai tiyu shihua* 20 (September 1988), 3–4.

49. Zhuang Yu, "Ertong tiyu lun," *Jiaoyu zazhi* 5.2 (10 May 1913), 23, 29, 25.

50. Xunwu, "Youxi zhi leibie," *Jiaoyu zazhi* 4.9 (10th day, 12th lunar month [16 January], 1913), 35.

51. Taixuan, "Ticao jiaoshou gexin zhi yanjiu," *Jiaoyu zazhi* 10.1 [20 January 1918], 72–74.

52. Xunwu, "Youxi zhi leibie," 37.

53. Jia Fengzhen, "Guomin tiyu buzhen zhi gu," *Jiaoyu zazhi* 10.12 (20 December 1918), 157–59.

54. Zhu Yuanshan, "Tiyu zhi jiazhi," *Jiaoyu zazhi* 7.11 (15 November 1915), 203, 207.

55. Xie Shouheng, "Youxichang yu zhiye jiaoyu zhi guanxi," in *Tiyu yanjiuhui huikan,* ed. Nanjing gaodeng shifan xuexiao tiyu yanjiuhui (Nanjing, 1918), 1.

56. Xie Shouheng, "Youxichang yu zhiye jiaoyu," 1–2.

57. Chin Yü Sung [Jin Yusong], "The Sixth Semi-Annual Field and Track Meet of Our School," *Xuesheng zazhi* 3.11 (20 November 1916), 6.

58. Hou Hongjian, "Canguan Jiangsu shengli di er nüzi shifan yundonghui ji," *Jiaoyu zazhi* 7.9 (15 September 1915), 69.

59. Philip J. Deloria, *Playing Indian* (New Haven, Conn.: Yale University Press, 1998), 113.

60. Lulu, "Renti zhi heping huiyi," *Tiyu zhoubao* 1 (9 December 1918), 6.

61. "Youji ziliao," *Tiyu zazhi* 1 (June 1914), 4–8.

62. Yuan Shichen, "Jingzheng youji," *Jiaoyu zazhi* 6.11 (15 December 1914), 46–47.

63. Wang Huaiqi, "Zui xin qicao (wu yue jiu ri)," *Jiaoyu zazhi* 8.9 (15 September 1916), 33.

64. Wang Huaiqi, "Zui xin qicao," 33–38.

65. Wang Huaiqi, "Gaodeng youji: Songpo qiu," *Jiaoyu zazhi* 9.4 (20 April 1917), 1–3.

66. Huanlong, "Canguan Jiangsu shengli xuexiao lianhe yundonghui jishi," *Jiaoyu zazhi* 6.10 (15 December 1914), 32.

67. Jiang Ang, "Canguan Jiangsu Di er nü shifan ji Changshou lianhe yundonghui ji," *Jiaoyu zazhi* 7.7 (15 July 1915), 47.

68. Other educators also questioned competitive sport for the potential moral harm it could bring to participants, for the original ties of these forms to the English nobility who exploited the remainder of their society, and for the behaviors of athletes at meets (being too competitive, competing under false names,

gambling, and taunting other athletes). Huanlong, "Canguan Jiangsu shengli xuexiao lianhe yundonghui jishi," 31; Taixuan, "Jiaoyuxue yu shehuixue (xu)," *Jiaoyu zazhi* 9.12 (20 December 1917), 48; Shenlong, "Canguan Jiangsu shengli xuexiao di si ci lianhe yundonghui ji," *Jiaoyu zazhi* 10.6 (20 June 1918), 21.

69. Jiang Ang, "Canguan Jiangsu Di er nü shifan ji Changshou lianhe yundonghui ji," 45.

70. Hou Hongjian, "Canguan Jiangsu shengli di er nüzi shifan yundonghui ji," 70.

71. Hou Hongjian, "Canguan Jiangsu shengli di er nüzi shifan yundonghui ji," 69–70.

72. Lufei Kui, "Minguo putong xuezhi yi," *Jiaoyu zazhi* 3.10 (10th day, 1st lunar month [27 February], 1912), 4–12; Wang Zengming, ed., *Jindai Zhongguo tiyu fagui* (Zhongguo tiyushi xuehui Hebei fenhui, 1988), 202–3, 310–14, 403–6; Hao Gengsheng, "Tiyu," in *Zhonghua minguo jiaoyu zhi*, vol. 2, ed. Wu Junsheng (Taibei: Zhonghua wenhua chuban shiye weiyuanhui, 1955), 2; "Dashi ji," *Jiaoyu zazhi* 4.11 (10th day, 2d lunar month [17 March], 1913).

73. Yibing [Xu Yibing], "Tiyu yu wuli bian," *Tiyu zazhi* 1 (June 1914), 2.

74. Xu Yibing, "Lun xuexiao tiyu," *Jiaoyu zazhi* 6.10 (15 December 1914), 190–92; Xu Yibing, "Ticao youxi ke danji jiaoshoufa zhi yanjiu," *Jiaoyu zazhi* 6.10 (15 December 1914), 219–21.

75. Jia Fengzhen, "Shixing junguomin jiaoyu zhi fangfa," *Jiaoyu zazhi* 7.7 (15 July 1915), 139–40.

76. Jia Fengzhen, "Duanlian zhuyi zhi jiaoyu," *Jiaoyu zazhi* 7.6 (15 June 1915), 116–26.

77. Hou Hongjian, "Duiyu Jiangsu di san jie sheng lianhe yundonghui ganlun," *Jiaoyu zazhi* 8.11 (15 November 1916), 184.

78. Xu Yibing, "Ershi nian lai ticao tan," *Tiyu zhoubao tekan* (Changsha: Tiyu zhoubao she, 1920), quoted in Hsu I-hsiung, "Xu Yibing tiyu sixiang chutan," *Taiwan tiyu* 39 (October 1988), 19.

79. For examples of this Social Darwinist notion of intramural competition, see writings of Ou Qujia cited in Prasenjit Duara, "Provincial Narrations of the Nation: Centralism and Federalism in Republican China," in *Cultural Nationalism in East Asia: Representation and Identity*, ed. Harumi Befu (Berkeley: Institute of East Asian Studies, University of California, 1993), 13.

80. Yun Daiying, "Xuexiao tiyu zhi yanjiu," *Qingnian jinbu* 4 (June 1917), 3. This drill-versus-sports debate was not unique to China; modern sports also horrified nineteenth-century German nationalists and Dutch educators. Allen Guttmann, *Games and Empires: Modern Sports and Cultural Imperialism* (New York: Columbia University Press, 1994), 46–47, 142–45.

81. Zhu Jianfan, "Jun guomin tiyu de jieguo," *Tiyu zhoubao* 29 (7 July 1919), 2.

82. The author also criticized the "athlete system" in schools, where pampered athletes became "indulgent and without any restraint." Wang Shiying, "Xianzai tiyu shang de liangge bibing," *Minguo ribao*, 4 November 1920, sec. 4, p. 1.

83. Zhang Baochen, "Xuexiao yingfou feizhi bingcao? (Yi)," *Tiyu zhoubao* 46 (24 November 1919), 5–6.

84. Jiang Xiaoxian, "Xuexiao yingfou feizhi bingcao? (Er)," *Tiyu zhoubao* 46 (24 November 1919), 9.

85. Huang Xing, "Xuexiao yingfou feizhi bingcao?" *Tiyu zhoubao* 46 (24 November 1919), 3.

86. Zeng Ruicheng, "Xin wenhua yundong shiqi Zhongguo zhi tiyu sixiang (yijiuyijiu—yijiuerqi)," *Guomin tiyu jikan* 20.1 (March 1991), 17–22.

87. S. S. Kwan (Guan Songsheng), "Sports in China," *China Today* 2.1 (January 1959), 5.

88. Hao Gengsheng, "Tiyu," 4.

89. Wu Yunrui, "Sanshiwu nian lai Zhongguo zhi tiyu," in *Zuijin sanshiwu nian zhi Zhongguo jiaoyu*, ed. Zhuang Yu (Shanghai: Shangwu yinshuguan, 1931), 231–34; Gu Shiquan, "Introduction to Ancient and Modern Chinese Physical Culture," in *Sport in China*, ed. Howard G. Knuttgen, Ma Qiwei, and Wu Zhongyuan (Champaign, Ill.: Human Kinetics Books, 1990), 16–17.

90. "Guli junjingjie xuexi tichang ji shishi jindai tiyu fangfa an," in *Tiyu shiliao di 16 ji: Zhongguo jindai tiyu yijuean xuanbian*, ed. Guojia tiwei tiyu wenshi gongzuo weiyuanhui and Quanguo tizong wenshi ziliao bianshen weiyuanhui (Beijing: Renmin tiyu chubanshe, 1990), 31.

91. Frantz Fanon, *The Wretched of the Earth* (New York: Grove Press, 1968), 210.

92. Italics are Duara's. Prasenjit Duara, *Rescuing History from the Nation: Questioning Narratives of Modern China* (Chicago: University of Chicago Press, 1995), 29.

93. Ernest Renan, "What Is a Nation?" in *Nation and Narration*, ed. Homi K. Bhabha (New York: Routledge, 1990), 19.

94. Peixian, "Tiyu shi," *Tiyujie* 1 (1st day, 3d lunar month [20 April], 1909), 3–5.

95. Xu Yibin [Xu Yibing], "Tiyu shi," *Tiyu zazhi* 1 (June 1914), 1.

96. Xu Yibin, "Tiyu shi," 1–5; Xu Yibin [Xu Yibing], "Tiyu shi (xu di yi qi)," *Tiyu zazhi* 2 (July 1914), 7–11.

97. Zeng Qiu, "Zhongguo gushi tiyu tan," in Nanjing gaodeng shifan xuexiao tiyu yanjiuhui, *Tiyu yanjiuhui huikan*, 1–2.

98. Guo Xifen, *Zhongguo tiyushi* (Shanghai: Shangwu yinshuguan, 1919; reprint, Shanghai: Shanghai wenyi chubanshe, 1993), 4–5 (page citations are to reprint edition); Zhu Liang, preface to Guo Xifen, *Zhongguo tiyushi*, 1.

99. Chang-tai Hung, *Going to the People: Chinese Intellectuals and Folk Literature, 1918–1937* (Cambridge, Mass.: Council on East Asian Studies, Harvard University, 1985), 21, 48, 105, 137–40, 148, 151.

100. Quoted in Hoh, *Physical Education in China*, 34.

101. Tang Leang-li, *Reconstruction in China* (Shanghai: China United Press, 1935), 94.

102. Guo Xifen, "Zhongguo tiyushi xulie," in *Zhongguo tiyushi*, 3–4; Guo

Xifen, *Zhongguo tiyushi*, 102, 113, 131. Guo's work also shows some ambiguity in what these new games are called. At different points he refers to baseball as *yeqiu* (from the Japanese *yakyū*) and in longhand as *yewai bangqiu* (literally "outdoor stickball").

103. Pierre Bourdieu, "Sport and Social Class," *Social Science Information* 17.6 (1978), 821–22.

104. Joseph R. Levenson, *Confucian China and Its Modern Fate: A Trilogy,* vol. 1, *The Problem of Intellectual Continuity* (Berkeley: University of California Press, 1958; reprint, 3 vols. in 1, Berkeley: University of California Press, 1972), 74–75 (page citation is to reprint edition).

105. One *New Youth* article on physical education, written by a young Mao Zedong under the pen name Twenty-Eight-Brushstroke Student, would decades later be officially recognized as a *tiyu* Holy Writ, a primal inspiration for the physical movements of every Chinese person under the sun. However, despite the later glorification of this article, its value lies mostly in its representation of the standard liberal take on *tiyu* of the age; Mao's idea that "the way of physical education is what makes possible an education in morality and wisdom" would not have seemed out of place in the inspired pep talks of any foreign missionary or YMCA track coach. Ershiba huasheng [Mao Zedong], "Tiyu zhi yanjiu," *Xin qingnian (La Jeunesse)* 3.2 (1 April 1917), 2. As recently as 1994, a volume of essays on Chairman Mao's contributions to Chinese physical culture included sixteen works analyzing and appraising this 1917 *New Youth* piece, which established the "correct definition" of modern Chinese *tiyu*. Guojia tiwei tiyu wenshi gongzuo weiyuanhui and Zhongguo tiyu kexue xuehui tiyushi fenhui, eds., *Mao Zedong yu tiyu wenji* (Chengdu: Sichuan jiaoyu chubanshe, 1994).

CHAPTER 3. "MIND, MUSCLE, AND MONEY"

1. Huang is not to be confused with another famous Huang Xing from Changsha, the Tongmenghui revolutionary who died in Shanghai in 1916. Huang the physical educator also went by the styled *zi* (alternate) name Shengbai, or "Vanquish-the-white."

2. W. S. [Huang Xing], "Shenme jiaozuo tiyu?" *Tiyu zhoubao* 25 (9 June 1919), 2.

3. Taixuan, "De-mo-ke-la-xi yu xunlian," *Jiaoyu zazhi* 11.9 (20 September 1919), 1.

4. Taixuan, "De-mo-ke-la-xi yu xunlian," 2–3.

5. E. D. Vernik, "Group Athletics," *Educational Review (Jiaoyu yuebao)* 12.4 (October 1920), 336–38.

6. B. A. Garside, "A Track-Meet for the Whole School," *Educational Review (Jiaoyu yuebao)* 17.3 (July 1924), 289.

7. Garside, "A Track-Meet," 292.

8. Takashi Fujitani, "Technologies of Power in Modern Japan: The Military,

the 'Local,' the Body," 14. This is the English original of the article that appears as T. Fujitani, "Kindai Nihon ni okeru kenryoku no tekunorojī: guntai, 'chihō,' shintai," trans. Umemori Naoyuki, *Shisō* 845 (November 1994).

9. Zhi Yongqing, "Daoyan" (preface), in *Youxi zhuanlun (Games and Sports)* (Shanghai: Shangwu yinshuguan, 1924), 3.

10. Fujitani, "Technologies of Power," 22–23.

11. Fujitani, "Technologies of Power," 15.

12. Wu Yunrui, "Woguo tiyu shang zhi zijue," *Qingnian jinbu* 41 (March 1921), 55.

13. Zhong Ruiqiu, "Jindai zhuming tiyujia: Wu Yunrui zhuanlüe," *Shanghai tiyu shihua* 4 (July 1983), 3.

14. Wu Yunrui, "Woguo tiyu shang zhi zijue," 55–56.

15. Wu Yunrui, "Woguo tiyu shang zhi zijue," 57.

16. Michael Taussig, *Mimesis and Alterity: A Particular History of the Senses* (New York: Routledge, 1993), xv.

17. Taussig, *Mimesis and Alterity,* 195.

18. Taussig, *Mimesis and Alterity,* 33.

19. Taussig, *Mimesis and Alterity,* xiii–xv, 255. Here, this "history" is of course the history of imperialism in China. However, my use of Taussig's model often displeases my Chinese colleagues, who at the present point in the history of their nation do not wish to be compared to the Cuna Indians.

20. Interview with Dong Hanwen, Taipei, Taiwan, 15 October 1995. Mr. Dong was later personally scouted and given a soccer scholarship by Zhang Xueliang, president/principal of the Northeastern University and High School; Dong owes this to his soccer skills and also to the fact that his father Dong Futing was a local military man of some renown.

21. Interview with Li Shiming, Beitou, Taiwan, 13 June 1996.

22. Interview with Cheng Jinguan, Suzhou, China, 2 March 1997.

23. *The Shanghai 1925 Volume X* (Shanghai: Shanghai College, 1925), 97.

24. Gunsun Hoh (Hao Gengsheng), *Physical Education in China* (Shanghai: Commercial Press, 1926), 157–58.

25. Zhang Jiwu, "Nankai zhi tiyu," in *Nankai daxue xiaoshi ziliaoxuan (1919–1949),* ed. Wang Wenjun et al. (Tianjin: Nankai daxue chubanshe, 1989), 540.

26. Yi Liang Chang, "A Few Encouraging Words to the Physical Training Society of Ai Kuo Girls School," *Tiyu huikan* 1 (June 1925), 1.

27. Heng, "Benxiao tiyu xin jiaoshou Shen Guoquan jun," *Nanyang zhoukan* 3.11 (15 December 1923), frontispiece.

28. Shen Guoquan narration, transcribed by Fei Zhendong, "Wo duiyu benxiao tiyu de sheshi he jihua," *Nanyang zhoukan* 3.11 (15 December 1923), 2. "Mind," "Muscle," and "Money" were all typeset in English with no Chinese translation.

29. Walter Benjamin, "On the Mimetic Faculty," in *Reflections: Essays, Aphorisms, Autobiographical Writings,* ed. Peter Demetz (New York: Harcourt Brace Jovanovich, 1978), 335–36.

30. Statistician Karl Pearson's concept, cited by Zhang Jiwu, "Nankai zhi tiyu," 540.

31. Benjamin's mention of the uses of ancient dance in producing similarity also underscores the importance of a bodily element of the mimetic faculty.

32. McCloy also had eight years' experience as a physical education instructor and administrator. Charles Harold McCloy, *Some Achievement Standards in Track and Field Athletic Events for Boys from Ten to Twenty Years of Age* (New York: A. S. Barnes, 1932), "Vita."

33. Mai Kele [Me K'e-lo; i.e., Charles McCloy], "Wushi nian lai Zhongguo zhi tiyu ji wushu," in *Zuijin zhi wushi nian* (Shanghai: Shenbaoguan, 1922; reprint, Shanghai: Shanghai shudian, 1987), 4 (page citations are to the reprint edition); Mai Kele [Charles H. McCloy], "De Rui Ying sanguo zhi tiyu," trans. Xie Shouheng and Zhang Yuanyang, in *Tiyu yanjiuhui huikan*, ed. Nanjing gaodeng shifan xuexiao tiyu yanjiuhui (Nanjing, 1918), 2; Wang Chien-tai, "Mai Kele (Charles Harold McCloy) dui Zhongguo jindai tiyu de yingxiang (yijiuyisan ~ yijiuerliu)" (M.S. thesis, Guoli tiyu xueyuan, 1993), 93.

34. Wang Chien-tai, "Mai Kele," 101. For example, see Xu Jiazhen, *Jiating ticao* (Shanghai: Shangwu yinshuguan, 1923).

35. Mai Kele [Charles H. McCloy], "Tiyu yu de-mo-ke-la-xi," *Tiyu yu weisheng* 3.1 (March 1924), 1–6.

36. Mai Kele, "Mai Kele jun yanci," *Wushu* 1.2 (February 1921), 2.

37. He stopped drawing a YMCA salary in October 1921, and his biographical file ends at this date. Biographical File for Charles Harold McCloy, Archives of the YMCA.

38. Mai Kele [Charles H. McCloy], "Yundong shang junzi de jingshen (Sportsmanship)," *Tiyu jikan* 1.2 (August 1922), 1–2.

39. Er-ai-li, "Gaodeng xiaoxue nannü xuesheng heli de yundong xitong," trans. Mai Kele [Charles H. McCloy], *Tiyu jikan* 1.2 (August 1922), 1–12.

40. Mai Kele [Charles H. McCloy], "Wenhua yu tiyu," *Tiyu jikan* 2.4 (December 1923), 1–9.

41. Mai Kele [Charles H. McCloy], "Yuandong yundonghui ji Zhongguo gedi yundonghui gaiyong mituzhi," *Tiyu jikan* 2.4 (December 1923), 1–3.

42. Mai Kele, "Wushi nian lai Zhongguo zhi tiyu ji wushu," 1.

43. Mai Kele, "Wushi nian lai Zhongguo zhi tiyu ji wushu," 3–6. The next year, McCloy would write (in English) on *wushu* as "the one uniquely Chinese physical training—the only true son of the soil." C. H. McCloy, "Physical Education in China," *Chinese National Association for the Advancement of Education Bulletin* 2.5 (1923), 1.

44. Mai Kele [Charles H. McCloy], "Quanguo yundonghui zhi yiyi," in *Di san ci quanguo yundong dahui tekan* (Hankou: Hankou jidujiao qingnianhui, 1924). The book is unpaginated.

45. Mai Kele, "Quanguo yundonghui zhi yiyi."

46. Mai Kele, "Quanguo yundonghui zhi yiyi." Italics added.

47. The picture becomes even more complicated when one considers that while doing research in the history of modern *tiyu* in China, I was often com-

pared to Mai Kele, as a fellow American expert in China. A professor with whom I worked in Hangzhou was fond of saying, when introducing me to other scholars, "Eighty years ago Mai Kele brought modern European American physical culture to China. Now Mao Anjun [my Chinese name] has come to take the history of our twentieth-century *tiyu* development back to America."

48. J. H. Gray, "The Present Status of Physical Education in China," *American Physical Education Review* 31.10 (December 1926), 1169. Italics in original.

49. The earliest known American-rules football team in China was organized at the Zhili Higher Normal School in Baoding in 1913–14, although the team was soon disbanded by officials who felt that the game (in Chinese, *qiangqiu*, or "seize-ball") was too violent. Shi Likang, "Ershi niandai Shanghai de ganlanqiu yundong," *Shanghai tiyu shihua* 17 (September 1987), 15.

50. Zhang Tianbai, "Ershi nian dai Yancheng Huaimei xuexiao kaizhan Meishi ganlanqiu yundong zhi jianjie," *Jiangsu tiyu wenshi* 19 (June 1991), 6.

51. Shi Likang, "Ershi niandai Shanghai de ganlanqiu yundong," 16.

52. Taussig, *Mimesis and Alterity*, 255.

53. *Beiyang huabao (Pei-Yang Pictorial News)* 126 (5 October 1927), 2.

54. Taussig, *Mimesis and Alterity*, 20.

55. The other seven topics were patriotism, respect for law, public morality, common knowledge, aesthetic appreciation, encouragement of industry, and public hygiene. Chai H. Chuang, "Movement for Educating Illiterates in China," *Chinese National Association for the Advancement of Education Bulletin* 2.2 (1923), 8.

56. Ads for *Jiuguo ribao*, *Shishi xinbao*, and *Hunan shiye zazhi*, in *Tiyu zhoubao* 49 (12 January 1920), inside front cover.

57. Yoshida Akinobu, "Yundong shenglixue," trans. Luo Heizi, *Tiyu zhoubao* 49 (12 January 1920), 5–10; Henry S. Curtis, "Youxi jiaoyu," trans. Wang Changping and Mu Haipeng, *Tiyu zhoubao* 49 (12 January 1920), 11–13.

58. Xing [Huang Xing], "Fang baozhu he weisheng," *Tiyu zhoubao* 49 (12 January 1920), 19–20.

59. Suxin, "Xinnian de youxi," *Tiyu zhoubao* 49 (12 January 1920), 18–19.

60. Huang Binsheng, "Biaozhun yundong de ceyan," *Tiyu jikan* 2.1 (April 1923), 1.

61. Wang Huaiqi and Zou Falu, *Tiyu ceyanfa* (1925; reprint, Shanghai: Zhongguo jianxueshe, 1929), 1 (page citations are to the reprint edition).

62. Wang Huaiqi and Zou Falu, *Tiyu ceyanfa*, 2, 4–57.

63. Mai Kele, "Chayan shenti fangfa (xu)," *Tiyu jikan* 2.4 (December 1923), 1–13.

64. Zhonghua quanguo tiyu yanjiuhui, "Tiyu jiaoyuan fenjifa," *Tiyu jikan* 2.1 (April 1923), 1–4.

65. Zhonghua quanguo tiyu yanjiuhui, "Tiyu jiaoyuan fenjifa," 2–4; quotations are from 1.

66. Fujitani, "Technologies of Power," 14–18.

67. Xie Siyan, *Tianjingsai de lilun yu shiji* (Shanghai: Kaiming shudian, 1927), 7.

68. Xie Siyan, *Tianjingsai de lilun yu shiji*, 7–9. "Gentleman" and "sportsman" were included in English type without Chinese translation.

69. Wang Huaiqi and Zou Falu, *Tiyu ceyanfa*, 62–65.

70. Wang Huaiqi and Zou Falu, *Tiyu ceyanfa*, 66–69.

71. Wang Huaiqi and Zou Falu, *Tiyu ceyanfa*, back of book. Xu Jiazhen's 1923 book *Home Exercises* was published by the Commercial Press as a small pocket volume. In addition to the book's forty-nine drawings of exercise poses, it included a table for the reader to record seventeen measurements of his or her body. These measurements were to be recorded once before beginning the exercise regimen and five times after. Xu Jiazhen, *Jiating ticao*, tables after 138.

72. Huang Xing, "Wo jiao ticao shi de zuiguo," *Tiyu zhoubao* 42 (27 October 1919), 2.

73. Huang Xing, "Wo jiao ticao shi de zuiguo," 3–4.

74. Luo Yidong, *Tiyuxue* (1924; reprint, Shanghai: Zhonghua shuju, 1931), 2–3, 10.

75. Beijing tushuguan, ed., *Minguo shiqi zongshumu (1911–1949): Jiaoyu, tiyu* (Beijing: Shumu wenxian chubanshe, 1995), 663; Commercial Press advertisement in *Tiyu jikan* 2.1 (April 1923).

76. Huang Binsheng, "Jingdou youxi," *Tiyu jikan* 2.1 (April 1923), 1–4.

77. Zhang Liuquan, "Zhongdeng xuexiao xiuxian xiguan zhi yanjiu," *Jiaoyu zazhi* 17.7 (20 July 1925), 5–17, 19, 20.

78. *Dongya tiyu xuexiao xiaokan* 2 (November 1920), 1–6, 1–7.

79. Sun Wangqiu, "Zhi biye tongxue shu," in *Zhejiang tiyu zhuanmen xuexiao yundong tekan* (Hangzhou, 1928), 105.

80. Hoh, *Physical Education in China*, 201–5.

81. The CAAU was now headed by Chair Zhang Boling (Tianjin), Vice Chair Guo Bingwen (Nanjing), Accountant Yuan Dunli (Beijing), and Secretary Charles McCloy (Nanjing). Gu Shiquan, "'Zhonghua yeyu yundong lianhehui' chengli qianhou," *Tiyu wenshi* 48 (March 1991), 39–40.

82. Eighty-three percent of these books were published in Shanghai. They could be divided evenly into martial arts, physical education, and sports subject matter categories. Beijing tushuguan, *Minguo shiqi zongshumu*, 661–737.

83. Hsu I-hsiung, *Woguo jindai tiyu baokan mulu suoyin* (Taibei: Shida shuyuan, 1994), 629–38.

84. Luo Yidong, *Tiyuxue*, 5–6.

85. Lao, "Yundong yu zhanzheng zhi bijiao," *Shenbao*, 31 May 1921, "The Far Eastern Olympic Games Supplement #2" section, 1.

86. Quoted in Wang Zengming, "Feng Yuxiang jiangjun yu tiyu," *Tiyu wenshi* 10 (June 1984), 10.

87. Gu Xin, "Tiyujia Chen Zhang'e," 48. Chen would later serve as the director of the Xiamen University Physical Education Department.

88. "*Tiyu zhoubao tekan* di yi hao zhounian jinianhao," *Minguo ribao*, 17 January 1920, sec. 4, p. 14.

89. Huang Xing, "Zhu lu," *Tiyu zhoubao* 32 (28 July 1919), 3–4.

90. Jizhe [Charles H. McCloy], "Shibai de yuanyin," *Tiyu jikan* 1.2 (August 1922), 1.

91. Wang Huaiqi, *Xingqiu guize* (Shanghai: Zhongguo jianxue she, 1928), front cover, 6–16.

92. Wang Huaiqi, *Xingqiu guize*, 57–59. Italics added.

93. Wang Huaiqi, *Xingqiu guize*, list inside front cover.

94. "All-China Sports," *North-China Daily News*, 28 May 1924, 7.

95. "Di qi jie Yuandong yundonghui quanguo yuxuanhui zhi jingguo," *Jiaoyu zazhi* 17.6 (20 June 1925), 8.

96. "Far Eastern Olympic Games," *North-China Daily News*, 29 August 1927, 19.

97. "The Far Eastern Olympic Games," *North-China Daily News*, 30 August 1927, 14.

98. *Fujian quansheng xuexiao lianhe yundong dahui baogao* (n.p.: Fujian jiaoyuting, 1921), 164–66.

99. "Yuandong yundonghui xiaoxi," *Shenbao*, 24 May 1921, 10.

100. *Bayun jianjie* (Shanghai: Zhonghua renmin gongheguo Di ba jie quanguo yundonghui jizibu, 1996), unpaginated.

101. *Di san ci quanguo yundong dahui tekan*, advertisements at front and back of publication.

102. Advertisement in *Liangyou* 16 (30 June 1927), 36.

103. *Tiyu jikan* 1.2 (August 1922); *Tiyu jikan* 2.1 (April 1923).

104. "Yuandong yundonghui xiaoxi," 10.

CHAPTER 4. NATIONALISM AND POWER

1. Hsu Yuan-ming, "Jindai Zhongguo canyu Yuandong yundonghui zhi tantao (1913–1934)," unpublished paper, 1993, 54.

2. Wu Wenzhong, *Zhongguo jin bai nian tiyu shi* (Taibei: Taiwan shangwu yinshuguan, 1967), 95.

3. Zhang Tianbai, "Zhonghua quanguo tiyu xiejinhui choubei chengli shimo," *Tiyu wenshi* 46 (November 1990), 30–31.

4. Zhang Tianbai, "Zhonghua quanguo tiyu xiejinhui," 31–32.

5. Zhang Gong, "'Zhonghua yeyu yundong lianhehui' jieti yu heshi?" *Tiyu wenshi* 50 (July 1991), 48.

6. Zhang Gong, "'Zhonghua yeyu yundong lianhehui,'" 49; Zhang Tianbai, "Zhonghua quanguo tiyu xiejinhui," 33.

7. "Fei-lü-bin Yuandong yundonghui zhi jingguo," *Jiaoyu zazhi* 11.6 (20 June 1919), 60.

8. The other two main planners were Zhonghua University President Chen Shi and Wuchang elementary school principal Huang Zhiduan. Hao Gengsheng, *Hao Gengsheng huiyilu* (Taibei: Zhuanji wenxue chubanshe, 1969), 22.

9. Gunsun Hoh, *Physical Education in China* (Shanghai: Commercial Press, 1926), 138. *Shenbao* referred to Gray as merely an "honorary advisor." "Quanguo yundonghui xuanshou jixu dao E," *Shenbao*, 23 May 1924, 10.

10. "Quanguo yundonghui yaoxun," *Shenbao*, 24 May 1924, 10.

11. Guojia tiwei tiyu wenshi gongzuo weiyuanhui and Zhongguo tiyushi xuehui, eds., *Zhongguo jindai tiyushi* (Beijing: Beijing tiyu xueyuan chubanshe, 1989), 148.

12. Hoh, *Physical Education in China*, 142, 144; "Quanguo yundonghui zongjiesu," *Shenbao*, 29 May 1924, 7.

13. Wang Qihua, "Guizhou Qingmo Minguo shiqi tiyu yundong jilüe," *Guizhou tiyu shiliao* 3 (November 1986), 30–31; Hao Gengsheng, *Hao Gengsheng huiyilu*, 25–26; 149.

14. "Quanguo yundonghui kaihui zhi di yi ri," *Shenbao*, 25 May 1924, 7.

15. The Central Air Force in Beijing sent twenty-one men and two aircraft to Wuhan just for the games. The final day of the meet, May 25, saw an appearance by the *Aifoluo*, which circled the stadium five times and then returned to Beijing that same day. Chen Tiesheng, "Di san jie quanguo yundonghui guocao jishi benmo," *Jingwu zazhi* 42 (15 June 1924), 19; Wang Zhenya, *Jiu Zhongguo tiyu jianwen* (Beijing: Renmin tiyu chubanshe, 1987), 147.

16. Wang Zhenya, *Jiu Zhongguo tiyu jianwen*, 147; Hoh, *Physical Education in China*, 141. These games were not the first to be filmed in China. The First Fujian Provincial Games in 1920, organized by the Fuzhou YMCA and the Southern Fujian Athletic Association (Minnan tiyu lianhehui), were filmed by a Commercial Press crew from Shanghai invited by Fujian Military Governor Li Houji. Cai Jinbo, "Quan Min yundonghui jixiang," *Qingnian jinbu* 42 (April 1921), 78.

17. "Quanguo yundonghui yaoxun," *Shenbao*, 22 May 1924, 7; "All-China Sports," *North-China Daily News*, 28 May 1924, 7.

18. "Quanguo yundonghui dahui kaihuiji," *Shenbao*, 27 May 1924, 10.

19. Hoh, *Physical Education in China*, 142–55, 160.

20. Chen Tiesheng, "Di san jie quanguo yundonghui guocao," 1–8.

21. Hao Gengsheng, *Hao Gengsheng huiyilu*, 22, 23.

22. Hao Gengsheng, *Hao Gengsheng huiyilu*, 23.

23. Hao Gengsheng, *Hao Gengsheng huiyilu*, 23–24.

24. In the early 1970s, Hao was run down and killed by a young motorcyclist on the National Taiwan University campus—itself a site known in local lore to be victimized by bad *fengshui*.

25. "China's Sovereign Rights on the Athletic Ground," *North-China Daily News*, 10 May 1924, 7.

26. Li Cimin, "Liang ci canjia Aoyunhui de guojiao—Li Huitang," in *Aoyunhui yu Zhongguo*, ed. Ji Hongmin, Yu Xingmao, and Lü Changfu (Beijing: Wenshi ziliao chubanshe, 1985), 110; Cai Yangwu, "Jiefang qian Gang-Hu zuqiu de fazhan jiqi shehue yuanyin," *Tiyu wenshi* 45 (September 1990), 29.

27. Hoh, *Physical Education in China*, 192.

28. Shen Guoquan narration, transcribed by Fei Zhendong, "Fu Aozhou saiqiu jianwenlu," *Nanyang zhoukan* 3.11 (15 December 1923), 68.

29. The relationship apparently ended after her grandmother wrote to Li telling him to break off this interracial relationship, but some Hong Kong news-

papers proudly reported that Li had wedded the woman. Li Huitang, "Li le mu-tai dao xianzai," *Liangyou* 45 (March 1930), 26–27.

30. Qiao Keqin and Guan Wenming, *Zhongguo tiyu sixiangshi* (Lanzhou: Gansu minzu chubanshe, 1993), 254.

31. "Tiyu wenti jueyian," *Xianqu* 18 (10 May 1923), 3. This document is incorrectly cited as a resolution of a Chinese Socialist Youth Brigade Central Committee meeting in *Tiyu shiliao di 16 ji: Zhongguo jindai tiyu yijuean xuanbian*, ed. Guojia tiwei tiyu wenshi gongzuo weiyuanhui and Quanguo tizong wenshi ziliao bianshen weiyuanhui (Beijing: Renmin tiyu chubanshe, 1990), 356.

32. Daiying [Yun Daiying], "Dadao jiaohui jiaoyu," *Zhongguo qingnian* 60 (3 January 1925), 159.

33. "Tongyi tiyu mingci ji kouling an," reprinted in Guojia tiwei and Quanguo tizong, *Tiyu shiliao di 16 ji*, 37–38.

34. Guojia tiwei and Zhongguo tiyushi xuehui, *Zhongguo jindai tiyushi*, 153.

35. Guojia tiwei and Zhongguo tiyushi xuehui, *Zhongguo jindai tiyushi*, 152; Chen Xianming, Liang Youde, and Du Kehe, *Zhongguo bangqiu yundongshi* (Wuhan: Wuhan chubanshe, 1990), 13.

36. Article in *Shaanxi ribao*, 13 May 1922, quoted in Wang Zengming, "Feng Yuxiang jiangjun yu tiyu," 9–10.

37. Prasenjit Duara, "De-Constructing the Chinese Nation," *Australian Journal of Chinese Affairs* 30 (July 1993), 9–11.

38. Xie Siyan, "Nüzi tiyu wenti," *Funü zazhi* 9.7 (July 1923), 2–5.

39. Tani E. Barlow, "Theorizing Woman: *Funü, Guojia, Jiating* (Chinese Woman, Chinese State, Chinese Family)," in *Body, Subject and Power in China*, ed. Angela Zito and Tani E. Barlow (Chicago: University of Chicago Press, 1994), 253.

40. Wang Zheng, *Women in the Chinese Enlightenment: Oral and Textual Histories* (Berkeley: University of California Press, 1999), 16–21.

41. Wendy Larson, *Women and Writing in Modern China* (Stanford, Calif.: Stanford University Press, 1998), 2–5, 110–22.

42. *Tiyu* 1.2 (15 June 1927).

43. Wang Zhenya, *Jiu Zhongguo tiyu jianwen*, 141–42.

44. Ruan Weicun, *Yuandong yundonghui lishi yu chengji* (Shanghai: Qin-fen shuju, 1933), 82. The sixteen-woman Chinese volleyball team was made up of five athletes from Shanghai schools, two from Suzhou, one from Ningbo, four from Guangzhou, two from Tianjin, and two from Beijing. Zhang Wanqing, "Huiyi Zhongguo shouci nüzi paiqiudui chuguo cansai," *Tiyu wenshi* 38 (July 1989), 53–54.

45. *Funü zazhi* 9.7 (1 July 1923) and 9.8 (1 August 1923).

46. Pan Zhiben, "Nüzi youxi—duiqiu shu," *Funü zazhi* 8.7 (July 1922), 81.

47. Guojia tiwei and Zhongguo tiyushi xuehui, eds., *Zhongguo jindai tiyushi*, 176; Fan Hong, *Footbinding, Feminism and Freedom: The Liberation of Women's Bodies in Modern China* (Portland, Ore.: Frank Cass, 1997), 137.

48. "Chinese Girls to Be in Far Eastern Games," *Millard's Review of the Far East* (28 May 1921), 695; "Yuandong yundonghui xiaoxi," *Shenbao*, 24 May

1921, 10; "The Far Eastern Olympic Games Supplement," *Shenbao,* 2 June 1921, 2.

49. Kristin Stapleton, "Yang Sen in Chengdu: Urban Planning in the Interior," in *Remaking the Chinese City: Modernity and National Identity, 1900–1950,* ed. Joseph W. Esherick (Honolulu: University of Hawai'i Press, 2000), 95.

50. Yi Runsheng and Mao Hongkai, "Yun Daiying yu you yici Chuannan lianhe yundonghui," *Sichuan tiyu shiliao* 6 (May 1984), 14–15.

51. Zhang Ruizhen, "Nüzi tianjingsai yundong shuo," *Tiyu jikan* 2.1 (April 1923), 1–2.

52. Zhang Ruizhen, "Nüzi tianjingsai yundong shuo," 2.

53. Kui, "Di san jie Huazhong yundonghui zhi di yi ri," *Shenbao,* 26 April 1925, 12.

54. Kui, "Di san jie Huazhong yundonghui zhi jieguo," *Shenbao,* 28 April 1925, 11.

55. "Far Eastern Olympic Games," *North-China Daily News,* 22 August 1927, 14.

56. Chien-ming Yu has written on this subject of "healthy beauty" in modern Chinese women's physical culture. "Jindai Zhongguo nüzi tiyu guan chutan," *Xin shixue* 7.4 (December 1996), 119–58. See also Larson, *Women and Writing,* 114–116.

57. Gao Shan, "Meirong de yundongfa," *Funü zazhi* 7.12 (December 1921), 81.

58. Xiao Liu, "Nüzi shinei ticao," *Funü zazhi* 8.1 (January 1922), 83.

59. Yang Binru, "Zhiye funü de yundong," *Funü zazhi* 10.6 (June 1924), 908.

60. Chen Yongsheng, *Nüzi meirong yundongfa* (Shanghai: Wenming shuju, 1924), 30–35.

61. Gao Shilin, "Women weishenme yao yundong," *Funü zazhi* 7.7 (July 1921), 80–81.

62. Fan Hong, *Footbinding, Feminism and Freedom,* 138.

63. Fan Hong, *Footbinding, Feminism and Freedom,* 137–38.

64. Yan Sui, "Nüzi de tiyu," *Chenbao,* 28 March 1921, 5, and 29 March 1921, 7.

65. For example, a piece by Saiga Kazumi from the journal *Research into the Japanese Family,* "Nüzi tiyu yanjiu," trans. Yan Wei, *Funü zazhi* 9.7 (July 1923), 6–10.

66. Agnes Fung, "Chinese Women and Physical Culture," *Tiyu shijie* 1 (30 March 1927), 39.

67. Lu Lihua, "Zhongguo nüzi tiyu yijian shu," in *Di san ci quanguo yundong dahui tekan* (Hankou: Hankou jidujiao qingnianhui, 1924).

68. Xiang Fuchun, "Wo de tiyu guan," *Tiyu huikan* 1 (June 1925), 8.

69. Ding Zengfang, "Wo duiyu tiyu zhi ganxiang," *Tiyu huikan* 1 (June 1925), 11.

70. Kathleen E. McCrone, *Playing the Game: Sport and the Physical Eman-*

cipation of English Women, 1879–1914 (Lexington: University Press of Kentucky, 1988), 206–212.

71. Wang Huaiqi, *Xingqiu guize* (Shanghai: Zhongguo jianxueshe, 1928), 2–3.

72. See Coubertin on the Olympics as an internationalized "republic of muscles" and his belief that his games could contribute to world peace, trade, and understanding of different nations and cultures. John J. MacAloon, *This Great Symbol: Pierre de Coubertin and the Origins of the Modern Olympic Games* (Chicago: University of Chicago Press, 1981), 136, 155.

73. Lao, "Yundong yu zhanzheng zhi bijiao," *Shenbao,* 31 May 1921, "The Far Eastern Olympic Games Supplement #2" section, 1. Underscoring this connection between sports and the military, the 1921 Chinese gold medal-winning basketball team was led by Qinghua University star Sun Liren, who would serve as commander of the Nationalist Army on Taiwan. Qu Ziqing, *Zhongguo lanqiu shihua* (Taibei: Weihua tiyu xunkanshe, 1961), 12.

74. Mo, "Di si ri huichang suo jian," *Shenbao,* 3 June 1921, "The Far Eastern Olympic Games Supplement #5" section, 1; untitled item in same, 2.

75. Mo, "Di yi ri huichang zhong suo jian," *Shenbao,* 31 May 1921, "The Far Eastern Olympic Games Supplement #2" section, 1.

76. Tsai Jen-hsiung, "Riju shidai 'Taiwan tiyu xiehui' chengli de lishi kaocha," paper presented at Di yi jie Dongbeiya tiyu yundongshi xueshu yantaohui, Taipei, Taiwan, 19–21 December 1995.

77. *Shenbao,* 5 June 1921, "The Far Eastern Olympic Games Supplement," 3. *Wansui* ("long life") is the Chinese term from which the Japanese *banzai* is derived.

78. Despite their internationalist goals, they employed traditional regionalist and nationalist stereotypes in attempting to deceive their captors. The armed anarchist (carrying four guns) first pretended that he was Cantonese and could not understand the language of the arresting officers but was unable to answer when spoken to in that language. He then admitted to carrying the guns but told police he carried weapons to protect himself from Japanese ruffians who had beaten him up. "Yundonghui zhong guojidang kaiqiang zhi waixun," *Shenbao,* 6 June 1921, 10; "Yundonghui zhong faxian guojidang zhi zuoxun," *Shenbao,* 7 June 1921, 10.

79. *Di qi jie Yuandong yundonghui quanguo yuxuan dahui tekan* (Shanghai: Di qi jie Yuandong yundonghui quanguo yuxuan dahui tekanshe, 1925), 64.

80. Ying Wen, "Sun Jinshun shouzhan Manila," *Shanghai tiyu shihua* 16 (July 1987), 18.

81. "Di qi jie Yuandong yundonghui jishi," *Jiaoyu zazhi* 17.7 (20 July 1925), 5; "No Settlement Reached with 'Strikers,'" *Manila Times,* 20 May 1925, 1.

82. "Strikers Punished," *Manila Times,* 22 May 1925, 1.

83. "Tokio to Withdraw Team from Olympics, Expected: Subsidy Likely to Be Ended," *Manila Times,* 21 May 1925, 1; Hsu Yuan-ming, "Jindai Zhongguo canyu Yuandong yundonghui," 53.

84. Takahara Tomiyasu, ed., *Showa supōtsu shi: Olinpikku 80 nen* (Tokyo: Mainichi shinbunsha, 1976), 24–25.

85. *Beiyang huabao* 140 (23 November 1927), 2.

86. *North-China Daily News,* 17 August 1927, 9.

87. "Far Eastern Olympic Games," *North-China Daily News,* 1 September 1927, 10.

88. *Beiyang huabao* 118 (3 September 1927), 2.

89. Jin Huating, "Yuandong yundonghui de duanpian," *Shenbao,* 3 September 1927, 12. Another *Shenbao* author wrote on the same banquet, ridiculing the Filipino men who didn't want to let go of their dancing partners when the music stopped, "their faces turning black," crying out, "oh, oh" for the women to accompany them to their rooms. Lin Zemin, "Niwu zalu," *Shenbao,* 4 September 1927, 10.

CHAPTER 5. "WE CAN ALSO BE THE CONTROLLERS AND OPPRESSORS"

1. *Quanguo yundong dahui zongbaogao* (Hangzhou, 1930), "Yanshuoci" section, 3.

2. This was a common trope in the 1930s. One writer described his worry that "our citizens might break the world records for the worst physiques and lowest level of hygiene." Tan Jihua, "Lun tiyu," *Yanjiu yu pipan* 1.6 (1 November 1935), 91.

3. Sichuan, Suiyuan, Liaoning, Heilongjiang (Harbin), and Anhui were all newcomers to the National Games. The fourteen provinces not represented in 1930 were Guangxi, Guizhou, Yunnan, Xikang, Xinjiang, Qinghai, Gansu, Ningxia, Shaanxi, Shanxi, Henan, Chahar, Rehe, and Jilin.

4. Zhu Jiahua, "Duiyu Quanguo yundong dahui de ganxiang yu jinhou de xiwang," in *Quanguo yundong dahui zongbaogao,* "Lunzhu" section, 5, 6.

5. Zhu Jiahua, "Quanguo yundong dahui zhi yiyi," in *Quanguo yundong dahui yaolan* (Hangzhou: Quanguo yundong dahui xuanchuanbu, 1930), 5–6.

6. Wu Wenzhong, *Zhongguo tiyu fazhan shi* (Taibei: Guoli jiaoyu ziliaoguan, 1981), 136; Dong Shouyi, "Aolinpike yu Zhongguo," in *Aoyunhui yu Zhongguo,* ed. Ji Hongmin, Yu Xingmao, and Lü Changfu (Beijing: Wenshi ziliao chubanshe, 1985), 19.

7. Guojia tiwei tiyu wenshi gongzuo weiyuanhui and Quanguo tizong wenshi ziliao bianshen weiyuanhui, eds., *Tiyu shiliao di 16 ji: Zhongguo jindai tiyu yijuean xuanbian* (Beijing: Renmin tiyu chubanshe, 1990), 66–91.

8. "Guomin tiyu fa," Education Department Directive #262, 16 April 1929, reprinted in *Jindai Zhongguo tiyu fagui,* ed. Wang Zengming (n.p.: Zhongguo tiyushi xuehui Hebei fenhui, 1988), 1–2.

9. *Quanguo yundong dahui zongbaogao,* "Yanshuoci" section, 6.

10. "Choubei zhi jingguo," *Shenbao,* 1 April 1930, 11.

11. Liang Desuo, "Bianzhe jiang hua," *Liangyou* 46 (April 1930), 2.

12. *Quanguo yundong dahui zongbaogao,* "Jiangpin zu" section, 7–100.

13. *Quanguo yundong dahui zongbaogao,* "Shiwu gu baogao" section, 27–28.

14. *Quanguo yundong dahui zongbaogao,* "Yanshuoci" section, 4.

15. Interview with Dong Hanwen, Taipei, 30 January 1997; Dai Shizeng, "Liuwang Beiping qijian de Dongbei tiyu xiejinhui," *Beijing tiyu wenshi* 1 (April 1984), 17.

16. *Quanguo yundong dahui zongbaogao,* "Zhaodai zu" section, 1; Pan Chuji, "Anhui sheng xuanshoutuan canjia si jie Quanyunhui de riji," *Anhui tiyu shiliao* 5 (October 1983), 31–32.

17. *Quanguo yundong dahui zongbaogao,* "Yundong chengji jilu" section, 34–36.

18. Zhu Jiahua, "Dahui zhi yiyi," *Shenbao,* 1 April 1930, 11.

19. Lloyd E. Eastman, *The Abortive Revolution: China under Nationalist Rule, 1927–1937* (Cambridge, Mass.: Council on East Asian Studies, Harvard University, 1974), 44–45; Frederic Wakeman, Jr., "A Revisionist View of the Nanjing Decade: Confucian Fascism," in *Reappraising Republican China,* ed. Frederic Wakeman, Jr., and Richard Louis Edmonds (New York: Oxford University Press, 2000), 173–77.

20. This dichotomy is also used to describe Soviet sports in Robert Edelman, *Serious Fun: A History of Spectator Sports in the USSR* (New York: Oxford University Press, 1993), 15.

21. Shang Shumei, "Minzhong tiyu," *Kexue de Zhongguo* 2.8 (15 October 1933), 32.

22. Wang Geng, *Minzhong tiyu shishifa* (Shanghai: Qinfen shuju, 1933), opposite 1.

23. Wang Geng, *Gonggong tiyuchang* (Hangzhou: Zhejiang sheng jiaoyuting, 1931), 2–3.

24. Wang Zhuangfei, *Tiyuchang zhinan* (Shanghai: Qinfen shuju, 1931), 65.

25. The only provinces listing no public athletic grounds were Jilin, Suiyuan, and Xinjiang.

26. Jiaoyubu Zhongguo jiaoyu nianjian bianzuan weiyuanhui, ed., "Bing bian," sec. 3 in *Di yi ci Zhongguo jiaoyu nianjian* (Nanjing, 1934; reprint, Taibei: Zongqing tushu gongsi, n.d.), 910–34 (page citations are to the reprint edition).

27. "Jinxiandai tiyu renwu," *Jiangsu tiyu wenshi* 11 (June 1989), 27.

28. Shang Shumei, "Minzhong tiyu," 34.

29. "Minzhong yeyu yundonghui banfa dawang," Education Department Directive #669, 8 April 1931, reprinted in *Zhongguo jindai tiyushi ziliao,* ed. Chengdu tiyu xueyuan tiyushi yanjiusuo (Chengdu: Sichuan jiaoyu chubanshe, 1988), 220–21.

30. Wang Zhuangfei, *Tiyuchang zhinan,* 8–14.

31. These comments were made with regard to the recent formation of the Shanghai First Municipal Public Athletic Grounds Laborer-Merchant Amateur Soccer Club. Wang Zhuangfei, *Tiyuchang zhinan,* 94.

32. "Guomin tiyu shishi fang'an," *Jiaoyubu gongbao* 4.43–44 (6 November 1932), 79.

33. Cheng Dengke, "Zhongguo jinhou minzhong tiyu yingyou zhi dong-xiang," *Guoshu, tiyu, junshi* 29 (17 May 1934) [Weekly feature in *Zhongguo ribao*], 8.

34. Wang Geng, "Minzhong tiyuchang zhi lilun yu shiji," *Jiaoyu yu minzhong* 4.6 (February 1933), 1008.

35. Yu Jinxiang, "Jinhou wuguo minzhong tiyu yingyou zhi dongxiang," *Tiyu zazhi* 1 (4 April 1935), 16; Shu Yifan, "Ruhe fazhan wuguo minzhong tiyu," *Hanxue yuekan* (1 May 1935), 32–33. Shu omitted the party, while Yu omitted merchants.

36. Yu Jinxiang, "Jinhou wuguo minzhong tiyu," 17.

37. Yu Zizhen, "Xiangcun xiaoxue tiyu jiaocai yu shebei," *Qinfen tiyu yuebao* 4.1 (October 1936), 44.

38. Huo Liangui, "Gaijin xiangcun xiaoxue tiyu de wojian," *Qinfen tiyu yuebao* 4.3 (December 1936), 253.

39. Zhang Zhenguo, "Nongcun qingnian suo xu de tiyu huodong," *Qinfen tiyu yuebao* 2.11 (August 1935), 751–52.

40. Chu Jianhong, "Shishi xiangcun tiyu juti fang'an," *Qinfen tiyu yuebao* 3.6 (March 1936), 475–78.

41. "Guomin tiyu shishi fang'an," 80.

42. "Guomin tiyu shishi fang'an," 81–82.

43. *Jiangxi shengli tiyuchang shishi gongzuo zongbaogao* (Nanchang: Jiangxi shengli tiyuchang, 1935), 2–3, tables after 58.

44. Zhang Jiwu, "Nankai xuexiao bannian lai quxiao xuanshouzhi hou de xin shiyan," *Tiyu zhoubao: Zhounian jinian tekan* (21 January 1933), 8. These English terms were used with Chinese translations.

45. "Yundong biaozhun ceyan zhi jieguo," *Nankai zhoukan* 120 (15 December 1931), and "Benxiao yundong chengji ceyan," *Nankai zhoukan* (29 November 1932), both reprinted in *Nankai daxue xiaoshi ziliaoxuan*, ed. Wang Wenjun et al. (Tianjin: Nankai daxue chubanshe, 1989), 583, 588.

46. Fan Hong, *Footbinding, Feminism and Freedom: The Liberation of Women's Bodies in Modern China* (Portland, Ore.: Frank Cass, 1997), 237.

47. "Nüzi yundong yingxiang shengyu," *Shenbao*, 18 June 1929, 3.

48. Wu Yunrui, "Wuguo minzu fuxing zhong nüzi tiyu zhi zhongyao," *Tiyu zazhi* 1.1 (4 April 1935), 1.

49. Ding Zuyin, "Tiyu de xinli yanjiu (shang)," *Xiaoxue jiaoshi banyuekan* 4.10 (1 February 1937), 29–32.

50. Zhou Xingjian, "Tan funü tiyu," *Renyan zhoukan* 12 (5 May 1934), 258.

51. Cheng Dengke, "Xie gei xin biye de tiyu tongzhimen," *Qinfen tiyu yuebao* 2.10 (July 1935), 669–71.

52. Xiang Xianggao, "Nüzi tiyu yu nüzi de jianglai," *Minguo ribao*, 23 January 1929, "Qingnian funü" section 1.

53. Xiang Xianggao, "Nüzi tiyu yu nüzi de jianglai," 2.

54. Naoruisi narration, transcribed by Tingtingdun, "Lao yu zhiwu de funü—chengle yijijia!" *Tiyu zhoubao* 2.16 (27 May 1933), 9.

55. Naoruisi, "Lao yu zhiwu de funü," 9–10; Naoruisi narration, transcribed by Tingtingdun, "Lao yu zhiwu de funü—chengle yijijia! (xu)," *Tiyu zhoubao* 2.17 (3 June 1933), 8–9.

56. Weiqin, "Nüzi tiyu yu shengli bianhua," *Qinfen tiyu yuebao* 1.7 (10 April 1934), 15–19; Weiqin, "Nüzi yuejing yu yundong zhi guanxi," *Qinfen tiyu yuebao* 1.5 (10 February 1934), 42–44.

57. Weiqin, "Nüzi tiyu yu shengli bianhua," 19.

58. Weiqin, "Nüzi yuejing yu yundong zhi guanxi," 44.

59. Zhang Naifeng, "Nüzi he yundong de xuyao," *Xin jiating* 1.3 (March 1931), 3.

60. Zhang Huilan, "Tige jianyan ji tiyu fenzu wenti," *Qinfen tiyu yuebao* 2.12 (September 1935), 801.

61. Zhang Huilan, "Tige jianyan ji tiyu fenzu wenti," 801.

62. Liu-Shao Jinying, "Tichang nüzi tiyu zhi wu jian," *Qinfen tiyu yuebao* 2.3 (10 December 1934), 212–13.

63. Yunsu, "San zhong butong de xuyao," *Nü qingnian yuekan* 13.6 (June 1934), 47.

64. Christina Kelley Gilmartin, *Engendering the Chinese Revolution: Radical Women, Communist Politics, and Mass Movements in the 1920s* (Berkeley: University of California Press, 1995), 204, 205.

65. Dai Mengqin, "Jianshen jianguo de tujing," *Shenghuo zhoukan* 6.26 (20 June 1931), 535, 536.

66. "Duzhe guwen," *Qinfen tiyu yuebao* 2.9 (June 1935), 639–40.

67. Chen Lifu, "Chuangzao shihe Zhongguo guoqing de yundong," in *Tiyu yu jiuguo*, ed. Zhongguo Guomindang zhongyang zhixing weiyuanhui xuanchuan weiyuanhui (Nanjing: Zhongguo Guomindang zhongyang zhixing weiyuanhui xuanchuan weiyuanhui, 1933), 101–2.

68. Chen Lifu, "Chuangzao shihe Zhongguo guoqing de yundong," 104. However, in his memoirs published in 1994, Chen remembered fondly his participation in soccer, tennis, basketball, track and field, and ice skating at Beiyang University. Sidney H. Chang and Ramon H. Myers, eds., *The Storm Clouds Clear over China: The Memoir of Ch'en Li-fu 1900–1993* (Stanford, Calif.: Hoover Press, 1994), 12–13.

69. Italicized terms were rendered in English with Chinese translations. Chen Lifu, "Chuangzao shihe Zhongguo guoqing de yundong," 104.

70. Chen Lifu, "Chuangzao shihe Zhongguo guoqing de yundong," 105, 106.

71. Wu Cheng, "Ding youyong wei guomin yundong de guanjian," *Guoshu, tiyu, junshi* 34 (28 June 1934) [Weekly feature in *Zhongguo ribao*], 8.

72. Yinting, "Sheng-tuo-mai-si yuanzheng qiudui li Hu ji," *Tiyu pinglun* 27 (15 April 1933), 54; Ma Chonggan, "Di wu jie Quanguo yundonghui zhi huigu," *Shenbao yuekan* 2.11 (15 November 1933), 79.

73. Quoted in Chen Xianming, Liang Youde, and Du Kehe, *Zhongguo bangqiu yundongshi* (Wuhan: Wuhan chubanshe, 1990), 31.

74. "Yi yue lai zhi haiwai tiyu," *Qinfen tiyu yuebao* 1.4 (10 January 1934), 69.

75. "Er zhounian zhengqiu da yundong," *Qinfen tiyu yuebao* 2.12 (September 1935).

76. "'Guomin youxi' xuanshang da'an jiexiao," *Qinfen tiyu yuebao* 3.5 (February 1936).

77. Huang Jianxing, "Wuguo ying caiyong zuqiu wei guomin youxi," *Qinfen tiyu yuebao* 3.5 (February 1936), 403–4.

78. Zhuang Wenchao, "Wuguo ying caiyong lanqiu wei guomin youxi," *Qinfen tiyu yuebao* 3.5 (February 1936), 405–7.

79. Shao Rugan, "Wei zhengqiu 'Woguo ying cai hezhong tiyu yundong wei guomin youxi' shuo jiju hua," *Qinfen tiyu yuebao* 3.5 (February 1936), 389.

80. Meng Guangpeng, "'Tiyu' yu 'Xin shenghuo,'" *Hubei sheng dang zheng jun xue tiyu cujin weiyuanhui huikan* 1.2 (10 May 1936), 9, 12. Italics added.

81. Simonetta Falasca-Zamponi, *Fascist Spectacle: The Aesthetics of Power in Mussolini's Italy* (Berkeley: University of California Press, 1997), 130–34.

82. Liu Shoupeng, "Tiyu yu guomin jingji jianshe," *Hubei sheng dang zheng jun xue tiyu cujin weiyuanhui huikan* 1.3 (10 September 1936), 4.

83. Wu Yunrui, "Wuguo minzu fuxing zhong nüzi tiyu zhi zhongyao," 1.

84. Xu Yongping, "Zhongguoren shengming de langfei zhi yanzhong kepaxing ji guomin tiyu de jianshe zhi poqie xuyaoxing lun," *Hanxue yuekan* 5.2 (1 May 1935), 1.

85. Xu Yongping, "Zhongguoren shengming de langfei," 1–2.

86. Xu Yongping, "Zhongguoren shengming de langfei," 2–3.

87. This program was not the first attempt to create national summer *tiyu* training. Beijing's Qinghua University held such a program three times between 1928 and 1931, boasting male and female physical education experts from Tianjin, Shanghai, Wuchang, Shanghai, Nanjing, Guangdong, and Fujian, as well as two American teachers. Huang Yanfu, "Woguo zaoqi peixun tiyu shizi de Qinghua shuqi tixiao," *Beijing tiyu wenshi* 4 (May 1989), 62–64.

88. "Jiaobu shuqi tiyuban tongxuehui xiaoxi (er)," *Qinfen tiyu yuebao* 1.3 (December 1933), 82–83; "Jiaoyubu tiyuban tongxuehui xiaoxi (san)," *Qinfen tiyu yuebao* 1.4 (January 1934), 81–83; parts 4–8 of same article, in *Qinfen tiyu yuebao* 1.5 (February 1934), 74–75; 1.6 (March 1934), 70–71; 1.7 (April 1934), 70–71; 1.8 (May 1934), 68–69; and 1.10 (July 1934), 60–61.

89. The weekly curriculum included twenty-three hours of theoretical courses and twelve hours of skills courses. "Jiaoyubu shuqi tiyu buxiban kecheng," *Tiyu zhoubao* 2.21 (1 July 1933), 9–11.

90. "Guanyu bennian shuqi tiyu xuexiao," *Tiyu zhoubao* 2.15 (20 May 1933), 1.

91. Yu Zizhen, "Dui Jiaobu shuqi tixiao jidian yijian," *Tiyu zhoubao* 2.20 (24 June 1933), 2–3.

92. "Schooling Physical Directors," *Illustrated Week-End Sporting World* 11.9 (6 March 1937), 3.

93. Hao Gengsheng, "Shi nian lai zhi Zhongguo tiyu," *Wenhua jianshe yuekan* 3.10 (10 July 1937), 118.

94. "Guoli Nanjing gaoshi, Dongnan daxue, Zhongyang daxue li jie biye tongxue zuijin diaocha biao," *Tiyu zazhi* 3 (June 1931), 127–40.

95. Wang Qihua, "Guizhou Qingmo Minguo shiqi tiyu yundong jilüe," *Guizhou tiyu shiliao* 3 (November 1986), 29.

96. Fan Hong, "'Iron Bodies': Women, War, and Sport in the Early Communist Movement in Modern China," *Journal of Sport History* 24.1 (Spring 1997), 6, 15. Or see Yu Jianyong, "Shilun hongse tiyu he Xin Zhongguo tiyu de neizai lianxi," *Tiyu wenshi* 47 (January 1991), 36–38.

97. Gu Shiquan, "Zhongyang Suqu shiqi Liening xiaoxue, Ertongtuan he Shaoxiandui de tiyu," *Tiyu wenshi* 22 (December 1986), 28; Zeng Biao, "Suqu xuexiao tiyu jiaocai yu jiaofa de gaige," *Tiyu wenshi* 67 (May 1994), 12–13.

98. Jie Jilin, "Hongjun zai Jiange shi de tiyu huodong," *Tiyu wenshi* 22 (December 1986), 3–4.

99. Qiu Liegao, "Shanghang Taiba qu de ge xuexiao jingsai dahui," *Qingnian shihua* 24, reprinted in Zeng Biao, ed., *Suqu tiyu ziliao xuanbian (1929–1934)* (Hefei: Anhui sheng tiyu shizhi bianjishi, 1985), 82–83.

100. "Da tabu maijin zhe de Changting xian," *Hongse Zhonghua*, 21 May 1934, 1.

101. Originally published in *Qingnian shihua* 2.18 (1 June 1933), quoted in Zeng Biao, "Gongchandang lingdao xia de zaoqi tiyu zuzhi," *Tiyu wenshi* 72 (March 1995), 29.

102. Zeng Biao, *Suqu tiyu ziliao xuanbian*, 27–31; Gu Shiquan, "Suqu shiqi 'Julebu' he 'Liening shi' de tiyu," *Tiyu wenshi* 21 (October 1986), 31–32.

103. Liang Tian, *Zhongguo tianjing fazhan jianshi* (n.p.: Guangdong tiyu kexue yanjiusuo and Guangdong tiyu wenshi weiyuanhui, 1982), 58–59.

104. Cheng Dengke narration, ed. Chen Weilin, "Sanshi niandai wo tichu 'tiyu junshihua' yinqi de yi chang lunzhan," *Sichuan tiyu shiliao* 7 (June 1984), 7.

105. Cheng Dengke, "Sanshi niandai wo tichu 'tiyu junshihua,'" 7.

106. Cheng Dengke, "Dadao buzhongshi ji fuhua de tiyu tongzhi," *Qinfen tiyu yuebao* 1.4 (10 January 1934), 4.

107. Cheng Dengke, *Shijie tiyushi gangyao*, Minguo congshu di yi bian #50 (Chongqing: Shangwu yinshuguan, 1945; reprint, Shanghai: Shanghai shudian, 1989), 229 (page citations are to the reprint edition).

108. Liu Shenzhan, *Tiyu geming* (Nanjing: Zhongguo ribao, 1933), 6, 11–12.

109. Chu Minyi, "Fuxing minzu yu tichang tiyu," *Hubei jiaoyu yuekan* 5 (January 1934), 13–14, 16.

110. John Fitzgerald, *Awakening China: Politics, Culture and Class in the Nationalist Revolution* (Stanford, Calif.: Stanford University Press, 1996), 215.

111. Liu Shenzhan, *Tiyu geming*, 32.

112. Liu Shenzhan, "Women yingdang zenyang de nuli," *Qinfen tiyu yuebao* 2.1 (10 October 1934), 5.

113. Liu Shenzhan, *Tiyu geming*, 40.

114. Liu Shenzhan, *Tiyu geming*, 20.

115. Liu Shenzhan, "Tiyu jiuguo lun (er)," *Qinfen tiyu yuebao* 2.11 (August 1935), 719.

116. Cheng Dengke, "Deguo xiaoxue tiyu shishi gaikuang ji ganyan," *Jiaoyu congkan* 2.2 (June 1935), 1.

117. Yuan Tao, "Mo-suo-li-ni yu Yi-da-li de jiankang," *Huanian zhoukan* 1.11 (25 June 1932), 210–12.

118. Fan Wenzhao, "Ou Mei ganxiang," *Zhongguo jianzhu* 24 (March 1936), 17–19.

119. Japanese athletes scored two medals in the 1920 Olympic Games, one in 1924, five in 1928, and eighteen in 1932. Takahara Tomiyasu, ed., *Showa supōtsu shi: Olinpikku 80 nen* (Tokyo: Mainichi shinbunsha, 1976), 43, 46, 56, 73.

120. Preface to Okamoto Noritsune, *Tiyu zhi kexue de jichu* [Original title *Taiiku kaibō*] , trans. Guo Renji (Shanghai: Xieqiao yiyuan, 1929), 3.

121. Yuan Zongze, "Riben shehui tiyu zhi sheshi," *Minzhong jiaoyu yuekan* 2.5 (1 March 1930), 37–38.

122. Li Shijun, "Tiyu jiaoyu jianguo lun," *Jiangxi jiaoyu* 18 (April 1936), 70.

123. Ruan Weicun, "Riben minzu tige yanjin shikuang," *Qinfen tiyu yuebao* 3.10 (July 1936), 901; tables and graphs are on 892–900. Ruan would later serve as one of the main physical culture leaders in Wang Jingwei's Nanjing government.

124. Zhou Weizhuo, "Riben tiyu kaocha ji," *Qinfen tiyu yuebao* 3.3 (December 1935), 271–74; parts 2–4 of same article, *Qinfen tiyu yuebao* 3.4 (January 1936), 353–56; 3.5 (February 1936), 423–24; 3.6 (March 1936), 494–96.

125. Yu Zizhen, "Kang Ri de biaoqingcao," *Tiyu zhoubao* 44 (3 December 1932), 22.

126. Hu Tong, "Xiaoxue aiguo youxi jiaocai," *Qinfen tiyu yuebao* 1.4 (10 January 1934), 46–52.

127. Cheng Dengke, "Deguo xiaoxue tiyu shishi gaikuang ji ganyan," 1.

128. Chen Kuisheng, "Woguo xiaoxue tiyu mubiao gaige wenti," *Qinfen tiyu yuebao* 1.3 (10 December 1933), 8.

129. "Shixian xian Zongli zhuzhang shi quanmin tiyuhua," *Jiaoyu zazhi* 25.2 (10 February 1935), 140–41.

130. Of the 9,282 actual participants, 34.9 percent were workers, 34.3 percent were merchants, and 16.1 percent were unemployed. Only 1.2 percent were farmers. Cheng Shikui, "Jiangxi shenghui de gongmin xunlian," *Jiaoyu zazhi* 25.1 (10 January 1935), 121–26.

131. "Guomin tiyu zhi yiban," *Hanxue yuekan* 5.2 (1 May 1935).

132. The Dang zheng jun xue tiyu cujinhui, a New Life–affiliated organization founded in Hubei in 1935, was one chief agent of the spread of militarized *tiyu*.

133. Deng Kanshun, "Wuzhuang wu xiang yundong bisai fangfa," *Qinfen tiyu yuebao* 3.5 (February 1936), 419.

134. Edward Y. K. Kwong, "Militarizing Sports," *China Critic* 14.8 (20 August 1936), 177–78.

135. Lujun di shiba jun quanjun yundong dahui, ed., "Gezhong junshi tiyu bisai guize," *Qinfen tiyu yuebao* 3.8 (May 1936), 773–79.

136. Military-ball was featured as a demonstration event at the Fourteenth Guangdong Provincial Games in 1936. Yu Jie, "Junshiqiu—yi zhong xin de qiuxi," *Tiyu jikan* 3.2 (June 1937), 178–82.

137. Cheng Dengke, "Geguo qingnian tiyu xunlian zhi shixiao ji wuguo jinhou qingnian tiyu yingyou zhi dongxiang," *Jiaoyu congkan* 3.1 (December 1935), 215–21.

138. Cheng Dengke, "Geguo qingnian tiyu xunlian zhi shixiao," 213–14.

139. Cheng Dengke narration, transcribed by Zhou Shouzang, "Zhongguo xian Qin tiyu," *Tiyu jikan* 3.2 (June 1937), 127.

140. Cheng Dengke, "Tiyu junshihua de jiaoxue chuyi," *Jiao yu xue* 1.7 (1 January 1936), 280, 282.

141. Qiao Keqin and Guan Wenming, *Zhongguo tiyu sixiangshi* (Lanzhou: Gansu minzu chubanshe, 1993), 248–49.

142. "Jiaoyu huabao," *Jiaoyu zazhi* 27.4 (10 April 1937).

143. Fang Xiebang, "Jindai tiyu zai Qinghai," *Qinghai tiyu shiliao* 2 (December 1987), 14.

144. *Guoli Qingdao daxue yilan* (Qingdao: Qingdao daxue, 1931), 11–12, 15, 157–67.

145. *Henan shengli Henan daxue xianxing zhangze huibian* (n.p.: Henan shengli Henan daxue, 1935), 83, 86, 98–99.

146. *Guangxi daxue min er wu ji biye jiniance* (Wuzhou, 1936).

147. Xu Longrui, "Fang Wanbang tiyu sixiang chulun," *Tiyu wenshi* 35 (January 1989), 8.

148. The book's frontispiece photograph showed Fang in his Columbia University graduation cap and gown. Fang Wanbang, *Tiyu yuanli* (Shanghai: Shangwu yinshuguan, 1933).

149. Fang Wanbang, "Woguo xianxing tiyu zhi shi da wenti jiqi jiejue tujing," *Jiaoyu zazhi* 25.3 (10 March 1933), 32–33.

150. Cheng Dengke, "Du Fang Wanbang xiansheng 'Woguo xianxing tiyu zhi shi da wenti jiqi jiejue tujing' zhong suo chi dui tiyu junshihua buqie shiyong de jiantao," *Tiyu jikan* 1.3 (July 1935), 358–61.

151. Zhang Jiwu, "Dule Fang Wanbang Cheng Dengke liang xiansheng de dazhu zhihou," *Tiyu jikan* 2.3 (September 1936), 348–49, quoted in Hsu Yuanming, "Zhanqian shinian Zhongguo tiyu sixiang zhi yanjiu" (M.S. thesis, Guoli Taiwan shifan daxue, 1990), 60–61.

152. Lin Liru, "Duiyu zhongxue kecheng zhong junshi xunlian di yi ge jianyi," *Jiaoyu zazhi* 26.1 (10 January 1936), 35–36.

153. Zhong Ruiqiu, "Jindai zhuming tiyujia: Wu Yunrui zhuanlüe," *Shanghai tiyu shihua* 4 (July 1983), 3.

154. Wu Yunrui, "Junshi xunlian yu tiyu," *Tiyu jikan* 3.1 (March 1937), 2–3.

155. Han Chunling, "Renwu jieshao: Cheng Dengke," *Tiyu wenshi* 54 (March 1992), 68–69.

156. Zhang Zengyuan, "Sichuan zui zao huode tiyu shuoshi xuewei de liu-xuesheng Liu Xuesong," *Sichuan tiyu shiliao* 14 (August 1985), 29.

157. Liu Xuesong, "Kefou jiang tiyu tongjun guoshu dacheng yipian," *Tiyu jikan* 3.1 (March 1937), 7–10.

CHAPTER 6. ELITE COMPETITIVE SPORT

Parts of this chapter were originally published in Andrew Morris, "'I Can Compete!': China in the Olympic Games, 1932 and 1936," *Journal of Sport History* 26.3 (fall 1999), 545–66.

1. Zhiyun, *Zhejiang quansheng yundong dahui xiaoshi* (Hangzhou: Tushu zhanwang yuekan, 1937), 2–3.

2. Yuan Zongze and Zhu Lin, "1914 nian—1937 nian Jiangsu sheng yun-donghui jianjie," *Jiangsu tiyu wenshi* 1 (October 1984), 27–39.

3. Ye Yuanlong, "Ye xu," in *Guizhou sheng di yi jie quansheng yundonghui zongbaogao*, ed. Guizhou sheng di yi jie quansheng yundonghui choubei weiyuanhui (Guiyang: Guizhou sheng zhengfu jiaoyuting, 1935), 2.

4. "Guoqu de he xianzai de yundonghui," *Guizhou chenbao yundonghui tekan*, 8 September 1935, reprinted in Guizhou sheng di yi jie quansheng yun-donghui choubei weiyuanhui, *Guizhou sheng di yi jie quansheng yundonghui zongbaogao*, 108.

5. Teams from Zhangbei, Xuanhua, and Saibei, all within thirty miles of the capital at Zhangjiakou, joined. Chahar sheng ershisan nian zhongdeng xuexiao qiuji yundong dahui choubei weiyuanhui, eds., *Chahar sheng ershisan nian zhongdeng xuexiao qiuji yundong dahui zongbaogao* (Zhangjiakou: Chahar sheng jiaoyuting mishushi, 1934), 1, 19.

6. Chahar sheng ershisan nian zhongdeng xuexiao qiuji yundong dahui choubei weiyuanhui, *Chahar sheng ershisan nian zhongdeng xuexiao qiuji yun-dong dahui zongbaogao*, 4.

7. *Gannan junmin lianhe er ci yundong dahui tekan* (n.p., 1934), 2.

8. *Gannan junmin lianhe er ci yundong dahui tekan*, photos before 1.

9. *Gannan junmin lianhe er ci yundong dahui tekan*, 2.

10. Benjamin Yang, *From Revolution to Politics: Chinese Communists on the Long March* (Boulder, Colo.: Westview Press, 1990), 69–70.

11. *Gannan junmin lianhe er ci yundong dahui tekan*, "Jiangpin" section, 1–4.

12. Ye Yuanlong, "Ye xu," 2.

13. Li Lixian, "Yunnan quansheng yundong dahui jixiang," *Qinfen tiyu yue-bao* 3.5 (February 1936), 438–41; "1900 nian—1949 nian Yunnan sheng tiyu dashi," *Yunnan tiyu wenshi* 10 (December 1988), 43.

14. Hung-Mao Tien, *Government and Politics in Kuomintang China, 1927–1937* (Stanford, Calif.: Stanford University Press, 1972), 97–103.

15. Zhao Botao, "Shengsili zhongdeng xuexiao qiuji yundonghui xu," in

Chahar sheng ershisan nian zhongdeng xuexiao qiuji yundong dahui choubei weiyuanhui, *Chahar sheng ershisan nian zhongdeng xuexiao qiuji yundong dahui zongbaogao,* 1.

16. Tien, *Government and Politics,* 156.

17. These eight were joined on the provincial team by eight Guizhou natives studying in Shanghai. In Guizhou sheng di yi jie quansheng yundonghui choubei weiyuanhui, *Guizhou sheng di yi jie quansheng yundonghui zong-baogao,* 95–96.

18. Xiao Guipei, "Jianguo qian Xinjiang sheng di yi jie yundonghui ji bufen tiyu huodong gaikuang," *Xinjiang tiyu shiliao* 1 (1985), 44; "Jianguo qian Xinjiang canjia di wu, liu, qi jie Quanguo yundonghui jianjie," *Xinjiang tiyu shiliao* 2 (1985), 10.

19. In the 1930s, these Huabei Games were joined by teams representing Shandong, Henan, Hebei, Shanxi, Shaanxi, Gansu, Liaoning, Jilin, Heilongjiang, Rehe, Suiyuan, Chahar, Beiping, Tianjin, Qingdao, Harbin, and Weihaiwei.

20. Following his ascent to power upon his father's death in 1928, Zhang quickly began working to spread modern physical culture in Liaoning. He began his first address to students at his Northeastern University by proclaiming, "The first thing I want to say to you today is to work for the cause of physical fitness." That same year, Zhang established a Department of Physical Education at Northeastern, staffing it with the most famed of national *tiyu* elites, and sponsored an international meet in Shenyang, inviting top Japanese and French track and field teams to join the competition, and carefully filming these foreign experts' skills and techniques for use in training Chinese athletes. *Shengjing shibao,* 18 September 1928, reprinted in *Zhang Xueliang jiangjun ziliaoxuan: Liaoning wenshi ziliao di shiba ji,* ed. Zhongguo renmin zhengzhi xieshang huiyi Liaoning sheng weiyuanhui and Wenshi ziliao yanjiu weiyuanhui (Shenyang: Liaoning renmin chubanshe, 1986), 158; Zhao Shouren, "Zhang Xueliang jiangjun yu Dongbei xiandai tiyu de xingqi," *Tiyu wenshi* 25 (June 1987), 51; Wang Zhenya, *Jiu Zhongguo tiyu jianwen* (Beijing: Renmin tiyu chubanshe, 1987), 11.

21. Zhao Shouren, "Zhang Xueliang jiangjun yu Dongbei xiandai tiyu," 51.

22. Interview with Dong Hanwen and Li Shiming, Beitou, Taiwan, 13 June 1996.

23. *Di shiwu jie Huabei yundonghui* (Ji'nan, 1931), "Tici" section, 1–2, "Dahui" section, 75–79.

24. "Huabei yundong chengji jinbu zhi kexi," *Shenghuo zhoukan* 6.24 (6 June 1931), 485.

25. Chunsheng, "Huabei yundonghui yu tichang tiyu zhong zhi cuowu guannian," *Beifang gonglun* 83 (1 November 1934), 11–12.

26. Guojia tiwei tiyu wenshi gongzuo weiyuanhui and Quanguo tizong wenshi ziliao bianshen weiyuanhui, eds., *Tiyu shiliao di 15 ji: Huabei yundonghui (1913–1934 nian)* (Beijing: Renmin tiyu chubanshe, 1989), 214; Liu Shipan, "Zaoqi Nankai tiyu shihua," *Tianjin tiyu shiliao* 6 (December 1985), 12.

27. Interview with Li Shiming and Dong Hanwen, 14 June 1996.

28. The Central China Games were convened six times between 1923 and 1936, with teams from Anhui, Hubei, Hunan, and Jiangxi provinces. A 1936 film made by the Central Military Commission made similar points about the regional character and national importance of this meet. Junshi weiyuanhui zhengxun chu dianying gu, prod., *Huazhong yundonghui di liu jie* (1936), film.

29. The Northwest Games were held once (Yinchuan, Ningxia, 1933), sponsored by Ningxia Provincial Chairman Ma Hongkui. These games featured teams from seven Northwest provinces—Ningxia, Qinghai, Gansu, Xinjiang, Suiyuan, Shaanxi, and Shanxi—and followed very orthodox Nationalist formulas for the planning of official meets, with several figures from the Beiping and Tianjin sporting communities recruited to plan the games. "Xibei yundonghui jianzhang ji jingsai guicheng," *Tiyu zhoubao* 2.24 (22 July 1933), 2.

30. Richard L. Jen, "The Changing Sports Page in the Chinese Press," *Chinese Republic* 3.15 (12 August 1933), 347, 353.

31. For example, some 325,000 *yuan* (U.S.$110,000) was spent to hold the Eighteenth Huabei Games in Tianjin in 1934, the majority paying for the new fifty-acre athletic grounds at Beining Park. Yu Henian, "Di shiba jie Huabei yundonghui jiyao," *Hebei yuekan* 2.11 (November 1934), 3; Dai Shizeng and Zhao Yafu, "Hebei sheng tiyuchang—Tianjin shi Beizhan tiyuchang xiujian shimo," *Tianjin tiyu shiliao* 5 (July 1985), 8–9.

32. Chen Xiping, "Zhongyang tiyuchang choujian shimo ji," *Zhongguo jianzhu* 1.3 (September 1933), 1; Xia Xingshi, "Zhongyang tiyuchang gaikuang," *Zhongguo jianzhu* 1.3 (September 1933), 8.

33. Liping Wang, "Creating a National Symbol: The Sun Yatsen Memorial in Nanjing," *Republican China* 21.2 (April 1996), 40–48.

34. Chu Minyi, "Quanguo yundong dahui choubei jingguo," *Qinfen tiyu yuebao* 1.2 (10 November 1933), 19.

35. The track stadium alone accommodated thirty-five thousand spectators. Xia Xingshi, "Zhongyang tiyuchang gaikuang," 17–24; Chu Minyi, "Quanguo yundong dahui choubei jingguo," 20.

36. Quoted in Pan Guxi, ed., *Nanjing de jianzhu* (Nanjing: Nanjing chubanshe, 1995), 115.

37. "Youguan zhengqiu Yijiusanyi nian Quanguo yundong dahui geci de wenjian," File 587 (10), Folder 5, Document 160, Second Historical Archives, Nanjing, China.

38. The committee later asked the famed linguist Zhao Yuanren, Tang Xueyong, and Du Tingxiu to compose scores to match these lyrics and selected Zhao's entry. File 587 (10), Folder 5, Documents 252 and 473, Second Historical Archives, Nanjing, China.

39. Min, "Quanyun yu shuizai," *Tiyu xinsheng* 1 (October 1931), 25.

40. Cai Zongxian narration, transcribed by An Yongxin and Fang Ruji, "Xinjiang di yi ci pai ren canjia Quanguo yundonghui," *Xinjiang tiyu shiliao* 1 (1985), 42–43.

41. Ma Chonggan, "Di wu jie Quanguo yundonghui zhi huigu," *Shenbao yuekan* 2.11 (15 November 1933): 77.

42. Planners expected delegations from all thirty provinces (including Mongolia and Tibet), seven municipalities (Nanjing, Shanghai, Qingdao, Tianjin, Hankou, Hong Kong, Harbin), and Chinese contingents from Java, Honolulu, Singapore, and the Philippines. "Minguo ershi nian Quanguo yundong dahui jingsai guicheng," *Jiaoyubu gongbao* 3.12 (29 March 1931), 59.

43. "Yijiusanyi nian Quanguo yundong dahui choubei weiyuanhui jieshu yijiao de wenjian," File 587 (10), Folder 9, Second Historical Archives, Nanjing, China.

44. The biggest rush at the fences came with the mass tai chi calisthenics demonstration at noon, when Boy Scouts had to save several would-be spectators trampled by the crowds. "Nanking Games Stampede," *North-China Daily News*, 11 October 1933, 12; Peng Zhou, "Di wu jie Quanguo yundong dahui ji," *Xin Zhonghua* 1.21 (10 November 1933), 34.

45. In his speech, Dai Jitao thanked Chiang for his message from the "bandit extermination battlefields." Ershier nian Quanguo yundong dahui choubei weiyuanhui, ed., *Ershier nian Quanguo yundong dahui zongbaogao shu* (Shanghai: Zhonghua shuju, 1934), sec. 2, 3–4.

46. Zhao, "Bianqu tichang tiyu zhi kunnan," in *Baihong tianjingsaidui jiniankan* (Shanghai: Baihong tianjingdui, 1931), 87.

47. "Yi yue lai zhi tiyu jie," *Qinfen tiyu yuebao* 1.3 (10 December 1933), 75; Fang Xiebang, "Qinghai jinxiandai tiyu fengyun renwu lu," *Qinghai tiyu shiliao* 1 (June 1987), 106–7.

48. Only Guangxi, Chahar, and Xikang provinces did not send teams. Ershier nian Quanguo yundong dahui choubei weiyuanhui, *Ershier nian Quanguo yundong dahui zongbaogao shu*, sec. 2, 22.

49. See Andrew Morris, "Native Songs and Dances: Southeast Asia in a Greater Chinese Sporting Community, 1920–1948," *Journal of Southeast Asian Studies* 31.1 (March 2000), 57–69.

50. Ershier nian Quanguo yundong dahui choubei weiyuanhui, *Ershier nian Quanguo yundong dahui zongbaogao shu*, sec. 2, 180.

51. Ma Chonggan, "Di wu jie Quanguo yundonghui zhi huigu," 78.

52. Ma Chonggan, "Di wu jie Quanguo yundonghui zhi huigu," 78.

53. Ma Chonggan, "Di wu jie Quanguo yundonghui zhi huigu," 77.

54. *Quanguo nü yundongyuan mingjiang lu* (Shanghai: Qinfen shuju, 1936), 4.

55. Qian's sporting efforts for her nation were repaid in cruel fashion. In 1950, she began coaching physical education at Fudan University in Shanghai, but in April 1968, during the havoc of the Cultural Revolution, she was killed for having been a star in this bourgeois realm of sport. Gemin, "Yidai tianjing nüjie—Qian Xingsu," *Shanghai tiyu shihua* 12 (December 1985), 42.

56. Wang Zhenya, *Jiu Zhongguo tiyu jianwen*, 159–60.

57. In 1936, Yang would be the star attraction at a Shanghai Aviation Association Swim Meet held to raise money to buy warplanes in honor of Chiang Kai-shek's birthday. In 1937, she married star Shanghai jockey Tao Bolin, and the couple left for Hong Kong at the outbreak of war soon after. Cheng Jinguan,

a classmate of Tao's at Fudan University High School, visited the couple in Hong Kong during and after the war and remembered Tao's violence that prompted Yang to divorce him and emigrate to Canada in 1947. "Yang Xiuqiong zuo pingqi de yaochuan," *Qinfen tiyu yuebao* 1.3 (10 December 1933), 75; Yiru, "Jiangxi shuishang yundonghui," *Qinfen tiyu yuebao* 1.11 (10 August 1934), 26–29; Fujian sheng difangzhi bianzuan weiyuanhui, ed., *Fujian shengzhi: Tiyu zhi* (Fuzhou: Fujian renmin chubanshe, 1993), 134; Wu Ningxing and Gu Qingfang, "'Meirenyu' quanjia Jinling yongtan xianji ji," *Jiangsu tiyu wenshi* 6 (January 1988), 49–50; "Yi yue lai zhi yundong bisai," *Qinfen tiyu yuebao* 3.10 (July 1936), 949; Feng Shaoer, "'Meirenyu' Yang Xiuqiong zai Shanghai," *Shanghai tiyu shihua* 24 (September 1989), 48; Interview with Cheng Jinguan, 3 March 1997, Suzhou, China.

58. The Hunan delegation boasted the highest turnout of loyal participants. Ershier nian Quanguo yundong dahui choubei weiyuanhui, *Ershier nian Quanguo yundong dahui zongbaogao shu*, sec. 2, 176.

59. Ershier nian Quanguo yundong dahui choubei weiyuanhui, *Ershier nian Quanguo yundong dahui zongbaogao shu*, sec. 3, 55–60, 29–30.

60. *Minguo ershier nian Quanguo yundonghui zhuankan* (Shanghai: Shidai tushu gongsi, 1933).

61. Peng Zhou, "Di wu jie Quanguo yundong dahui ji," 38.

62. Ershier nian Quanguo yundong dahui choubei weiyuanhui, *Ershier nian Quanguo yundong dahui zongbaogao shu*, sec. 2, 80.

63. Ma Chonggan, "Di wu jie Quanguo yundonghui zhi huigu," 80; Peng Zhou, "Di wu jie Quanguo yundong dahui ji," 35–36.

64. Chen Jianxiao, "Quanguo yundonghui de jiaoxun," *Xiandai xuesheng* 3.2 (November 1933), 6.

65. The Shanxi runner Gu Desheng, the second-place finisher, was later awarded the championship, but on the Jiangsu delegation leader's request, an unofficial "rematch" was held on the last day of the meet between the top three finishers. Before an over-capacity crowd of some fifty thousand fans, Jin won the rematch and with it the "Sportsmanlike Struggle" (*junzi zhi zheng*) cup donated for this race by the *Xinwenbao* press. Yan Duhe, "Junzi zhi zheng," *Xinwenbao*, 19 October 1933, reprinted in Ershier nian Quanguo yundong dahui choubei weiyuanhui, *Ershier nian Quanguo yundong dahui zongbaogao shu*, sec. 4, 189; Wang Zhenya, *Jiu Zhongguo tiyu jianwen*, 160.

66. Shu Sheng-min, "Sportsmanship and Playing the Game," *Chinese Republic* 4.4 (14 April 1934), 81, 94–95.

67. Chen Jianxiao, "Quanguo yundonghui de jiaoxun," 6–8.

68. Wu Yunrui, "Duiyu Zhongyang tiyuchang jianzhu fangmian zhi piping," in Ershier nian Quanguo yundong dahui choubei weiyuanhui, *Ershier nian Quanguo yundong dahui zongbaogao shu*, sec. 4, 176–77.

69. Chu Minyi, "Fuxing minzu yu tichang tiyu," *Hubei jiaoyu yuekan* 5 (January 1934), 15.

70. Zhang Yuanruo, "Guofang yu tiyu," *Fuxing yuekan* 2.3 (1 November 1933): 1. Ershier nian Quanguo yundong dahui choubei weiyuanhui, *Ershier*

nian Quanguo yundong dahui zongbaogao shu, sec. 3, 47, gives the expense figure.

71. Shi Nong, "Shijie tiyu de xin qushi," *Guoshu, tiyu, junshi* 3 (2 November 1933) [Weekly feature in *Zhongguo ribao*], 8.

72. "Po quanguo? Quanguo xin? Luo Jialun tanhua, Xiaozu de yijian," *Tiyu pinglun* 54 (21 October 1933), 161.

73. For reasons of space I do not provide details on the Sixth National Games, held in Shanghai, 10–20 October 1935. In July 1935 the Games Planning Committee took out a 3.5 million–*yuan* loan from the Central Government, this sum including the costs of building Jiangwan Stadium at what was to be the new civic center in the northeast reaches of Shanghai. This immense stadium, built to hold sixty thousand spectators, still functions today and in 1993 hosted the First East Asian Games.

Some 2,285 athletes (1649 male, 636 female) represented thirty-eight provinces at this meet, with teams representing Guangxi, Xikang, Chahar, Mongolia, Tibet, and Malaya joining for the first time. Several new men's demonstration events were added for these games as well: polo, speedwalking, weightlifting, diving, mini-soccer, cycling, ping-pong, and Mongolian wrestling. These would be the last National Games held until 1948; the Seventh National Games, scheduled for Nanjing 1937, were canceled with the outbreak of total war with Japan. Xing, "Di liu jie Quanguo yundonghui jilüe," *Shenbao yuekan* 4.11 (15 November 1935), 123; "Di liu jie Quanguo yundonghui jiyao," *Jiaoyu zazhi* 25.12 (10 December 1935), 109–18; "Gezhong biaoyan," *Qinfen tiyu yuebao* 3.2 (November 1935), 209–12; Wang Zhenya, *Jiu Zhongguo tiyu jianwen,* 161–75.

74. "Di jiu jie Yuandong yundonghui zhi huigu," *Jiaoyu zazhi* 22.6 (20 June 1930), 233.

75. The one exception to this trend was in soccer, where Chinese teams, almost always made up of Hong Kong all-stars, won nine of the ten FECG titles from 1913 to 1934.

76. Chen Xianming, Liang Youde, and Du Kehe, *Zhongguo bangqiu yundongshi* (Wuhan: Wuhan chubanshe, 1990), 30.

77. Extra Public Security officers were hired for one reception, after it was rumored that Communists were plotting a disturbance of some sort for the evening. "Chinese Athletes in Shanghai," *North-China Daily News,* 14 April 1930, 16; "Athletics," *North-China Daily News,* 9 May 1930, 16.

78. "Chinese Team off for Japan," *North-China Daily News,* 16 May 1930, 18; Interview with Cheng Jinguan, 2 March 1997, Suzhou, China.

79. This four-man Indian team, their first FECG delegation, was the focus of the most noteworthy event of this meet—a protracted diplomatic struggle over which "Indian" flag (the Indian National Congress banner or the Union Jack) would fly over Meiji Stadium. The Indians were eventually forced to march behind a Union Jack, but they won praise from Chinese observers for their nationalist spirit. "Trouble-Makers in Japan," *North-China Daily News,* 23 May 1930, 11; "Di jiu jie Yuandong yundonghui zhi huigu," 233, 241; *Di*

jiu jie Yuandong yundonghui (Shanghai: Liangyou tushu yinhua youxian gongsi, 1930), 3, 54.

80. After the China-Japan title game ended in a tie, the Chinese wanted to play into overtime to determine a true champion, but the Japanese team and Japanese referees maintained that the game was over, no doubt pleased to escape with a tie with the traditionally strong Chinese footballers.

81. Interview with Cheng Jinguan, 2 March 1997, Suzhou, China.

82. "Di jiu jie Yuandong yundonghui zhi huigu," 241; *Di jiu jie Yuandong yundonghui,* 52.

83. Qin Jin, quoted in Yuri, "Zhong-Ri Yuandong juesui shi," *Tiyu wenshi* 42 (March 1990), 48.

84. "Di jiu jie Yuandong yundonghui zhi huigu," 241.

85. "Yuandong yundong dahui Zhong-Ri-Fei choubei qingxing," *Qinfen tiyu yuebao* 1.7 (10 April 1934), 52.

86. Zhou Dingchang, "Yuandong yundonghui Zhong-Ri-Fei changhui jingguo," *Qinfen tiyu yuebao* 1.8 (10 May 1934), 13–14; "Dispute over Olympics," *New York Times,* 10 April 1934, 16; "Japanese Ultimatum Is Expected in Manchukuoan Issue—Manila Firm in Olympics Row," *New York Times,* 15 April 1934, 24.

87. The only teams not selected on the basis of direct competition were the swim team, the selection of whose members was simply entrusted to the Hong Kong Swimming Federation, and the tennis team, to which Shanghai's Qiu Feihai, Singapore's Lin Wangsu, and Indonesia's Xu Chengji were directly selected by CNAAF officials. Guo Yungong, "Yuandong yundonghui Quanguo yuxuan ji," *Qinfen tiyu yuebao* 1.8 (10 May 1934), 19–20.

88. A saying in 1930s sports circles used to describe the state of sprinting in China was "Cheng in the south, and Liu in the north" (*nan Cheng bei Liu*).

89. Interview with Cheng Jinguan, 2 March 1997, Suzhou, China.

90. Cheng Jinguan won the one-hundred-meter (10.9 seconds) and two-hundred-meter (22.6) races to lead the Chinese team. Pin Chen, "Woguo Yuandong tianjing xuanshou duikang Xilian chengji," *Qinfen tiyu yuebao* 1.8 (10 May 1934), 51–52.

91. Interview with Cheng Jinguan, 2 March 1997, Suzhou, China.

92. You Yinzu, "Yuanyun qianjing (Ma-ni-la tongxin)," *Renyan zhoukan* 16 (26 May 1934), 324.

93. Interview with Cheng Jinguan, 2–3 March 1997, Suzhou, China.

94. The Chinese women's swim team, led by Hong Kong phenom Yang "The Mermaid" Xiuqiong, "shocked the Philippine islands" with their victory in the women's swimming demonstration event. Ma Chonggan, "Di shi jie Yuandong yundonghui huigu," *Shenbao yuekan* 3.6 (15 June 1934), 40.

95. The Indonesian soccer team included five ethnic Chinese players, moving one author to describe them as "talent from our nation being employed by another (*Chu cai Jin yong,* literally "talent of the Chu kingdom being employed by the Jin")—what a pity that they cannot fight for glory for the nation!" You Yinzu, "Yuanyun qianjing," 323.

96. "China, Japan All Even in Far East Olympics," *New York Times*, 14 May 1934, 22; Wang Zhenya, *Jiu Zhongguo tiyu jianwen*, 218.

97. "Rain Washes out Olympic Games," *North-China Daily News*, 18 May 1934, 14.

98. "New Quarrel Mars Opening of Far Eastern Olympic Games," *North-China Daily News*, 14 May 1934, 12; "Victorious March of Filipinos," *North-China Daily News*, 16 May 1934, 13; "Riotous Scene at Far Eastern Games," *North-China Daily News*, 20 May 1934, 17.

99. Jizhe, "Yuandong tiyu xiehui feifa jiesan zhi jingguo," *Qinfen tiyu yuebao* 1.9 (10 June 1934), 71–72.

100. Chinese observers rightfully found it ironic that the Japanese had clung to Article 3 for dear life when it was proposed in 1930 that Korea join the Far Eastern organization. Richard L. Jen, "Japan's Manila 'Stunt' and What It Means," *China Weekly Review* 69.3 (16 June 1934), 104; Wu Hongyi, "Yuandong tiyu xiehui jiesan," *Shidai gonglun* 3.9 (25 May 1934), 23.

101. Jizhe, "Yuandong tiyu xiehui feifa jiesan," 72; "The Passing of the F. E. Olympic Association," *Chinese Affairs* 5.24 (30 May 1934), 392.

102. "Chuxi Yuanyunhui ge daibiao tanhua," *Qinfen tiyu yuebao* 1.9 (10 June 1934), 9. After Japan had gotten its way, Consul Kimura received a death threat, informing him (in Chinese) that he would be killed in Cervantes Plaza in front of the Consulate. "Threat to Assassinate Japanese Consul at Manila," *China Weekly Review* 69.1 (2 June 1934), 7.

103. Hao Gengsheng, *Hao Gengsheng huiyi lu* (Taibei: Zhuanji wenxue chubanshe, 1969), 36.

104. Philippines President Quezon offered a personal apology to Wang Zhengting, and the *Manila Daily* opined that the decision was "cowardly and devoid of faith." "Chuxi Yuanyunhui ge daibiao tanhua," 8–9; "Manchukuo Recognized—Public Is Critical," *New York Times*, 22 May 1934, 41; Jizhe, "Yuandong tiyu xiehui feifa jiesan," 74.

105. This new association was to include Japan, the Philippines, Manzhouguo, Indonesia, India, Vietnam, and Malaya, and an invitation was extended to China as well. The first AAAO Games were planned for Tokyo, 1938, and Philippines President Quezon was nominated to serve as AAAO honorary chairman. "A Dramatic Move Concludes Olympic Games," *North-China Daily News*, 22 May 1934, 12; Jizhe, "Yuandong tiyu xiehui feifa jiesan," 74; Jen, "Japan's Manila 'Stunt,'" 104.

106. Hao Gengsheng, *Hao Gengsheng huiyilu*, 37.

107. "Dr. C. T. Wang Says Dissolution of Far Eastern Athletic Association Is Illegal," *China Weekly Review* 69.1 (2 June 1934), 7; "F. E. Games Quarrel Not Yet Over," *North-China Daily News*, 24 May 1934, 13; Wu Hongyi, "Yuandong tiyu xiehui jiesan," 23.

108. Wu Hongyi, "Yuandong tiyu xiehui jiesan," 23.

109. "Passing of the F. E. Olympic Association," 392.

110. Ma Chonggan, "Di shi jie Yuandong yundonghui huigu," 41.

111. Zhuang Zexuan, "Yuandong tixie de jiesan shi Zhongguo de qichi daru," *Shenbao*, 25 May 1934, 14.

112. Only once, at the Second Games held in Shanghai in 1915, did the Chinese team win the overall championship.

113. Song Ruhai, *Wo neng bi ya: Shijie yundonghui conglu* (Shanghai: Shangwu yinshuguan, 1930), preface 1.

114. Song Ruhai, *Wo neng bi ya*.

115. John J. MacAloon, *This Great Symbol: Pierre de Coubertin and the Origins of the Modern Olympic Games* (Chicago: University of Chicago Press, 1981), 137.

116. Li Sheng, "Di yi ge daibiao Zhongguo canjia Aoyunhui bisai de Liu Changchun," *Tiyu wenshi* 5 (February 1984), 34; Liu Changchun, "Wo daibiao Zhongguo canjia Di shi jie Aoyunhui shimo," in *Aoyunhui yu Zhongguo*, ed. Ji Hongmin, Yu Xingmao, and Lü Changfu (Beijing: Wenshi ziliao chubanshe, 1985), 57–88; Interview with Dong Hanwen, 4 June 1996, Taipei, Taiwan.

117. Jizhe, "Liu Changchun chuxi Shijiehui zhi yunniang," *Tiyu zhoubao* 23 (9 July 1932), 18.

118. The International Olympic Committee saw no problem with the participation of this puppet government, merely stating that Manzhouguo would have to wait, along with Afghanistan, for official IOC recognition of their nation. The IOC also asked Manzhouguo officials to submit their national flag and anthem for use in Los Angeles. *New York Times*, 26 May 1932, 32; "Wei xuanshou chuxi Shijiehui," *Tiyu zhoubao* 20 (18 June 1932), 1; "Weiguo xuanshou chuchang wenti," *Tiyu zhoubao* 20 (18 June 1932), 19.

119. Wang Guan, "Guanyu weiguo de qianpai Yu Liu ji qita," *Tiyu zhoubao* 20 (18 June 1932), 18–19.

120. Liu Changchun, "Wo daibiao Zhongguo," 64.

121. A rejoicing *Sporting Weekly* published a file photo of Liu over the caption, "Liu Changchun, who will not be a puppet." "Liu Changchun zishu," *Tiyu zhoubao* 20 (18 June 1932), 20.

122. Shi Ji, "Zhongguo canjia Di shi jie Aoyunhui jingguo," *Tiyu wenshi* 5 (February 1984), 16.

123. Zhou was a former secretary to Zhang Xueliang, and his son Zhou Changxing was also a standout athlete during the early 1930s. Interview with Dong Hanwen, November 1995, Taipei, Taiwan.

124. Liu Changchun, "Wo daibiao Zhongguo," 66.

125. Interview with Li Shiming, 17 May 1996, Taipei, Taiwan; Hu Shiliu, "Di shi jie Shijie yundong dahui ji," *Shenbao yuekan* 1.3 (15 September 1932), 121.

126. "Ben jie Ou-lin-pi-ke yundong dahui zhi qianzhan (xu ba)," *Tiyu zhoubao* 26 (30 July 1932), 22.

127. "Ben jie Ou-lin-pi-ke yundong dahui zhi qianzhan," 22.

128. Liu led after the first fifty meters in his one-hundred-meter heat on 31 July and led after 150 meters in his two-hundred-meter heat on 2 August before faltering at the end of both races. "Liu Changchun de riji," *Tiyu zhoubao*

32 (10 September 1932), 21–22; Hu Shiliu, "Di shi jie Shijie yundong dahui ji," 122.

129. "Liu Changchun de riji," 23.

130. "Liu Changchun de riji," 23.

131. David B. Welky, "Viking Girls, Mermaids, and Little Brown Men: U.S. Journalism and the 1932 Olympics," *Journal of Sport History* 24.1 (Spring 1997), 39–41.

132. Hu Shiliu, "Di shi jie Shijie yundong dahui ji," 117; "Liu Changchun bei shou huanying," *Tiyu zhoubao* 27 (6 August 1932), 1.

133. Jizhe, "Liu Changchun chuxi Shijiehui," 18–19.

134. "Liu Changchun bei shou huanying," 1.

135. "Quanguo tixiehui jihua canjia Shijie yundonghui gexiang banfa," *Shishi xinbao,* 5 November 1934, reprinted in *Jiaoyu zazhi* 25.1 (10 January 1935), 423.

136. A five-week Summer Physical Education Lecture Series and a five-day Summer Physical Education Conference were also scheduled in conjunction with the Olympic Training Camp. "Shuqi tiyu taolunhui guicheng," *Qinfen tiyu yuebao* 2.9 (June 1935), 624–27; "Shuqi tiyu jiangxihui guicheng," *Qinfen tiyu yuebao* 2.9 (June 1935), 627–29; File Number 53–1–2216, Zhejiang Provincial Archives, 2–26.

137. Interviews with Dong Hanwen, November 1995, 10 and 17 May 1996, Taipei, Taiwan; Qu Ziqing, *Zhongguo lanqiu shihua* (Taibei: Weihua tiyu xunkanshe, 1961), 17.

138. Olga Lang, *Chinese Family and Society* (New Haven, Conn.: Yale University Press, 1946), 184.

139. "Shuqi tiyu xunlianhui guicheng," *Qinfen tiyu yuebao* 2.9 (June 1935), 633–35.

140. Li broke the 2:05 standard in the eight hundred meters again on 3 August. However, he failed to qualify for the two-hundred-meter dash and the javelin after several trials in each event. "Yi yue lai zhi yundong bisai," *Qinfen tiyu yuebao* 2.12 (September 1935), 839–40.

141. "Yi yue lai zhi yundong bisai," *Qinfen tiyu yuebao* 3.10 (July 1936), 948.

142. *Chuxi Di shiyi jie Shijie yundonghui Zhonghua daibiaotuan baogao* (Shanghai: Zhonghua quanguo tiyu xiejinhui, 1937), sec. 1, 5.

143. Li, running the four hundred and eight hundred meters, won two gold medals in 1933 and two silvers in 1934, finishing second in both events to life-long friend and almost-Olympian Yu Xiwei. Interview with Li Shiming, 17 May 1996, Taipei, Taiwan; "Li ci wei Man yundonghui chengji," *Jilin tiyu shiliao* 1983.2 (October 1983), 32.

144. For more information on the Manzhouguo *tiyu* project and the dilemmas faced by athletes like Li, see Andrew Morris, "Cultivating the National Body: A History of Physical Culture in Republican China" (Ph.D. diss., University of California, San Diego, 1998), 555–62.

145. Qiao Ji, "Weiguo tiyu jinkuang yi shu," *Tiyu zhoubao* 2.20 (24 June 1933), 7.

146. History was repeated for Li in 1937 when Beiping fell to the Japanese. He chose to stay, eventually joining and captaining the "national" track team sponsored by the Wang Jingwei regime in eastern China.

147. Many in the Shanghai sporting establishment were less than thrilled about the Hong Kong carpetbaggers' complete appropriation of the soccer entry. Several Shanghai papers published items from the European press questioning the amateur status of the Hong Kong team, whose members allegedly "were receiving 'retainers' from undisclosed sources to enable them to play football." "What Is an Amateur?" *Illustrated Week-End Sporting World* 10.43 (9 May 1936), 5.

148. The team won twenty-three of the matches, tying four and losing none, and outscoring their opponents 113–27. *Chuxi Di shiyi jie Shijie yundonghui,* sec. 1, 8–9.

149. The boxers trained with a British coach and Chen Hanqiang, an Austrian Chinese who came to China after reigning as European light middleweight champion. *Chuxi Di shiyi jie Shijie yundonghui,* sec. 1, 10.

150. *Chuxi Di shiyi jie Shijie yundonghui,* sec. 1, 16.

151. *Chuxi Di shiyi jie Shijie yundonghui,* sec. 1, 17–18; Interview with Cheng Jinguan, Suzhou, China, 2 March 1997.

152. *Chuxi Di shiyi jie Shijie yundonghui,* sec. 1, 18–19.

153. *Chuxi Di shiyi jie Shijie yundonghui,* sec. 1, 21.

154. Chen Yongsheng, *Ouzhou tiyu kaocha riji* (Shanghai: Nansheng chubanshe, 1938), 7.

155. Interview with Cheng Jinguan, Suzhou, China, 2 March 1997.

156. Chen Yongsheng, *Ouzhou tiyu kaocha riji,* 31–34.

157. Chen Yongsheng, *Ouzhou tiyu kaocha riji,* 36; *Chuxi Di shiyi jie Shijie yundonghui,* sec. 1, 24.

158. Interview with Cheng Jinguan, Suzhou, China, 2 March 1997.

159. Lin Yin-feng, "Weekly Interviews—Mr. Williams Z. L. Sung," *China Critic* 15.1 (1 October 1936): 18.

160. The Olympic trip was funded by a 170,000 *yuan* central government grant, plus 30,568.88 *yuan* (U.S.$9,230) from twenty-eight donors, including Chen Jitang, Wu Tiecheng, Bai Chongxi, Li Zongren, Yang Sen, Yan Xishan, He Yingqin, Dai Jitao, Chen Yi, and several Chinese in Southeast Asia and Europe. *Chuxi Di shiyi jie Shijie yundonghui,* sec. 1, 2–3.

161. Jiang Huaiqing, "Bo-lin mian qu ba!" *Guomin tiyu huikan* 1 (1 January 1936), 19.

162. Lin Yin-feng, "Weekly Interviews," 18–19.

163. Ambassador Cheng Tianfang seems to be returning the gesture in another photo taken at the station. *Chuxi Di shiyi jie Shijie yundonghui,* sec. 1, 25; Interview with Cheng Jinguan, Suzhou, China, 2 March 1997.

164. *Chuxi Di shiyi jie Shijie yundonghui,* sec. 1, 33.

165. Interview with Cheng Jinguan, Suzhou, China, 2 March 1997.

166. This author also expressed solidarity with the Jewish members of the American Olympic Committee who quit the body as a protest against Germany's

ban on German Jews' participation in the games. He also pointed out sardonically that the hurdles and other iron sports equipment used in these Olympics
were manufactured by the Krupp Corporation, which also produced the German tanks that terrorized so many in Europe. Suizhi, "Di shiyi jie Shijie yundonghui de jingguo jiqi tezhi," *Zhongxuesheng* 67 (September 1936), 65.

167. Ma Chonggan, "Di shiyi jie Shijie yundonghui gaishu," *Shenbao
zhoukan* 1.33 (23 August 1926), 792.

168. Unfortunately for the former Olympian, a substantial anti-Cheng
campaign was begun in Suzhou, persecuting him for having served as a "foreign spy." The proof, of course, was that he had been to Japan, the Philippines,
and Germany and had seen Hitler, Goebbels, and Japanese fascist and Philippine
collaborationist officials with his own eyes! Before the campaign got too far, in
1969 Cheng and his wife were sent to Xiangshui County in northeast Jiangsu
for two years. Cheng had to render incomplete his commemorative set of
Olympic photo cards by burning one Hitler card but was able to stash other
photos and clippings in friends' homes. He was also able to keep his Olympic
necktie; no one noticed that his son wore it for years as a belt. Interview with
Cheng Jinguan, Suzhou, China, 2 March 1997.

169. "Editorial Commentary," *T'ien Hsia Monthly* 3.2 (September 1936), 86.

170. Interview with Cheng Jinguan, Suzhou, China, 2 March 1997.

171. China's greatest basketball honor at Berlin was that Shu Hong, assistant coach for the Chinese Olympic team (also a Springfield College graduate
and Zhejiang University Physical Education Director), was selected to officiate
the basketball gold medal contest. (The United States defeated Canada, 12–8.)
Qu Ziqing, *Zhongguo lanqiu shihua*, 19.

172. *Chuxi Di shiyi jie Shijie yundonghui*, sec. 1, 34–40.

173. *Chuxi Di shiyi jie Shijie yundonghui*, sec. 1, 19, 23, 29–30.

174. "Yi yue lai zhi tiyu xingzheng," *Qinfen tiyu yuebao* 2.12 (September
1935), 837.

175. *Chuxi Di shiyi jie Shijie yundonghui*, sec. 1, 42.

176. *Chuxi Di shiyi jie Shijie yundonghui*, sec. 1, 37–38, 44.

177. "Echo of Olympic Sportsmanship," *Illustrated Week-End Sporting
World* 10.58 (22 August 1936), 4.

178. Suizhi, "Di shiyi jie Shijie yundonghui," 65–66.

179. "Editorial Commentary," 85.

180. Suizhi, "Di shiyi jie Shijie yundonghui," 66.

181. Interview with Cheng Jinguan, Suzhou, China, 2 March 1997; Suizhi,
"Di shiyi jie Shijie yundonghui," 62.

182. Fengshen, "Di shiyi jie Shijie yundonghui de niaokan," *Zhongwai
yuekan* 1.9 (1 October 1936), 127–30.

183. Tong Zhixuan, "Shiyunhui Zhongguodui shibai hou guoren duiyu tiyu
yingyou zhi renshi yu nuli," *Jiao yu xue* 2.3 (1 September 1936), 13.

184. "Editorial Commentary," 86, 85.

185. Zhao Baozhong, "Jiji de jiankang jiaoyu," *Shanxi minzhong jiaoyu*
3.5–6 (15 October 1936), 1–3.

186. Zhang Junjun, *Huazu suzhi zhi jiantao* (Chongqing: Shangwu yin-shuguan, 1943), 6. This discussion is also cited in Lung-Kee Sun, *The Chinese National Character: From Nationhood to Individuality* (Armonk, N.Y.: M. E. Sharpe, 2002), 172.

187. "Shijie yundongchang shang zhi yingjie," *Zhonghua yuebao* 4.7 (1 July 1936), 6–8.

188. "The Life for an Athlete," *China Critic* 14.12 (17 September 1936), 275.

189. Xie Siyan, "Woguo canjia ben jie Shiyunhui shibai hou de jiaoxun," *Tiyu* 4.11 (30 November 1936), 4.

190. "China and the Next Olympiad," *Illustrated Week-End Sporting World* 10.61 (12 September 1936), 3.

191. Chang Bo, "Cong Shiyunhui dedao de jiaoxun," *Kang-Zang qianfeng* 3.12 (August 1936), 13.

192. Chang Bo, "Cong Shiyunhui dedao de jiaoxun," 14.

CHAPTER 7. FROM MARTIAL ARTS TO NATIONAL SKILLS

1. Lin Boyuan, "Zhongguo jindai qianqi wushujia xiang chengshi de yidong yiji dui wushu liupai fenhua de yingxiang," *Tiyu wenshi* 79 (May 1996), 14–16.

2. Hsu I-hsiung, "Wan Qing tiyu sixiang zhi xingcheng: Yi ziqiang baozhong sixiang wei zhongxin de tantao," *Tiyu xuebao* 10 (December 1988), 8–9.

3. My translation of *Jingwu* as "Pure Martial" is not literal but instead plays on the definition of "essence" (*jing*) as an elementary, constituent, or pure substance that is highly sought after.

4. Kuang Wennan and Hu Xiaoming, *Zhongguo tiyu shihua* (Chengdu: Badu shushe, 1989), 219; Wu Wenzhong, *Zhongguo jin bai nian tiyu shi* (Taibei: Taiwan shangwu yinshuguan, 1967), 40; Jiang Zhihe, "Aiguo de Jingwu tiyuhui," *Shanghai tiyu shihua* 30 (February 1991), 36; Han Xizeng, "Jianping Chen Yingshi faqi chuangban Jingwuhui," *Shanghai tiyu shihua* 29 (December 1990), 32.

5. Chen Tiesheng, "Huizhi zhi lishi," in *Jingwu benji*, ed. Chen Tiesheng (1920; reprint, Shanghai: n.p., 1922), 9.

6. Gu Liuxin, "Aiguo wushujia Huo Yuanjia," *Shanghai tiyu shihua* 4 (July 1983), 11; Huo Wenting, "Xianzu Huo Yuanjia gong shengzu niankao," *Shanghai tiyu shihua* 30 (February 1991), 21.

7. Chai Weiliang, "Liu Baichuan jibai Kang-tai-er shimo," *Tiyu wenshi* 59 (January 1993), 47.

8. Luo Mujin, "Chuantong tiyu guoshu jiaoxue zhi wojian," *Guomin tiyu jikan* 23.4 (December 1994), 17.

9. Parts of this section were originally published in Andrew Morris, "Mastery without Enmity : Athletics, Modernity and the Nation in Early Republican China." *Republican China* 22.2 (April 1997), 3–39; and Andrew Morris, "'To Make the 400 Million Move,' : The Late Qing Dynasty Origins of Modern Chinese Sport and Physical Culture." *Comparative Studies in Society and History* 42.4 (October 2000), 876–906.

10. The association also held violin and piano classes and had its own Can-

tonese orchestra, Western string orchestra, go and chess clubs, and camera club. Chen Tiesheng, *Jingwu benji*, 107–33; Kuang Wennan and Hu Xiaoming, *Zhongguo tiyu shihua*, 220–21.

11. Chen Tiesheng, "Yundonghui ji," in Chen Tiesheng, *Jingwu benji*, 21–35.

12. Huang Wanxiang, "Huncheng zhi youxi," in Chen Tiesheng, *Jingwu benji*, 146.

13. Shen Shuting, "Tichang guoji chuyan," in *Tiyu yanjiuhui huikan*, ed. Nanjing gaodeng shifan xuexiao tiyu yanjiuhui (Nanjing, 1918), 1.

14. Xiao Rulin, "Shu Jingwu tiyuhui shi," *Xin qingnian* 1.5 (January 1916), 2.

15. *Shangwu yinshuguan* advertisements, *Jiaoyu zazhi* 9.6 (20 June 1917); 10.7 (20 July 1918).

16. Jia Fengzhen, "Duanlian zhuyi zhi jiaoyu," *Jiaoyu zazhi* 7.6 (15 June 1915), 116–17, 120.

17. Xu Yuxin, *Quanshuxue jiaokeshu* (1913; reprint, Shanghai: Zhonghua tushuguan, 1916), "Xu," 3–4.

18. Xu Yuxin, *Quanshuxue jiaokeshu*, "Fanlie," 2.

19. Wang Huaiqi, "Batuanjin ticao," *Jiaoyu zazhi* 7.11 (15 November 1915), 11–14.

20. Sun Shan, "Jiji shifou shiyi xuexiao jiaoshou," in *Jiangsu shengli xuexiao di yi ci lianhe yundonghui huibian* (Nanjing: Jiangsu xun'anshi gongshu, 1914), "Wenyi" section, 6–7.

21. Yibing [Xu Yibing], "Zhengdun quanguo xuexiao tiyu shang Jiaoyubu wen," *Tiyu zazhi* 2 (July 1914), 3–4.

22. Lin Boyuan, "Zhongguo jindai xuexiao wushu kecheng de shezhi yu fazhan," paper presented at Di yi jie Dongbeiya tiyu yundongshi xueshu yantaohui, Taipei, Taiwan, 19–21 December 1995, 6–9.

23. Wang Daoping, "Qingmo Minchu Jiaoda de jiji yundong," *Shanghai tiyu shihua* 6 (March 1984), 14.

24. Fei Futao, ed., *Nanyang daxue jijibu shi zhou jiniance* (Shanghai, 1922), 30.

25. Zhou Renshan and Fei Futao, "Wuxiao jijibu shinian yange shi," in Fei Futao, *Nanyang daxue jijibu shi zhou jiniance*, 37–38.

26. Zhong Ruiqiu, "Lun Jingwu tiyuhui yu Xin wenhua yundong," *Shanghai tiyu shihua* 29 (December 1990), 41.

27. Chen Tiesheng, *Jingwu benji*; Cai Yangwu, "Jingwu shukan xi," *Shanghai tiyu shihua* 29 (December 1990), 44.

28. Zhou Peiyu, "Lun Jingwu nüjie," *Shanghai tiyu shihua* 30 (February 1991), 32.

29. Huang Xing, "Weishenme tichang jing de tiyu?" *Tiyu zhoubao* 10 (24 February 1919), 2. Italics in original.

30. Huang Xing, "Weishenme tichang jing de tiyu?" 2.

31. Wu Wenzhong, *Zhongguo tiyu fazhan shi* (Taibei: Guoli jiaoyu ziliaoguan, 1981), 84; Lin Boyuan, "Zhongguo jindai xuexiao wushu kecheng," 9.

32. Lu Xun, "Sui gan lu (sanshiqi)," *Xin qingnian* 5.5 (15 October 1918), 514–15.

33. Chen would go on to edit the Pure Martial Association's three-hundred-page *Record of the Pure Martial* in 1920 and later serve as publisher of their magazine, *Jingwu zazhi*, from 1920 to 1925.

34. "Quanshu yu quanfei," *Xin qingnian* 6.2 (15 February 1919), 218–19. This exchange between Lu Xun and Chen is also described in Paul A. Cohen, *History in Three Keys: The Boxers as Event, Experience, and Myth* (New York: Columbia University Press, 1997), 230–33.

35. Chen's letter was accompanied by a response from Lu Xun, but this piece was uncharacteristically defensive and lacking in iconoclastic energy. "Quanshu yu quanfei," 218–21.

36. Duxiu [Chen Duxiu], "Sui gan lu (bashi): Qingnian tiyu wenti," *Xin qingnian* 7.2 (1 January 1920), 157.

37. Guo briefly described the "dedication" of Qing boxers, listed the skills of five standout Qing masters, and listed the fifty-five brands of boxing and sixty-four of weapon fighting in the Yellow River Valley *wushu* school and the nineteen styles of boxing and nine of weaponry in the Yangtze Valley school. Guo Xifen, *Zhongguo tiyushi*, 29–47.

38. Gunsun Hoh [Hao Gengsheng], *Physical Education in China* (Shanghai: Commercial Press, 1926), 30–32, 62–89.

39. Quoted in Wang Zengming, "Feng Yuxiang jiangjun yu *tiyu*," *Tiyu wenshi* 10 (June 1984), 10.

40. Daiying [Yun Daiying], "Yubei shujia de xiangcun yundong," *Zhongguo qingnian* 32 (24 May 1924), 4, 7; "Hanjiaqi zhong women de gongzuo," *Zhongguo qingnian* 58 (20 December 1924), 124.

41. Lu Weichang, in Chen Tiesheng, *Jingwu benji*, quoted in Jiang Zhihe, "Aiguo de Jingwu tiyuhui," 37.

42. Lu Weichang, "Zhongguo wushu zhi jianglai," in *Di san ci quanguo yundong dahui tekan*.

43. Cai Yangwu, "Jingwu shukan xi," 43.

44. Chen Tiesheng, "Jingwu tiyuhui jiji congkan (xu): Damojian di er lu," *Xuesheng zazhi* 3.11 (20 November 1916), 27–34; Chen Tiesheng, "Jingwu tiyuhui jiji congkan (xu): Tantui di si lu," *Xuesheng zazhi* 3.12 (20 December 1916), 35–42; Cai Yangwu, "Jingwu shukan xi," 43.

45. Chen Tiesheng, "Da Jingwu zhuyi," in Chen Tiesheng, *Jingwu benji*, 1–5.

46. Chen Tiesheng, "Wu ku," in Chen Tiesheng, *Jingwu benji*, 93–94.

47. Cai Yangwu, "Jingwu shukan xi," 43.

48. T.K. Yaoheng Own, "Chin Woo," *Jingwu zazhi* 38 (15 February 1924), 2.

49. Chen Gongzhe, *Wushu fazhan shi (Jingwuhui wushi nian)* (Taibei: Hualian chubanshe, 1973), 39–41.

50. Cai Yangwu, "Jingwu shukan xi," 45–46.

51. Hsu I-hsiung, "Zhongguo jindai minzu zhuyi tiyu sixiang zhi tezhi," *Tiyu xuebao* 12 (December 1990), 9–10.

52. Sun Wen, "Jingwu benji xu," in Chen Tiesheng, *Jingwu benji*, 1.

53. Chen Tiesheng, *Jingwu benji*, insert after 12.

54. For both the quoted comments of Chen Tiesheng and the 1923 trip to Beijing, see Cai Yangwu, "Jingwu shukan xi," 46.

55. Ruth Rogaski expounds on the Pure Martial leaders' bourgeois backgrounds and attitudes in "Fists of Fury? Or the *Jingwu hui* before Bruce Lee," paper presented in the panel "Creating, Selling, and Remembering Martial Arts in Modern China" at the annual meeting of the Association for Asian Studies, San Diego, 9 March 2000.

56. Chen Gongzhe, *Wushu fazhan shi*, 19–20.

57. Yang Jiahua, "Shilun 'Jingwu san gongsi' lihe de shehui yinsu," *Shanghai tiyu shihua* 30 (February 1991), 45; Chen Gongzhe, *Wushu fazhan shi*, 122.

58. *Jingwu zazhi* 38 (15 February 1924); *Jingwu zazhi* 46 (1 December 1924).

59. "Shanghai Jingwu zhengqiudui jiming," *Jingwu zazhi* 38 (15 February 1924), 3–7; "Zhengqiu jianzhang," *Jingwu zazhi* 38 (15 February 1924), 18.

60. "Shanghai Jingwu fashou henianpian," *Jingwu zazhi* 46 (1 December 1924), 37.

61. Pang Yizhi, "Hangzhou xingyi ji," *Jingwu zazhi* 43 (15 July 1924), 57–60.

62. Huang Wanxiang, "Nüzi yu jiji zhi guanxi," in Chen Tiesheng, *Jingwu benji*, 247.

63. Cai Zinan, "Bian nüzi wei ruozhi shuo," in Chen Tiesheng, *Jingwu benji*, 248.

64. Chen Tiesheng, "Pingpan Songjiang yundonghui ji," in Chen Tiesheng, *Jingwu benji*, 71.

65. Thanks to Susan Brownell for reminding me of this point.

66. For more on this topic, see Andrew Morris, "Native Songs and Dances: Southeast Asia in a Greater Chinese Sporting Community, 1920–1948," *Journal of Southeast Asian Studies* 31.1 (March 2000), 51–57.

67. Yu Juean, "Jingwu nan chuan jiqi fazhan zhi chutan," *Shanghai tiyu shihua* 30 (February 1991), 41.

68. Cai Yangwu, "Jingwu shukan xi," 45; Zhou Peiyu, "Lun Jingwu nüjie," 34.

69. Luo Xiaoao, *Jingwu waizhuan* (Shanghai: Jingwu tiyuhui, 1921), 28–29.

70. Yu Juean, "Jingwu nan chuan jiqi fazhan zhi chutan," 42–43.

71. Yu Juean, "Jingwu shiliao," *Shanghai tiyu shihua* 24 (September 1989), 16–17.

72. "Ji Furong Jingwu huanyinghui," *Jingwu zazhi* 38 (15 February 1924), 64.

73. Quoted in Jian Shijian, "Huanying Lu Yao liang zhuren huiguo ji," *Jingwu zazhi* 40 (15 April 1924), 59–64.

74. Zhong Ruiqiu, "Lun Jingwu tiyuhui yu Xin wenhua yundong," 40.

75. Chen Tiesheng, "Di san jie quanguo yundonghui guocao jishi benmo," *Jingwu zazhi* 42 (15 June 1924), 6–8. This was not the first inclusion of martial arts in a large-scale athletic meet in China. At the 1921 Fifth Far Eastern Championship Games, held in Shanghai, Wu Zhiqing of the Chinese Wushu Associa-

tion of Shanghai led more than four hundred students in a demonstration of what Wu called "practical martial arts," or the "Chinese new calisthenics" (*Zhongguo xin ticao*). The press praised students for their demonstration of the "national essence" before a crowd including so many foreign spectators, and Wu was complimented for designing a new martial arts based on the sciences of psychology, education, and physiology. *Shanghai Zhonghua wushuhui di san jie zhengqiu dahui tekan* (Shanghai, 1921), 10.

76. *Liangyou* 24 (29 February 1928), 22.

77. Drawing by Shen Bocheng, in Chen Tiesheng, *Jingwu benji*, 237.

78. Yang Jiahua, "Shilun 'Jingwu san gongsi' lihe de shehui yinsu," 45.

79. Jiang Rongqiao, "Chen Gongzhe xiansheng shenghuo pianduan," ed. Cao Hongxun, *Shanghai tiyu shihua* 9 (December 1984), 35.

80. Chen Gongzhe, *Wushu fazhan shi*, 106–7.

81. Jiang Xingyu and Li Jinrong, "Kang Ri zhanzheng qian de Zhongyang guoshuguan duanyi," *Jiangsu tiyu wenshi* 2 (February 1985), 43; Lin Boyuan, *Zhongguo wushu shi* (Taibei: Wuzhou chubanshe, 1996), 447–48; Fan Zhengzhi, "Zhongyang guoshuguan shi," *Zhonghua guoshu jikan* 2.2 (1 October 1985), 45.

82. These connections definitely helped Zhang's bid, as another martial arts figure, Shanghai *neiquan* master Chen Weiming, had the support of Guomindang Chairman Tan Yankai for his proposal for a national martial arts organization. Wu Zhiqing, *Guoshu lilun gaiyao*, Minguo congshu di yi bian #50 (Shanghai: Dadong shuju, 1935; reprint, Shanghai: Shanghai shudian, 1989), 24 (page citations are to the reprint edition).

83. Lin Boyuan, *Zhongguo wushu shi*, 448.

84. "Wushu qigong yu minsu tiyu," chap. 1 of *Jiangsu shengzhi: Tiyu zhi*, published in *Jiangsu tiyu wenshi* 14 (March 1990), 42. Director Zhang Zhijiang was also a devout Christian. One account of the early academy years mentions that students were required to study the Bible with a priest for one hour each morning. Jiang Xingyu and Li Jinrong, "Kang Ri zhanzheng qian de Zhongyang guoshuguan duanyi," 44.

85. Lin Boyuan, *Zhongguo wushu shi*, 448; Yang Songshan, "Jiu Zhongguo Zhongyang guoshuguan huiyi pianduan," in *Zhongguo jindai tiyushi ziliao*, ed. Chengdu tiyu xueyuan tiyushi yanjiusuo (Chengdu: Sichuan jiaoyu chubanshe, 1988), 71.

86. However, four years later, Tang Hao was detained and jailed by Zhang Zhijiang for his suspected involvement with the Communist Party. He Fusheng, "Huiyi Tang Hao xiansheng," *Tiyu wenshi* 3 (August 1983), 40.

87. Wu Wenzhong, *Zhongguo jin bai nian tiyu shi*, 220.

88. Daniel A. Segal and Richard Handler, "How European Is Nationalism?" *Social Analysis* 32 (December 1992), 9.

89. Wu Wenzhong, *Zhongguo jin bai nian tiyu shi*, 220. As could be expected, however, these numbers are a suspiciously low estimate of the diverse types of martial arts in practice across the Republic. Where Guomindang figures counted seventy-three types of boxing extant in the Yellow River Valley, Shanxi Province

itself boasts sixty-five types of boxing. Shanxi sheng difangzhi bianzuan weiyuanhui, ed., *Shanxi tongzhi di sishier juan: Tiyu zhi* (Beijing: Zhonghua shuju, 1995), 18–19.

90. Wu maintains that the *shu* (skills) element explicitly referred to *wushu* and not just any other *jishu* (technique). Wu Wenzhong, "Zhongguo wushu de pingjia yu gaijin fazhan de tujing," *Guoshu yuekan* 1.3 (1 March 1972), 3.

91. Chen Jiaxuan, "Cong guoshu shuo dao guocui," in *Zhejiang guoshu youyihui huikan* (1930), 26.

92. Li Dingfang, "Guoshu de diwei he jiazhi," in *Zhejiang guoshu youyihui huikan*, 9.

93. "Zhongyang guoshuguan zuzhi dawang," "Shengshi guoshuguan zuzhi dawang," "Xian guoshuguan zuzhi dawang," and "Qu guoshushe ji cunli guoshushe zuzhi dawang," all in *Jindai Zhongguo tiyu fagui*, ed. Wang Zengming (n.p.: Zhongguo tiyushi xuehui Hebei fenhui, 1988), 107–8, 109–10, 111–12, 113–14.

94. Jiaoyubu Zhongguo jiaoyu nianjian bianzuan weiyuanhui, ed., *Di yi ci Zhongguo jiaoyu nianjian* (Nanjing, 1934; reprint, Taibei: Zongqing tushu gongsi, n.d.), 911–12 (page citations are to the reprint edition); "Wushu qigong yu minsu tiyu," 44–45; Wang Tianyu, "Gansu sheng guoshuguan yu Wang Fuchen," *Gansu tiyu shiliao zhuanji* 4 (December 1985), 14; Li Peihe and Jin Ying, "Ma Fengtu xiansheng zai Zhangye de wushu huodong," *Gansu tiyu shiliao* 12 (June 1988), 32; Shandong sheng difang shizhi bianzuan weiyuanhui, ed., *Shandong shengzhi: Tiyu zhi* (Ji'nan: Shandong renmin chubanshe, 1993), 34; Shanxi sheng difangzhi bianzuan weiyuanhui, *Shanxi tongzhi di sishier juan*, 15; Hong Zhengfu, Lin Yinsheng, and Su Yinghan, "Sanbai nian lai de Yongchun baihequan," *Tiyu wenshi* 19 (July 1986), 31; "Quanguo guoshu gaikuang diaocha (wu)," *Guoshu zhoukan* 133 (9 December 1934), 7.

95. Lin Boyuan, *Zhongguo wushu shi*, 449.

96. "Quanguo guoshu gaikuang diaocha (san)," *Guoshu zhoukan* 131 (25 November 1934), 8; parts 4, 6, 8 of same article, *Guoshu zhoukan* 132 (2 December 1934), 8; 134 (16 December 1934), 7–8; 136–37 (20 January 1935), 13–15; "Shandong sheng guoshu gaikuang," *Xiahun* 1 (10 October 1936), 51–52.

97. "Wushu qigong yu minsu tiyu," 43.

98. *Guoshu zhoukan* 135 (23 December 1934), 7–8; *Guoshu zhoukan* 138–39 (2 October 1935).

99. Qiu Shan, quoted in Tian Zhenfeng, "Jiji mantan," *Qiushi jikan* 1.2 (10 January 1935), 1; Tian Zhenfeng, "Jiji mantan," 2.

100. "Quanguo guoshu gaikuang diaocha (yi)," *Guoshu zhoukan* 129 (11 November 1934), 8; "Quanguo guoshu gaikuang diaocha (ba)," 13.

101. Even the Training Program, which offered no official degree, attracted students from afar. The 144 graduates (114 men, 30 women) of the 1934 training course came from the following provinces: Hebei 56, Jiangsu 24, Anhui 23, Shandong 15, Henan 13, Fujian 4, Sichuan 3, Jiangxi 2, Yunnan 1, Hunan 1, Hubei 1, Zhejiang 1. "Zhongyang guoshuguan ershisan nian zhong jiangxi ban ji lianxi ban nan xueyuan tongxue lu," *Guoshu zhoukan* 136–137 (20 January

1935), 19–24; "Zhongyang guoshuguan ershisan nian zhong lianxi nü xueyuan tongxue lu," *Guoshu zhoukan* 136–137 (20 January 1935), 24.

102. Wang Bingyi and Zhou Yong, "Long shang wushujia Tiejianchan shi," *Gansu ribao*, 1 March 1989, reprinted in *Gansu tiyu shiliao* 13 (March 1989), 55.

103. Pang Lintai and Bu Bingquan, "Xingyiquan mingjia Bu Xuekuan," *Tiyu wenshi* 14 (June 1985), 23–24.

104. Li Peihe and Jin Ying, "Ma Fengtu xiansheng zai Zhangye de wushu huodong," 31.

105. Ichisada Miyazaki, *China's Examination Hell: The Civil Service Examinations of Imperial China,* trans. Conrad Schirokauer (New Haven, Conn.: Yale University Press, 1981), 103; "Guoshu kaoshi tiaoli," in Wang Zengming, *Jindai Zhongguo tiyu fagui,* 117.

106. Miyazaki, *China's Examination Hell,* 103.

107. Those finishing in first place were crowned *hanwei* ("defender"), and second and third place were awarded the titles *fuwei* and *yiwei* (both meaning "assistant defender"). "Guoshu kaoshi tiaoli," 116; Lin Boyuan, *Zhongguo wushu shi,* 460–61.

108. "Guoshuguan zhi guokao," *Shenbao,* 17 October 1928, 7; "Guoshuguan zhi guokao," *Shenbao,* 19 October 1928, 7; "Guoshu kaoshi zuo gao zhongjie," *Shenbao,* 20 October 1928, 7. *Shenbao's* coverage of the Guoshu Exam was all located in the "Important Bulletins" sections of the newspaper and not on the sports page.

109. *Ershier nian Quanguo yundong dahui zongbaogao shu,* sec. 2, 136; Lin Boyuan, *Zhongguo wushu shi,* 461.

110. "Guoshu kaoshi xize," in Wang Zengming, *Jindai Zhongguo tiyu fagui,* 119–29.

111. Local and provincial exams were held after 1933 in China's martial arts strongholds. Henan held their Sixth Provincial Exam in 1936, and Shandong held a spectacular Third Provincial Exam in 1935 that featured vicious brawling between rival factions in the provincial academy system. "Yu guoshu shengkao ji qishe dahui," *Tiyu* 4.10 (30 October 1936), 15–16; Guo Hongru, "Shengkao fengchao liang ri ji," *Qiushi yuekan* 2.10 (10 July 1936), 353–55.

112. Fangwu, "Shanxi sheng guoshu cujinhui shilüe," *Qiushi jikan* 1.1 (10 October 1934), 53–56; Shanxi sheng difangzhi bianzuan weiyuanhui, *Shanxi tongzhi di sishier juan,* 15–16.

113. Hong Zhengfu, Lin Yinsheng, and Su Yinghan, "Sanbai nian lai de Yongchun baihequan," 31–32.

114. Liu Yongkang, "Jiefang qian Kunming wushu huodong," *Kunming tiyu wenshi* 2 (1987), 35.

115. Zhang Zhiliu, "Liang zhi dixia wushudui," *Shanghai tiyu shihua* 19 (June 1988), 33.

116. Wu Zhiqing, *Guoshu lilun gaiyao,* 1.

117. Wu Zhiqing, *Guoshu lilun gaiyao,* 39–56.

118. Liu Liqing, "Zhongguo wushu zuijin de qushi," *Nanfang zazhi* 1.6 (1 November 1932), 157.

119. Cohen describes Chinese interpretations of the Boxers in the 1920s in *History in Three Keys*, 243–60.

120. Xu Zhen, "Fakan ci," *Qiushi jikan* 1.1 (10 October 1934), 1.

121. Xie Xie, "Xie xu," in Wu Zhiqing, *Kexuehua de guoshu* (Shanghai: Dadong shuju, 1931), 1.

122. Mucheng, "Huabei guoshu yanjiuhui zhuiyilu," *Qiushi yuekan* 2.10 (10 July 1936), 351.

123. Xie Siyan, "Ping *Dagongbao* qi ri sheping," *Tiyu zhoubao* 30 (27 August 1932), 2.

124. Liu Shenzhan, *Tiyu geming* (Nanjing: Zhongguo ribao, 1933), 15–16.

125. Wu Zhiqing, *Kexuehua de guoshu*.

126. Wu Zhiqing, *Guoshu lilun gaiyao*, 30–34, 57–63, 81–93.

127. Wu Zhiqing, *Guoshu lilun gaiyao*, 1.

128. Shen Jiazhen, "He wei taijiquan wudang quan (xu)," *Tiyu* 4.12 (30 December 1936), 6–14.

129. However, not every martial artist in the 1930s sought to characterize *guoshu* as a literate realm. The allied *Seek Truth* and "Chivalrous Soul" factions of Ji'nan worked hard to cultivate anti-intellectual stances that would privilege the martial arts themselves over any words that could be written about them: "We are martial men, and don't know a thing about 'A-B-C' or 'a-i-u.' We are simply unsophisticated martial men, researching the martial arts." Mucheng, "Benkan de shiming," *Xiahun* 1 (10 October 1936), 3.

130. Chu Minyi, "Zhongwei Chu Minyi shi zhi datan guoshu—feng wei renlei de fuyin," *Jiaoyu zazhi* 20.12 (20 December 1928), 3–4.

131. Jiang Xiahun, "Guoshu yu tongyi," *Guoshu tongyi yuekan* 1.2 (20 November 1934), 4.

132. Wu Zhiqing, *Guoshu lilun gaiyao*, 77–78.

133. Qian Moming, "Guoshu jie xuyao he buxuyao de lingxiu," *Qiushi yuekan* 2.3 (10 December 1935), 107.

134. Zhenfeng [Tian Zhenfeng], "Hezuo yu guoshu," *Qiushi yuekan* 1.6 (10 July 1935), 235–36.

135. Chu Minyi, "Fakan ci," *Guoshu tongyi yuekan* 1.1 (20 July 1934), 2.

136. "Bian qian," *Qiushi jikan* 1.2 (10 January 1935), 2.

137. "Benguan changwu dongshi Su Jingyou xiansheng zhici" and "Wang Ziqing yanci," both in *Zhejiang guoshu youyihui huikan*, 18, 20.

138. For example, see Tian Zhenfeng, "Huayun jishi," *Qiushi jikan* 1.1 (10 October 1934), 58, 78.

139. Tian Zhenfeng, "Guan'gan hou de jianyi," *Qiushi jikan* 1.1 (10 October 1934), 17–18.

140. "Yi yue lai zhi tiyu xingzheng," *Qinfen tiyu yuebao* 2.9 (June 1935), 643.

141. Wang Geng, *Gonggong tiyuchang* (Hangzhou: Zhejiang sheng jiaoyuting, 1931), 122–27.

142. Cheng Dengke, "Tiyu junshihua de jiaoxue chuyi," *Jiao yu xue* 1.7 (1 January 1936), 282, 287–88.

143. Zhang Zhijiang, *Guoshu yu guonan* (Nanjing: Zhongyang guoshuguan, 1932), 1–2.

144. Chu Minyi, *Taijicao zhi shuoming ji kouling* (Shanghai: Dadong shuju, 1933), 1–10.

145. Chu asked teachers to join him for three to five practice sessions before they devoted two to three months teaching the routine to their students. *Ershier nian Quanguo yundong dahui zongbaogao shu*, sec. 1, 54–55. The next year, Chu led a similar *taijicao* demonstration of 960 elementary students at the Eighteenth North China Games, held in Tianjin. Yu Henian, "Di shiba jie Huabei yundonghui jiyao," *Hebei yuekan* 2.11 (November 1934), 5.

146. Chu Minyi, "Tichang tiyu zhi zhen yiyi," *Dalu zazhi* 1.6 (1 December 1932), 23.

147. Partha Chatterjee, *The Nation and Its Fragments: Colonial and Postcolonial Histories* (Princeton, N.J.: Princeton University Press, 1993), 36–41, 72–75.

148. Quoted in Lin Dazu and Pan Cangshui, "Chu Minyi xiansheng yanjiang taijicao de yuanli," *Guoshu tongyi yuekan* 1.1 (20 July 1934), 1.

149. Chu Minyi, *Taijicao zhi shuoming ji kouling*, 11–37.

150. Four scholarships were available to students submitting the most outstanding essays on the principles of *taijicao*. "Ben tongxuehui zhuban Taijicao hanshou xuexiao," *Qinfen tiyu yuebao* 2.1 (10 October 1934), 110–11.

151. Chu Minyi, "Taijicao zhi tuanti biaoyan," *Kangjian zazhi* 1.3 (1 July 1933), 3.

152. Taijicao hanshou xuexiao and Taijicao yanjiuhui, "Taijicao," *Qinfen tiyu yuebao* 2.6 (March 1935), 415.

153. "Yi yue lai zhi tiyu xingzheng," *Qinfen tiyu yuebao* 2.12 (September 1935), 837.

154. "Chu Minyi yu Menggu wanggong saima," *Tiyu zhoubao* 46 (17 December 1932), 2.

155. *Liangyou* 25 (April 1928), 24; "Tiyu zhuanjia Chu Minyi boshi zhi tige," *Xiandai xuesheng* 3.1 (October 1933), photo before 1.

156. In 1930, Shanghai's Sino-French Engineering School began manufacturing these devices, which were based on Song dynasty *taiji* implements. Ying Ji, "Tiyu jie zhenwen ji changshi," in *Quanguo yundong dahui yaolan* (Hangzhou: Quanguo yundong dahui xuanchuanbu, 1930), 36–37.

157. "Jiaoyubu canjia gezhong jinian huodong de wenjian," File 2078, Folder 52, Second Historical Archives, Nanjing, China.

158. Sun Wen, "Jingwu benji xu," 1.

CHAPTER 8. *TIYU* THROUGH WARTIME AND "LIBERATION"

1. "Di qi jie quanyunhui choubei weiyunahui de wenjian," File 587 (10), Folder 10, Second Historical Archives, Nanjing, China.

2. "Di qi jie Quanguo yundong dahui zuzhi guicheng," *Qinfen tiyu yuebao* 4.9 (June 1937), 710.

3. For more information on the wartime *tiyu* projects of the Nationalist, Communist, Manzhouguo, and Nanjing "puppet" regimes, see Andrew Morris, "Cultivating the National Body: A History of Physical Culture in Republican China" (Ph.D. diss., University of California, San Diego, 1998), 516–600; Andrew Morris, "'All China Has Muscles Now, and We Know How to Use Them': Nationalist and Communist Sporting Cultures during Wartime, 1937–45," paper presented at the annual meeting of the Association for Asian Studies, Washington, D.C., 5 April 2002, available at www.calpoly.edu/~admorris/AAS2002Paper.

4. Hubert Freyn, *Chinese Education in the War* (Shanghai: Kelly & Walsh, 1940; reprint, Taipei: Ch'eng Wen Publishing, 1974), 11 (page citations are to the reprint edition).

5. Hu Xingyi, "Shuidongping kang Ri jiuguo yundonghui," *Yunnan tiyu wenshi* 7 (December 1986), 45–46.

6. This is unlike Japan, where the pressures of war drove the Japanese sports world further and further into outright fascist forms and models. For example, the national Meiji Jingū Athletic Meet by 1942 became known as the Meiji Jingū Citizen Training Games, its former sporting events replaced totally by militaristic drills, gymnastics, and martial arts. Imamura Yoshio, *Nihon taiikushi* (Tokyo: Kaneko Shobō, 1951), 308–9.

7. Chongqing shi tiyu yundong weiyuanhui and Chongqing shizhi zongbianshi, eds., *Kangzhan shiqi peidu tiyu shiliao* (Chongqing: Chongqing chubanshe, 1988), photo before 1; I am also drawing on an untitled film in my possession on Chongqing physical culture highlights of the year 1940.

8. "Shiyunhui zuo yuanman jieshu," *Dagongbao*, 13 October 1942, 3.

9. Zhang Guotao's Red Fourth Front Army even held a three-day May First Athletic Meet during the Long March itself. The meet was held on a grassy plateau behind a Lama temple in Luhuo, northeastern Xikang (now part of the Garzē Zang Autonomous Prefecture, Sichuan). Zhang Xinyun, Lan Cao, and Han Lei, "Changzheng zhong de yundonghui," *Tiyu wenshi* 24 (April 1987), 5–6.

10. Shaan-Gan-Ning bianqu tiyushi bianshen weiyuanhui, eds., *Shaan-Gan-Ning bianqu tiyushi* (Xi'an: Shaanxi renmin chubanshe, 1990), 34.

11. Qiao Keqin and Guan Wenming, *Zhongguo tiyu sixiangshi* (Lanzhou: Gansu minzu chubanshe, 1993), 310, 315.

12. Zhou Zikun, "Jinian 'Wu sa' yundonghui zongjie," *Kangdi bao*, 11 June 1939, reprinted in *Zhongguo jindai tiyushi ziliao*, ed. Chengdu tiyu xueyuan tiyushi yanjiusuo (Chengdu: Sichuan jiaoyu chubanshe, 1988), 667.

13. Wu Jiangping, "Yi Yan'an," *Xin tiyu* 2–3 (1957), reprinted in *Shaan-Gan-Ning bianqu tiyu shiliao*, ed. Shaanxi sheng tiyu wenshi gongzuo weiyuanhui (Xi'an: Shaanxi sheng tiyu wenshi gongzuo weiyuanhui, 1986), 200.

14. Dongfang Ming, "Huaxu," *Jiefang ribao*, 5 September 1942, and Tiewu, "Yundong dahui duiyu women," *Xin Zhonghua bao*, 29 July 1937, both reprinted

in Shaanxi sheng tiyu wenshi gongzuo weiyuanhui, *Shaan-Gan-Ning bianqu tiyu shiliao*, 340, 237.

15. "'Wu yi' yundong dahui de weisheng," *Xin Zhonghua bao*, 9 May 1937, "Quzi Xian 'Wu sa' xuesheng jianyue yundong dahui baogao," and "Guoji qing-nianjie kuoda yundonghui zhengji dahui jiangpin qishi," *Jiefang ribao*, 22 August 1942, all reprinted in Shaanxi sheng tiyu wenshi gongzuo weiyuanhui, *Shaan-Gan-Ning bianqu tiyu shiliao*, 229–30, 267, 270, 294.

16. "Tixie lishihui," *Dagongbao*, 8 September 1945, 3.

17. Lü Rongling, "Duiyu jiujiu Tiyujie de qiwang," in *Zhonghua quanguo tiyu xiejinhui Guangxi sheng fenhui huikan: Sanshiliu nian "jiujiu" Tiyujie teji* (Guilin, 1947), 25.

18. Chen Zhang'e, *Tiyu mantan* (Shanghai: Dongnan chubanshe, 1948).

19. Wang Xuezheng, *Tiyu yu jiaoyu* (Chongqing: Shangwu yinshuguan, 1945; reprint, Taibei: Taiwan shangwu yinshuguan, 1966), 62–70 (page citations are to the reprint edition).

20. Cheng Qian, "Fayang yundong jingshen jianshe xin Zhongguo," in *Hubei di jiu jie quan sheng yundong dahui tekan* (Hankou, 1947), 1.

21. "Yi ge Xian minjiaoguan zhang de kuzhong: Qing choukuan jiudian bufu," *Xinjiang tiyu shiliao* 5 (1991), 33.

22. Li Jiaxiao, "Kao qiangganzi qusheng de lanqiusai," *Yunnan tiyu wenshi* 12 (October 1990), 55.

23. Tong Xiangzhao, "Cong Taiwan xuanshou tanqi," *Zhengyanbao*, 11 May 1948, "Quanyun tekan" section, 4.

24. For a more thorough analysis, see Andrew Morris, "Baseball, History, the Local and the Global in Taiwan," in *The Minor Arts of Daily Life: Popular Culture in Taiwan*, ed. David K. Jordan, Andrew Morris, and Marc L. Moskowitz (Honolulu: University of Hawai'i Press, 2004), 180–82.

25. Su Jinzhang, *Jiayi bangqiu shihua* (Taibei: Lianjing chuban shiye gongsi, 1996), 27.

26. *Taiwan sheng di yi jie quansheng yundong dahui* (Taibei: Taiwan sheng di yi jie quansheng yundong dahui xuanchuan zu, 1946), first 12 unnumbered pages.

27. Hsieh Chang-an, "Development of Physical Education in China," *China Weekly Review* 110.3 (19 June 1948), 84.

28. Dong Shouyi, "Aolinpike yu Zhongguo," in *Aoyunhui yu Zhongguo*, ed. Ji Hongmin, Yu Xingmao, and Lü Changfu (Beijing: Wenshi ziliao chubanshe, 1985), 29–30.

29. Gu Bingfu, "China's Participation in the Olympics (II)," trans. Xin Yu, *China Sports* 336 (September 1996), 6–7; "Woguo canjia Di shisi jie shijie yundong canzao shibai," in *Shuilibu saqi nian qiuji yundonghui tekan* (Nanjing: Shuilibu, 1948), 31–32. The one bright spot was the Chinese basketball team, which finished with a 5–3 record and set an Olympic record by beating the Iraqi team 125–25. Tang Mingxin, *Woguo canjia guoji lanqiusai lishi* (Taibei: Zhonghua quanguo lanqiu weiyuanhui, 1963), 29–31.

30. Dong Shouyi, "Aolinpike yu Zhongguo," 35–36.

31. Yang Zhengyan, "Xin Zhongguo de di yi ci yundonghui," *Tiyu wenshi* 9 (August 1984), 24–25; "Zhonghua renmin gongheguo tiyu yundong dashiji," *Tiyu wenshi* 9 (August 1984), 91.

32. *China Handbook* Editorial Committee, *Sports and Public Health*, trans. Wen Botang (Beijing: Foreign Languages Press, 1983), 48–49.

33. Jonathan Kolatch, *Sports, Politics and Ideology in China* (New York: Jonathan David Publishers, 1972), 135–40.

34. "Inter Camp Olympics, 1952 Pyuktong D.P.R.K." (P.O.W. Camps Administration in the Democratic People's Republic of Korea, 1952), retrieved 26 February 2003 from www.kmike.com/POW_Olympics/pow/index.htm.

35. Xie Jin, dir., *Nülan wu hao* (Beijing: Tianma dianying zhipianchang, 1957), film.

36. Shi Chuanxiang, "Women taofen gongren ye you le tiyu huodong," *Xin tiyu* (February 1965), 24.

37. Liang Heng and Judith Shapiro, *Son of the Revolution* (New York: Vintage Books, 1983), 211–21.

38. Andrew Morris, "'I Believe You Can Fly': Basketball Culture in Postsocialist China," in *Popular China: Unofficial Culture in a Globalizing Society*, ed. Perry Link, Richard P. Madsen, and Paul G. Pickowicz (Lanham, Md.: Rowman & Littlefield Publishers, Inc., 2002), 9–38.

39. Of the twenty-five members of the old ROC Chinese Olympic Committee, nineteen were now in Taiwan. Kolatch, *Sports, Politics and Ideology*, 224.

40. Liu Chin-ping, "Zhonghua minguo Aolinpike weiyuanhui huiji yanbian zhi lishi kaocha, 1949–1981" (M.S. thesis, Guoli Taiwan shifan daxue, 1995), 29–30.

41. The PRC translates "Chinese Taipei" (also in other official settings, like the Asia-Pacific Economic Cooperation, which have adopted the "Olympic model") as *Zhongguo Taibei*, or, literally, "*China's* Taipei." The 1981 "Olympic model," which the PRC's Chinese Olympic Committee formally accepted in 1990, also forbids that the ROC national flag and anthem appear in any Olympic context. When Taiwan athletes win medals, the flag of the Chinese Taipei Olympic Committee is raised and the Olympic anthem played. Possessing an ROC flag at the Olympics (technically, any "flags other than those of participating countries") actually becomes an extraterritorially illegal act; two Taiwanese fans were arrested after fighting with police who tried to remove them from the stands for waving the ROC flag during the women's table tennis championships at the Atlanta Olympics of 1996. "Taiwanese Spectators Arrested," Associated Press, 1 August 1996.

42. Liu Chin-ping, "Zhonghua minguo Aolinpike weiyuanhui," 30–32; *Dangdai Zhongguo* congshu bianji weiyuanhui, eds., *Dangdai Zhongguo tiyu* (Beijing: Zhongguo shehui kexue chubanshe, 1984), 402–4; Gu Bingfu, "China's Participation in the Olympics (II)," 7; Kolatch, *Sports, Politics and Ideology*, 171–73.

43. Liu Chin-ping, "Zhonghua minguo Aolinpike weiyuanhui," 38–39.

44. Yang's disappointing fifth-place finish puzzled the sporting world, but

he only learned of this plot in 1978 from an ROC intelligence agent. "Sports Legend Alleges Foul Play," *China Post*, 5 April 1997; Rafer Johnson, *The Best That I Can Be: An Autobiography* (New York: Doubleday, 1998), 172.

45. Morris, "Baseball, History," 182–86.

46. Ma Tongbin and Qin Yuanyuan, *Beijing 2008: Shen Ao de taiqian muhou* (Beijing: Beijing tiyu daxue chubanshe, 2001), 20–21. My thanks to Susan Brownell for providing this source.

47. "New Beijing, Great Olympics—Our Bid—Our Vision," from "Official Website of Beijing 2008 Olympic Games Bid Committee," retrieved 30 August 2000 from www.beijing-olympic.org.cn/xbxa/sbsb/xbxa_sbsb_ssln.htm.

48. "Emblem of Beijing 2008 Olympic Games Bid Committee," from "Official Site of the Beijing 2008 Olympic Games Bid Committee," retrieved 19 May 2000 from www.beijing-olympic.org.cn/eindex.shtm.

49. "The Emblem, Slogan and Official Web Site in Beijing's Bid for the Host of the 2008 Olympic Games Were Officially Announced," 1 February 2000, retrieved 19 May 2000 from "Official Site of the Beijing 2008 Olympic Games Bid Committee—News Center," www.beijing-olympic.org.cn/enws/bidnews/31.shtm.

50. Beijing Organizing Committee for the Games of the XXIX Olympiad, "National, Regional and City Characteristics," retrieved 6 February 2003 from www.beijing-2008.org/eolympic/ztq/5–1/5–1.html.

51. "Beijing: Human Rights Issue No Excuse against Olympic Bid," retrieved 30 August 2000 from "Official Website of Beijing 2008 Olympic Games Bid Committee—News," www.beijing-olympic.org.cn/xbxa/xwxw/bidn/369.shtm; Mei Hui and Wu Yiyi, "Olympics Seen to Bring Higher Living Standards," *China News Digest*, 6 February 2001; Li Xin, "One Slogan, Many Objectives," *China Daily*, 23 November 2000; Sue Bruell and Wu Yiyi, "No 'One-China' Agreement, No Olympic Cooperation: Beijing," *China News Digest*, 2 July 2000; Willy Lam, "Beijing Playing 'Taiwan Card,'" *CNN.com*, 15 May 2001; Li Yan, "Sports Circles: Promote Cross-Straits Cooperation," *People's Daily*, 26 July 2001; "In Olympics Bid, Beijing's Bathrooms Face Scrutiny," Associated Press, 4 December 2000.

52. "Gallup Poll: 94.9 Percent of Beijingers Support Bid for 2008 Games," Xinhua News Agency, Beijing, 20 February 2001.

Bibliography

A note regarding citations of Chinese publications with English subtitles: The English titles that accompany many Republican-era publications often give insight to how an author or publisher understood a certain work and are thus too valuable to discard or replace with my own translations. Therefore, Chinese publications that carry English subtitles are cited to include both of these, as follows: "*Jiaoyu zazhi (Chinese Educational Review)*." This is opposed to publications for which I provide translations, which appear as, for example: "*Hanxue yuekan* [Sweat and blood monthly]," with square brackets and unitalicized English translations.

For reasons of space, some 311 items (mostly articles from newspapers, PRC-era Chinese "*tiyu* history" journals, ROC-era English-language journals, and minor pieces from ROC-era Chinese journals) have been cut from this bibliography. These sources are all cited in full in the notes of this book, and interested readers can view a full list of them at www.calpoly.edu/~admorris/TiyuExtendedBibliography.

American Physical Education Review. Boston.
Anhui tiyu shiliao 安徽体育史料 [Materials from the history of Anhui physical culture]. Hefei.
Annual Reports of the Foreign Secretaries of the International Committee, October 1, 1907 to September 30, 1908. New York: International Committee, YMCA, 1908.
Annual Reports of the Foreign Secretaries of the International Committee, October 1, 1909 to September 30, 1910. New York: International Committee, YMCA, 1910.
Annual Reports of the Foreign Secretaries of the International Committee,

October 1, 1911 to September 30, 1912. New York: International Committee, YMCA, 1912.

Annual Reports of the Foreign Secretaries of the International Committee, October 1, 1912 to September 30, 1913. New York: International Committee, YMCA, 1913.

Annual Reports of the Foreign Secretaries of the International Committee, October 1, 1913 to September 30, 1914. New York: International Committee, YMCA, 1914.

Association Men. Chicago.

Baihong tianjingsaidui jiniankan 白虹田徑賽隊紀念刊 [Commemorative publication of the White Rainbow Track and Field Club]. Shanghai: Baihong tianjingdui, 1931.

Bailey, Paul J. *Reform the People: Changing Attitudes towards Popular Education in Early Twentieth-Century China.* Edinburgh: Edinburgh University Press, 1990.

Barlow, Tani E. "Theorizing Woman: *Funü, Guojia, Jiating* (Chinese Woman, Chinese State, Chinese Family)." In *Body, Subject and Power in China,* edited by Angela Zito and Tani E. Barlow, 253–89. Chicago: University of Chicago Press, 1994.

Bayun jianjie 八運簡介 *(Brief Introduction to the 8th National Games).* Shanghai: Zhonghua renmin gongheguo Di ba jie quanguo yundonghui jizibu, 1996.

Befu, Harumi, ed. *Cultural Nationalism in East Asia: Representation and Identity.* Berkeley: Institute of East Asian Studies, University of California, 1993.

Beifang gonglun 北方公論 [Northern opinion]. Beiping.

Beijing Organizing Committee for the Games of the XXIX Olympiad. "National, Regional and City Characteristics." Retrieved 6 February 2003 from www.beijing-2008.org/eolympic/ztq/5–1/5–1.html.

———. "Olympics 2008: Our Vision." Retrieved 7 January 2003 from www.beijing-2008.org/eolympic/xay/xay_index.htm.

Beijing tiyu wenshi 北京体育文史 [Materials from the history of Beijing physical culture]. Beijing.

Beijing tushuguan 北京图书馆, ed. *Minguo shiqi zongshumu (1911–1949): Jiaoyu, tiyu* 民国时期总书目 (1911–1949): 教育, 体育 [Index of Republican-era books (1911–1949): Education, physical education]. Beijing: Shumu wenxian chubanshe, 1995.

Beiyang huabao 北洋畫報 *(Pei-Yang Pictorial News).* Tianjin.

"Ben jie Ou-lin-pi-ke yundong dahui zhi qianzhan (xu ba)" 本居歐林匹克運動大會之前瞻 (續八) [Preview of this Olympiad (Part 8)]. *Tiyu zhoubao (Sporting Weekly)* 26 (30 July 1932): 22–23.

Benjamin, Walter. "On the Mimetic Faculty." In *Reflections: Essays, Aphorisms, Autobiographical Writings,* edited by Peter Demetz, 333–36. New York: Harcourt Brace Jovanovich, 1978.

Bennett, Tony. "The Exhibitionary Complex." In *Culture/Power/History: A Reader in Contemporary Social Theory,* edited by Nicholas B. Dirks, Geoff

Eley, and Sherry B. Ortner, 123–54. Princeton, N.J.: Princeton University Press, 1994.

Bhabha, Homi K. *Nation and Narration*. New York: Routledge, 1990.

Bocobo-Olivar, Celia. *History of Physical Education in the Philippines*. Quezon City: University of the Philippines Press, 1972.

Bourdieu, Pierre. "Sport and Social Class." *Social Science Information* 17.6 (1978): 819–40.

Brownell, Susan. *Training the Body for China: Sports in the Moral Order of the People's Republic*. Chicago: University of Chicago Press, 1995.

Cai Jinbo 蔡金波. "Quan Min yundonghui jixiang 全閩運動會紀詳 (The Fukien Athletic Meet)." *Qingnian jinbu (Association Progress)* 42 (April 1921): 78–80.

Cai Zinan 蔡梓柟. "Bian nüzi wei ruozhi shuo" 辨女子為弱質説 [An argument against the line that women are weak in constitution]. In *Jingwu benji*, edited by Chen Tiesheng, 248. 1920; reprint, Shanghai: n.p., 1922.

Carr, Kevin Gray. "Making Way: War, Philosophy, and Sport in Japanese *Jūdō*." *Journal of Sport History* 20.2 (Summer 1993): 167–88.

Chahar sheng ershisan nian zhongdeng xuexiao qiuji yundong dahui choubei weiyuanhui 察哈爾省二十三年中等學校秋季運動大會籌備委員會, eds. *Chahar sheng ershisan nian zhongdeng xuexiao qiuji yundong dahui zongbaogao* 察哈爾省二十三年中等學校秋季運動大會總報告 [Chahar Province 1934 High School Autumn Games Official Report]. Zhangjiakou: Chahar sheng jiaoyuting mishushi, 1934.

Chang Bo 昌伯. "Cong Shiyunhui dedao de jiaoxun" 從世運會得到的教訓 [Lessons learned from the Olympics]. *Kang-Zang qianfeng* 3.12 (August 1936): 12–15.

Chang, Sidney H., and Ramon H. Myers, eds. *The Storm Clouds Clear over China: The Memoir of Ch'en Li-fu 1900–1993*. Stanford, Calif.: Hoover Press, 1994.

Chatterjee, Partha. *The Nation and Its Fragments: Colonial and Postcolonial Histories*. Princeton, N.J.: Princeton University Press, 1993.

Chen Gongzhe 陳公哲. *Wushu fazhan shi (Jingwuhui wushi nian)* 武術發展史(精武會五十年) [The history of the development of martial arts (Fifty years of the Pure Martial Association)]. Taibei: Hualian chubanshe, 1973.

Chen Jianxiao 陳劍僪. "Quanguo yundonghui de jiaoxun" 全國運動會的教訓 [Lessons from the National Games]. *Xiandai xuesheng (Modern Student)* 3.2 (November 1933): 1–9.

Chen Kuisheng 陳奎生. "Woguo xiaoxue tiyu mubiao gaige wenti" 我國小學體育目標改革問題 [The question of reforming the goals of our nation's elementary school physical education]. *Qinfen tiyu yuebao (Chin Fen Sports Monthly)* 1.3 (10 December 1933): 7–8.

Chen Lifu 陳立夫. "Chuangzao shihe Zhongguo guoqing de yundong" 創造適合中國國情的運動 [Creating a sport suitable to the Chinese national condition]. In *Tiyu yu jiuguo*, edited by Zhongguo Guomindang zhongyang zhixing weiyuanhui xuanchuan weiyuanhui, 101–2. Nanjing: Zhongguo

Guomindang zhongyang zhixing weiyuanhui xuanchuan weiyuanhui, 1933.

Chen Tiesheng 陳鐵生. "Da Jingwu zhuyi" 大精武主義 [The great Pure Martial-ism]. In *Jingwu benji*, edited by Chen Tiesheng, 1–5. 1920; reprint, Shanghai: n.p., 1922.

———— 陳鐵笙. "Di san jie quanguo yundonghui guocao jishi benmo" 第三屆 全國運動會國操紀事本末 [A full account of the national calisthenics demonstration at the Third National Games]. *Jingwu zazhi* 42 (15 June 1924): 1–24.

———— 陳鐵生. "Huizhi zhi lishi" 會址之歷史 [The history of the association's locations]. In *Jingwu benji*, edited by Chen Tiesheng, 9. 1920; reprint, Shanghai: n.p., 1922.

————. "Jingwu tiyuhui jiji congkan (xu): Damojian di er lu" 精武體育會技 擊叢刊（續）：達摩劍第二路 [The Pure Martial Athletic Association martial arts series (continued): Bhodidharma-style swords, routine #2]. *Xuesheng zazhi (Students' Magazine)* 3.11 (20 November 1916): 27–34.

————. "Jingwu tiyuhui jiji congkan (xu): Tantui di si lu" 精武體育會技擊叢 刊（續）：潭腿第四路 [The Pure Martial Athletic Association martial arts series (continued): *Tantui*, routine #4]. *Xuesheng zazhi (Students' Magazine)* 3.12 (20 December 1916): 35–42.

————. "Pingpan Songjiang yundonghui ji" 評判松江運動會紀 [Record of my officiating at the Songjiang (martial arts) meet]. In *Jingwu benji*, edited by Chen Tiesheng, 71. 1920; reprint, Shanghai: n.p., 1922.

————. "Wu ku" 武庫 [Martial library]. In *Jingwu benji*, edited by Chen Tiesheng, 93–94. 1920; reprint, Shanghai: n.p., 1922.

————. "Yundonghui ji" 運動會紀 [Record of the athletic meets]. In *Jingwu benji*, edited by Chen Tiesheng, 21–35. 1920; reprint, Shanghai: n.p., 1922.

————, ed. *Jingwu benji* 精武本紀 [Record of the Pure Martial]. 1920; reprint, Shanghai: n.p., 1922.

Chen Xianming 陈显明, Liang Youde 梁友德, and Du Kehe 杜克和. *Zhongguo bangqiu yundongshi* 中国棒球运动史 [The history of baseball in China]. Wuhan: Wuhan chubanshe, 1990.

Chen Xiping 陳希平. "Zhongyang tiyuchang choujian shimo ji" 中央體育場 籌建始末記 [A record of the entire process of the planning and construction of Central Stadium]. *Zhongguo jianzhu (Chinese Architect)* 1.3 (September 1933): 1–7.

Chen Yongsheng 陳詠聲. *Nüzi meirong yundongfa* 女子美容運動法 [Regimen for women's beauty exercise]. Shanghai: Wenming shuju, 1924.

————. *Ouzhou tiyu kaocha riji* 歐洲體育考察日記 [Diary of the Olympic inspection tour of European physical culture]. Shanghai: Nansheng chubanshe, 1938.

Chen Zhang'e 陳掌諤. *Tiyu mantan* 體育漫談 [Informal discussions on sport]. Shanghai: Dongnan chubanshe, 1948.

Chenbao 晨報 *(Morning Post)*. Beijing.

Cheng Dengke 程登科. "Dadao buzhongshi ji fuhua de tiyu tongzhi" 打倒不 忠實及腐化的體育同志 [Overthrow our disloyal and corrupt *tiyu* comrades]. *Qinfen tiyu yuebao (Chin Fen Sports Monthly)* 1.4 (10 January 1934): 3–5.

———. "Deguo xiaoxue tiyu shishi gaikuang ji ganyan" 德國小學體育實施概況及感言 [An account of and my feelings on the German implementation of elementary physical education programs]. *Jiaoyu congkan (Educational Research)* 2.2 (June 1935): 1–22.

———. "Du Fang Wanbang xiansheng 'Woguo xianxing tiyu zhi shi da wenti jiqi jiejue tujing' zhong suo chi dui tiyu junshihua buqie shiyong de jiantao" 讀方萬邦先生'我國現行體育之十大問題及其解決途徑'中所持對體育軍事化不切實用的檢討 [A discussion of the unrealistic and impractical notions held in Mr. Fang Wanbang's "The ten greatest problems with our nation's current physical education programs and the paths we should take to solve them"]. *Tiyu jikan (Physical Education Quarterly)* 1.3 (July 1935): 353–61.

———. "Geguo qingnian tiyu xunlian zhi shixiao ji wuguo jinhou qingnian tiyu yingyou zhi dongxiang" 各國青年體育訓練之實效及吾國今後青年體育應有之動向 [The results of youth *tiyu* training in other countries and the directions our nation's youth *tiyu* training should take from this day on]. *Jiaoyu congkan (Educational Research)* 3.1 (December 1935): 209–24.

———. *Shijie tiyushi gangyao* 世界體育史綱要 [The essential history of world sport]. Minguo congshu di yi bian #50. Chongqing: Shangwu yinshuguan, 1945; reprint, Shanghai: Shanghai shudian, 1989.

———. "Tiyu junshihua de jiaoxue chuyi" 體育軍事化的教學芻議 [My humble opinions on pedagogy for a militarized physical education]. *Jiao yu xue* 1.7 (1 January 1936): 280–97.

———. "Xie gei xin biye de tiyu tongzhimen" 寫給新畢業的體育同志們 [A letter to my newly graduated comrades in physical culture]. *Qinfen tiyu yuebao (Chin Fen Sports Monthly)* 2.10 (July 1935): 665–71.

———. "Zhongguo jinhou minzhong tiyu yingyou zhi dongxiang" 中國今後民眾體育應有之動向 [The direction Chinese mass *tiyu* should take from this day forward]. *Guoshu, tiyu, junshi* 29 (17 May 1934) [Weekly feature in *Zhongguo ribao*]: 8.

———. "Zhongguo xian Qin tiyu" 中國先秦體育 [Chinese physical culture of the pre-Qin era]. Transcribed by Zhou Shouzang 周壽臧. *Tiyu jikan (Physical Education Quarterly)* 3.2 (June 1937): 127–38.

Cheng Shikui 程時煃. "Jiangxi shenghui de gongmin xunlian" 江西省會的公民訓練 [Citizen training in the Jiangxi provincial capital]. *Jiaoyu zazhi (Educational Review)* 25.1 (10 January 1935): 121–38.

Chengdu tiyu xueyuan tiyushi yanjiusuo 成都体育学院体育史研究所, ed. *Zhongguo jindai tiyushi ziliao* 中国近代体育史资料 [Materials from modern Chinese physical culture history]. Chengdu: Sichuan jiaoyu chubanshe, 1988.

Chengdu tiyu xueyuan xuebao 成都體育學院學報 *(Journal of Chengdu Physical Education Institute)*. Chengdu.

Chin Yü Sung [Jin Yusong 金育松]. "The Sixth Semi-Annual Field and Track Meet of Our School." *Xuesheng zazhi (Students' Magazine)* 3.11 (20 November 1916): 5–6.

China Critic. Shanghai.

China Daily. Beijing.

China Handbook Editorial Committee. *Sports and Public Health.* Translated by Wen Botang. Beijing: Foreign Languages Press, 1983.

China Leader (Zhonghua daobao 中華導報*).* Nanjing.

China News Digest. Gaithersburg, Md.

China Post. Taipei.

China Tomorrow. Peiping.

China Weekly Review. Shanghai.

China's Young Men. Tianjin.

Chinese Affairs. Shanghai.

Chinese National Association for the Advancement of Education Bulletin. Peking.

Chinese Recorder and Missionary Journal. Shanghai.

Chinese Republic. Shanghai.

Chongqing shi tiyu yundong weiyuanhui 重庆市体育运动委员会 and Chongqing shizhi zongbianshi 重庆市志总编室, eds. *Kangzhan shiqi peidu tiyu shiliao* 抗战时期陪都体育史料 [Historical materials from wartime physical culture in the provisional capital]. Chongqing: Chongqing chubanshe, 1988.

Chu Jianhong 儲劍虹. "Shishi xiangcun tiyu juti fang'an" 實施鄉村體育具體 方案 [Concrete proposal for the implementation of village *tiyu*]. *Qinfen tiyu yuebao (Chin Fen Sports Monthly)* 3.6 (March 1936): 475–79.

Chu Minyi 褚民誼. "Fakan ci" 發刊辭 [Words to introduce this periodical]. *Guoshu tongyi yuekan* 1.1 (20 July 1934): 1–2.

———. "Fuxing minzu yu tichang tiyu" 復興民族與提倡體育 [Revitalizing the nation-race and promoting physical culture]. *Hubei jiaoyu yuekan* 5 (January 1934): 11–17.

———. "Quanguo yundong dahui choubei jingguo" 全國運動大會籌備經過 [The process of planning the National Games]. *Qinfen tiyu yuebao (Chin Fen Sports Monthly)* 1.2 (10 November 1933): 19–26.

———. *Taijicao zhi shuoming ji kouling* 太極操之説明及口令 [Tai chi calisthenics instructions and commands]. Shanghai: Dadong shuju, 1933.

———. "Taijicao zhi tuanti biaoyan" 太極操之團體表演 [Group *taijicao* demonstrations]. *Kangjian zazhi (Good Health Magazine)* 1.3 (1 July 1933): 2–7.

———. "Tichang tiyu zhi zhen yiyi" 提倡體育之真意義 [Promote the true meaning of physical fitness]. *Dalu zazhi (La Terre)* 1.6 (1 December 1932): 17–24.

———. "Zhongwei Chu Minyi shi zhi datan guoshu—feng wei renlei de fuyin" 中委褚民誼氏之大談國術－奉為人類的福音 [Central Executive Committee member Chu Minyi's great hopes for *guoshu*: Presenting glad tidings to all humanity]. *Jiaoyu zazhi (Educational Review)* 20.12 (20 December 1928): 3–4.

"Chu Minyi yu Menggu wanggong saima" 褚民誼與蒙古王公賽馬 [Chu Minyi rides with the Mongol princes]. *Tiyu zhoubao (Sporting Weekly)* 46 (17 December 1932): 2.

Chunsheng 春生. "Huabei yundonghui yu tichang tiyu zhong zhi cuowu guannian" 華北運動會與提倡體育中之錯誤觀念 [The North China Games and some incorrect notions that exist within the promotion of physical culture]. *Beifang gonglun* 83 (1 November 1934): 11–12.

Chuxi Di shiyi jie Shijie yundonghui Zhonghua daibiaotuan baogao 出席第十一屆世界運動會中華代表團報告 *(Official Report of the Chinese Delegation to the XIth Olympiad, Berlin, 1936).* Shanghai: Zhonghua quanguo tiyu xiejinhui, 1937.

Cohen, Paul A. *History in Three Keys: The Boxers as Event, Experience, and Myth.* New York: Columbia University Press, 1997.

Corbett, Charles Hodge. *Shantung Christian University (Cheeloo).* New York: United Board for Christian Colleges in China, 1955.

Curtis, Henry S. "Youxi jiaoyu" 遊戲教育 [Games instruction]. Translated by Wang Changping 王長平 and Mu Haipeng 穆海鵬. *Tiyu zhoubao* 49 (12 January 1920): 11–13.

Cuyler, P. L. *Sumo: From Rite to Sport.* New York: Weatherhill, 1979.

Dagongbao 大公報 *(L'Impartial).* Chongqing.

Dai Mengqin 戴夢琴. "Jianshen jianguo de tujing" 健身健國的途徑 [The way to build a healthy body and a healthy nation]. *Shenghuo zhoukan (Life Weekly)* 6.26 (20 June 1931): 535–36.

Daiying 代英. "Dadao jiaohui jiaoyu" 打倒教會教育 [Defeat missionary education]. *Zhongguo qingnian* 60 (3 January 1925): 158–61.

———. "Yubei shujia de xiangcun yundong" 預備暑假的鄉村運動 [Preparing for the summer vacation rural movement]. *Zhongguo qingnian* 32 (24 May 1924): 4–10.

Dalu zazhi 大陸雜志 *(La Terre).* Nanjing.

Dangdai Zhongguo congshu bianji weiyuanhui 当代中国丛书编辑委员会, eds. *Dangdai Zhongguo tiyu* 当代中国体育 [Sports and physical culture in contemporary China]. Beijing: Zhongguo shehui kexue chubanshe, 1984.

Dazhuan tiyu 大專體育 [University and college physical education]. Taibei.

Deloria, Philip J. *Playing Indian.* New Haven, Conn.: Yale University Press, 1998.

Demetz, Peter, ed. *Reflections: Essays, Aphorisms, Autobiographical Writings.* Translated by Edmund Jephcott. New York: Harcourt Brace Jovanovich, 1978.

Deng Kanshun 鄧堪舜. "Wuzhuang wu xiang yundong bisai fangfa" 武裝五項運動比賽方法 [Rules of competition for the fully armed pentathlon]. *Qinfen tiyu yuebao (Chin Fen Sports Monthly)* 3.5 (February 1936): 419–20.

Di jiu jie Yuandong yundonghui 第九屆遠東運動會 [The Ninth Far Eastern Championship Games]. Shanghai: Liangyou tushu yinhua youxian gongsi, 1930.

"Di jiu jie Yuandong yundonghui zhi huigu" 第九屆遠東運動會之回顧 [A look back at the Ninth Far Eastern Championship Games]. *Jiaoyu zazhi (Educational Review)* 22.6 (20 June 1930): 233–42.

"Di liu jie Quanguo yundonghui jiyao" 第六屆全國運動會紀要 [Outline of the Sixth National Games]. *Jiaoyu zazhi (Educational Review)* 25.12 (10 December 1935): 109–39.

Di qi jie quanguo yundonghui huakan 第七屆全國運動會畫刊 [Seventh National Games Official Pictorial]. Shanghai: Shenbaoguan, 1948.

Di qi jie quanguo yundonghui jinian shouce 第七屆全國運動會紀念手冊 [Seventh National Games Commemorative Program]. Shanghai: Shenbaoguan, 1948.

"Di qi jie quanyunhui choubei weiyuanhui de wenjian" 第七屆全運會籌備委員會的文件 [Documents from the Seventh National Games Planning Committee]. File 587 (10), Folder 10. Second Historical Archives, Nanjing, China.

Di qi jie Yuandong yundonghui quanguo yuxuan dahui tekan 第七屆遠東運動會全國預選大會特刊 [Special publication of the National Selection Meet for the Seventh Far Eastern Championship Games]. Shanghai: Di qi jie Yuandong yundonghui quanguo yuxuan dahui tekanshe, 1925.

"Di qi jie Yuandong yundonghui quanguo yuxuanhui zhi jingguo" 第七屆遠東運動會全國預選會之經過 [Events at the Seventh Far Eastern Championship Games National Selection Meet]. *Jiaoyu zazhi (Chinese Educational Review)* 17.6 (20 June 1925): 6–9.

Di san ci quanguo yundong dahui tekan 第三次全國運動大會特刊 [Special Publication of the Third National Games]. Hankou: Hankou jidujiao qingnianhui, 1924.

Di shiwu jie Huabei yundonghui 第十五屆華北運動會 [The Fifteenth North China Games]. Ji'nan, 1931.

Dikötter, Frank. *The Discourse of Race in Modern China*. Stanford, Calif.: Stanford University Press, 1992.

Ding Zengfang 丁曾芳. "Wo duiyu tiyu zhi ganxiang" 我對於體育之感想 [My feelings about physical education]. *Tiyu huikan* 1 (June 1925): 11.

Ding Zuyin 丁祖蔭. "Tiyu de xinli yanjiu (shang)" 體育的心理研究(上) [Psychological research into physical education, Part 1]. *Xiaoxue jiaoshi banyuekan* 4.10 (1 February 1937): 28–32.

Dirks, Nicholas B., Geoff Eley, and Sherry B. Ortner, eds. *Culture/Power/History: A Reader in Contemporary Social Theory*. Princeton, N.J.: Princeton University Press, 1994.

Djung, Lu-Dzai [Zhong Luzhai 鐘魯齋]. *A History of Democratic Education in Modern China*. Shanghai: Commercial Press, 1934.

Dong Shouyi 董守义. "Aolinpike yu Zhongguo" 奧林匹克与中国 [The Olympics and China]. In *Aoyunhui yu Zhongguo*, edited by Ji Hongmin, Yu Xingmao, and Lü Changfu, 1–56. Beijing: Wenshi ziliao chubanshe, 1985.

Dongya tiyu xuexiao xiaokan 東亞體育學校校刊 [Journal of the East Asia Physical Education School]. Shanghai.

"Dongya yundonghui di yi ci dahui ji" 東亞運動會第一次大會記 [Record of the First Far Eastern Championship Games]. *Zhenxiang huabao (True Record [Illustrated Magazine])* 17 (1 March 1913): 1–2.

Duara, Prasenjit. "Provincial Narrations of the Nation: Centralism and Federalism in Republican China." In *Cultural Nationalism in East Asia: Representation and Identity,* edited by Harumi Befu, 9–35. Berkeley: Institute of East Asian Studies, University of California, 1993.

————. *Rescuing History from the Nation: Questioning Narratives of Modern China.* Chicago: University of Chicago Press, 1995.

Duxiu 獨秀. "Sui gan lu (bashi): Qingnian tiyu wenti" 隨感錄(八十): 青年體育問題 [Random jottings (#80): Problems in youth physical education]. *Xin qingnian (La Jeunesse)* 7.2 (1 January 1920): 157.

Dyck, Noel, ed. *Games, Sports and Cultures.* New York: Berg, 2000.

Eastman, Lloyd E. *The Abortive Revolution: China under Nationalist Rule, 1927–1937.* Cambridge, Mass.: Council on East Asian Studies, Harvard University, 1974.

Edelman, Robert. *Serious Fun: A History of Spectator Sports in the USSR.* New York: Oxford University Press, 1993.

Educational Review (Jiaoyu yuebao 教育月報). Shanghai.

Er-ai-li 爾愛理. "Gaodeng xiaoxue nannü xuesheng heli de yundong xitong" 高等小學男女學生合理的運動系統 [Appropriate exercise regimens for male and female higher primary school students]. Translated by Mai Kele 麥克樂 [Charles H. McCloy]. *Tiyu jikan (Physical Education Quarterly)* 1.2 (August 1922): 1–12.

Ershiba huasheng 二十八畫生 (Mao Zedong 毛澤東). "Tiyu zhi yanjiu" 體育之研究 [Research on physical education]. *Xin qingnian (La Jeunesse)* 3.2 (1 April 1917): 1–11.

Ershier nian Quanguo yundong dahui choubei weiyuanhui 二十二年全國運動大會籌備委員會, ed. *Ershier nian Quanguo yundong dahui zongbaogao shu* 二十二年全國運動大會總報告書 [1933 National Games Official Report]. Shanghai: Zhonghua shuju, 1934.

Esherick, Joseph W., ed. *Remaking the Chinese City: Modernity and National Identity, 1900–1950.* Honolulu: University of Hawai'i Press, 2000.

Falasca-Zamponi, Simonetta. *Fascist Spectacle: The Aesthetics of Power in Mussolini's Italy.* Berkeley: University of California Press, 1997.

Fan Hong. "The Female Body, Missionary and Reformer: The Reconceptualization of Femininity in Modern China." *International Journal of the History of Sport* 10.2 (August 1993): 133–58.

————. *Footbinding, Feminism and Freedom: The Liberation of Women's Bodies in Modern China.* Portland, Ore.: Frank Cass, 1997.

————. "'Iron Bodies': Women, War, and Sport in the Early Communist Movement in Modern China." *Journal of Sport History* 24.1 (Spring 1997): 1–23.

Fan Jun 樊駿. "Duiyu guoji zhi ganyan" 對於國猞之感言 [Thoughts on martial arts]. In *Tiyu yanjiuhui huikan,* edited by Nanjing gaodeng shifan xuexiao tiyu yanjiuhui, 1–2. Nanjing: n.p., 1918.

Fan Wenzhao 范文照. "Ou Mei ganxiang" 歐美感想 [Thoughts on Europe and America]. *Zhongguo jianzhu* 24 (March 1936): 11–19.

Fang Wanbang 方萬邦. *Tiyu yuanli* 體育原理 [Principles of physical education]. Shanghai: Shangwu yinshuguan, 1933; reprint 1935.

————. "Woguo xianxing tiyu zhi shi da wenti jiqi jiejue tujing" 我國現行體育之十大問題及其解決途徑 [The ten greatest problems with our nation's current physical education programs and the paths we should take to solve them]. *Jiaoyu zazhi (Educational Review)* 25.3 (10 March 1933): 29–38.

Fanon, Frantz. *The Wretched of the Earth*. New York: Grove Press, 1968.

Fei Futao 費福燾, ed. *Nanyang daxue jijibu shi zhou jiniance* 南洋大學技擊部十週紀念冊 [Nanyang University Boxing Team tenth anniversary commemorative volume]. Shanghai, 1922.

"Fei-lü-bin Yuandong yundonghui zhi jingguo" 菲律賓遠東運動會之經過 [The events of the Philippines Far Eastern Championship Games]. *Jiaoyu zazhi (Chinese Educational Review)* 11.6 (20 June 1919): 58–60.

Fengshen 鳳申. "Di shiyi jie Shijie yundonghui de niaokan" 第十一屆世界運動會的鳥瞰 [A bird's-eye view of the Eleventh Olympiad]. *Zhongwai yuekan (Sino-Foreign Monthly)* 1.9 (1 October 1936): 123–32.

Fitzgerald, John. *Awakening China: Politics, Culture and Class in the Nationalist Revolution*. Stanford, Calif.: Stanford University Press, 1996.

Freyn, Hubert. *Chinese Education in the War*. Shanghai: Kelly and Walsh, 1940; reprint, Taipei: Ch'eng Wen Publishing, 1974.

Fujian quansheng xuexiao lianhe yundong dahui baogao 福建全省學校聯合運動大會報告 [Official report of the Fujian Provincial Interscholastic Games]. N.p.: Fujian jiaoyuting, 1921.

Fujian sheng difangzhi bianzuan weiyuanhui 福建省地方志編纂委员会, ed. *Fujian shengzhi: Tiyu zhi* 福建省志:体育志 [Fujian provincial gazetteer: Chronicle of physical culture]. Fuzhou: Fujian renmin chubanshe, 1993.

Fujitani, Takashi. "Technologies of Power in Modern Japan: The Military, the 'Local,' the Body." English original of the article that appears as: T. Fujitani. "Kindai Nihon ni okeru kenryoku no tekunorojī: guntai, 'chihō', shintai." Translated by Umemori Naoyuki. *Shisō* 845 (November 1994).

Funü zazhi 婦女雜誌 *(Ladies' Journal)*. Shanghai.

Funü zazhi 婦女雜誌 [Women's magazine]. Beijing.

Fuxing yuekan 復興月刊 [Renaissance monthly]. Shanghai.

Gannan junmin lianhe er ci yundong dahui tekan 贛南軍民聯合二次運動大會特刊 [Special Publication of the Second Southern Jiangxi Military-Citizenry United Athletic Meet]. N.p., 1934.

Gansu tiyu shiliao 甘肅体育史料 [Materials from the history of Gansu physical culture]. Lanzhou.

Gansu tiyu shiliao zhuanji 甘肅体育史料专辑 [Collection of materials from the history of Gansu physical culture]. Lanzhou.

Gao Mingkai 高名凱 and Liu Zhengyan 刘正琰. *Xiandai Hanyu wailaici yanjiu* 现代汉语外来词研究 [Research into terms of foreign origin in the modern Chinese language]. Beijing: Wenxue geming chubanshe, 1958.

Gao Shan 高山. "Meirong de yundongfa" 美容的運動法 [Beauty exercise regimen]. *Funü zazhi (Ladies' Journal)* 7.12 (December 1921): 81–82.

Gao Shilin 高石麟. "Women weishenme yao yundong" 我們為甚麼要運動 [Why we should exercise]. *Funü zazhi (Ladies' Journal)* 7.7 (July 1921): 80–81.

Gilmartin, Christina Kelley. *Engendering the Chinese Revolution: Radical Women, Communist Politics, and Mass Movements in the 1920s.* Berkeley: University of California Press, 1995.

Goldman, Merle, and Elizabeth J. Perry, eds. *Changing Meanings of Citizenship in Modern China.* Cambridge, Mass.: Harvard University Press, 2002.

Graham, Gael. "Exercising Control: Sports and Physical Education in American Protestant Mission Schools in China, 1880–1930." *Signs: Journal of Women in Culture and Society* 20.1 (Autumn 1994): 23–48.

Gu Bingfu. "China's Participation in the Olympics (II)." Translated by Xin Yu. *China Sports* 336 (September 1996): 6–8.

Gu Shiquan (谷世权). "Introduction to Ancient and Modern Chinese Physical Culture." In *Sport in China,* edited by Howard G. Knuttgen, Ma Qiwei, and Wu Zhongyuan, 3–24. Champaign, Ill.: Human Kinetics Books, 1990.

———. *Zhongguo tiyu shi (xia ce—jindai bufen)* 中国体育史(下册－近代部分) [The history of Chinese physical culture (vol. 2, Modern section)]. Beijing: Beijing tiyu xueyuan chubanshe, 1989.

Guangxi daxue min er wu ji biye jiniance 廣西大學民二五級畢業紀念冊 [Guangxi University Class of 1936 yearbook]. Wuzhou, 1936.

Guangxi tiyu shiliao 广西体育史料 [Materials from the history of Guangxi physical culture]. Nanning.

Guizhou sheng Di yi jie quansheng yundonghui choubei weiyuanhui 贵州省第一届全省運動會籌備委員會, eds. *Guizhou sheng Di yi jie quansheng yundonghui zongbaogao* 贵州省第一届全省運動會總報告 [Official report of the First Guizhou Provincial Games]. Guiyang: Guizhou sheng zhengfu jiaoyuting, 1935.

Guizhou sheng Zunyi diqu difangzhi bianzuan weiyuanhui 贵州省遵义地区地方志编纂委员会, eds. *Zhejiang daxue zai Zunyi* 浙江大学在遵义 [Zhejiang University in Zunyi]. Hangzhou: Zhejiang daxue chubanshe, 1990.

Guizhou tiyu 贵州体育 [Guizhou physical culture]. Guiyang.

Guizhou tiyu shiliao 贵州体育史料 [Materials from the history of Guizhou physical culture]. Guiyang.

Guo Hongru 果鸿儒. "Shengkao fengchao liang ri ji" 省考風潮兩日記 [A diary of two days of unrest at the Provincial Guoshu Exam]. *Qiushi yuekan* 2.10 (10 July 1936): 353–55.

Guo Xifen 郭希汾. *Zhongguo tiyushi* 中國體育史 [The history of Chinese physical culture]. Shanghai: Shangwu yinshuguan, 1919. Shanghai: Shanghai wenyi chubanshe, 1993.

Guojia tiwei tiyu wenshi gongzuo weiyuanhui 国家体委体育文史工作委员会 and Quanguo tizong wenshi ziliao bianshen weiyuanhui 全国体总文史资料编审委员会, eds. *Tiyu shiliao di 15 ji: Huabei yundonghui (1913–1934 nian)* 体育史料第15辑: 华北运动会(1913–1934年)[Historical materials on physical education, vol. 15: The North China Games (1913–1934)]. Beijing: Renmin tiyu chubanshe, 1989.

———. *Tiyu shiliao di 16 ji: Zhongguo jindai tiyu yijuean xuanbian* 体育史料

第16辑:中国近代体育议决案选编 [Historical materials on physical education, vol. 16: Collection of resolutions on modern Chinese physical education]. Beijing: Renmin tiyu chubanshe, 1990.

Guojia tiwei tiyu wenshi gongzuo weiyuanhui 国家体委体育文史工作委员会 and Zhongguo tiyu kexue xuehui tiyushi fenhui 中国体育科学学会体育史分会, eds. *Mao Zedong yu tiyu wenji* 毛泽东与体育文集 [Essays on Mao Zedong and physical culture]. Chengdu: Sichuan jiaoyu chubanshe, 1994.

Guojia tiwei tiyu wenshi gongzuo weiyuanhui 国家体委体育文史工作委员会 and Zhongguo tiyushi xuehui 中国体育史学会, eds. *Zhongguo jindai tiyushi* 中国近代体育史 [The history of modern Chinese sport]. Beijing: Beijing tiyu xueyuan chubanshe, 1989.

"Guoli Nanjing gaoshi, Dongnan daxue, Zhongyang daxue li jie biye tongxue zuijin diaocha biao" 國立南京高師東南大學中央大學歷屆畢業同學最近調查表 [Data from recent survey of alumni from each Nanjing Higher Normal, Southeastern University, and Central University graduating class]. *Tiyu zazhi* 3 (June 1931): 127–40.

Guoli Qingdao daxue yilan 國立青島大學一覽 [Tour of National Qingdao University]. Qingdao: Qingdao daxue, 1931.

Guomin tiyu huikan 國民體育彙刊 (*Olympic Physical Review*). Shanghai.

Guomin tiyu jikan 國民體育季刊 (*Physical Education Quarterly*). Taibei.

"Guomin tiyu shishi fang'an" 國民體育實施方案 [Program for the implementation of citizens' *tiyu*]. *Jiaoyubu gongbao* 4.43–44 (6 November 1932): 70–89.

"Guomin tiyu zhi yiban" 國民體育之一斑 [Scenes from the citizens' physical culture]. *Hanxue yuekan* 5.2 (1 May 1935).

Guoshu, tiyu, junshi 國術，體育，軍事 [*Guoshu*, sports, paramilitary training] (Weekly feature in *Zhongguo ribao*, 1933–34.). Nanjing.

Guoshu tongyi yuekan 國術統一月刊 [*Guoshu* unification monthly]. Shanghai.

Guoshu yuekan 國術月刊 (*National Gymnastics Monthly*). Taibei.

Guoshu zhoukan 國術週刊 [*Guoshu* weekly]. Nanjing.

Guttmann, Allen. *Games and Empires: Modern Sports and Cultural Imperialism.* New York: Columbia University Press, 1994.

"Hanjiaqi zhong women de gongzuo" 寒假期中我們的工作 [Our work for the winter vacation period]. *Zhongguo qingnian* 58 (20 December 1924): 120–125.

Hanxue yuekan 汗血月刊 [Sweat and blood monthly]. Shanghai.

Hao Gengsheng 郝更生. *Hao Gengsheng huiyilu* 郝更生回憶錄 [Memoirs of Hao Gengsheng]. Taibei: Zhuanji wenxue chubanshe, 1969.

———. "Shi nian lai zhi Zhongguo tiyu" 十年來之中國體育 [Chinese physical culture over the last ten years]. *Wenhua Jianshe yuekan* 3.10 (10 July 1937): 111–124.

———. "Tiyu" 體育 [Physical education]. In *Zhonghua minguo jiaoyu zhi*, vol. 2, edited by Wu Junsheng, 1–25. Taibei: Zhonghua wenhua chuban shiye weiyuanhui, 1955.

He Yousheng 何酉生 and Wu Mengfei 吳夢非. "Zhejiang quansheng yundonghuige" 浙江全省運動會歌 [Song of the Zhejiang Provincial Games]. *Tushu zhanwang* 2.7 (May 1937).

Hebei yuekan 河北月刊 [Hebei monthly]. Shijiazhuang.

Henan shengli Henan daxue xianxing zhangze huibian 河南省立河南大學現行章則彙編 [Current constitution and other data from Henan Provincial University]. N.p.: Henan shengli Henan daxue, 1935.

Heng 恆. "Benxiao tiyu xin jiaoshou Shen Guoquan jun" 本校體育新教授申國權君 [Our school's new P.E. professor, Mr. Shen Guoquan]. *Nanyang zhoukan (Nanyang Weekly)* 3.11 (15 December 1923).

Hoh, Gunsun [Hao Gengsheng]. *Physical Education in China*. Shanghai: Commercial Press, 1926.

Hongse Zhonghua 紅色中華 [Red China]. Ruijin.

Hou Hongjian 侯鴻鑑. "Canguan Jiangsu shengli di er nüzi shifan yundonghui ji" 參觀江蘇省立第二女子師範運動會記 [A record of observations from the Second Jiangsu Provincial Women's Normal School Meet]. *Jiaoyu zazhi (Chinese Educational Review)* 7.9 (15 September 1915): 68–70.

———. "Duiyu Jiangsu di san jie sheng lianhe yundonghui ganlun" 對於江蘇第三屆省聯合運動會感論 [My feelings on the Third Jiangsu Provincial Games]. *Jiaoyu zazhi (Chinese Educational Review)* 8.11 (15 November 1916): 182–187.

Hsu I-hsiung [Xu Yixiong] 許義雄. "Wan Qing tiyu sixiang zhi xingcheng: Yi ziqiang baozhong sixiang wei zhongxin de tantao" 完全體育思想之形成：以自強保種思想為中心的探討 [The formation of a philosophy of physical culture in the late Qing: An investigation made with the philosophy of self-strengthening and racial preservation at the base]. *Tiyu xuebao (Bulletin of Physical Education)* 10 (December 1988): 7–17.

———. *Woguo jindai tiyu baokan mulu suoyin* 我國近代體育報刊目錄索引 [Catalogued index of modern Chinese sports periodicals]. Taibei: Shida shuyuan, 1994.

———. "Xu Yibing tiyu sixiang chutan" 徐一冰體育思想初探 [A preliminary investigation into Xu Yibing's philosophy of physical education]. *Taiwan tiyu (Taiwan Sports)* 39 (October 1988): 17–20.

———. "Zhongguo jindai minzu zhuyi tiyu sixiang zhi tezhi" 中國近代民族主義體育思想之特質 [Special characteristics of modern Chinese nationalistic philosophies of physical culture]. *Tiyu xuebao (Bulletin of Physical Education)* 12 (December 1990): 1–18.

Hsu Yuan-ming [Xu Yuanmin] 徐元民. "Jindai Zhongguo canyu Yuandong yundonghui zhi tantao (1913–1934)" 近代中國參與遠東運動會之探討 [A study of China's participation in the Far Eastern Championship Games (1913–1934)]. Unpublished paper, 1993.

———. "Zhanqian shinian Zhongguo tiyu sixiang zhi yanjiu (1928–1937)" 戰前十年中國體育思想之研究 (1928–1937) [Research into Chinese physical education philosophy during the prewar decade (1928–1937)]. M.S. thesis, Guoli Taiwan shifan daxue, 1990.

Hu Shiliu 胡師柳. "Di shi jie Shijie yundong dahui ji" 第十屆世界運動大會記 [Record of the Tenth Olympiad]. *Shenbao yuekan* 1.3 (15 September 1932): 117–25.

Hu Tong 胡通. "Xiaoxue aiguo youxi jiaocai" 小學愛國游戲教材 [Patriotic games for elementary school instruction]. *Qinfen tiyu yuebao (Chin Fen Sports Monthly)* 1.4 (10 January 1934): 46–52.

Huabei tiyu yuebao 華北體育月報 [North China sports monthly]. Beijing.

"Huabei yundong chengji jinbu zhi kexi" 華北運動成績進步之可喜 [Joy at the progress seen in the North China Games]. *Shenghuo zhoukan (Life Weekly)* 6.24 (6 June 1931): 485–86.

Huang Binsheng 黃斌生. "Biaozhun yundong de ceyan" 標準運動的測驗 [Standard athletic tests]. *Tiyu jikan (Chinese Journal of Physical Education)* 2.1 (April 1923): 1–7.

———. "Jingdou youxi" 競鬥游戲 [Competitive games]. *Tiyu jikan (Chinese Journal of Physical Education)* 2.1 (April 1923): 1–4.

Huang Jianxing 黃健行. "Wuguo ying caiyong zuqiu wei guomin youxi" 吾國應採用足球為國民遊戲 [Our nation should take soccer as its national pastime]. *Qinfen tiyu yuebao (Chin Fen Sports Monthly)* 3.5 (February 1936): 403–4.

Huang Wanxiang 黃畹香. "Huncheng zhi youxi" 混成之游戲 [Hybrid game]. In *Jingwu benji*, edited by Chen Tiesheng, 146. Shanghai, 1920; reprint 1922.

———. "Nüzi yu jiji zhi guanxi" 女子與技擊之關係 [The relationship between females and martial arts]. In *Jingwu benji*, edited by Chen Tiesheng, 247. 1920; reprint, Shanghai: n.p., 1922.

Huang Xing 黃醒. "Weishenme tichang jing de tiyu?" 為甚麼提倡靜的體育 [Why advocate tranquil exercise?]. *Tiyu zhoubao* 10 (24 February 1919): 2–3.

———. "Wo jiao ticao shi de zuiguo" 我教體操時的罪過 [My past sins as a calisthenics instructor]. *Tiyu zhoubao* 42 (27 October 1919): 2–4.

———. "Xuexiao yingfou feizhi bingcao?" 學校應否廢止兵操 [Should schools abolish military drill?]. *Tiyu zhoubao* 46 (24 November 1919): 3–5.

———. "Zhu lu" 築路 [Road construction]. *Tiyu zhoubao* 32 (28 July 1919): 3–5.

Huanian zhoukan 華年周刊 [Chinese weekly]. Shanghai.

Huanlong 幻龍. "Canguan Jiangsu shengli xuexiao lianhe yundonghui jishi" 參觀江蘇省立學校聯合運動會記事 [Record of observations on the Jiangsu Provincial School Athletic Meet]. *Jiaoyu zazhi (Chinese Educational Review)* 6.10 (15 December 1914): 31–40.

Hubei di jiu jie quan sheng yundong dahui tekan 湖北第九屆全省運動大會特刊 *(The Special Publishing of Hubeh Provincial Athletic Meet)*. Hankou, 1947.

Hubei jiaoyu yuekan 湖北教育月刊 [Hubei education monthly]. Hankou.

Hubei sheng dang zheng jun xue tiyu cujin weiyuanhui huikan 湖北省黨政軍學體育促進委員會會刊 [Hubei Province Party-Government-Military-Scholastic Physical Culture Promotion Society Publication]. Wuchang.

Hubei wuxue 湖北武學 [Hubei Military Academy]. n.p., 1900.

Hunan sheng difangzhi bianzuan weiyuanhui 湖南省地方志编纂委员会, ed. *Hunan shengzhi, di ershier juan: Tiyu zhi* 湖南省志, 第二十二卷:体育志 [Hunan provincial gazetteer, vol. 22: Chronicle of physical culture]. Changsha: Hunan chubanshe, 1994.

Hung, Chang-tai. *Going to the People: Chinese Intellectuals and Folk Literature, 1918–1937*. Cambridge, Mass.: Council on East Asian Studies, Harvard University, 1985.

Huo Liangui 霍連貴. "Gaijin xiangcun xiaoxue tiyu de wojian" 改進鄉村小學體育的我見 [My opinions on reforming village elementary school physical instruction]. *Qinfen tiyu yuebao (Chin Fen Sports Monthly)* 4.3 (December 1936): 252–253.

Illustrated Week-End Sporting World (Jingle huabao 競樂畫報). Shanghai.

Imamura Yoshio 今村嘉雄. *Nihon taiikushi* 日本体育史 [The history of Japanese physical culture]. Tokyo: Kaneko Shobō, 1951.

"Inter Camp Olympics, 1952 Pyuktong D.P.R.K." P.O.W. Camps Administration in the Democratic People's Republic of Korea, 1952. Retrieved 26 February 2003 from www.kmike.com/POW_Olympics/pow/index.htm.

Ji Hongmin 纪红民, Yu Xingmao 俞兴茂, and Lü Changfu 吕长赋, eds. *Aoyunhui yu Zhongguo* 奥运会与中国 [The Olympics and China]. Beijing: Wenshi ziliao chubanshe, 1985.

Jia Fengzhen 賈豐臻. "Duanlian zhuyi zhi jiaoyu" 鍛煉主義之教育 [A training-ist education]. *Jiaoyu zazhi (Chinese Educational Review)* 7.6 (15 June 1915): 116–26.

———. "Guomin tiyu buzhen zhi gu" 國民體育不振之故 [The causes of our citizens' poor physical fitness]. *Jiaoyu zazhi (Chinese Educational Review)* 10.12 (20 December 1918): 157–62.

———. "Shixing junguomin jiaoyu zhi fangfa" 實行軍國民教育之方法 [Methods of instituting military citizenship education]. *Jiaoyu zazhi (Chinese Educational Review)* 7.7 (15 July 1915): 139–147.

Jian Shijian 簡世鑑. "Huanying Lu Yao liang zhuren huiguo ji" 歡迎盧姚兩主任回國紀 [On the welcome-home reception for Directors Lu and Yao]. *Jingwu zazhi* 40 (15 April 1924): 59–64.

Jiang Ang 蔣昂. "Canguan Jiangsu Di er nü shifan ji Changshou lianhe yundonghui ji" 參觀江蘇第二女師範及常熟聯合運動會紀 [Record of observations on the Second Jiangsu Provincial Women's Normal School Meet and the Changshou Athletic Meet]. *Jiaoyu zazhi (Chinese Educational Review)* 7.7 (15 July 1915): 45–47.

Jiang Huaiqing 蔣槐青. "Bo-lin mian qu ba!" 柏林免去吧 [Don't just go to Berlin!]. *Guomin tiyu huikan (Olympic Physical Review)* 1 (1 January 1936): 19.

Jiang Xiahun 姜俠魂. "Guoshu yu tongyi" 國術與統一 [*Guoshu* and unification]. *Guoshu tongyi yuekan* 1.2 (20 November 1934): 3–5.

Jiang Xiaoxian 江孝賢. "Xuexiao yingfou feizhi bingcao? (Er)" 學校應否廢止兵操(二) [Should schools abolish military drill? (Two)]. *Tiyu zhoubao* 46 (24 November 1919): 8–9.

Jiangsu shengli xuexiao di yi ci lianhe yundonghui huibian 江蘇省立學校第一次聯合運動會彙編 [First Jiangsu Provincial Interscholastic Meet Report]. Nanjing: Jiangsu xun'anshi gongshu, 1914.

Jiangsu tiyu wenshi 江苏体育文史 [Materials from the history of Jiangsu physical culture]. Nanjing.

Jiangxi jiaoyu 江西教育 [Jiangxi education]. Nanchang.

Jiangxi shengli tiyuchang shishi gongzuo zongbaogao 江西省立體育場實施工作總報告 [Jiangxi Provincial Athletic Grounds final work report]. Nanchang: Jiangxi shengli tiyuchang, 1935.

Jianzhe 健者. "Di shi jie Ou-lin-bi-ke yundong dahui huizhi" 第十屆歐林匹克運動大會彙誌 [Collected reports on the Tenth Olympiad]. *Qingnian jinbu (Association Progress)* 139 (January 1931): 100–102; 140 (February 1931): 78–80; 141 (March 1931): 92–94.

Jiao yu xue 教與學 [Teaching and learning]. Nanjing.

Jiaoyu congkan 教育叢刊 *(Educational Research)*. Shanghai.

Jiaoyu yu minzhong 教育與民眾 [Education and the masses].

Jiaoyu zazhi 教育雜誌 *(Chinese Educational Review)*. Shanghai.

Jiaoyu zazhi 教育雜誌 *(Educational Review)*. Shanghai. [Continues above with different English title.]

Jiaoyu ziliao jikan 教育資料季刊 [Educational information quarterly]. Taibei.

"Jiaoyubu canjia gezhong jinian huodong de wenjian" 教育部參加各種紀念活動的文件 [Documents from Department of Education participation in any type of commemorative event]. File 2078, Folder 52. Second Historical Archives, Nanjing, China.

Jiaoyubu gongbao 教育部公報 [Bulletin of the Department of Education]. Nanjing.

"Jiaoyubu shuqi tiyu buxiban kecheng" 教育部暑期體育補習班課程 [Education Department Summer *Tiyu* Session curriculum]. *Tiyu zhoubao (Sporting Weekly)* 2.21 (1 July 1933): 9–11.

Jiaoyubu Zhongguo jiaoyu nianjian bianzuan weiyuanhui 教育部中國教育年鑑編纂委員會, ed. *Di yi ci Zhongguo jiaoyu nianjian* 第一次中國教育年鑑 [First Chinese education yearbook]. Nanjing, 1934; reprint, Taibei: Zongqing tushu gongsi, n.d.

Jilin tiyu shiliao 吉林体育史料 [Materials on the history of Jilin physical culture]. Changchun.

Jingwu zazhi 精武雜誌 [Pure Martial magazine]. Shanghai.

Jizhe 記者. "Liu Changchun chuxi Shijiehui zhi yunniang" 劉長春出席世界會之醞釀 [The story of how Liu Changchun's participation in the Olympics came about]. *Tiyu zhoubao (Sporting Weekly)* 23 (9 July 1932): 18–22.

Jizhe 記者. "Yuandong tiyu xiehui feifa jiesan zhi jingguo" 遠東體育協會非法解散之經過 [The story of the unlawful dissolution of the Far Eastern Athletic Association]. *Qinfen tiyu yuebao (Chin Fen Sports Monthly)* 1.9 (10 June 1934): 71–75.

Jizhe 記者 [Charles H. McCloy]. "Shibai de yuanyin" 失敗的原因 [The reasons for failure]. *Tiyu jikan (Physical Education Quarterly)* 1.2 (August 1922): 1–2.

———. "Zhonghua quanguo tiyu yanjiuhui" 中華全國體育研究會 [The Chinese National Tiyu Research Society]. *Tiyu jikan (Chinese Journal of Physical Education)* 2.1 (April 1923): 1–2.

Johnson, Rafer. *The Best That I Can Be: An Autobiography.* New York: Doubleday, 1998.

Jordan, David K., Andrew D. Morris, and Marc L. Moskowitz, eds. *The Minor Arts of Daily Life: Popular Culture in Taiwan.* Honolulu: University of Hawai'i Press, 2004.

Judge, Joan. "Citizens or Mothers of Citizens? Gender and the Meaning of Modern Chinese Citizenship." In *Changing Meanings of Citizenship in Modern China,* edited by Merle Goldman and Elizabeth J. Perry, 23–43. Cambridge, Mass.: Harvard University Press, 2002.

———. *Print and Politics: "Shibao" and the Culture of Reform in Late Qing China.* Stanford, Calif.: Stanford University Press, 1996.

Junshi weiyuanhui zhengxun chu dianying gu 軍事委員會政訓處電影股 production. *Huazhong yundonghui di liu jie* 華中運動會第六屆 [The Sixth Central China Games]. 1936 film.

Jusdanis, Gregory. *The Necessary Nation.* Princeton, N.J.: Princeton University Press, 2001.

Kang-Zang qianfeng 康藏前鋒 [The Xikang-Tibet Vanguard]. Nanjing.

Kangjian zazhi 康健雜誌 (*Good Health Magazine*). Shanghai.

Kexue de Zhongguo 科學的中國 [Scientific China]. Nanjing.

Kexue huabao 科學畫報 (*Popular Science*). Shanghai.

Knuttgen, Howard G., Ma Qiwei, and Wu Zhongyuan, eds. *Sport in China.* Champaign, Ill.: Human Kinetics Books, 1990.

Kolatch, Jonathan. *Sports, Politics and Ideology in China.* New York: Jonathan David Publishers, 1972.

Kuang Wennan 旷文楠 and Hu Xiaoming 胡小明. *Zhongguo tiyu shihua* 中国体育史话 [Items from the history of Chinese athletics]. Chengdu: Badu shushe, 1989.

Kunming tiyu wenshi 昆明体育文史 [Materials from the history of Kunming physical culture]. Kunming.

Kwan, S. S. [Guan Songsheng 關頌聲]. "Sports in China." *China Today* 2.1 (January 1959): 1–10.

Lang, Olga. *Chinese Family and Society.* New Haven, Conn.: Yale University Press, 1946.

Lao She. *Ma and Son.* Translated by Jean M. James. 1935. San Francisco: Chinese Materials Center, 1980.

Larson, Wendy. *Women and Writing in Modern China.* Stanford, Calif.: Stanford University Press, 1998.

Lazarus, Neil. *Nationalism and Cultural Practice in the Postcolonial World.* New York: Cambridge University Press, 1999.

Lee, Leo Ou-fan. *Shanghai Modern: The Flowering of a New Urban Culture in China, 1930–1945.* Cambridge, Mass.: Harvard University Press, 1999.

Levenson, Joseph R. *Confucian China and Its Modern Fate: A Trilogy.* Berkeley: University of California Press, 1958; reprint (3 vols. in 1), Berkeley: University of California Press, 1972.

Li Cimin 李次民. "Liang ci canjia Aoyunhui de guojiao—Li Huitang" 兩次參加

奥运会的国脚－李惠堂 [Two-time soccer Olympian Li Huitang]. In *Aoyun-hui yu Zhongguo*, edited by Ji Hongmin, Yu Xingmao, and Lü Changfu, 104–19. Beijing: Wenshi ziliao chubanshe, 1985.

Li Huitang 李惠堂. "Li le mutai dao xianzai" 離了母胎到現在 [My life from the womb to today]. *Liangyou (Young Companion)* 45 (March 1930): 12–13, 26–27, 34, 36.

Li Lixian 李立賢. "Yunnan quansheng yundong dahui jixiang" 雲南全省運動大會紀詳 [Record of the Yunnan Provincial Games]. *Qinfen tiyu yuebao (Chin Fen Sports Monthly)* 3.5 (February 1936): 438–41.

Li Shijun 李世駿. "Tiyu jiaoyu jianguo lun" 體育教育建國論 [On *tiyu* education and nation building]. *Jiangxi jiaoyu* 18 (April 1936): 61–72.

Liang Heng and Judith Shapiro. *Son of the Revolution.* New York: Vintage Books, 1983.

Liang Tian 梁田. *Zhongguo tianjing fazhan jianshi* 中国田径发展简史 [A simple history of the development of track and field in China]. N.p.: Guangdong tiyu kexue yanjiusuo and Guangdong tiyu wenshi weiyuanhui, 1982.

Liangyou 良友 *(Young Companion)*. Shanghai.

Lin Boyuan 林伯原. "Zhongguo jindai xuexiao wushu kecheng de shezhi yu fazhan" 中国近代学校武术课程的设置与发展 [The design and development of martial arts curricula in modern Chinese schools]. Handwritten manuscript presented at Di yi jie Dongbeiya tiyu yundongshi xueshu yantaohui 第一屆東北亞體育運動史學術研討會 [First Conference on the History of Physical Education and Sport in Northeast Asia], National Taiwan Normal University, Taipei, Taiwan, 19–21 December 1995.

———. *Zhongguo wushu shi* 中國武術史 [The history of Chinese martial arts]. Taibei: Wuzhou chubanshe, 1996.

Lin Dazu 林達祖 and Pan Cangshui 潘蒼水. "Chu Minyi xiansheng yanjiang taijicao de yuanli" 褚民誼先生演講太極操的原理 [Mr. Chu Minyi's lectures on the principles of *taijicao*]. *Guoshu tongyi yuekan* 1.1 (20 July 1934): 1–2.

Lin, Julia C. *Modern Chinese Poetry: An Introduction.* Seattle: University of Washington Press, 1972.

Lin Liru 林礪儒. "Duiyu zhongxue kecheng zhong junshi xunlian di yi ge jianyi" 對於中學課程中軍事訓練底一個建議 [A suggestion regarding military training in the middle school curriculum]. *Jiaoyu zazhi (Educational Review)* 26.1 (10 January 1936): 34–38.

Lin Mingyi 林明毅. "Qingmo xuexiao tiyu" 清末學校體育 [Physical education in late Qing schools]. *Shida tiyu*, no. 31 (1990): 18–24.

Liu Changchun 刘长春. "Wo daibiao Zhongguo canjia Di shi jie Aoyunhui shimo" 我代表中国参加第十届奥运会始末 [The whole story of my representing China at the Tenth Olympiad]. In *Aoyunhui yu Zhongguo*, edited by Ji Hongmin, Yu Xingmao, and Lü Changfu, 57–88. Beijing: Wenshi ziliao chubanshe, 1985.

"Liu Changchun bei shou huanying" 劉長春備受歡迎 [Liu Changchun's welcome]. *Tiyu zhoubao (Sporting Weekly)* 27 (6 August 1932): 1–2.

"Liu Changchun de riji" 劉長春的日記 [Liu Changchun's diary]. *Tiyu zhoubao (Sporting Weekly)* 32 (10 September 1932): 21–24.***

Liu Chin-ping [Liu Jinping] 劉進枰. "Zhonghua minguo Aolinpike weiyuan-hui huiji yanbian zhi lishi kaocha, 1949–1981" 中華民國奧林匹克委員會會籍演變之歷史考察1949–1981 (A Historical Survey of the Changes of ROC's Olympic Committee Membership from 1949 to 1981). M.S. thesis, Guoli Taiwan shifan daxue, 1995.

Liu Liqing 劉蘂青. "Zhongguo wushu zuijin de qushi" 中國武術最近的趨勢 [Recent trends in Chinese martial arts]. *Nanfang zazhi* 1.6 (1 November 1932): 153–159.

Liu, Lydia H. *Translingual Practice: Literature, National Culture, and Trans-lated Modernity — China, 1900–1937.* Stanford, Calif.: Stanford University Press, 1995.

Liu Shenzhan 劉慎旃. *Tiyu geming* 體育革命 [The physical culture revolution]. Nanjing: Zhongguo ribao, 1933.

———. "Tiyu jiuguo lun (er)" 體育救國論 (二) [On a physical education for national salvation (Part 2)]. *Qinfen tiyu yuebao (Chin Fen Sports Monthly)* 2.11 (August 1935): 713–719.

———. "Women yingdang zenyang de nuli" 我們應當怎樣的努力 [How we should be striving]. *Qinfen tiyu yuebao (Chin Fen Sports Monthly)* 2.1 (10 October 1934): 4–5.

Liu Shoupeng 劉壽朋. "Tiyu yu guomin jingji jianshe" 體育與國民經濟建設 [Physical culture and the reconstruction of the national economy]. *Hubei sheng dang zheng jun xue tiyu cujin weiyuanhui huikan* 1.3 (10 September 1936): 1–4.

Liu Xuesong 劉雪松. "Kefou jiang tiyu tongjun guoshu dacheng yipian" 可否將體育童軍國術打成一片 [Would it be possible to unite as one *tiyu*, Boy Scout training and *guoshu*?]. *Tiyu jikan (Physical Education Quarterly)* 3.1 (March 1937): 7–10.

Liu-Shao Jinying 劉邵錦英. "Tichang nüzi tiyu zhi wu jian" 提倡女子體育之吾見 [My opinions on promoting a women's physical culture]. *Qinfen tiyu yuebao (Chin Fen Sports Monthly)* 2.3 (10 December 1934): 212–13.

Lo, Jung-Pang, ed. *K'ang Yu-Wei: A Biography and a Symposium.* Tucson: University of Arizona Press, 1967.

Loud Family. *Interbabe Concern.* Burbank, Calif.: Alias Records, 1996.

Louie, Kam. *Theorizing Chinese Masculinity: Society and Gender in China.* New York: Cambridge University Press, 2002.

Lu Lihua 陸禮華. "Zhongguo nüzi tiyu yijian shu" 中國女子體育意見書 [An essay on my opinions on Chinese women's physical education]. In *Di san ci quanguo yundong dahui tekan.* Hankou: Hankou jidujiao qingnianhui, 1924.

Lu Weichang 盧煒昌. "Zhongguo wushu zhi jianglai" 中國武術之將來 [The future of Chinese martial arts]. In *Di san ci quanguo yundong dahui tekan.* Hankou: Hankou jidujiao qingnianhui, 1924.

Lu Xun 魯迅. "Sui gan lu (san qi)" 隨感錄(三七)[Random jottings (#37)]. *Xin qingnian (La Jeunesse)* 5.5 (15 October 1918): 514–15.

Lufei Kui 陸費逵. "Minguo putong xuezhi yi" 民國普通學制議 [Opinions on the public school system for the Republic]. *Jiaoyu zazhi (Chinese Educational Review)* 3.10 (10th day, 1st lunar month [27 February], 1912): 4–12.

Lujun di shiba jun quanjun yundong dahui 陸軍第十八軍全軍運動大會, ed. "Gezhong junshi tiyu bisai guize" 各種軍事體育比賽規則[Rules for several types of militarized *tiyu* competitions]. *Qinfen tiyu yuebao (Chin Fen Sports Monthly)* 3.8 (May 1936): 773–79.

Lulu 碌鹿. "Renti zhi heping huiyi" 人體之和平會議 [A human body peace conference]. *Tiyu zhoubao* 1 (9 December 1918): 6.

Luo Mujin 駱木金. "Chuantong tiyu guoshu jiaoxue zhi wojian" 傳統體育國術教學之我見 [My views on traditional physical culture and martial arts pedagogy]. *Guomin tiyu jikan (Physical Education Quarterly)* 23.4 (December 1994): 16–20.

Luo Xiaoao 羅嘯璈. *Jingwu waizhuan* 精武外傳 [An alternative history of the Pure Martial Association]. Shanghai: Jingwu tiyuhui, 1921.

Luo Yidong 羅一東. *Tiyuxue* 體育學 [The science of physical fitness]. 1924; reprint, Shanghai: Zhonghua shuju, 1931.

Ma Chonggan 馬崇淦. "Di shi jie Yuandong yundonghui huigu" 第十屆遠東運動會回顧 [A look back at the Tenth Far Eastern Championship Games]. *Shenbao yuekan* 3.6 (15 June 1934): 37–42.

———. "Di shiyi jie Shijie yundonghui gaishu" 第十一屆世界運動會概述 [A brief narrative of the Eleventh Olympiad]. *Shenbao zhoukan* 1.33 (23 August 1926): 791–92.

———. "Di wu jie Quanguo yundonghui zhi huigu" 第五屆全國運動會之回顧 [A look back at the Fifth National Games]. *Shenbao yuekan* 2.11 (15 November 1933): 77–82.

Ma Tongbin 马同斌 and Qin Yuanyuan 秦圓圓. *Beijing 2008 – Shen Ao de taiqian muhou* 北京2008—申奥的台前幕后[Beijing 2008: The official and behind-the-scenes details of the Olympic bid]. Beijing: Beijing tiyu daxue chubanshe, 2001.

MacAloon, John J. *This Great Symbol: Pierre de Coubertin and the Origins of the Modern Olympic Games.* Chicago: University of Chicago Press, 1981.

Mai Kele 麥克樂 [Charles H. McCloy]. "Chayan shenti fangfa (xu)" 查驗身體方法(續) [How to conduct physical examinations (continued)]. *Tiyu jikan (Chinese Journal of Physical Education)* 2.4 (December 1923): 1–13.

———. "Mai Kele jun yanci" 麥克樂君演辭 [Speech by Mr. Mai Kele (Charles McCloy)]. *Wushu* 1.2 (February 1921): 1–3.

———. "Quanguo tiyu yanjiuhui di yi nian de chengji baogao" 全國體育研究會第一年的成績報告[Report on the accomplishments of the Chinese National Tiyu Research Society in its first year]. *Tiyu jikan (Chinese Journal of Physical Education)* 2.4 (December 1923): 1–5.

———. "Quanguo yundonghui zhi yiyi" 全國運動會之意義 [The significance of these National Games]. In *Di san ci quanguo yundong dahui tekan.* Hankou: Hankou jidujiao qingnianhui, 1924.

———. "Tiyu yu de-mo-ke-la-xi" 體育與德謨克拉西 [Physical culture and democracy]. *Tiyu yu weisheng (Journal of Physical Education and Hygiene)* 3.1 (March 1924): 1–6.

———. "Wenhua yu tiyu" 文化與體育 [Culture and physical education]. *Tiyu jikan (Chinese Journal of Physical Education)* 2.4 (December 1923): 1–9.

——— ["Me K'e-lo"]. "Wushi nian lai Zhongguo zhi tiyu ji wushu" 五十年來中國之體育及武術 ("China's Physical Culture & Athletics for the Past 50 Years"). In *Zuijin zhi wushi nian (The Past Fifty Years)*, 1–7. Shanghai: Shenbaoguan, 1922; Shanghai: Shanghai shudian, 1987.

———. "Yuandong yundonghui ji Zhongguo gedi yundonghui gaiyong mituzhi" 遠東運動會及中國各地運動會改用米突制 [On the switch to the metric system in the Far Eastern Games and in track meets all over China]. *Tiyu jikan (Chinese Journal of Physical Education)* 2.4 (December 1923): 1–3.

———. "Yundong shang junzi de jingshen (Sportsmanship)" 運動上君子的精神 (Sportsmanship) [The gentleman's spirit (sportsmanship) as applied to athletics]. *Tiyu jikan (Physical Education Quarterly)* 1.2 (August 1922): 1–7.

Manchuria: A Monthly Review. Xinjing.

Manila Times. Manila.

Mao Anjun 毛岸俊 [Andrew Morris]. "1909–1919 nian *Jiaoyu zazhi* tiyu wenzhang fenxi de chubu" 1909–1919「教育雜誌」體育文章分析的初步 [A preliminary analysis of physical education–related articles in the *Chinese Educational Review, 1909–1919*]. *Tiyu xuebao (Bulletin of Physical Education)* 21 (June 1996): 47–58.

———. "Zhongguo cong ticao dao tiyu de zhuanbian" 中国从体操到体育的转变 [The Chinese transition from calisthenics and gymnastics to athletics]. *Tiyu wenshi (Journal of Sport History and Culture)* 87 (September 1997): 33–35.

McCloy, Charles Harold. *Some Achievement Standards in Track and Field Athletic Events for Boys from Ten to Twenty Years of Age.* New York: A. S. Barnes, 1932.

McCrone, Kathleen E. *Playing the Game: Sport and the Physical Emancipation of English Women, 1879–1914.* Lexington: University Press of Kentucky, 1988.

Meng Guangpeng 孟廣澎. "'Tiyu' yu 'Xin shenghuo'" '體育'與'新生活' ["Physical culture" and "New Life"]. *Hubei sheng dang zheng jun xue tiyu cujin weiyuanhui huikan* 1.2 (10 May 1936): 8–13.

Millard's Review of the Far East. Shanghai.

Min 敏. "Quanyun yu shuizai" 全運與水災 [The National Games and the flooding]. *Tiyu xinsheng (Athletic China)* 1 (October 1931): 25.

"Minguo ershi nian Quanguo yundong dahui jingsai guicheng" 民國二十年全國運動大會競賽規程 [Competition rules and regulations for the 1931 National Games]. *Jiaoyubu gongbao* 3.12 (29 March 1931): 58–68.

Minguo ershier nian Quanguo yundonghui zhuankan 民國二十二年全國運動會專刊 *(National Athletic Meet Special 1933)*. Shanghai: Shidai tushu gongsi, 1933.

Minguo ribao 民國日報 *(Republican Daily News)*. Nanjing.

Minzhong jiaoyu yuekan 民眾教育月刊 [Mass education monthly]. Nanjing.

Morris, Andrew. "'All China Has Muscles Now, and We Know How to Use Them': Nationalist and Communist Sporting Cultures during Wartime, 1937–45." Paper presented at the Association for Asian Studies Annual Meeting, Washington, D.C., 5 April 2002. www.calpoly.edu/~admorris/AAS2002Paper.

———. "Baseball, History, the Local and the Global in Taiwan." In *The Minor Arts of Daily Life: Popular Culture in Taiwan*, edited by David K. Jordan, Andrew Morris, and Marc L. Moskowitz, 175–203. Honolulu: University of Hawai'i Press, 2004.

———. "Cultivating the National Body: A History of Physical Culture in Republican China." Ph.D. diss., University of California, San Diego, 1998.

———. "'I Believe You Can Fly': Basketball Culture in Postsocialist China." In *Popular China: Unofficial Culture in a Globalizing Society*, edited by Perry Link, Richard P. Madsen, and Paul G. Pickowicz, 9–38. Lanham, Md.: Rowman & Littlefield Publishers, 2002.

———. "'I Can Compete!': China in the Olympic Games, 1932 and 1936." *Journal of Sport History* 26.3 (Fall 1999): 545–66.

———. "Mastery without Enmity: Athletics, Modernity and the Nation in Early Republican China." *Republican China* 22.2 (April 1997): 3–39.

———. "Native Songs and Dances: Southeast Asia in a Greater Chinese Sporting Community, 1920–1948." *Journal of Southeast Asian Studies* 31.1 (March 2000): 48–69.

———. "'To Make the 400 Million Move': The Late Qing Dynasty Origins of Modern Chinese Sport and Physical Culture." *Comparative Studies in Society and History* 42.4 (October 2000): 876–906.

Mucheng 慕澄. "Huabei guoshu yanjiuhui zhuiyilu" 華北國術研究會追憶錄 [Looking back on the North China Guoshu Research Association]. *Qiushi yuekan* 2.10 (10 July 1936): 351–353.

Nanfang zazhi 南方雜誌 [Southern magazine]. Nanning.

Nanjing gaodeng shifan xuexiao tiyu yanjiuhui 南京高等師範學校體育研究會, ed. *Tiyu yanjiuhui huikan* 體育研究會會刊 [Physical Education Research Society journal]. Nanjing, 1918.

Nanyang zhoukan 南洋周刊 *(Nanyang Weekly)*. Shanghai.

Naoruisi 腦瑞偲 narration. Transcribed by Tingtingdun 亭廷頓. "Lao yu zhiwu de funü—chengle yijijia!" 勞於職務的婦女 — 成了藝技家 [Women laboring at their professions—who become acrobats!]. *Tiyu zhoubao (Sporting Weekly)* 2.16 (27 May 1933): 9–10; 2.17 (3 June 1933): 8–9.

New York Times. New York.

North-China Daily News. Shanghai.

Nü qingnian yuekan 女青年月刊 [Young woman monthly]. Shanghai.

"Official Website of Beijing 2008 Olympic Games Bid Committee." Retrieved 30 August 2000 from www.beijing-olympic.org.cn/eindex.shtm.

Okamoto Noritsune 岡本規矩. *Tiyu zhi kexue de jichu* 體育之科學的基礎 [The scientific foundations of physical education; original title *Taiiku kaibō* 體育

解剖: Physical education and anatomy]. Translated by Guo Renji 郭人驥. Shanghai: Xieqiao yiyuan, 1929.

Own, T. K. Yaoheng. "Chin Woo." *Jingwu zazhi* 38 (15 February 1924): 1–3.

Pan Guxi 潘谷西, ed. *Nanjing de jianzhu* 南京的建筑 [Nanjing architecture]. Nanjing: Nanjing chubanshe, 1995.

Pan Zhiben 潘知本. "Nüzi youxi—duiqiu shu" 女子游戲－隊球術 [A game for women—volleyball]. *Funü zazhi (Ladies' Journal)* 8.7 (July 1922): 81–86.

Pang Yizhi 龐宜之. "Hangzhou xingyi ji" 杭州行役記 [Record of the official trip to Hangzhou]. *Jingwu zazhi* 43 (15 July 1924): 57–60.

Peixian 佩弦. "Tiyu shi" 體育史 [The history of physical culture]. *Tiyujie* 1 (1st day, 3d lunar month [20 April], 1909): 3–5.

Peng Zhou 蓬洲. "Di wu jie Quanguo yundong dahui ji" 第五屆全國運動大會記 [Diary of the Fifth National Games]. *Xin Zhonghua (New China Magazine)* 1.21 (10 November 1933): 33–39.

People's Daily. Beijing.

Philippines Free Press. Manila.

"Po quanguo? Quanguo xin? Luo Jialun tanhua, Xiaozu de yijian" 破全國?全國新?羅家倫談話，小卒的意見[Breaking the entire nation? New for the entire nation? Luo Jialun speaks, and Xiaozu's opinion]. *Tiyu pinglun (Sports Review)* 54 (21 October 1933): 161.

Qian Moming 錢莫名. "Guoshu jie xuyao he buxuyao de lingxiu" 國術界需要和不需要的領袖 [Types of leaders that the *guoshu* community needs and does not need]. *Qiushi yuekan* 2.3 (10 December 1935): 107–108.

Qiang Gong 強公. "Fakan ci" 發刊詞 [Words to introduce this periodical]. *Wushu* 1.1 (January 1921): 1–2.

Qiao Keqin 乔克勤 and Guan Wenming 关文明. *Zhongguo tiyu sixiangshi* 中国体育思想史 [The history of Chinese physical education philosophy]. Lanzhou: Gansu minzu chubanshe, 1993.

Qinfen tiyu yuebao 勤奮體育月報 *(Chin Fen Sports Monthly).* Shanghai.

Qingdao shi tiyu xiejinhui 青島市體育協進會, eds. *Liang zhounian gongzuo zongbaogao* 兩週年工作總報告 [Official report of two years' work]. Qingdao: Qingdao tiyu xiejinhui chuban weiyuanhui, 1935.

Qinghai tiyu shiliao 青海体育史料 [Materials from the history of Qinghai physical culture]. Xining.

Qingnian jinbu 青年進步 *(Association Progress).* Shanghai.

Qiushi jikan 求是季刊 [Seek truth quarterly]. Ji'nan.

Qiushi yuekan 求是月刊 [Seek truth monthly]. Ji'nan. [Continues above.]

Qiwu 七五 (Xu Yibing 徐一冰). "Jinggao jiaoyujie" 敬告教育界 [A warning to the education community]. *Tiyujie* 1 (1st day, 3d lunar month [20 April], 1909): 1–2.

Qu Lihe 瞿立鶴. *Qingmo Minchu minzu zhuyi jiaoyu sichao* 清末民初民族主義教育思潮 [The late Qing–early Republic nationalist education tide of thought]. Taibei: Zhonghua wenhua fuxing yundong tuixing weiyuanhui, 1984.

Qu Ziqing 瞿子清. *Zhongguo lanqiu shihua* 中國籃球史話 [Stories from the history of basketball in China]. Taibei: Weihua tiyu xunkanshe, 1961.

"Quanguo guoshu gaikuang diaocha (yi)" 全國國術概況調查(一) [Investigation into *guoshu* conditions across the nation (Part 1)]. *Guoshu zhoukan* 129 (11 November 1934): 8. Parts 3–6, 8 of same article in *Guoshu zhoukan* 131 (25 November 1934): 8; 132 (2 December 1934): 8; 133 (9 December 1934): 7–8; 134 (16 December 1934): 7–8; 136–137 (20 January 1935): 13–15.

Quanguo nü yundongyuan mingjiang lu 全國女運動員名將錄 [Roll of the nation's women athletes]. Shanghai: Qinfen shuju, 1936.

Quanguo yundong dahui yaolan 全國運動大會要覽 [Guided tour of the National Games]. Hangzhou: Quanguo yundong dahui xuanchuanbu, 1930.

Quanguo yundong dahui zongbaogao 全國運動大會總報告 [The National Games official report]. Hangzhou, 1930.

Quanguo yundonghui tuhua zhuankan 全國運動會圖畫專刊 *(The 4th "National Atheletic Meet")*. Shanghai: *Liangyou* tushu yinshua gongsi, 1930.

"Quanshu yu quanfei" 拳術與拳匪 [Boxing and Boxer bandits]. *Xin qingnian (La Jeunesse)* 6.2 (15 February 1919): 218–21.

"Quanyun bimu zhi ci," 全運閉幕之辭 *Guizhou chenbao yundonghui tekan*, 17 September 1935. Reprinted in *Guizhou sheng di yi jie quansheng yundonghui zongbaogao*, ed. Guizhou sheng di yi jie quansheng yundonghui choubei weiyuanhui, 115. Guiyang: Guizhou sheng zhengfu jiaoyuting, 1935.

Renan, Ernest. "What Is a Nation?" In *Nation and Narration*, edited by Homi K. Bhabha, 8–22. New York: Routledge, 1990.

Renyan zhoukan 人言周刊 [Weekly critique]. Shanghai.

Reynolds, Douglas R. *China, 1898–1912: The Xinzheng Revolution and Japan.* Cambridge, Mass.: Council on East Asian Studies, Harvard University, 1993.

Riben pinglun 日本評論 *(Japanese Affairs Review)*. Nanjing.

Riordan, James. *Sport in Soviet Society: Development of Sport and Physical Education in Russia and the USSR.* New York: Cambridge University Press, 1977.

Rogaski, Ruth. "Fists of Fury? Or the *Jingwu hui* before Bruce Lee." Paper presented at the annual meeting of the Association for Asian Studies, San Diego, 9 March 2000.

Ruan Weicun 阮蔚村. "Riben minzu tige yanjin shikuang" 日本民族體格演進實況 [Specifics on the evolution of the physique(s) of the Japanese race]. *Qinfen tiyu yuebao (Chin Fen Sports Monthly)* 3.10 (July 1936): 892–901.

———. *Riben tiyu kaocha baogao* 日本體育考察報告 [Report on my investigations into Japanese physical culture]. Beijing: Jingshengshe, 1940.

———. *Yuandong yundonghui lishi yu chengji* 遠東運動會歷史與成績 [History and records of the Far Eastern Championship Games]. Shanghai: Qinfen shuju, 1933.

Saiga Kazumi 雜賀三省. "Nüzi tiyu yanjiu" 女子體育研究 [A study of women's physical education]. Translated by Yan Wei 嚴畏. *Funü zazhi (Ladies' Journal)* 9.7 (July 1923): 6–10.

Sasajima Kōsuke 世島恆輔. *Jindai Zhongguo tiyu yundong shi* 近代中國體育運動史 [The history of the physical education movement in modern China]. Translated by Wu Enlian 武恩蓮. N.p.: Zhongguo tiyushi xuehui bianjibu, 1985.

Schwartz, Benjamin. *In Search of Wealth and Power: Yen Fu and the West.* New York: Harper & Row, 1964.

Schwartz, Vanessa R. *Spectacular Realities: Early Mass Culture in Fin-de-Siècle Paris.* Berkeley: University of California Press, 1998.

Shaan-Gan-Ning bianqu tiyushi bianshen weiyuanhui 陕甘宁边区体育史编审委员会, eds. *Shaan-Gan-Ning bianqu tiyushi* 陕甘宁边区体育史 [The history of physical culture in the Shaanxi-Gansu-Ningxia border region]. Xi'an: Shaanxi renmin cubanshe, 1990.

Shaanxi sheng tiyu wenshi gongzuo weiyuanhui 陕西省体育文史工作委员会, ed. *Shaan-Gan-Ning bianqu tiyu shiliao* 陕甘宁边区体育史料 [Historical materials from Shaanxi-Gansu-Ningxia border region physical culture]. Xi'an: Shaanxi sheng tiyu wenshi gongzuo weiyuanhui, 1986.

Shandong sheng difang shizhi bianzuan weiyuanhui 山东省地方史志编纂委员会, ed. *Shandong shengzhi: Tiyu zhi* 山东省志:体育志 [Shandong provincial gazetteer: Chronicle of physical culture]. Ji'nan: Shandong renmin chubanshe, 1993.

"Shandong sheng guoshu gaikuang" 山東省國術概況 [The state of *guoshu* in Shandong province]. *Xiahun* 1 (10 October 1936): 51–52.

Shang Shumei 尚樹梅. "Minzhong tiyu" 民眾體育 [Physical culture for the masses]. *Kexue de Zhongguo* 2.8 (15 October 1933): 32–36.

The Shanghai 1925 Volume X (Hujiang yichou niankan 滬江乙丑年刊*).* Shanghai: Shanghai College, 1925.

Shanghai tiyu shihua 上海体育史话 [Items from the history of Shanghai physical culture]. Shanghai.

Shanghai Zhonghua wushuhui di san jie zhengqiu dahui tekan 上海中華武術會第三屆徵求大會特刊 [Special publication of the Chinese Wushu Association of Shanghai's Third Fundraising Drive]. Shanghai, 1921.

Shanxi minzhong jiaoyu 山西民眾教育 [Shanxi mass education]. Taiyuan.

Shanxi sheng difangzhi bianzuan weiyuanhui 山西省地方志编纂委员会, ed. *Shanxi tongzhi di sishier juan: Tiyu zhi* 山西通志第四十二卷:体育志 [Shanxi provincial gazetteer, vol. 42: Chronicle of physical culture]. Beijing: Zhonghua shuju, 1995.

Shao Rugan 邵汝幹. "Di wu jie Quanguo yundong dahui yu minzu fuxing" 第五屆全國運動大會與民族復興 [The Fifth National Games and the revitalization of the nation-race]. *Xin Zhonghua (New China Magazine)* 1.19 (10 October 1933): 25–27.

———. "Wei zhengqiu 'Woguo ying cai hezhong tiyu yundong wei guomin youxi' shuo jiju hua" 為徵求'我國應採何種體育運動為國民遊戲'説幾句話 [A few words on the call, "Which sport should be taken by our nation as the national pastime?"]. *Qinfen tiyu yuebao (Chin Fen Sports Monthly)* 3.5 (February 1936): 389.

Shen Guoquan 申國權. "Fu Aozhou saiqiu jianwenlu" 赴澳州賽球見聞錄 [Record of what I saw and heard on the road trip to Australia]. Transcribed by Fei Zhendong 費振東. *Nanyang zhoukan (Nanyang Weekly)* 3.11 (15 December 1923): 65–69.

———. "Wo duiyu benxiao tiyu de sheshi he jihua" 我對於本校體育的設施和計劃[My thoughts and plans on our school's *tiyu*]. *Nanyang zhoukan (Nanyang Weekly)* 3.11 (15 December 1923): 2–5.

Shen Jiazhen 沈家楨. "He wei taijiquan wudang quan (xu)" 何為太極拳武當拳(續) [What are *taijiquan* and *wudangquan?* (Continued)]. *Tiyu* 4.12 (30 December 1936): 3–14.

Shenbao 申報 [Shanghai times]. Shanghai.

Shenbao yuekan 申報月刊 [*Shenbao* monthly]. Shanghai.

Shenbao zhoukan 申報週刊 [*Shenbao* weekly]. Shanghai.

Shenghuo zhoukan 生活週刊 *(Life Weekly)*. Shanghai.

Shenyang shi tiyu zhi 沈阳市体育志 [Shenyang municipal chronicle of physical culture]. Shenyang: Shenyang chubanshe, 1989.

Shi Chuanxiang 时传祥. "Women taofen gongren ye you le tiyu huodong" 我们掏粪工人也有了体育活动 [We night-soil carriers also take part in athletic activities now]. *Xin tiyu* (February 1965): 24–25.

Shi Nong 是儂. "Shijie tiyu de xin qushi" 世界的新趨勢 [The new trend in international physical culture]. *Guoshu, tiyu, junshi* 3 (2 November 1933) [Weekly feature in *Zhongguo ribao*]: 8.

Shida tiyu 師大體育[National Taiwan Normal University physical education]. Taibei.

Shidai gonglun 時代公論 [Current public opinion]. Nanjing.

"Shijie yundongchang shang zhi yingjie" 世界運動場上之英傑 [Heroes on the international athletic stage]. *Zhonghua yuebao (Central China Monthly)* 4.7 (1 July 1936): 6–8.

Shu Yifan 束以範. "Ruhe fazhan wuguo minzhong tiyu" 如何發展吾國民眾體育 [How to develop our nation's mass *tiyu*]. *Hanxue yuekan* (1 May 1935): 31–45.

Shuilibu saqi nian qiuji yundonghui tekan 水利部卅七年秋季運動會特刊 [Special publication of the Water Conservancy Department Autumn 1948 Athletic Meet]. Nanjing: Shuilibu, 1948.

Sichuan tiyu shiliao 四川体育史料 [Materials from the history of Sichuan physical culture]. Chengdu.

Song Ruhai 宋如海. *Wo neng bi ya: Shijie yundonghui conglu* 我能比呀：世界運動會叢錄 *(Records of Olympic Meetings)*. Shanghai: Shangwu yinshuguan, 1930.

St. John's University 1879–1929. Shanghai: St. John's University Alumni Association, 1929. reprint, Taipei, n.p., 1972.

Stapleton, Kristin. "Yang Sen in Chengdu: Urban Planning in the Interior." In *Remaking the Chinese City: Modernity and National Identity, 1900–1950*, edited by Joseph W. Esherick, 90–106. Honolulu: University of Hawai'i Press, 2000.

Strand, David. "Citizens in the Audience and at the Podium." In *Changing Meanings of Citizenship in Modern China*, edited by Merle Goldman and Elizabeth J. Perry, 44–69. Cambridge, Mass.: Harvard University Press, 2002.

Su Jinzhang 蘇錦章. *Jiayi bangqiu shihua* 嘉義棒球史話 [Stories from Jiayi baseball history]. Taibei: Lianjing chuban shiye gongsi, 1996.

Suizhi 遂之. "Di shiyi jie Shijie yundonghui de jingguo jiqi tezhi" 第十一屆世界運動會的經過及其特質 [Events and special qualities of the Eleventh Olympiad]. *Zhongxuesheng* 67 (September 1936): 55–68.

Sun, Lung-Kee. *The Chinese National: From Nationhood to Individuality.* Armonk, N.Y.: M.E. Sharpe, 2002.

Sun Wen 孫文. "Jingwu benji xu" 精武本紀序 [Preface to *Record of the Pure Martial*]. In *Jingwu benji*, edited by Chen Tiesheng, 1–2. 1920; reprint, Shanghai: n.p., 1922.

Suxin 素心. "Xinnian de youxi" 新年的遊戲 [New Year's games]. *Tiyu zhoubao* 49 (12 January 1920): 18–19.

Taijicao hanshou xuexiao 太極操函授學校 and Taijicao yanjiuhui 太極操研究會. "Taijicao" 太極操 *[Taijicao]. Qinfen tiyu yuebao (Chin Fen Sports Monthly)* 2.6 (March 1935): 415–417.

Taiwan sheng di yi jie quansheng yundong dahui 台灣省第一屆全省運動大會 [The First Taiwan Provincial Games]. Taibei: Taiwan sheng di yi jie quansheng yundong dahui xuanchuan zu, 1946.

Taiwan tiyu 臺灣體育 *(Taiwan Sports).* Taibei.

Taixuan 太玄. "De-mo-ke-la-xi yu xunlian" 德謨克拉西與訓練 [Democracy and training]. *Jiaoyu zazhi (Chinese Educational Review)* 11.9 (20 September 1919): 1–4.

———. "Jiaoyuxue yu shehuixue (xu)" 教育學與社會學(續) [Pedagogy and sociology (continued)]. *Jiaoyu zazhi (Chinese Educational Review)* 9.12 (20 December 1917): 39–48.

———. "Ticao jiaoshou gexin zhi yanjiu" 體操教授革新之研究 [Research into the reform of physical education instruction]. *Jiaoyu zazhi (Chinese Educational Review)* 10.1 (20 January 1918): 69–76.

Takahara Tomiyasu 高原富保, ed. *Showa supōtsu shi: Olinpikku 80 nen* 昭和スポーツ史：オリンピック80年 [The history of Showa sports: Eighty years of the Olympic movement]. Tokyo: Mainichi shinbunsha, 1976.

Tan, G. G. [Chen Zhang'e 陳掌諤]. "Chinese Origins of Diverse Types of Modern Ball Games." *China Today* 2.10 (October 1959): 71–75.

Tan Jihua 譚吉華. "Lun tiyu" 論體育 [On physical culture]. *Yanjiu yu pipan* 1.6 (1 November 1935): 89–92.

Tan Sitong quanji 譚嗣同全集 [The complete collection of Tan Sitong's writings]. Beijing: Sanlian shudian, 1954.

Tang Leang-li. *Reconstruction in China.* Shanghai: China United Press, 1935.

Tang Mingxin 湯銘新. *Woguo canjia guoji lanqiusai lishi* 我國參加國際籃球賽歷史 [The history of our nation's participation in international basketball competition]. Taibei: Zhonghua quanguo lanqiu weiyuanhui, 1963.

Tao, W. Tchishin [Tao Zhixing 陶知行] and C. P. Chen [Cheng Qibao 程其保]. *Education in China, 1924.* Shanghai: Commercial Press, 1925.

Taussig, Michael. *Mimesis and Alterity: A Particular History of the Senses.* New York: Routledge, 1993.

Tian Zhenfeng 田鎮峰. "Guan'gan hou de jianyi" 觀感後的建議 [Suggestions after viewing (the Eighteenth North China Games)]. *Qiushi jikan* 1.1 (10 October 1934): 17–25.

——. "Huayun jishi" 華運紀實 [A true record of the North China Games]. *Qiushi jikan* 1.1 (10 October 1934): 56–87.

——. "Jiji mantan" 技擊漫談 [A discussion of martial arts]. *Qiushi jikan* 1.2 (10 January 1935): 1–7.

Tianjin shi difangzhi bianxiu weiyuanhui 天津市地方志编修委员会, ed. *Tianjin tongzhi: Tiyu zhi* 天津通志: 体育志 *(Overall Annals of Tianjin: Sports Volume)*. Tianjin: Tianjin shehui kexueyuan chubanshe, 1994.

Tianjin tiyu shiliao 天津体育史料 [Materials from the history of Tianjin physical culture]. Tianjin.

T'ien Hsia Monthly. Shanghai.

Tien, Hung-Mao. *Government and Politics in Kuomintang China, 1927–1937.* Stanford, Calif.: Stanford University Press, 1972.

Tientsin Young Men. Tianjin.

Tiyu 體育 [Physical culture]. Beiping.

Tiyu huikan 體育彙刊 [Physical education journal]. Shanghai.

Tiyu jikan 體育季刊 *(Physical Education Quarterly)*. Shanghai. 1922.

Tiyu jikan 體育季刊 *(Chinese Journal of Physical Education)*. Shanghai. [Continues above with different English title.]

Tiyu jikan 體育季刊 *(Physical Education Quarterly)*. Shanghai. 1935–37. [Different journal from the 1922 *Tiyu jikan* above.]

Tiyu pinglun 體育評論 *(Sports Review)*. Shanghai.

Tiyu shijie 體育世界 *(Sports World)*. Shanghai.

Tiyu wenshi 体育文史 [Materials on the history of sport]. Beijing.

Tiyu wenshi 体育文史 *(Sport History)*. Beijing. [Continues above with English title.]

Tiyu wenshi 体育文史 *(Sports History)*. Beijing. [Continues above with different English title.]

Tiyu wenshi 体育文史 *(Journal of Sport History and Culture)*. Beijing. [Continues above with different English title.]

"Tiyu wenti jueyian" 體育問題決議案 [Resolution on the problem of sports]. *Xianqu (Poineer)* [sic] 18 (10 May 1923): 3–4.

Tiyu xinsheng 體育新聲 *(Athletic China)*. Shanghai.

Tiyu xuebao 體育學報 *(Bulletin of Physical Education)*. Taibei.

Tiyu yu weisheng 體育與衛生 *(Journal of Physical Education and Hygiene)*. Shanghai. [Continues *Tiyu jikan*.]

"Tiyu yu weisheng zu" 體育與衛生組 [P.E. and Hygiene Division]. *Xin jiaoyu* 11.2 (September 1925): 290–294.

Tiyu yuekan 體育月刊 [Physical culture monthly]. Beijing.

Tiyu yundong jiaoxue cankao ziliao 体育运动教学参考资料 [Sports and physical education teaching information]. Hangzhou.

Tiyu zazhi 體育雜誌 [Physical culture magazine]. Nanjing. 1931.

Tiyu zazhi 體育雜誌[Physical culture magazine]. Nanjing. 1935. [Different magazine from the 1931 *Tiyu zazhi* above.]

Tiyu zazhi 體育雜誌[Physical culture magazine]. Shanghai.

Tiyu zhoubao 體育週報 [Physical culture weekly]. Changsha.

Tiyu zhoubao 體育周報 *(Sporting Weekly)*. Tianjin.

Tiyujie 體育界 [Physical education world]. Shanghai.

Tiyushi wenji 体育史文集 [Collection of writings on the history of physical culture]. Chengdu: Chengdu tiyu xueyuan tiyushi yanjiushi, 1983.

Tong Zhixuan 童致旋. "Shiyunhui Zhongguodui shibai hou guoren duiyu tiyu yingyou zhi renshi yu nuli" 世運會中國隊失敗後國人對於體育應有之認識與努力[On the physical culture understanding and efforts our people should have and make after the Chinese team's Olympic failure]. *Jiao yu xue* 2.3 (1 September 1936): 11–14.

Tsai Jen-hsiung [Cai Zhenxiong] 蔡禎雄. "Riju shidai 'Taiwan tiyu xiehui' chengli de lishi kaocha" 日據時代'臺灣體育協會' 成立的歷史考察[A historical investigation into the Taiwan Athletic Federation established during the Japanese colonial period]. Paper presented at Di yi jie Dongbeiya tiyu yundongshi xueshu yantaohui 第一屆東北亞體育運動史學術研討會[First Conference on the History of Physical Education and Sport in Northeast Asia], National Taiwan Normal University, Taipei, Taiwan, 19–21 December 1995.

Tushu zhanwang 圖書展望 [Literary forecast]. Hangzhou.

W. S. [Huang Xing]. "Shenme jiaozuo tiyu?" 甚麼叫做體育 [What is *tiyu?*]. *Tiyu zhoubao* 25 (9 June 1919): 2–3.

Wakeman, Frederic, Jr. "A Revisionist View of the Nanjing Decade: Confucian Fascism." In *Reappraising Republican China*, edited by Frederic Wakeman, Jr., and Richard Louis Edmonds, 141–78. New York: Oxford University Press, 2000.

Wakeman, Frederic, Jr., and Richard Louis Edmonds, eds. *Reappraising Republican China*. New York: Oxford University Press, 2000.

Wang Chien-tai [Wang Jiantai] 王建臺. "Mai Kele (Charles Harold McCloy) dui Zhongguo jindai tiyu de yingxiang (yijiuyisan ~ yijiuerliu)" 麥克樂 (Charles Harold McCloy) 對中國近代體育的影響 (一九一三~一九二六) [Charles Harold McCloy's influence on modern Chinese physical education (1913–1926)]. M.S. thesis, Guoli tiyu xueyuan, 1993.

Wang Geng 王庚. *Gonggong tiyuchang* 公共體育場 [Public athletic grounds]. Hangzhou: Zhejiang sheng jiaoyuting, 1931.

———. *Minzhong tiyu shishifa* 民眾體育實施法[Mass *tiyu* implementation methods]. Shanghai: Qinfen shuju, 1933.

———. "Minzhong tiyuchang zhi lilun yu shiji" 民眾體育場之理論與實際 [Mass athletic grounds, theory and practice]. *Jiaoyu yu minzhong* 4.6 (February 1933): 987–1023.

———. "Tiyu zhi kexue de yanjiu" 體育之科學的研究 [Research into the science of physical education]. *Xiandai xuesheng (Modern Student)* 3.1 (October 1933): 1–16.

Wang Guan 王關. "Guanyu weiguo de qianpai Yu Liu ji qita" 關於偽國的遣派于劉及其他 [On the bogus government's sending Yu and Liu, among other things]. *Tiyu zhoubao (Sporting Weekly)* 20 (18 June 1932): 18–19.

Wang Huaiqi 王懷琪. "Batuanjin ticao" 八團錦體操 [*Batuanjin* (Eight-stretch routine) calisthenics]. *Jiaoyu zazhi (Chinese Educational Review)* 7.11 (15 November 1915): 11–14.

———. "Gaodeng youji: Songpo qiu" 高等遊技：松坡球 [An advanced game: Songpo-ball]. *Jiaoyu zazhi (Chinese Educational Review)* 9.4 (20 April 1917): 1–3.

———. *Guochi jinian ticao* 國恥紀念體操 [National humiliation commemorative calisthenics]. Shanghai: Zhongguo jianxueshe, 1929.

———. *Xingqiu guize* 星球規則 [Starball regulations]. Shanghai: Zhongguo jianxueshe, 1928.

———. "Zui xin qicao (wu yue jiu ri)" 最新旗操（五月九日） [A new flag calisthenics routine (May Ninth)]. *Jiaoyu zazhi (Chinese Educational Review)* 8.9 (15 September 1916): 33–38.

Wang Huaiqi and Zou Falu 鄒法魯. *Tiyu ceyanfa* 體育測驗法 [Physical education standards testing]. 1925; reprint, Shanghai: Zhongguo jianxueshe, 1929.

Wang, Liping. "Creating a National Symbol: The Sun Yatsen Memorial in Nanjing." *Republican China* 21.2 (April 1996): 23–63.

Wang Wenjun 王文俊, Liang Jisheng 梁吉生, Yang Xun 杨珣, Zhang Shujian 张书俭, and Xia Jiashan 夏家善, eds. *Nankai daxue xiaoshi ziliaoxuan (1919–1949)* 南开大学校史资料选 [Selected materials on the history of Nankai University, 1919–1949]. Tianjin: Nankai daxue chubanshe, 1989.

Wang Xuezheng 王學政. *Tiyu yu jiaoyu* 體育與教育 [Physical culture and education]. Chongqing: Shangwu yinshuguan, 1945; reprint, Taibei: Taiwan shangwu yinshuguan, 1966.

Wang Zengming 王增明, ed. *Jindai Zhongguo tiyu fagui* 近代中国体育法规 [Modern Chinese physical culture laws and regulations]. N.p.: Zhongguo tiyushi xuehui Hebei fenhui, 1988.

Wang Zheng. *Women in the Chinese Enlightenment: Oral and Textual Histories.* Berkeley: University of California Press, 1999.

Wang Zhenya 王振亚. *Jiu Zhongguo tiyu jianwen* 旧中国体育见闻 [Glimpses of physical culture in the old China]. Beijing: Renmin tiyu chubanshe, 1987.

Wang Zhuangfei 王壯飛. *Tiyuchang zhinan* 體育場指南 [Public athletic grounds guide]. Shanghai: Qinfen shuju, 1931.

Wasserstrom, Jeffrey N. *Student Protests in Twentieth-Century China: The View from Shanghai.* Stanford, Calif.: Stanford University Press, 1991.

"Wei xuanshou chuxi Shijiehui" 偽選手出席世界會 [Bogus athletes to participate in Olympics]. *Tiyu zhoubao (Sporting Weekly)* 20 (18 June 1932): 1–2.

Weiqin 葳芩. "Nüzi tiyu yu shengli bianhua" 女子體育與生理變化 [Women's *tiyu* and physiological changes]. *Qinfen tiyu yuebao (Chin Fen Sports Monthly)* 1.7 (10 April 1934): 15–19.

———. "Nüzi yuejing yu yundong zhi guanxi" 女子月經與運動之關系 [The

relationship between women's menstruation and exercise]. *Qinfen tiyu yue-bao (Chin Fen Sports Monthly)* 1.5 (10 February 1934): 42–44.

Welky, David B. "Viking Girls, Mermaids, and Little Brown Men: U.S. Journalism and the 1932 Olympics." *Journal of Sport History* 24.1 (Spring 1997): 24–49.

Wenhua jianshe yuekan 文化建設月刊 [Cultural reconstruction monthly]. Shanghai.

Wilber, Francis E. Photo Album. 3 vols. YMCA Archives, University of Minnesota, St. Paul.

Wu Cheng 吳澂. "Ding youyong wei guomin yundong de guanjian" 定游泳為國民運動的管見 [My humble opinion on establishing swimming as a national sport]. *Guoshu, tiyu, junshi* 34 (28 June 1934) [Weekly feature in *Zhongguo ribao*]: 8.

Wu, Chih-Kang. "The Influence of the YMCA on the Development of Physical Education in China." Ph.D. diss., University of Michigan, 1956.

Wu Hongyi 伍宏儀. "Yuandong tiyu xiehui jiesan" 遠東體育協會解散 [The dissolution of the Far Eastern Athletic Association]. *Shidai gonglun* 3.9 (25 May 1934): 23.

Wu Junsheng 吳俊升, ed. *Zhonghua minguo jiaoyu zhi* 中華民國教育誌 [Chronicle of education in the Republic of China]. 2 vols. Taibei: Zhonghua wenhua chuban shiye weiyuanhui, 1955.

Wu Tingfang (伍廷芳). *America through the Spectacles of an Oriental Diplomat.* New York: Frederick A. Stokes, 1914; Taipei: Ch'eng-wen Publishing, 1968.

Wu Wenzhong 吳文忠. *Zhongguo jin bai nian tiyu shi* 中國近百年體育史 [The history of Chinese physical culture over the last century]. Taibei: Taiwan shangwu yinshuguan, 1967.

———. *Zhongguo tiyu fazhan shi* 中國體育發展史 [The history of the development of Chinese sport]. Taibei: Guoli jiaoyu ziliaoguan, 1981.

———. "Zhongguo wushu de pingjia yu gaijin fazhan de tujing" 中國武術的評價與改進發展的途徑 [The value of Chinese martial arts and the path of its development and evolution]. *Guoshu yuekan (National Gymnastics Monthly)* 1.3 (1 March 1972): 1–6.

Wu Yunrui 吳蘊瑞. "Junshi xunlian yu tiyu" 軍事訓練與體育 [Military training and physical education]. *Tiyu jikan (Physical Education Quarterly)* 3.1 (March 1937): 1–6.

———. "Sanshiwu nian lai Zhongguo zhi tiyu" 三十五年來中國之體育 [Athletics in China over the last thirty-five years]. In *Zuijin sanshiwu nian zhi Zhongguo jiaoyu,* edited by Zhuang Yu, 225–41. Shanghai: Shangwu yinshuguan, 1931.

———. "Tiyu kexuehua" 體育科學化 [The scientization of physical culture]. *Kexue huabao* 3.5 (1 October 1935): 161.

———. "Woguo tiyu shang zhi zijue" 我國體育上的自覺 ("China's Realization along the Line of Physical Education)." *Qingnian jinbu (Association Progress)* 41 (March 1921): 54–57.

———. "Wuguo minzu fuxing zhong nüzi tiyu zhi zhongyao" 吾國民族復興中女子體育之重要 [The importance of women's physical education in the revival of our nation-race]. *Tiyu zazhi* 1.1 (4 April 1935): 1–2.

Wu Zhiqing 吳志青. *Guoshu lilun gaiyao* 國術理論概要 [An outline of *guoshu* theory]. Minguo congshu di yi bian #50. Shanghai: Dadong shuju, 1935; reprint, Shanghai: Shanghai shudian, 1989.

———. *Kexuehua de guoshu* 科學化的國術 [A scientized *guoshu*]. Shanghai: Dadong shuju, 1931.

Wushu 武術 [Martial arts]. Shanghai.

Xia Xingshi 夏行時. "Zhongyang tiyuchang gaikuang" 中央體育場概況 [A look at Central Stadium]. *Zhongguo jianzhu (Chinese Architect)* 1.3 (September 1933): 8–27.

Xiahun 俠魂 [Chivalrous soul]. Ji'nan.

Xiandai xuesheng 現代學生 *(Modern Student)*. Shanghai.

Xiang Fuchun 項富春. "Wo de tiyu guan" 我的體育觀 [My views on physical education]. *Tiyu huikan* 1 (June 1925): 8–9.

Xiao Liu 小柳. "Nüzi shinei ticao" 女子室內體操 [Indoor calisthenics for women]. *Funü zazhi (Ladies' Journal)* 8.1 (January 1922): 83–86.

Xiao Rulin 蕭汝霖. "Shu Jingwu tiyuhui shi" 述精武體育會事 [On the Pure Martial Athletic Association]. *Xin qingnian (La Jeunesse)* 1.5 (January 1916): 1–2.

Xiaoxue jiaoshi banyuekan 小學教師半月刊 [Elementary teachers' fortnightly].

"Xibei yundonghui jianzhang ji jingsai guicheng" 西北運動會簡章及競賽規程 [Northwest Games consitution and rules of competition]. *Tiyu zhoubao (Sporting Weekly)* 2.24 (22 July 1933): 2–4.

Xie Jin 謝晉, dir. *Nülan wu hao* 女籃五号 [Woman Basketball Player No. 5]. Beijing: Tianma dianying zhipianchang, 1957 film.

Xie Siyan 謝似顏. "Nüzi tiyu wenti" 女子體育問題 [Questions of women's physical education]. *Funü zazhi (Ladies' Journal)* 9.7 (July 1923): 2–5.

———. "Ping *Dagongbao* qi ri sheping" 評大公報七日社評 [A critique of the social commentary published in *L'Impartial* on the 7th]. *Tiyu zhoubao (Sporting Weekly)* 30 (27 August 1932): 1–4.

———. *Tianjingsai de lilun yu shiji* 田徑賽的理論與實際 [Track and field theory and practice]. Shanghai: Kaiming shudian, 1927.

Xin jiaoyu 新教育 [New education]. Beijing.

Xin qingnian 新青年 *(La Jeunesse)*. Shanghai.

Xin shixue 新史學 [New historiography]. Taibei.

Xin tiyu 新體育 [New physical culture]. Beijing.

Xin Zhonghua 新中華 *(New China Magazine)*. Shanghai.

Xing 行. "Di liu jie Quanguo yundonghui jilüe" 第六屆全國運動會記略 [Brief record of the Sixth National Games]. *Shenbao yuekan* 4.11 (15 November 1935): 123–24.

Xing 醒. "Fang baozhu he weisheng" 放爆竹和衛生 [Firecrackers and hygiene]. *Tiyu zhoubao* 49 (12 January 1920): 19–20.

Xinhua News Agency. Beijing.

Xinhua ribao 新華日報 [New China daily]. Chongqing.

Xinjiang tiyu shiliao 新疆体育史料 [Materials from the history of Xinjiang physical culture]. Urumqi.

Xu Jiazhen 須家楨 (Su Chia-cheng). *Jiating ticao* 家庭體操 *(Home Exercises)*. Shanghai: Shangwu yinshuguan, 1923.

Xu Yibin 徐益彬 [Xu Yibing 徐一冰]. "Tiyu shi" 體育史 [History of physical culture]. *Tiyu zazhi* 1 (June 1914): 1–5.

———. "Tiyu shi (xu di yi qi)" 體育史續第一期 [History of physical culture (Continued from Issue #1)]. *Tiyu zazhi* 2 (July 1914): 7–11.

Xu Yibing 徐一冰. "Lun xuexiao tiyu" 論學校體育 [On school physical education]. *Jiaoyu zazhi (Chinese Educational Review)* 6.10 (15 December 1914): 189–92.

———. "Ticao youxi ke danji jiaoshoufa zhi yanjiu" 體操游戲科單級教授法之研究 [Research into class level-specific calisthenics and games instruction]. *Jiaoyu zazhi (Chinese Educational Review)* 6.10 (15 December 1914): 218–24.

Xu Yongping 徐詠平. "Zhongguoren shengming de langfei zhi yanzhong kepaxing ji guomin tiyu de jianshe zhi poqie xuyaoxing lun" 中國人生命的浪費之嚴重可怕性及國民體育的建設之迫切需要性論 [On the serious and frightening nature of the waste of Chinese lives and the urgency of the need to reconstruct a citizens' physical culture]. *Hanxue yuekan* 5.2 (1 May 1935): 1–5.

Xu Yuxin 徐愚忻. *Quanshuxue jiaokeshu* 拳術學教科書 [A textbook for the study of boxing]. 1913; Shanghai: Zhonghua tushuguan, 1916.

"Xuebu caijing" 學部財經 [Board of Education finances]. File 241. First Historical Archives, Beijing, China.

Xuesheng zazhi 學生雜誌 *(Students' Magazine)*. Shanghai.

Xunwu 巽吾. "Youxi zhi leibie" 遊戲之類別 [Different categories of games]. *Jiaoyu zazhi (Chinese Educational Review)* 4.9 (10th day, 12th lunar month [16 January], 1913): 35–38.

Yang, Benjamin. *From Revolution to Politics: Chinese Communists on the Long March*. Boulder, Colo.: Westview Press, 1990.

Yang Binru 楊彬如. "Zhiye funü de yundong" 職業婦女的運動 [Exercise for professional women]. *Funü zazhi (Ladies' Journal)* 10.6 (June 1924): 908–15.

Yanjiu yu pipan 研究與批判 [Research and criticism]. Shanghai.

Yibing 一冰 [Xu Yibing 徐一冰]. "Tiyu yu wuli bian" 體育與武力辨 [The differences between physical education and military force]. *Tiyu zazhi* 1 (June 1914): 2–4.

———. "Zhengdun quanguo xuexiao tiyu shang Jiaoyubu wen" 整頓全國學校體育上教育部文 [Text of petition to Education Department on the correcting of physical education in the nation's schools]. *Tiyu zazhi* 2 (July 1914): 1–6.

"Yijiusanyi nian Quanguo yundong dahui choubei weiyuanhui jieshu yijiao de wenjian" 一九三一年全國運動大會籌備委員會結束移交的文件 [Documents relating to the closing and handover of the 1931 National Games Planning Committee]. File 587 (10), Folder 9. Second Historical Archives, Nanjing, China.

Ylanan, Regino R., and Carmen Wilson Ylanan. *The History and Development of Physical Education and Sports in the Philippines*. Quezon City: University of the Philippines Press, 1974.

Yoshida Akinobu 吉田章信. "Yundong shenglixue" 運動生理學 [Sports physiology]. Translated by Luo Heizi 羅黑子. *Tiyu zhoubao* 49 (12 January 1920): 5–10.

You Yinzu 尤蔭祖. "Yuanyun qianjing (Ma-ni-la tongxin)" 遠運前景 (馬尼剌通信) [A Far Eastern Games preview (Letter from Manila)]. *Renyan zhoukan* 16 (26 May 1934): 323–24.

"Youguan zhengqiu Yijiusanyi nian Quanguo yundong dahui geci de wenjian" 有關徵求一九三一年全國運動大會歌詞的文件 [Documents on the search for 1931 National Games Official Song lyrics]. File 587 (10), Folder 5, Document 160. Second Historical Archives, Nanjing, China.

"Youji ziliao" 遊技資料 [Materials on games]. *Tiyu zazhi* 1 (June 1914): 1–10.

Yu, Chien-ming [You Jianming] 游鑑明. "Jindai Zhongguo nüzi tiyu guan chutan" 近代中國女子體育觀初探 ("A Probe into Views on Women's Physical Education in Modern China"). *Xin shixue* 7.4 (December 1996): 119–58.

"Yu guoshu shengkao ji qishe dahui" 豫國術省考暨騎射大會 [The Henan Provincial *Guoshu* Exam and Horsemanship-Archery Meet]. *Tiyu* 4.10 (30 October 1936): 15–16.

Yu Henian 于鶴年. "Di shiba jie Huabei yundonghui jiyao" 第十八屆華北運動會紀要 [Report on the Eighteenth North China Games]. *Hebei yuekan* 2.11 (November 1934): 1–17.

Yu Jie 俞杰. "Junshiqiu—yi zhong xin de qiuxi" 軍事球——一種新的球戲 [Military-ball: A new type of ballgame]. *Tiyu jikan (Physical Education Quarterly)* 3.2 (June 1937): 178–82.

Yu Jinxiang 俞晉祥. "Jinhou wuguo minzhong tiyu yingyou zhi dongxiang" 今後吾國民眾體育應有之動向 [Directions our nation's mass *tiyu* should follow from this day on]. *Tiyu zazhi* 1 (4 April 1935): 14–26.

Yu Zizhen 俞子箴. "Dui Jiaobu shuqi tixiao jidian yijian" 對教部暑期體校幾點意見 [Some opinions on the Education Department Summer *Tiyu* School]. *Tiyu zhoubao (Sporting Weekly)* 2.20 (24 June 1933): 2–3.

———. "Kang Ri de biaoqingcao" 抗日的表情操 [An anti-Japanese expressive calisthenics routine]. *Tiyu zhoubao (Sporting Weekly)* 44 (3 December 1932): 22–24.

———. "Xiangcun xiaoxue tiyu jiaocai yu shebei" 鄉村小學教育教材與設備 [Physical education instruction materials and equipment for village elementary schools]. *Qinfen tiyu yuebao (Chin Fen Sports Monthly)* 4.1 (October 1936): 44–56.

Yuan Shichen 袁士琛. "Jingzheng youji" 競爭遊技 [Competitive games]. *Jiaoyu zazhi (Chinese Educational Review)* 6.11 (15 December 1914): 46–48.

Yuan Tao 遠濤. "Mo-suo-li-ni yu Yi-da-li de jiankang" 墨索里尼與意大利的

健康 [Mussolini and the health of Italy]. *Huanian zhoukan* 1.11 (25 June 1932): 208–212.

Yuan Zongze 袁宗澤. "Riben shehui tiyu zhi sheshi" 日本社會體育之設施 [Physical education practices in Japanese society]. *Minzhong jiaoyu yuekan* 2.5 (1 March 1930): 27–40.

Yun Daiying 惲代英. "Xuexiao tiyu zhi yanjiu" 學校體育之研究 [Research on school physical education]. *Qingnian jinbu (Association Progress)* 4 (June 1917): 1–6.

Yunnan tiyu shiliao 云南体育史料 [Materials from the history of Yunnan physical culture]. Kunming.

Yunnan tiyu wenshi 云南体育文史 [Materials from the history of Yunnan physical culture]. Kunming. [Continues above with different title.]

Yunsu 蘊素. "San zhong butong de xuyao" 三種不同的需要 [Three different needs]. *Nü qingnian yuekan* 13.6 (June 1934): 45–48.

Zeng Biao 曾飙, ed. *Suqu tiyu ziliao xuanbian (1929–1934)* 苏区体育资料选编 (1929–1934) [Selected historical materials from Soviet base area physical culture (1929–1934)]. Hefei: Anhui sheng tiyu shizhi bianjishi, 1985.

Zeng Ruicheng 曾瑞成. "Xin wenhua yundong shiqi Zhongguo zhi tiyu sixiang (yijiuyijiu—yijiuerqi)" 新文化運動時期中國之體育思想(一九一九～一九二七) [Chinese physical culture philosophy during the New Culture Movement (1919–1927)]. *Guomin tiyu jikan (Physical Education Quarterly)* 20.1 (March 1991): 16–28.

Zhang Baochen 張寶琛. "Xuexiao yingfou feizhi bingcao? (Yi)" 學校應否廢止兵操? (一) [Should schools abolish military drill? (One)]. *Tiyu zhoubao* 46 (24 November 1919): 5–8.

Zhang Jiwu 章輯五. "Dule Fang Wanbang Cheng Dengke liang xiansheng de dazhu zhihou" 讀了方萬邦程登科兩先生的大著之後 [Upon reading Messrs. Fang Wanbang's and Cheng Dengke's important works]. *Tiyu jikan (Physical Education Quarterly)* 2.3 (September 1936): 348–49.

———."Nankai xuexiao bannian lai quxiao xuanshouzhi hou de xin shiyan" 南開學校半年來取消選手制後的新試驗 [Nankai School's new experiments half a year after ending the athete system]. *Tiyu zhoubao: Zhounian jinian tekan* (21 January 1933): 8–10.

Zhang Juefei 張覺非. *Xin guomin cao* 新國民操 [New citizens' calisthenics]. Shanghai: Zhonghua shuju, 1948.

Zhang Junjun 張君俊. *Huazu suzhi zhi jiantao* 華族素質之檢討 [An investigation into the quality of our Chinese race]. Chongqing: Shangwu yinshuguan, 1943.

Zhang Liuquan 章柳泉. "Zhongdeng xuexiao xiuxian xiguan zhi yanjiu" 中等學校休閒習慣之研究 [Research into recreational habits of high school students]. *Jiaoyu zazhi (Chinese Educational Review)* 17.7 (20 July 1925): 1–22.

Zhang Naifeng 張乃豊. "Nüzi he yundong de xuyao" 女子和運動的需要 [Women and the need for exercise]. *Xin jiating* 新家庭 *(Modern Home)* 1.3 (March 1931): 1–6.

Zhang Ruizhen 張瑞珍. "Nüzi tianjingsai yundong shuo" 女子田徑賽運動説

[On women's participation in track and field competitions]. *Tiyu jikan (Chinese Journal of Physical Education)* 2.1 (April 1923): 1–2.

Zhang Yuanruo 章淵若. "Guofang yu tiyu" 國防與體育 [National defense and physical culture]. *Fuxing yuekan* 2.3 (1 November 1933): 1–7.

Zhang Zhenguo 張振國. "Nongcun qingnian suo xu de tiyu huodong" 農村青年所需的體育活動 [The *tiyu* activities that village youth need]. *Qinfen tiyu yuebao (Chin Fen Sports Monthly)* 2.11 (August 1935): 751–752.

Zhang Zhijiang 張之江. *Guoshu yu guonan* 國術與國難 [*Guoshu* and the national crisis]. Nanjing: Zhongyang guoshuguan, 1932.

Zhao Baozhong 趙寶忠. "Jiji de jiankang jiaoyu" 積極的健康教育 [An activist health education]. *Shanxi minzhong jiaoyu* 3.5–6 (15 October 1936): 1–6.

Zhejiang guoshu youyihui huikan 浙江國術游藝會彙刊 [Publication of the Zhejiang Guoshu Fair]. 1930.

Zhejiang tiyu zhuanmen xuexiao yundong tekan 浙江體育專門學校運動特刊. Hangzhou, 1928.

Zhenfeng 鎮峰. "Hezuo yu guoshu" 合作與國術 [Cooperation and *guoshu*]. *Qiushi yuekan* 1.6 (10 July 1935): 235–237.

Zhengyanbao. 正言報 [The whole truth]. Shanghai.

Zhenxiang huabao 真相畫報 *(True Record (Illustrated Magazine)).* Shanghai.

Zhi Yongqing 治永清. *Youxi zhuanlun* 遊戲專論 *(Games and Sports).* Shanghai: Shangwu yinshuguan, 1924.

Zhiyun 植耘. *Zhejiang quansheng yundong dahui xiaoshi* 浙江全省運動大會小史 [A short history of the Zhejiang Provincial Games]. Hangzhou: Tushu zhanwang yuekan, 1937.

Zhongguo Guomindang zhongyang zhixing weiyuanhui xuanchuan weiyuanhui 中國國民黨中央執行委員會宣傳委員會, eds. *Tiyu yu jiuguo* 體育與救國 [Physical culture and national salvation]. Nanjing: Zhongguo Guomindang zhongyang zhixing weiyuanhui xuanchuan weiyuanhui, 1933.

Zhongguo jianzhu 中國建築 *(Chinese Architect).* Nanjing.

Zhongguo qingnian 中國青年 [Chinese youth]. Shanghai.

Zhongguo renmin zhengzhi xieshang huiyi Liaoning sheng weiyuanhui 中国人民政治协商会议辽宁省委员会 and Wenshi ziliao yanjiu weiyuanhui 文史资料研究委员会, eds. *Zhang Xueliang jiangjun ziliaoxuan: Liaoning wenshi ziliao di shiba ji* 张学良将军资料选: 辽宁文史资料第十八辑 [Selected historical materials on General Zhang Xueliang: Liaoning Historical Materials, Vol. 18]. Shenyang: Liaoning renmin chubanshe, 1986.

Zhongguo ribao 中國日報 [China daily]. Nanjing.

Zhongguo tiyu wenshi ziliao bianshen weiyuanhui 中国体育文史资料编审委员会, eds. *Tiyu shiliao, di shi ji* 体育史料, 第十辑 [Materials on the history of physical culture, vol. 10]. Beijing: Renmin tiyu chubanshe, 1984.

Zhonghua guoshu jikan 中國國術季刊 *(Chinese Kuo Shu Quarterly).* Taibei.

Zhonghua quanguo tiyu xiejinhui Guangxi sheng fenhui huikan: Sanshiliu nian "jiujiu" Tiyujie teji 中華全國體育協進會廣西省分會會刊：三十六年"九九"體育節特輯 [Publication of the Guangxi Provincial Branch of the Chinese National Amateur Athletic Federation: Special "September 9th" Sports Day 1947 Issue]. Guilin, 1947.

Zhonghua quanguo tiyu yanjiuhui 中華全國體育研究會. "Tiyu jiaoyuan fenjifa" 體育教員分級法 [Method for classifying physical education instructors]. *Tiyu jikan (Chinese Journal of Physical Education)* 2.1 (April 1923): 1–4.

Zhonghua yuebao 中華月報 *(Central China Monthly)*.

Zhongwai yuekan 中外月刊 *(Sino-Foreign Monthly)*. Nanjing.

Zhongxuesheng 中學生 [Middle school student]. Shanghai.

"Zhongyang guoshuguan ershisan nian zhong jiangxi ban ji lianxi ban nan xueyuan tongxue lu" 中央國術館二十三年終講習班暨練習班男學員同學錄 [List of male graduates from the Central Guoshuguan Lecture and Practice Section concluding in 1934]. *Guoshu zhoukan* 136–137 (20 January 1935): 19–24.

"Zhongyang guoshuguan ershisan nian zhong lianxi nü xueyuan tongxue lu" 中央國術館二十三年終練習女學員同學錄 [List of female graduates from the Central Guoshuguan Practice Section concluding in 1934]. *Guoshu zhoukan* 136–137 (20 January 1935): 24.

Zhongyang ribao 中央日報 [Central daily]. Chongqing.

Zhou Dingchang 周鼎昌. "Yuandong yundonghui Zhong-Ri-Fei changhui jingguo" 遠東運動會中日菲常會經過 [Events at the Chinese-Japanese-Filipino Far Eastern Championship Games Standing Committee meeting]. *Qinfen tiyu yuebao (Chin Fen Sports Monthly)* 1.8 (10 May 1934): 13–15.

Zhou Renshan 周仁山 and Fei Futao 費福燾. "Wuxiao jijibu shinian yange shi" 吾校技擊部十年沿革史 [A history of the development of our school's Boxing Team]. In *Nanyang daxue jijibu shi zhou jiniance*, edited by Fei Futao, 37–39. Shanghai, 1922.

Zhou Xingjian 周行健. "Tan funü tiyu" 談婦女體育 [On women's sports]. *Renyan zhoukan* 12 (5 May 1934): 257–258.

Zhu Jiahua 朱家驊. "Duiyu Quanguo yundong dahui de ganxiang yu jinhou de xiwang" 對於全國運動大會的感想與今後的希望 [Thoughts on the National Games and hopes for the future]. In *Quanguo yundong dahui zongbaogao, Lunzhu* 論著 section, 5–7. Hangzhou, 1930.

———. "Quanguo yundong dahui zhi yiyi" 全國運動大會之意義 [The significance of the National Games]. In *Quanguo yundong dahui yaolan*, 5–6. Hangzhou: Quanguo yundong dahui xuanchuanbu, 1930.

Zhu Jianfan 朱劍凡. "Jun guomin tiyu de jieguo" 軍國民體育的結果 [The consequences of military *tiyu* training]. *Tiyu zhoubao* 29 (7 July 1919): 2–3.

Zhu Yuanshan 朱元善. "Tiyu zhi jiazhi" 體育之价值 [The value of physical education]. *Jiaoyu zazhi (Chinese Educational Review)* 7.11 (15 November 1915): 201–8.

Zhuang Wenchao 莊文潮. "Wuguo ying caiyong lanqiu wei guomin youxi" 吾國應采用藍球為國民遊戲 [Our nation should take basketball as its national pastime]. *Qinfen tiyu yuebao (Chin Fen Sports Monthly)* 3.5 (February 1936): 405–407.

Zhuang Yu 莊俞. "Ertong tiyu lun" 兒童體育論 [On physical education for children]. *Jiaoyu zazhi (Chinese Educational Review)* 5.2 (10 May 1913): 23–31.

———, ed. *Zuijin sanshiwu nian zhi Zhongguo jiaoyu* 最近三十五年之中國教育 [Education in China over the last thirty-five years]. Shanghai: Shangwu yinshuguan, 1931.

Zito, Angela, and Tani E. Barlow, eds. *Body, Subject and Power in China.* Chicago: University of Chicago Press, 1994.

Zuijin zhi wushi nian 最近之五十年 *(The Past Fifty Years).* Shanghai: Shenbaoguan, 1922; Shanghai: Shanghai shudian, 1987.

Glossary of Names

Bai Baokun　白寶琨
Bai Chongxi　白崇禧
Bu Xuekuan　布學寬
Cai E (Songpo)　蔡鍔（松坡）
Cai Juezai　蔡倔哉
Cai Yuanpei　蔡元培
Cai Zongxian　蔡宗賢
Chen Baiyuan　陳百元
Chen Duxiu　陳獨秀
Chen Gongbo　陳公博
Chen Gongzhe　陳公哲
Chen Guofu　陳果夫
Chen Hanqiang　陳漢強
Chen Jiageng　陳嘉庚
Chen Jitang　陳濟棠
Chen Lifu　陳立夫
Chen Qimei　陳其美
Chen Shi　陳時
Chen Shichao　陳士超
Chen Tiesheng　陳鐵生（笙）
Chen Weiming　陳微明
Chen Yi　陳儀
Chen Zhang'e　陳掌諤
Chen Zhenggong　陳正公
Cheng Hanzhang　程瀚章

Cheng Jinguan　程金冠
Cheng Qian　程潛
Cheng Tianfang　程天放
Chi You　蚩尤
Chiang Kai-shek　蔣介石
Dai Jitao　戴季陶
Diao Zuoqian　刁作謙
Ding Wenjiang　丁文江
Dong Futing　董福亭
Dong Hanwen　董漢文
Dong Shouyi　董守義
Du Tingxiu　杜庭修
Duan-fang　端方
Feng Yuxiang　馮玉祥
Fu Baolu　符保盧
Fu Ziyun　傅子筼
Gao Zhendong　高振東
Ge-lei　葛雷
Gu Desheng　谷得勝
Gu Jiegang　顧頡剛
Gu Jilai　顧極來
Guo Bingwen　郭秉文
Guo Shaoyu　郭紹虞
Guo Xifen　郭希汾
Hao Boyang　郝伯陽

339

Hao Gengsheng　郝更生

He Haohua　何浩華

He Long　賀龍

He Yingqin　何應欽

He Zhiliang　賀志良

Hu Hanmin　胡漢民

Hu Shi　胡適

Huang Qiangya　黃強亞

Huang Xing　黃興

Huang Xing (Shengbai)　黃醒
　（勝白）

Huang Yanpei　黃炎培

Huang Zhiduan　黃芷端

Huo Dong'ge　霍東閣

Huo Yuanjia　霍元甲

Inoue Akio　井上昭夫

Jiang Baili　蔣百里

Jiang Xiangqing　蔣湘青

Jiang Xiaoxian　江孝賢

Jiao Xiangzong　焦湘宗

Jin Guidi　靳桂第

Jin Zhongkang　金仲康

Kang Youwei　康有為

Kong Xiangxi　孔祥熙

Li Bailian　李百練

Li Houji　李厚基

Li Jinglin　李景林

Li Lili　黎莉莉

Li Sen　李森

Li Shiming　李世明

Li Yuanhong　黎元洪

Li Zongren　李宗仁

Liang Qichao　梁啓超

Liao Zhongkai　廖仲凱

Lin Boqu　林伯渠

Lin Boyuan　林伯原

Lin Daiyu　林黛玉

Lin Sen　林森

Lin Wangsu　林望蘇

Liu Bei　劉備

Liu Changchun　劉長春

Liu Qingxu　劉清徐

Liu Shaoqi　劉少奇

Liu Shenzhan　劉慎旃

Liu Sijiu　劉思久

Liu Yinhu　劉印虎

Liu Zhensheng　劉振聲

Lu Lihua　陸禮華

Lu Peixuan　陸佩萱

Lu Weichang　盧煒昌

Luo Jialun　羅家倫

Ma Hongkui　馬鴻逵

Ma Liang　馬良

Ma Yuehan　馬約瀚

Ma Yufu　馬裕甫

Ma Zizhen　馬子貞

Mai Kele　麥克樂

Mao Zedong　毛澤東

Meng Zhuang　孟壯

Nie Rongzhen　聶榮臻

Nie Yuntai　聶雲台

Niu Yongjian　鈕永建

Nong Jinsun　農勁蓀

Noto Tokushige　納戶德重

Qian Xingsu　錢行素

Qin Jin　秦晉

Qiu Feihai　邱飛海

Shang Qiyu　商啓宇

Shao Rugan　邵汝幹

Shao Yuanchong　邵元沖

Shen Guoquan　申國權

Shen Siliang　沈嗣良

Shi Kefa　史可法

Shu Hong　舒鴻

Song Jiaoren　宋教仁

Song Junfu　宋君復

Song Meiling　宋美齡

Song Ruhai　宋如海

Song Zheyuan　宋哲元

Song Ziwen　宋子文

Sun Baoxin　孫寶信

Sun Chuanfang　孫傳芳

Sun Cunzhou　孫存周

Sun Diyun　孫迪雲

Sun Guiyun　孫桂雲

Sun Hebin　孫和賓

Sun Jinshun　孫錦順

Sun Ke　孫科

Sun Lutang　孫祿堂

Sun Shan　孫山

Sun Yat-sen (Wen)　孫逸仙（文）

Taixuan　太玄

Tan Wenbiao　譚文彪

Tan Yankai　譚延闓

Tanaka Ryūzō　田中隆三

Tang Baokun　唐寶堃

Tang Hao　唐豪

Tang Weizhi　唐蔚芝

Tang Xueyong　唐學詠

Wang Jingwei　汪精衛

Wang Jingxi　王精熹

Wang Shijie　王世傑稛

Wang Shiying　王世穎

Wang Zhengting　王正庭

Wang Zhuangfei　王壯飛

Wang Ziping　王子平

Wang Ziqing　王子慶

Wei Yuan　魏源

Wu Bangwei　吳邦偉

Wu Tiecheng　吳鐵城

Wu Tingfang　伍廷芳

Wu Weizhen　吳維楨

Wu Wenmei　武問梅

Wu Yunrui　吳蘊瑞

Wu Zhi　吳志

Wu Zhihui　吳稚暉

Wu Zhiqing　吳志青

Wu Zhongxin　吳忠信

Xiao Qin　蕭芹

Xiao Yaonan　蕭耀南

Xie Jin　謝晉

Xu Chengji　許承基

Xu Minhui　許民輝

Xu Teli　徐特立

Xu Yibing　徐一冰

Xu Yusheng　許禹生

Xue Ziliang　薛子良

Yan Fu　嚴復

Yan Xishan　閻錫山

Yan Xiu　嚴修

Yang Cheng　楊晟

Yang Chuanguang　楊傳廣

Yang Sen　楊森

Yang Shaochuan　楊少川

Yang Xiaochuan　楊小川

Yang Xiuqiong　楊秀瓊

Yang-Liu Gufang　楊劉谷芳

Yang-Tian Hengqiu　楊田衡秋

Yao Chanbo　姚蟾伯

Yu Hanmou　余漢謀

Yu Xiwei　于希渭

Yu Youren　于右任

Yuan Baozhu　遠葆珠

Yuan Dunli　袁敦禮

Yuan Shikai　袁世凱

Yue Fei　岳飛

Yun Daiying　惲代英

Zhang Baochen　張寶琛

Zhang Boling　張伯苓

Zhang Dongping　張東屏

Zhang Guotao　張國燾

Zhang Jian　張謇

Zhang Jiwu　章輯五

Zhang Renjun　張人駿

Zhang Shouren　張壽仁

Zhang Shusheng　張樹聲

Zhang Suhui　張素慧

Zhang Taiyan　章太炎

Zhang Xueliang　張學良

Zhang Yu　張裕

Zhang Zhijiang　張之江

Zhao Yuanren　趙元任

Zhou Changxing　周長星

Zhou Dawen　周大文

Zhou Enlai　周恩來

Zhou Xisan　周錫三

Zhou Zuoren　周作人

Zhu De　朱德

Zhu Liang　朱亮

Zhu Zhixin　朱執信

Zhu Zhongming　朱重明

Glossary of Terms

Aifoluo 愛佛羅

Asahi Shinbun 朝日新聞

baduanjin 八段錦

baguaquan 八卦拳

baquan 八拳

batuanjin 八團錦

bibang 彼邦

bingcao 兵操

bunka 文化

caoyan 操演

chise tiyu 赤色體育

chongtu 沖突

Chu cai Jin yong 楚材晉用

Chuannan lianhe yundonghui
川南聯合運動會

Chudeng xiaoxuetang 初等小學堂

chuiwan 捶丸

chulei bacui 出類拔萃

cuju 蹴踘

Dadong shuju 大東書局

Dagongbao 大公報

dahui 大會

Daiakan 大亞環

Damojian 達摩劍

Dang zheng jun xue tiyu cujinhui
黨政軍學體育促進會

daoyan 導言

dawo 大我

Di san ci quanguo yundong dahui
第三次全國運動大會

Di yi ci quanguo lianhe yundong dahui 第一次全國聯合運動大會

dianbao 電報

ding 鼎

dong sheng 東省

dong tequ 東特區

Dong Ya bingfu 東亞病夫

Dongbei tiyu xiejinhui 東北體育
協進會

Dongfang ba daxue yundonghui
東方八大學運動會

Dongfang zazhi 東方雜志

Dongwu daxue 東吳大學

duanlian zhuyi 鍛煉主義

duiqiu 隊球

Dujunshu wushudui 督軍署武
術隊

duo zi duo sun zhuyi 多子多孫
主義

dutong　都統

fabi　法幣

fan tiyu　反體育

fanlie　凡例

fei tiyu　非體育

fengjian buluo　封建部落

fengshui　風水

fuli　福利

fuwei　輔衛

ganqing lianluo　感情聯絡

Gaodeng xiaoxuetang　高等小學堂

Gaodeng zhongxuetang　高等中
　學堂

gaoji di yi lei　高級第一類

gexin　革新

gonggong tiyuchang　公共體育場

gou'an　苟安

gouqiu　鉤球

Guangfu　光復

guanshu　灌輸

gudai tiyu　古代體育

guidao zhuyi　鬼道主義

guizuhua　貴族化

gunshu　棍術

guo　國

guocao　國操

guocui tiyu　國粹體育

guohua　國華

guohuo　國貨

guoji　國技

guojia　國家

Guokao　國考

guomin bisai　國民比賽

guomin de yundong　國民的運動

Guomin tiyu jikan　國民體育季刊

Guomin tiyu shu　國民體育署

guomin youxi　國民游戲

guomin zhi shangwu jingshen
　國民之尚武精神

guominxing　國民性

guoqing　國情

guoshi　國士

Guoshu yanjiuguan　國術研究館

guowu　國武

Guowu huiyi　國務會議

guozu　國族

guyou　固有

hanwei　捍衛

Hanwen chuanxisuo　漢文傳習所

Hanyu pinyin　漢語拼音

haoshang　好尚

Hexing　和興

hongburang　紅不讓

hongse tiyu　紅色體育

Hongse Zhonghua　紅色中華

Hongxian　洪憲

hua　華

Huabei　華北

Huabei yundonghui　華北運動會

Huabei Zhi　華北直

Huadong Su　華東蘇

Huanan　華南

huanqiu da yundonghui　寰球大運
　動會

Huaqiao　華僑

Huazhong E Wenhua　華中鄂文華

Huazhong yundonghui　華中運
　動會

Huazu suzhi zhi jiantao　華族素質
　之檢討

Hubao　滬報

Huguo yundong　護國運動

jiadeng　甲等

jianchashi　監察使

Jiangnan daxue tiyuhui　江南大學體育會

jiangpin zu　獎品組

Jianguo jiaoyu　建國教育

jiankang mei　健康美

jianshen jiuguo　健身救國

jianshencao　健身操

jianxian　劍仙

Jiao yu xue　教與學

jiaolian　教練

Jiaoyu tongxun　教育通訊

Jiaoyu yu rensheng　教育與人生

jiaoyuan　教員

jie　界

Jiefang ribao　解放日報

jieji guannian　階級觀念

jiji　技擊

Jijibu　技擊部

jijishu　技擊術

jinbiao zhuyi　錦標主義

Jingwu　精武

Jingwu tiyuhui　精武體育會

jingzheng　競爭

jishu　技術

jiti　機體

jiyong　技勇

jūdō　柔道

jue　爵

juewu　覺悟

Julebu　俱樂部

jun guomin tiyu　軍國民體育

junguo zhuyi　軍國主義

junxun　軍訓

junzi de jingshen　君子的精神

junzi haoran　君子浩然

junzi zhi zheng　君子之爭

juzi　鉅資

Kangdi bao　抗敵報

kelikoutuo　克立扣脱

laladui　啦啦隊

leitai　擂臺

li　力

lianghao fenzi　良好分子

Liantai　聯泰

Liening shi　列寧室

liuwang xuanshou　流亡選手

lixue　理學

Lizhi she　勵志社

lunzhu　論著

luohou　落後

luohou jiu yao aida　落後就要挨打

Meiji Jingū　明治神宮

meiri de mianbao　每日的麵包

men　門

Mengxuetang　蒙學堂

Minnan tiyu lianhehui　閩南體育聯合會

Minzhengting　民政廳

minzhong tiyu　民眾體育

minzhong zhi jiankanglü　民眾之健康率

minzoku　民族

minzu　民族

minzu tige　民族體格

minzu tizhi　民族體質

minzu zhuyi　民族主義

modeng nülang　摩登女郎

mu　畝

muyecha　母夜叉

nan Cheng bei Liu　南程北劉

nanquan　南拳

nanren shan yong　南人善泳

neidiren　內地人

neimu　內幕

Nichinichi Shinbun 日日新聞

nong 農

nüxing taotai 女性淘汰

nüxing zhishu 女性指數

OuMei ren 歐美人

paiqiu 排球

pingmin zhuyi 平民主義

pingminhua 平民化

Pingyingtuan 平英團

po quanguo 破全國

puji 普及

qiangqiu 搶球

qiangshu 槍術

qianqian wanwan 千千萬萬

qigong 氣功

qili 氣力

Qingmingjie 清明節

Qingnian shihua 青年實話

qipao 旗袍

quanfei 拳匪

quanguo xin 全國新

Quanguo xuexiao qufendui di yi ci tiyu tongmenghui 全國學校區分隊第一次體育同盟會

Quanguo yundong dahui 全國運動大會

quanjiao 拳腳

quanjie duilian 勸戒對聯

quanshi 拳師

quanshu 拳術

quanyi 拳藝

quanyong 拳勇

qun 群

qunxing 群性

ren'ai 仁愛

rendao zhuyi 人道主義

renlei zhi genben 人類之根本

renmin 人民

renti yundongxue 人體運動學

rouruan ticao 柔軟體操

san gongsi 三公司

seiji 政治

Shaan-Gan-Ning 陝甘寧

Shanghai Dongya tiyu xuexiao 上海東亞體育學校

shangwu jingshen 尚武精神

Shaolin 少林

Shaonian xianfengdui 少年先鋒隊

shehui quanti 社會全體

shehui tili 社會體力

shehui tiyu 社會體育

Shenbao 申報

shengchanhua 生產化

Shengjing shibao 盛京時報

shenquan 神拳

shenti de zuzhi 身體的組織

shenti jiaoyu 身體教育

shenti zuzhi 身體組織

shenxin 身心

shi 士

Shibao 時報

shiwu gu baogao 事務股報告

shoubo 手搏

shu 術

shuaijiao 摔角

shui tu bufu 水土不服

shuyu 術語

sumō 相撲

suqing feihuo 肅清匪禍

ta 她

taiiku 体育

taijicao 太極操

taijiquan 太極拳

taisō 体操

tantui 潭腿

ti 體

ticao 體操

Ticao yiming 體操譯名

tici 體詞

tidenghui 提燈會

tige jiancha 體格檢查

tili 體力

tiyu 體育

Tiyu jie 體育節

Tiyu jikan 體育季刊

Tiyu shiyanqu 體育實驗區

tiyujia 體育家

tiyushi 體育史

Tiyu zazhi 體育雜志

Tiyuxue 體育學

Tongyi tiyu mingci ji kouling an 統一體育名詞及口令案

tongzhi 同志

tongzhi 統制

tongzhizhe 統制者

tu 土

undō 運動

undōkai 運動会

wang le 亡了

wangguo nu 亡國奴

wangguo wanyi 亡國玩藝

Wanmu caotang 萬木草堂

wansui 萬歲

Weimei 維梅

wen 文

wenhua 文化

wenruo 文弱

wenyi 文藝

Wo neng bi ya 我能比呀

Women Zhongguoren 我們中國人

wu 武

wu de youxi 武的游戲

wu he zhi zhong 烏合之眾

wu jiu 五九

Wudang 武當

wuguan 武館

wuhua 武化

Wuning 吳寧

wushi 武士

wushu 武術

wuyi 武藝

wuzhuang wu xiang yundong 武裝五項運動

wuzu gonghe 五族共和

Xia 夏

xiaobang 小邦

Xibei yundonghui 西北運動會

xin 心

xin Beijing, xin Aoyun 新北京，新奧運

Xin tiyu 新体育

Xin Zhonghua bao 新中華報

xingyi 行意

Xinminbao 新民報

Xinxin 新新

xuanshou zhi 選手制

yadan 鴨蛋

yakyū 野球

yang 洋

yangbiao 揚鑣

yangnu 洋奴

yang-tu 洋土

yanshuoci 演說辭

yaojing 妖精

yapo 壓迫

yapozhe 壓迫者

yeqiu 野球

yewai bangqiu 野外棒球

yeyu yundong 業餘運動

yingyou 應有

yiqi yongshi 意氣用事

Yiqunbao 益群報

yiwei 翊衛

yong 用

youse renzhong 有色人種

youxian youqian 有閒有錢

Yufan 裕繁

yun 運

yundong 運動

yundong chengji jilu 運動成績紀錄

yundong daode 運動道德

yundong jianjiang 運動健將

yundong pinxing 運動品性

yundong pinxing ziping jilu 運動品性自評紀錄

yundonghui 運動會

yundongyuan shici 運動員誓詞

yundongyuan timing 運動員題名

yuzhong 育種

Zangwen chuanxisuo 藏文傳習所

zhandou zhi jingshen 戰鬥之精神

zhaodai zu 招待組

zhaopai 招牌

zhengdang 正當

Zhengyibao 正義報

zhengzhi 政治

Zhongguo jianxueshe 中國健學社

Zhongguo minxing 中國民性

Zhongguo Taibei 中國台北

Zhongguo Ticao Xuexiao 中國體操學校

Zhongguo wushu 中國武術

Zhongguo xin ticao 中國新體操

Zhonghua quanguo tiyu xiejinhui 中華全國體育協進會

Zhonghua shuju 中華書局

Zhonghua Taibei 中華台北

Zhonghua tiyu xiehui 中華體育協會

Zhonghua xin wushu 中華新武術

Zhonghua yeyu yundong lianhehui 中華業余運動聯合會

Zhongxuetang 中學堂

Zhongyang guoshuguan 中央國術館

Zhongyang tiyuchang 中央體育場

zhuangshi 壯士

Zhuangzi 庄子

zhuti 主體

zhuyihua 主義化

zijue 自覺

ziqixin 自啓心

Zongli 總理

Index